CLARE AND THE WAR OF INDEPENDENCE

CLARE AND THE WAR OF INDEPENDENCE

JOE POWER

Eastwood

First published by Eastwood Books, 2020
Dublin, Ireland

www.eastwoodbooks.com
www.wordwellbooks.com
@eastwoodbooks

First Edition

Eastwood Books is an imprint of The Wordwell Group

Eastwood Books
The Wordwell Group
Unit 9, 78 Furze Road
Sandyford
Dublin, Ireland

ISBN: 978-1-9161375-9-2 (paperback)
ISBN: 978-1-8380416-8-7 (mobi)
ISBN: 978-1-8380416-9-4 (epub)

British Library Cataloguing in Publication Data.
A catalogue record for this book is available from the British Library.

Typeset in Ireland by Wordwell Ltd
Copy-editor: Myles McCionnaith
Cover design and artwork: Ger Garland
Printed by: SprintPrint, Dublin

CONTENTS

PREFACE

This study of the War of Independence examines, in comprehensive detail, the revolutionary history of County Clare between the rise of Sinn Féin in the early twentieth century and the truce on 11 July 1921. It does not pursue a heroic narrative but thoroughly examines the campaign for independence from a broad perspective. Using contemporary and historical sources and looking at the impact of the military campaign in economic, social and political terms, the main events of these turbulent times are highlighted and thoroughly investigated.

My mission was to discover and establish, as accurately as possible, the facts about each major incident during these momentous years, describing the impact of these events in a scholarly yet highly readable manner. The sources used include contemporary newspapers (national and local), witness statements, police records and private memoirs. The role of the Catholic Church in relation to the Irish Volunteers and the IRA is also examined.

The book is structured as a chronological narrative over four chapters. It deals with the years in which the country changed from being in favour of Home Rule with limited independence to largely being in favour of an independent Irish republic. The shift to the latter perspective took place between the Easter Rising of 1916 and the general election of 1918. Despite the overwhelming victory for Sinn Féin, the republican party, in the 1918 election, the British government would not grant this level of freedom and the IRA fought a war of independence over the next three years, 1919–21, to secure an Irish republic.

Chapter One focuses on the growth of Sinn Féin in Clare, from small beginnings in around 1905 to political dominance after the general election of December 1918. This chapter also examines the impact of the First World War and the sharp rise of the National Volunteers under John Redmond during 1914, which led to the split in the national movement and the reorganisation of the Irish Volunteers under Eoin MacNeill. The impact of the Easter Rising is also studied, and the political legacy of that momentous event is examined through the famous East Clare by-election of 1917, which saw de Valera elected for Sinn Féin.

Emboldened by this historic election, the Irish Volunteers of Clare, led by men such as Michael Brennan of Meelick, defiantly asserted their republicanism by organising public parades, although they were banned under military rule. The leaders were arrested, and they went on hunger strike in Mountjoy Jail, which led to the death and martyrdom of Thomas Ashe in September 1917, thus reviving the spirit of 1916. Thereafter, until the end of the First World War, the county was largely under military rule.

The Irish Volunteers were prominent in organising resistance to the introduction of conscription in the spring of 1918. Dr Fogarty, the Bishop of Killaloe, who privately praised the sacrifice of the 1916 martyrs, became an open convert to Sinn Féin after the East Clare by-election of 1917. He was prominently associated with Sinn Féin during the hunger strike of 1917, the conscription crisis in early 1918, and the general election of December 1918 after the end of the First World War. Although the war had finally ended on 11 November 1918, the Irish Republican Army (IRA), the military arm of the Sinn Féin movement, were preparing a new military campaign against the British government.

Chapter Two focuses on the first year of the War of Independence in Clare. The IRA were reorganised from one brigade into three – the East, Mid- and West Clare brigades – and they began to prepare for rebellion. Hampered by a shortage of weapons and ammunition, the IRA initiated a series of armed raids on the Big Houses of Clare, usually occupied by Protestant landed gentry. After the First Dáil met in January 1919, de Valera announced a policy of ostracising the Royal Irish Constabulary (RIC), the Irish police force, as enemies of Ireland; thereafter, they were publicly boycotted all around the county. In late June the Dáil authorised armed rebellion against the forces of the Crown and the War of Independence officially commenced. The IRA in Clare were in the vanguard of the rebellion, launching a guerrilla war with attacks on police patrols and RIC barracks, which resulted in the death of two policemen and the wounding of several others in July 1919. Bishop Fogarty gave strong moral support to the IRA during the year.

Chapter Three examines the state of the county in 1920, with the three Clare brigades involved in open and active rebellion against the Crown. A policeman was killed by the IRA in both Kilrush and Kilmihil, but their most successful operation against the British forces occurred at Rineen in September, when six policemen were killed. However, the Crown forces killed at least four people in reprisal for that attack, and they wreaked havoc in the towns of Ennistymon, Lahinch and Miltown Malbay. The calibre of the RIC changed significantly during this year. Because of early retirements and resignations due to public ostracism and IRA attacks, there were many vacancies in the police force, who were mainly from rural Catholic farming areas. These vacancies were filled by men largely recruited in England from urban, Protestant, working-class backgrounds. These men were called Black and Tans, because of their distinctive uniform. They were assisted by another paramilitary force known as the Auxiliaries, which was formed from ex-army officers.

The police authorities also consolidated and reinforced their organisation with the closure of many small barracks. The British government introduced tough new policies to deal with the IRA, including reprisals and 'shoot-to-kill' tactics. Victims of these policies included four men killed at Killaloe, the Bloody Sunday victims and two Doonbeg Volunteers. Besides these murders, three other IRA men were killed during operations at Cooraclare, Inagh and Kilmihil. The Black and Tans and Auxiliaries introduced a reign of terror in Clare; even priests were attacked, and there was an attempt to murder Bishop Fogarty.

The IRA also changed their military strategies in 1920 with the formation of flying columns in each brigade during the summer. This year also marked the first instance in which the IRA in Clare executed a civilian accused of being a spy. Towards the end of the year Dr Patrick Clune, the Clare-born Archbishop of Perth, was requested by the prime minister, Lloyd George, to negotiate a truce with Sinn Féin and the IRA. However, the talks failed, largely because of the British insistence that the IRA should surrender their arms as a precondition to a truce.

Chapter Four examines the third year of the war, up to the truce in July 1921. Despite the introduction of martial law in January, the IRA launched two successful ambushes on the Crown forces at Glenwood and Cratloe, killing eight policemen. The Crown forces replied with reprisals in the Sixmilebridge and Cratloe areas, burning at least eighteen homes. Two IRA members, Captain Patrick Gleeson and Captain Christopher McCarthy, were killed during an IRA ambush at Cratloe in June. Volunteer and ex-RIC man Thomas Healy died during an ambush at Newmarket-on-Fergus. Another IRA man, Captain Patrick White, was shot dead while a prisoner on Spike Island. All four of these IRA men belonged to the East Clare Brigade. Towards the end of the conflict, the IRA also retaliated by destroying the homes of loyalists.

To frustrate the IRA, the British used convoys of three or more heavily armed trucks with machine guns in joint police and military operations. The IRA responded with a war on communications aimed at paralysing the Crown forces; they seriously hindered their transport with road and rail obstructions and the destruction of telephonic networks. Besides this, the IRA carried out an economic war by stealing the county council rate books, robbing rate money from the rate collectors and organising their own rate collections. The Crown forces continued their 'terror tactics', with many civilians shot 'while running away' from the police or army. The IRA campaign against collaborators continued with the controversial execution of two men accused of being spies.

By early July conditions were ripe for a truce between the IRA and the Crown forces. Although the IRA may have controlled the rural areas, they were handicapped by a shortage of ammunition, preventing them from carrying out major attacks on the heavily armed British forces in the towns. The British government, having appeased most Ulster unionists with partition and the opening of a parliament at Stormont in June, was anxious to reach an accommodation with Sinn Féin and the IRA. There was a stalemate, and with the majority on both sides anxious for peace after more than two years of bitter conflict, a truce was negotiated on 11 July 1921. Given that there had been almost one hundred deaths associated with the county, this development was joyfully welcomed in Clare.

ACKNOWLEDGEMENTS

I wish to thank many people for their assistance in my research over the past four years. Without them, this work would not have been completed. My late father, Bernard Power, who was born in 1901, told me several stories about life in Clarecastle, which was a British garrison during the 'troubles'. For example, he told how he and many young men around the village were rounded up by the Black and Tans in order to repair Latoon bridge, which had been blown up by the IRA several times in 1920 and 1921. He also told me about the burning of the Protestant church in the village in 1920 and about the attack on the army barracks by anti-Treaty forces in 1922. Bernard Power was secretary of the memorial committee and he gave the oration at the unveiling of a monument to a local republican, Tommy Kinnane, on 22 July 1950 at Clarehill, Clarecastle.[1] My late mother, Peggy Power, née Ryan, of Kilcommon, Co. Tipperary told me the story of her 36-year-old aunt, Mrs Margaret Ryan, who was shot by an Auxiliary during the funeral of an RIC man in Callan, Co. Kilkenny on 21 December and who died on 23 December 1920.[2] Special thanks also to Eoin Shanahan for his assistance.

At primary school in Clarecastle, my teacher in second, third and fourth class was Mrs Maura Hanley, née Falvey, who had been commanding officer (OC) of the Ballyea Company, 2nd Battalion, Mid-Clare Brigade Cumann na mBan during the War of Independence. She was a formidable woman whose favourite expression as she administered corporal punishment was, 'There will be wigs on the Green!' I remember being moved by George Morrison's film *Mise Éire*, with haunting music by Seán Ó Riada, which I saw first in 1960 at Ennis cinema when I was 9 years old. I was 15 years old on the fiftieth anniversary of the Easter Rising, and the documentaries and publicity on RTÉ One and in the newspapers were very impressive. President de Valera undertook a farewell tour of Co. Clare before his retirement in 1973, and I remember the time he passed through the old village of Clarecastle in which a guard of honour was provided by some surviving members of the 2nd Battalion, Mid-Clare Brigade, including Bernie Barrett, Jim O'Reilly, John Bradley, Mick Carmody and Joe Reidy.

Growing up in Clarecastle during the 1950s, I heard of some of the exploits of old republicans from the parish, such as the Barretts of Bearnageeha, Tommy Kinnane of Clarecastle and Marty Slattery from Darragh, who had been involved in the War of Independence. I was also fortunate to have had an interview around 30 July 1977 with an old republican named Jim O'Reilly of Ardsollus, Quin, who gave me first-hand information about his role in the formation of a Sinn Féin club in Clarecastle in 1917 – of drilling the local Volunteers in 1917 and the wrecking of the Sinn Féin club house by Scottish soldiers of the Black Watch Regiment in 1918. Jim also told me about the Manusmore cattle drive of February 1918. He was one of the organisers of that operation and was imprisoned for several months, but he was later released without charge. The killing of John Ryan by the RIC during the cattle drive precipitated the introduction of military rule in the county at that time. Jim O'Reilly was prominent in the formation of the Volunteers at Clarecastle, and the county police inspector, Mr Gelston, stated in October 1917, 'James O'Reilly appeared to be their leader [...] sooner or later he will have to be arrested. He is a very disturbing element in Clarecastle.'[3]

I owe an enormous debt to the many historians, both at local and national level, who have written about and published works on the War of Independence. Most of my early research was done at local level, especially at the Local Studies Centre, Ennis, Clare and Clare County Library, and I am very grateful to the staff of both for their support and assistance over many years. I am indebted to the staff of many other libraries and institutions for their assistance over the years: the Irish National Archives, Dublin; the Military Archives at Cathal Brugha Barracks, Dublin; the Archive Collection, UCD, Dublin; the National Library, Dublin; the Royal Irish Academy, Dublin; Trinity College, Dublin; NUI Galway; the Glucksman Library, University of Limerick; the Killaloe Diocesan Archives, Westbourne, Ennis; and the Limerick Diocesan Archives. I am also indebted to Dr Paul O'Brien, Mary Immaculate College, Limerick for giving me access to the Joe Barrett papers and the State Library of Western Australia, Perth for information about Dr Clune. My sincere thanks also to Cailean MacLellan and to my daughter Maria for their assistance with the manuscript in Perth. I am thankful to George Stacpoole, Adare, for showing me the Helen Keane memoir. I am also grateful to Mrs Grania Weir, née O'Brien, Whitegate, Clare for allowing me to access some of her family papers from Dromoland Castle. I am grateful to Ronan Colgan and Una McConville at Wordwell for supporting my project and publishing this work, and Myles McCionnaith for his forensic editorial work and Nick Maxwell for his editorial assistance.

Finally, I wish to thank my wife Fionnuala and my daughters Maria, Rachel and Bronwyn for their love and support, and to whom this book is dedicated.

1
REVOLUTIONARY ROOTS

From small beginnings in the early twentieth century, Sinn Féin became the dominant political force in County Clare and in Ireland by 1918. This extraordinary political development was due to local, national and international factors that undermined the Irish Parliamentary Party, led by John Redmond, between the years 1914 and 1918. During that crucial four-year period, the Irish Parliamentary Party was undermined and discredited, and Sinn Féin, led by Éamon de Valera, became the political voice of Irish nationalism in Ireland after the Easter Rising. Despite the military failure of the Easter Rising, the Volunteers – later the IRA – were preparing to launch another rebellion at the end of 1918.

Early years

In August 1924 John Devoy, the Fenian leader in America, who was on a visit to Ireland for the first time since he was exiled, acknowledged Clare County Council's unanimous vote in welcoming him to Ireland. In a letter to the council, Devoy wrote:

> The Fenian movement was introduced into Clare by Edmond O'Donovan, son of the great scholar, John O'Donovan [...] I had the privilege of meeting the recognised Fenians of Clare in Ennis and Crusheen in 1879 during the presidency of Bryan Clune and can bear testimony to the efficiency of their work for the national cause. They were the backbone of the land movement in Clare in its fighting days and set an example at the Bodyke evictions of 1887 to the rest of the country.

John Devoy was in Ennis at the time of the New Departure, when James O'Gorman Mahon won the 1879 Clare by-election. The New Departure was the term used to describe the political relationship between Charles Stewart Parnell, the leader of the Irish

Parliamentary Party, and the Fenians, who represented the Irish republican movement.

Sinn Féin was founded by Arthur Griffith in 1905 to promote a more advanced form of nationalism than that being advocated by the Irish Parliamentary Party led by John Redmond, which was supported by most Irish nationalists. Sinn Féin grew slowly, and the first Sinn Féin branches in Clare were formed during 1906–7. The Irish Republican Brotherhood (IRB), also known as the Fenians, were originally founded in 1858 and organised a rising in 1867. The IRB movement went into decline after the failure of this rebellion, and this period witnessed the rise of constitutional nationalism following the formation of the Irish Parliamentary Party by Isaac Butt in 1874. However, the IRB were also reorganising in the early twentieth century under Bulmer Hobson and Denis McCullough, and some trusted Clare men were recruited among them.[4]

A Royal Irish Constabulary (RIC) informant code-named 'Peter' mentioned that secret meetings of the IRB were being held in Clare and Limerick as early as 1905. One IRB organiser was a man named Thomas O'Loughlin from Carron. According to RIC reports, an IRB circle was formed at a meeting in Carron on 29 September 1906. It seems that the RIC were confusing the open political organisation of Sinn Féin with the secret military organisation, the IRB. The meetings the informant observed were those of the first Sinn Féin club established in Clare. He stated that the Carron club members were more interested in the land question than in Irish independence, seeking the division of the large grazing estates in north Clare. At meetings held on 15 and 19 March 1908, resolutions were passed committing the members to cattle drives. Cattle drives were a common agrarian outrage in Clare which sought to force the large landowners and graziers to divide up their lands among small landholders by making it difficult and uneconomic to farm. On 25 October 1908 a total of forty-six men attended the Sinn Féin meeting at Carron. Thomas O'Loughlin was the president and there were a total of sixty members. Some of this group, including O'Loughlin, were IRB men. The club had acquired some Colt Reaper rifles in 1909 and sought to purchase more. In 1909 Thomas

O'Loughlin purchased a rifle from Keogan's of Dublin for the training of IRB members.[5]

A second Sinn Féin club was formed at Crusheen in November 1907. Tadgh McNamara, an Irish teacher and a member of the IRB, was responsible for this. This club was revived in 1909 by Seamus Mór O'Gríofa, who swore Sean McNamara and Sean O'Keefe into this IRB circle. About fourteen IRB members met regularly at McNamara's home.[6]

In September 1908 an IRB organiser named John McDermott came to west Clare and convened a meeting at Farrihy, Kilkee to form an IRB circle in this district, but it seems that he was not successful. An RIC report states:

> September 1908, Sinn Féin suspect and organiser, John McDermott, addressed a small meeting at Farrihy, Kilkee on 10 September with the intention of forming a branch. A Mrs Dryhurst of London, believed to be engaged in literature there, also spoke at the meeting. The audience were indifferent, no enthusiasm was aroused. No branch of the IRB was established there.

However, it seems that John McDermott and Cathal Brugha were successful in organising an IRB circle at Kilrush in 1910.[7] Note that John McDermott (Seán Mac Diarmada) was executed in 1916 as one of the leaders of the Easter Rising, and Cathal Brugha was a minister in the first Sinn Féin government of 1919 and a prominent opponent of the Treaty, who was killed during the civil war.

Another 1916 leader named Con Colbert, from Kerry, was active in the Tullycrine district of west Clare. While visiting his relations, the O'Donnells of Tullycrine, he persuaded his first cousin Art O'Donnell, a young national school teacher, to join the IRB and swore him into the organisation. Thus, a new IRB centre was formed in west Clare at the O'Donnells' in 1908.

Thomas O'Loughlin of Carron was active in recruiting members of the IRB in north Clare around this time, and it seems that he chose and inducted men such as Martin Devitt and John Joe Neylon of Ennistymon into the organisation. Martin Devitt subsequently set up an IRB circle at Cloonagh outside Ennistymon. According to John Joe 'Tosser' Neylon, 'Devitt had not much faith in townsmen and always maintained that one countryman was as good as half a dozen townsmen.' Andrew O'Donoghue of Kilfenora was also sworn into the IRB by Thomas O'Loughlin in 1913 when he was 16 years old.

In mid-Clare another IRB circle was formed in the Darragh area in 1908. Joe Barrett of Bearnageeha states:

> I was sworn into the Fenian Brotherhood on 15 August 1908. It was the practice in our part of the country to invite the eldest sons of all the old Fenians to become members of the Brotherhood, and my father, Sylvester Barrett, was an old Fenian in his time. Fifteen of us were sworn in from three or four parishes around. After about six or eight months the circle numbered 30 men.

Over in east Clare the Brennan brothers of Meelick joined the IRB between 1909 and 1911; Paddy was sworn into the organisation in 1909 while his younger brother Michael joined in 1911. Michael Brennan states that he was sworn into the IRB when he was 15 years old. Another east Clare man, Michael O'Dea of Tulla, states that he joined the IRB in 1914.

In the Kildysart area, several young men joined the organisation. Peadar Clancy was one of the founders of a Sinn Féin cumann (branch) in Kildysart in January 1907. In neighbouring Ballynacally, Hugh Hehir states that he was sworn into the IRB in 1911 at 15 years of age.[8]

Thus, by 1912 there was a small network of Sinn Féin clubs and IRB circles in Clare in places such as Carron, Cloonagh, Clooney, Crusheen, Darragh, Doora-Barefield, Kilfenora, Kildysart, Kilrush, Meelick and Tullycrine. It is significant that almost all these Sinn Féin clubs were in rural areas; perhaps this reflected Martin Devitt's observation that 'one countryman was as good as half a dozen townsmen.' Most of the above-named, who had joined the IRB before 1912, played a prominent part in the War of Independence. Members of the IRB were plotting and waiting for a suitable opportunity to renew the old Fenian struggle against English rule in Ireland.

Home Rule

Ireland in 1912 was in a political ferment owing to the third Home Rule bill, which became lawful despite fierce Ulster Unionist Party and Conservative Party opposition in the House of Commons and its rejection in the House of Lords. The Irish Parliamentary Party was the dominant nationalist political force and had seemingly achieved the unlikely prospect of Home Rule for Ireland through constitutional means. Most Irish people felt that Home Rule was imminent despite being delayed by Tory parliamentary tactics for two more years.

Nationalist Ireland expected that the country would have Home Rule in 1914, and even Patrick Pearse, a former editor of the Conradh na Gaeilge (Gaelic League) journal *An Claidheamh Soluis*, gave a qualified welcome to the prospect of this limited independence. There was a monster meeting on Sackville Street (now O'Connell Street), Dublin on 31 March 1912 in support of the Home Rule bill. The third speaker that day, after John Redmond and Eoin MacNeill, was Pearse. Speaking in Irish, he said, 'We have no wish to destroy the British, we only want our freedom in some shape or another [...] The bill we support today will be for the good of Ireland [...] let us unite and win a good Act from the British.' However, Pearse ended his speech prophetically with the following militant warning:

> If we are tricked this time, there is a party in Ireland and I am one of them that will advise the Gael to have no course or dealing with the Gall, but to answer henceforth with the strong arm and the sword's edge [...] if we are cheated once more then there will be red war in Ireland.

In his early career, Pearse was more of a cultural than a militant nationalist, but after determined and effective opposition to the Home Rule bill from the Ulster Unionist Party, the Conservative Party and the Ulster Volunteer Force (a unionist militia) between 1912 and 1914, Pearse concluded, like many others, that force was necessary to secure Irish freedom. Four years after addressing the Sackville Street meeting in favour of Home Rule, Pearse stood on the steps of the General Post Office (GPO) in Sackville Street, Dublin and publicly read from the Proclamation of the Irish Republic, of which he was one of the seven signatories.[9]

The Irish Volunteers

The unity of the Irish Volunteers was shattered and its membership significantly affected when, during a speech in Woodenbridge, Co. Wicklow in September 1914, John Redmond urged the Irish Volunteers to enlist and fight for Britain in the First World War. This was seen as a means of securing the independence offered by the Home Rule bill. Those that followed Redmond's call, about 180,000 Irishmen, were named the National Volunteers. A significant minority (about 10 per cent) refused Redmond's call and remained with Eoin MacNeill, who first established and led the Irish Volunteers; they remained known as the Irish Volunteers and declared that they would only fight in Ireland for Ireland. This split was also seen in Clare, where between 300 and 400 men joined MacNeill's group. Naturally, supporters of the Irish Volunteers were more disposed to Sinn Féin than to the Irish Parliamentary Party.

The split was clear towards the end of October 1914, when a county parade of the National Volunteers was due to be held in Ennis. Edward MacLysaght of Raheen in east Clare wrote to Bishop Fogarty of Killaloe that he 'was afraid of the split in west Clare'. Dr Fogarty replied that 'Ennistymon and Carron branches have unanimously refused to come to the review, in other districts there is division also.' Significantly, only about 700 National Volunteers out of a total of approximately 3,500 members from all over Clare turned up for the parade in Ennis.[10]

Urged by John Redmond and the Irish Parliamentary Party to fight for Home Rule by supporting the war effort, hundreds of thousands of National Volunteers enlisted in the British army and navy. In all, about 250,000 Irishmen joined the services. It is estimated that more than 4,000 men associated with Clare enlisted in the armed services of America, Australia, Britain, Canada, France, New Zealand and other Commonwealth countries; most of them were enlisted in the British army and navy. It seems that most of those from Clare who enlisted in the British services came from urban areas such as Ennis, Kilrush, Ennistymon and Killaloe, with very few from rural areas.[11]

The IRB, abiding by the old Fenian slogan that 'England's difficulty was Ireland's opportunity', began to plan a rebellion to take advantage of Britain's war difficulties. A secret military council began preparing for this rebellion, and they planned to use the Irish Volunteers as their fighting cohort – with the help of arms from Germany or other enemies of Britain.[12]

Organising the Irish Volunteers

With this project in mind, the IRB began to reorganise around the country. Members were sent from headquarters in Dublin to revive the old Fenian circles and recruit new members. One of the men who travelled around Clare on this mission, in 1915 and early 1916, was Ernest Blythe, a Presbyterian from Co. Antrim. The Bureau of Military History was established by the Irish government, in 1947, to record the witness statements of the men and women who fought for Irish independence between 1913 and 1921. In his witness statement, written in 1947, Blythe recalled his experiences in the county at this time. He gives some idea of the state of Sinn Féin and the IRB in the county, indicating that it had declined since the passage of the Home Rule bill in 1912. Blythe was disappointed with what he found out in 1915, but he seemed more hopeful when he returned in early 1916. One difficulty he experienced in his mission was that he was constantly being shadowed by Special Branch detectives of the RIC, and this factor may have inhibited local republicans from meeting him. Significantly, he seemed to have made more progress in rural areas rather than in towns like Ennis and Ennistymon:

> When I proceeded to Clare, I found that I was back in a worse atmosphere than I had experienced in Cork […] I think that Clare must, at that time, have been the very worst county in the country […] It was noticeable at the time in Limerick and still more in Clare, that the country areas were very much better than the towns [for recruitment of IRB Volunteers] […] Even a man like Frank Barrett was not willing to be seen with me at that time. I met him in a public house [in Ennis] one night and found that he was a Sinn Féiner, but I noticed that he was not willing to be seen in the street with me. Once or twice, when he saw me coming in the distance, he turned the corner so as not to meet me […]
>
> I started a company at Inch and another at Quin, but, of course, I could do nothing in Ennis itself. Ennis was not the only

> place where I experienced difficulty in getting accommodation. Two factors operated to cause people like me to be refused admission. One was that the feeling against Sinn Féin or pro-Germans, as they were called, was fairly bitter amongst certain sectors; and the other was the continual presence of a policeman outside the hotel where I was staying [...] from the time I went south at the beginning of 1915 right on until the rising, I was constantly shadowed and followed by police [...] they generally followed me at 20 or 30 yards distance [...]
>
> I remember it proved impossible to do anything in the town of Ennistymon, but I was able to get a couple of companies going a mile or two outside the town [...] On the whole, I did not succeed in making good progress in Clare [...] In Killadysart, I got a couple of people together, about 8 or 10 and got a premises, but I did not actually succeed in forming a company. I formed a company at Carrigaholt and another composed mainly of Irish-speakers at Kilbaha. With assistance from Sean MacNamara, I got a few men together at Crusheen [...] In Tuamgraney and Scariff, I met odd individuals, but could not form any companies. Clare was even at that time in June 1915, even worse than Cork at the beginning of the year but it was steadily improving [...] On 11 July at 8.30 am I was in Miss McCormack's Hotel in Lisdoonvarna, when I was ordered to leave Ireland under the Defence of the Realm Act [DORA].

However, after a short time in England, Blythe secretly returned to continue his work:

> In November 1915, up to March 1916, I was in Limerick and Clare mainly [...] Limerick was much easier to get results from work. Nevertheless, Clare had improved a good deal and we got companies going in a number of areas and older companies were strengthened. To the very last, however, I found it impossible to do anything at all in the town of Ennis. I was arrested again under DORA, in March 1916, just before the Rising.[13]

Blythe was arrested in Ennistymon and he was ordered out of the country. According to a newspaper report:

> Mr Blythe had been busy in Clare for some weeks, having made Ennis his HQ; he was subject to rigid police surveillance, with plain clothes policemen constantly detailed to keep him under observation in his trips around the county. He was endeavouring to organise a corps of the Irish Volunteers, but, according to the

> report in the Saturday Record, his efforts in Ennis at any rate had borne little fruit.

He had in fact reviewed the Ennis corps of the National Volunteers and was endeavouring to subvert their allegiance to John Redmond until they discovered his identity and mission.[14]

Michael Brennan of Meelick reveals in his memoirs how he and others helped to organise Irish Volunteer companies throughout east Clare after the split with Redmond. It must be remembered that Blythe stated he had made little progress in east Clare during 1915. Brennan first started in Meelick and Oatfield, his native parish. To increase their numbers and publicise their cause, the Volunteers used to hold parades after Sunday Mass and on popular social occasions, when hurling matches and tug o'war tournaments were held. Through these means they set up Irish Volunteer companies all over east and mid-Clare in parishes such as Clonlara, Cratloe, Newmarket-on-Fergus, Clarecastle, Crusheen, Ennis, Feakle, O'Callaghan's Mills, Ogonelloe, Scariff, Sixmilebridge and Tulla. They sang 'A Soldier's Song' over the hills of Clare. They did, however, encounter some strong vocal opposition on occasions from the wives of men serving in the British forces, 'separation women', whom Brennan referred to as 'viragoes'.[15]

One IRB man who was active in south-west Clare was Art O'Donnell of Tullycrine. Shortly after the war broke out, he began distributing anti-recruitment literature in the Kildysart region at sports meetings, dances and football matches – wherever a crowd was gathered in the district. The literature distributed by O'Donnell had the following lines, 'What will England do? She will recruit Irishmen to fight the Germans for her. She will then, when finished with them, fling them back to the workhouses of Ireland reeking with foul filthy diseases.' According to O'Donnell there was a strong body of National Volunteers in Kildysart led by John Bianconi O'Connell, who encouraged them to enlist. However, after about a month of warfare, their enthusiasm waned as they feared that the National Volunteers would be conscripted into the British army.[16]

Fear of conscription

With the war of attrition taking place on the Western Front during

1915, there was a huge demand for recruits; there were genuine fears that conscription would be introduced, as many British generals and politicians were calling for its extension to Ireland. Many young Irishmen, especially from the farming community, decided to emigrate to America to avoid being conscripted. They were attacked at ports such as Liverpool and called cowards and shirkers, but they were stoutly defended by Bishop Edward O'Dwyer of Limerick.

The *Clare Journal* highlighted the issue:

> For the past week or two there has been a steady exodus of young Clare people mostly able-bodied sturdy youths of the agricultural class for America, and the number that have left and are still going is attracting much public comment [...] Queenstown having been closed to emigrants since the beginning of the war they have to travel to Dublin [...] For the past week nearly 300 have left North Wall Dublin, about 50 of these from County Clare [...] and it was noticeable that most of them came from West Clare, and some from the most extreme part of the county [...] It is freely stated that the 'rush to emigrate' was attributed to statements made in certain quarters that a policy of conscription was about to be adopted by the present coalition government [...] Another batch of emigrants packed the Ennis station today.[17]

About six months later, avoiding conscription through emigration to America was virtually closed off. In an article headed 'The White Feathers' (a symbol of cowardice), the *Clare Journal* reported that twenty young men from Clare had been sent home from Liverpool. They were from the Tulla, Kilnamona and Inagh districts. These would-be emigrants were made to feel unwelcome in Liverpool and were assaulted. They received a sarcastic 'welcome home' from the *Clare Journal*. The White Star Line, a British shipping company, followed the Cunard shipping line's example in refusing to book men of military age attempting to emigrate to America. Also, further restrictions were put on the issuing of passports.[18]

Bishop O'Dwyer

The treatment of the Irish emigrants at Liverpool outraged Bishop O'Dwyer of Limerick, who publicly rebuked John Redmond. Redmond had rashly stated in an interview with the Press Association that 'it was very cowardly of them to try and emigrate.'

In a public letter Bishop O'Dwyer attacked Redmond for his remarks and his failure to defend the would-be emigrants:

> The treatment of the poor Irish emigrants at Liverpool is enough to make any Irishman's blood boil with anger and indignation! They do not want to be forced into the English army and sent to fight English battles in some part of the world [...] these poor Connaught peasants [...] Why should they die for England?

This letter caused a national sensation after it was published in the *Cork Examiner* and the *Limerick Chronicle* on 11 November 1915, and copies of it were found by the RIC in seventeen counties. Copies of the letter were distributed at chapel gates around the country by members of the Irish Volunteers and Sinn Féin. Bishop Fogarty wrote to Bishop O'Dwyer in support of his letter. He stated, 'it is past time that someone would tell the truth though few beside yourself have the courage to do so. By the way, the whole body of people have rallied to you and your letter to the emigrants. It has opened their eyes.'[19]

The Ennis Brian Boru branch of Sinn Féin also passed a resolution condemning 'the threats meted out to brother Irishmen by a Liverpool rabble'.[20] Such public attacks on Redmond must have seriously damaged the recruitment cause in the region. The following extract from a police report for Clare shows that Bishop O'Dwyer's letter was widely circulated in Clare by the Irish Volunteers:

> On 5 Dec 1915 Michael Brennan led about 20 Meelick armed men to Kilkishen and addressed a crowd stating: 'We want men to join the Irish Volunteers, we are against recruiting for England [...] Copies of the Bishop of Limerick's letter were distributed. Anti-enlistment posters were put up in Carrigaholt and Tubber on 19 December. Copies of Bishop of Limerick's letter of 10 November were also circulated at Kildysart and Carrigaholt. Besides these, copies of an extract from Mr John Dillon's speech against conscription at Armagh on 31 October 1915 were circulated at Sixmilebridge.[21]

Preparing for Rebellion

In east Clare the Irish Volunteers were drilling and playing their own war games in preparation for an expected rebellion. Three Brennan brothers, Austin, Michael and Patrick, along with other farmers' sons from the Meelick district were arrested in early January 1916 by a party of RIC from Killaloe. They were bound to the peace for twelve months on sureties of £20 each. This did not deter them, as two months later Captain Michael Brennan was arrested under DORA for drilling illegally and shooting on Glenomra Mountain. Justice Sharman stated at the trial, 'It was a very serious thing to have armed men marching around the country roads of Clare.' Brennan had publicly told the Irish Volunteers before a route march at Meelick on St Patrick's Day that 'if an attempt was made to seize their arms then they should use them, shoot anybody who attempted to seize their arms, it was self-defence and not murder [...] If their weapons were taken, then he said that the next thing would be conscription.' Brennan was sentenced to three months' imprisonment with hard labour for this seditious speech. Pending an appeal, he was released from Limerick Prison after a week. At his trial, Brennan refused to recant; instead he defiantly repeated the statement in court before the resident magistrate in Clare, George McElroy.[22]

By April 1916, with about 440 Irish Volunteers, the IRB decided to set up a military structure in Clare by dividing it into four battalions: East Clare under Michael Brennan; Mid-Clare under Sean McNamara; North Clare under H.J. Hunt; and West Clare under Éamon Fennell.[23] County Inspector Gelston, who had spent twenty-six years in the RIC and three years in Clare, gave testimony to an enquiry into the Easter Rising, which was set up by the British government in July 1916. Describing the rise of Sinn Féin in the county since 1914, he stated that the first branch of the Irish Volunteers was formed in March 1914:

> There were four branches with a membership of about 400. When the split occurred in September 1914, the majority of about 300 seceded from Mr Redmond's party and became the Sinn Féin Volunteers. A Sinn Féin branch was organised in the county by Thomas O'Loughlin of Carron, but nothing was done until May 1915, when a paid organiser, Mr Ernest Blythe came to the county and made himself very active. He went on creating branches until July 1915, when he came to be looked upon as a danger and a deportation order was served upon him [...] When Blythe left the county the movement stood still until a man named O'Hurley, a Gaelic teacher and organiser, became very active, with the result that by the beginning of this year, there

> were ten branches with a membership of 440 in the county. They drilled and some of them wore uniforms and practised shooting with miniature rifles [...] In the whole county they had about 35 rifles. They were not well-armed, but they had plenty of shotguns and miniature rifles. These branches became aggressive in some parts of the county and people got afraid of them.

Gelston said that some of the younger priests had Sinn Féin tendencies, but the older priests, as a rule, did not have these tendencies; he also noted that parish priests had spoken against the movement in some areas. There were several seditious sermons or remarks made by priests. One young priest, Fr Culligan of Carrigaholt, told the people:

> to arm themselves and if they could not get rifles then to get shotguns, which were very useful in the hands of Irishmen. If they couldn't get shotguns, he told them to get revolvers. If they failed to get revolvers, then they should arm themselves with pikes that the blacksmiths could make them. If pikes were not available, then they should get a hatchet or a slasher.

Fr Culligan was not arrested for this seditious speech. Shortly afterwards Fr Culligan was transferred to the parish of Silvermines in Tipperary. His departure affected Sinn Féin activities in the Carrigaholt area for a while; according to a police report for March 1916, 'Since the removal of Fr Culligan, the main mover in this area, to Tipperary, no drills or meetings have been held since then.' But that did not silence him or curtail his Sinn Féin activities.[24]

The Easter Rising

The IRB military council's plans for the Easter Rising were quite advanced and ready for action on Easter Sunday, 23 April 1916. They planned to have uprisings in many parts of the country, but their plans were stymied and ruined by the capture of a German ship, the *Aud*, with a shipment of 20,000 rifles and a couple of million rounds of ammunition for the Irish Volunteers. The role of the Irish Volunteers in Clare was utterly dependent on the successful landing of this arms shipment on Good Friday. Some leading Irish Volunteers in the county, such as the Brennans of Meelick, Sean McNamara of Crusheen and Thomas O'Loughlin of Carron, were privy to the plans a few days before the operation was due to begin.

Because of the *Aud*'s capture, the plans for a national turnout of all Irish Volunteers on Easter Sunday were countermanded at the last minute by Eoin MacNeill, leader of the Irish Volunteers, who was not aware of the IRB's plans until Holy Thursday.

Despite the confusion and last-minute cancellation, several hundred Irish Volunteers turned out in various parts of Clare on Easter Sunday to take part in manoeuvres. Groups of men assembled in places such as Bunratty, Carrigaholt, Cloonagh, Corofin, Crusheen, Darragh, Feakle and Killaloe. They had limited weapons, mostly shotguns and a few revolvers. They waited in vain for orders and eventually received instructions from Michael Colivet, commandant of the Limerick and Clare Brigade, to disband until further notice.[25]

The Easter Rising began belatedly in Dublin on Monday, 23 April. Despite the manoeuvres of the local Irish Volunteers over the Easter weekend in Clare, it was, according to local police, magistrates, clergy and journalists, relatively quiet during the week of conflict. Sarsfield Maguire, editor of the *Clare Journal*, wrote:

> It is highly satisfactory to state [...] that County Clare has not witnessed a solitary outbreak or disturbance of any kind. Today, practically normal conditions prevail, but it was very evident that during last week there was a considerable atmosphere of unrest and suppressed excitement, which found however, no actual vent; and the news of the surrender of the leaders of the Dublin rebellion on Saturday, which spread like wildfire, had a powerful effect of bringing home to possibly disaffected circles, limited and without influence as they may be, an idea and appreciation of the realities of the situation.

The *Clare Journal*'s Kilrush correspondent wrote, 'up to the time of writing, I am glad to say that things remain in the usual state of peace in West Clare; a young man named Art O'Donnell from the Tullycrine district an ex-teacher was arrested in Kilrush.' He had 'turned up in Kilrush on Saturday, dressed in a Volunteer uniform, with a revolver and ammunition and was arrested'.[26]

The resident magistrate George McElroy spoke of 'the admirable conduct of the people of Clare during the Dublin crisis.' He said that there were no disturbances of any kind in Clare, 'they should thank the National Volunteers of Ennis, Kildysart and other places for helping to keep law and order.'[27]

County Inspector Gelston testified at the enquiry into the Easter Rising. He stated, 'at the time of the rising there was considerable activity, organisers were moving about, and the Sinn Féiners were evidently anticipating something. On Easter Monday many of the Sinn Féiners met along the banks of the Shannon, evidently anticipating the landing of arms from the Kerry side of the river.' Gelston's testimony is corroborated by Michael Brennan's memoir, in which he describes how he mobilised about one hundred men from Meelick, Oatfield, Cratloe and Newmarket-on-Fergus, and how they marched to Bunratty and waited all day in the rain for orders to join the rebellion, but the orders never came.

Gelston attributed the fact that there was no uprising in Clare to the failure to land arms in Kerry:

> The Sinn Féin movement was very small, but it grew rapidly at the end of 1915 and the beginning of 1916. We had a record of over 400 Sinn Féiners in the county, but of course there were a great many sympathisers, who did not openly join, but showed themselves in sympathy with the Sinn Féin movement. My own opinion is that if they had had a rising in Clare we would have had a great many more than 400, we would have probably had three times that number. The older clergy, as a rule, the parish priests in a number of cases have spoken against the Sinn Féin movement [...] They assisted to the extent of denouncing the Rising from the pulpit. In one case a parish priest addressed the Sinn Féiners and asked them to give up their rifles to us. That was the only case in which rifles were given up to us.[28]

Judge McElroy's observations on the state of Clare during the Rising were corroborated by Judge Bodkin at the Ennis quarter sessions held on Wednesday, 1 June 1916. The quarter sessions were courts held every three months on the Munster Circuit in various counties. Judge Bodkin was presented with white gloves, as there were no indictable cases before the court. By custom, white gloves were given to justices by the court clerk if there were no cases to be tried before the court. During the recent troubles Judge Bodkin noted that 'County Clare remained perfectly peaceable, with not a single disturbance. Clare was an example to the rest of Ireland.'[29]

Ennis Urban Council, largely Redmondite in its composition, unanimously passed a resolution condemning the Easter Rising:

> That we, the members of Ennis Urban Council, while sympathising with the families of those who have fallen on both sides in the combat in the metropolis of Ireland, deeply deplore this awful bloodshed, and on behalf of those whom we have the honour to represent, we disassociate ourselves and deeply detest the actions of those on whose shoulders lies the responsibility for so many innocent victims being cut down in the prime of manhood […] We repose full confidence in John Redmond, the wise and noble leader of the Home Rule party.

Kilrush Urban Council also adopted a resolution on 1 May condemning 'the recent deplorable outrages in Dublin as detrimental to the real political and industrial interests and calling on nationalist Irishmen to support John Redmond's constitutional policy.'[30]

A sea change

Within a week or two of the Easter Rising, the mood of the country began to change as the leaders of the rising were court-martialled, sentenced to death and executed. The 'blood sacrifice' idea, promoted by leaders such as Patrick Pearse and James Connolly, had begun to take root and sprout. About a week after several of the rebel leaders had been executed, members of Ennis Rural District Council met and passed a resolution 'condemning the actions of the British government in shooting our brave and patriotic Irishmen who took part in the recent Irish rebellion'. Also, the Ennis District of the Ancient Order of Hibernians passed a resolution 'deeply regretting that the government found it necessary to shoot our countrymen after they had surrendered, and we strongly appeal to them not to shoot any more prisoners and to deal leniently with our fellow countrymen who participated in the recent rebellion.' A sea change in the political mood of the county was occurring as the condemned leaders were becoming martyrs. At the end of May, Clare County Council passed a resolution, which included the following, 'We hereby place on record our abhorrence of the drastic punishment meted out to the patriotic, but misguided leaders of the late attempt to set up an Irish Republic.'[31]

About a month later Bishop Fogarty, speaking at Ruan, said, 'If the actions of these brave but misguided youths, who gave their lives for what they believed to be was the cause of Ireland had the effect of stirring up of the national spirit and stemming the tide of Saxonism, then their blood was not shed in vain.'[32]

Meanwhile, in private letters to Bishop O'Dwyer dated 17 September, Dr Fogarty expressed his horror at the executions and said that the public were outraged by them. He also attacked the hypocrisy of the British and the slavish mentality of the Irish Parliamentary Party MPs and local councillors:

> Most people don't want rebellion, but the brutal shooting and deportation of these young irregulars after surrender has filled the country with indignation and raised such an anti-English feeling as I never saw before [...] One of the most disgusting things in our recent public life is the way our public bodies, county councils, urban councils etc., have all rushed up with sickening resolutions undermining the rebels. The national door of Ireland is half-closed [...] You have your critics among the sober birds, but the great body of the people, especially the young, male and female, are in boundless admiration of you.[33]

The Easter Rising had a hugely negative impact on recruitment in Ireland, and one of its benefits was that it probably saved tens of thousands of Irishmen from being slaughtered on the Western Front and in many other theatres of war from April 1916 up to the end of the First World War on 11 November 1918.

Arrests in Clare

Shortly after the rising began, the country was placed under military rule, and in the weeks following the Easter Rising many Sinn Féin activists and others were arrested throughout Clare. Among those arrested and deported were Austin, Michael and Patrick Brennan of Meelick and Art O'Donnell of Tullycrine. Other Clare men who were deported around this time included: H.J. Hunt and W. Hunt, Corofin; W. Byrne, Cloyne South, Ennistymon; Martin Crowe, Corofin; Denis Healy, a county councillor, Bodyke; Éamon Waldron, a Gaelic teacher, Ennistymon; Pat Comer, a Gaelic teacher, Killaloe; M.J. Shannon, Quin, formerly of Fountain; Thomas Kierse, Corofin;

and Colman O'Loughlin, Carron. O'Loughlin was a prominent Irish Volunteer and Sinn Féin leader in Clare who had been one of the signatories, along with Patrick Pearse, Thomas MacDonagh, Eoin MacNeill and others, of the document founding the Irish Volunteers in September 1914, after the split with John Redmond. The Volunteers who remained loyal to John Redmond were known as the National Volunteers.

Gelston noted that twenty-three persons had been arrested in the county, 'some of them dangerous leaders, others are dupes, they are of no importance, but they had to be arrested all the same.' One newspaper noted that the young men were sent from Ennis to Limerick and that there was 'no excitement over the arrests and only a few people watched their departure from the station'. The men were deported to England. The *Saturday Record* noted sarcastically that all those who had been arrested were farmers' sons.[34]

The combination of martial law, the arrest of Sinn Féin and Irish Volunteer leaders, and the searches for arms had a significant impact on the activities of the Irish Volunteers in the county. For most of the rest of the year they kept a low profile and there was very little activity – there were no public meetings or drills under martial law. Those who were arrested were gradually released. Seven of the men who were arrested in May were released in August and returned home, but according to County Inspector Gelston there were no demonstrations of welcome (this was probably due to martial law). Gelston also noted in December, when martial law had been relaxed, that the release of the remaining three prisoners caused no excitement or demonstrations.

However, Michael Brennan, in his memoir, contrasts the way he and other republicans were treated immediately after the Easter Rising with the reception they received eight months later when they returned from English prisons:

> At Limerick station we had been sent off by a crowd of British soldiers and separation allowance ladies, viragoes, who howled insults, pelted us with anything handy and several times had to be forced back physically by the military escort, when they tried to get us with fists or nails [...] Eight months later, when I got off the train in the same station, I was met by a crowd numbering several thousands, who cheered themselves hoarse and

> embarrassed us terribly by carrying me on their shoulders through the streets. It was all very bewildering, but it made clear that the Rising had already changed the people.[35]

Though the county seemed outwardly quiet, County Inspector Gelston observed:

> an undercurrent of unrest and disloyalty; there were republican slogans on walls, people were wearing badges and Sinn Féin flags were flown. Because of the rebellion in Dublin the Sinn Féin movement received an impetus and vast numbers of persons who had disapproved of the rebellion accorded their open sympathy to the rebels. Many of the National Volunteers regretted that they had not partaken in the Rising.

Gelston also remarked on a notable change in attitude among the Catholic clergy towards Sinn Féin and the Irish Volunteers:

> Before the Rising a number of Catholic clergymen were in favour of the Irish Volunteers but took no open part except Fr Culligan of Carrigaholt and Fr Crowe of Doora. After the rebellion practically all the clergy showed open sympathy with and approval of the actions of the rebels. This was most apparent among the younger clergy. And it was reported to me that Canon O'Dea of this town [Ennis], stated that the men of Co Clare ought to be ashamed of themselves for not having taken any part in the rebellion. The older clergy and those in high offices also showed their sympathies in their addresses to their congregations and took no public action to restrain the Sinn Féiners or to try and discourage the increase in the public feeling in favour of the rebels.[36]

A new Clare command

After their release, the Sinn Féin prisoners quietly resumed their operations in the county. Incarceration had not cowed them. Indeed, the opposite was the case, as the prison experience had hardened them and made them more determined to renew the struggle of 1916. The Clare Sinn Féiners sought and secured a separate military command for the county, which had been under the Limerick command in 1916. Therefore, in early 1917 a new Clare division under the command of Patrick Brennan of Meelick was formed; Michael Brennan acted as adjutant. Some of the released leaders were closely watched. For example, RIC men watched Michael

Brennan, captain of the Meelick Volunteers, as he spoke to the Volunteers on 14 January. At the same time, his brother Patrick was seen at Carrigaholt associating with some IRB men.[37]

Gelston found that the Sinn Féiners were becoming 'oppressive' in the early months of the new year. He noted that in each place where an ex-prisoner had returned, Sinn Féin had begun to meet again; he also observed that they were using 'seditious expressions' and had begun to defy the authorities. The most serious incident around this time occurred when Constable Johns was shot and wounded in the neck and shoulder on 5 March 1917. The police assumed that he was shot because he could identify some of the marchers in an illegal Sinn Féin-organised parade at Ennistymon led by Éamon de Bhaldraithe (Edward Waldron). This was a significant departure for Sinn Féin – allegedly the first attempt to kill a policeman in the county. Constable Johns's special duty on that day had been to watch the passengers arriving and departing at Ennistymon Railway Station.[38]

Leading Volunteers such as Michael Brennan were constantly watched by the police, and he was sentenced by magistrates to three months' prison on 4 April 1917 'for an attempt to cause sedition'. Brennan had earlier been arrested, along with many other leading republicans from all over the country, on 24 February 1917. He and about twenty-three others, including Thomas MacCurtain and Terence MacSwiney, were deported to England. This was Brennan's second deportation to England. The deportees were held under 'house arrest' in Ripon, but although watched closely, Brennan escaped and secretly returned to Ireland in early May. Éamon de Bhaldraithe, the Conradh na Gaeilge organiser in Ennistymon, was deported in April.[39]

Meanwhile, the first anniversary of the Easter Rising at the end of April was quietly marked in the county by a concelebrated Requiem Mass at the Franciscan Friary, Ennis for 'the repose of the souls of the men who died for Ireland'. The chief celebrant was Rev. Fr Leopold, OFM (Order of Friars Minor); he was assisted by Fr Peter, OFM and Fr M. McGrath, CC (Catholic curate), Clarecastle. Fr Molony, CC, Ennis, was master of ceremonies. In the choir were Rev. Fr J. Scanlan, PP (parish priest), Doora; Rev. D. Courtney, PP,

Kilmaley; Rev. Fr Molloy; Rev. Fr Gleeson; and Rev. Fr O'Donoghue (all of whom were from St Flannan's College); Rev. M. Crowe, CC, Doora; Rev. Fr Heenan, CC, Corofin; and Rev. Patrick, OFM.[40] Tricolours were also flown around the county to mark the occasion, but according to the police, there were no parades or processions organised by Sinn Féin. In May, Gelston remarked:

> though the county was quiet, there is a decided increase in Sinn Féinism through the wearing of badges, outspoken remarks and the flying of flags, it has now spread to older men, encouraged by all the younger clergy and some of the older ones. There is an ill-disguised hostility shown by Sinn Féiners towards the policemen as armed servants of the Crown.[41]

The East Clare by-election of 1917

The death of Major Willie Redmond, the MP for the East Clare constituency who was killed at Messines Ridge in Belgium on 7 June, necessitated a by-election. Major Redmond had been a Home Rule MP for East Clare since 1893, and the last election had occurred in 1910. This was a golden opportunity for Sinn Féin to advance their political struggle, both nationally and locally. Shortly after the death was announced, a meeting of Sinn Féin sympathisers took place in Ennis to secure the return of a Sinn Féin candidate. The meeting was held in the Clare Hotel, and after some discussion on the merits of various candidates, it was unanimously agreed that Peadar Clancy of Cranny should be the candidate in the forthcoming election. Peadar Clancy fought during the Easter Rising; he had initially been sentenced to death, but this sentence was commuted to a ten-year sentence of penal servitude. After selecting their candidate, the members formed a provisional election committee and appointed three men as joint secretaries: Rev. Michael Crowe, CC; Michael O'Brien; and Sean McNamara.

The provisional election committee then decided to summon a convention at the Old Ground Hotel, Ennis at noon on Thursday, 14 June to select a Sinn Féin candidate and to form an election committee. More than two hundred delegates attended the Sinn Féin convention. Rev. A. Clancy, PP, acted as chairman while Rev. M. Crowe acted as secretary. Sean Milroy, a member of the national executive of Sinn Féin, addressed the meeting; after this, nominations for the vacancy took place. Five candidates were proposed and seconded. After a full discussion, the names of four of the candidates were withdrawn in favour of Éamon de Valera; he was recently released from incarceration in England, had commanded the rebel forces at Boland's Mill during the Easter Rising and was subsequently elected president of Sinn Féin. Clearly, the national executive of Sinn Féin overruled the local choice. The Catholic clergy played a prominent part in the Sinn Féin organisation; acting as chairmen or secretaries, they would have been a very influential moderate group among the other delegates.[42]

The *Clare Champion* described the 'affecting scenes the wild enthusiasm and the tremendous reception given to de Valera when he arrived in Ennis just before the election'. The words of 'A Soldier's Song' were boldly printed on the front page of the newspaper, and his visit was comprehensively covered. The paper noted that 'a frenzied effort was being made to frighten the voters of Clare into the belief that de Valera is a desperado and an anarchist out for revolution, bloodshed and strife.' Meanwhile, the *Clare Journal* observed that the contest 'would be an historic one between Commandant de Valera, who represented the spirit of 1916, and Mr Lynch, of old Clare stock, representing constitutional methods, which won so much for Ireland.'[43]

Just before the election, leaflets were circulated throughout the county by the Sinn Féin organisation and Cumann na mBan members warning voters that the choice was between de Valera and conscription. One leaflet asked the question, 'Who will you follow, the men who fought for you in Dublin, or the men who would have sent you to meet German guns?' County Inspector Gelston described the scene:

> The state of the county is intense due to the flooding of the county by Sinn Féiners [people such as Éamon de Valera, Eoin MacNeill, Arthur Griffith and Countess Markiewicz] and released prisoners canvassing for the East Clare election [...] violent, disloyal and inflammatory speeches are being made, resulting in excitement and unrest [...] Sinn Féin has advanced since the opening of the election campaign. The extremists are fighting some of the moderates [...] the election contest is being fiercely fought and a bitter spirit exists [between Home Rulers and Sinn Féiners]. Sinn Féin regard the

> election as a vital one and as one speaker said: 'they would win by fair means, or by other means!' de Valera made a moderate speech. Sinn Féin clubs are being formed and I think before long many more clubs will be formed.[44]

The passions aroused by the 1917 election electrified the county. Edward MacLysaght, from Raheen, Tuamgraney, who supported de Valera, describes the powerful emotions at that time, 'Most people under sixty find it hard to realize the spirit, at once enthusiastic and indomitable, which then permeated almost our entire population, and many of those who shared that exhilarating experience cannot now recapture it.'[45]

On his journey to Clare before the election, de Valera paid a courtesy visit to Bishop O'Dwyer of Limerick, who by then had become a public supporter of Sinn Féin. With an ecclesiastical blessing from the most nationalistic of bishops, an endorsement from the *Clare Champion* and a strong campaign from members of the IRB, Sinn Féin, the Irish Volunteers and Cumann na mBan, de Valera won the election by a huge margin, defeating Patrick Lynch, the Irish Parliamentary Party candidate, by a total of 5,010 votes to 2,035. This was a major triumph for Sinn Féin, and the spirit of 1916, over the Irish Parliamentary Party. De Valera stated after the election, 'I regarded the victory in Clare as a monument to the dead.'

Even staunch unionists in Clare were impressed by de Valera. Colonel George O'Callaghan Westropp of Lismehane, Tulla wrote to the editor of the *Irish Times* on 25 June 1917:

> Yesterday, I heard Mr McNeill and Mr de Valera speak at Tulla in the East Clare election. This is not the place to criticise their policy, however, after thirty years' experience of public life I say that I have never heard a cause pleaded with more transparent honesty and lofty patriotism [...] be they right or wrong, it was Ireland first, last and all the time and no national convention can be complete and authoritative without such as they.

In a second letter to the *Irish Times* on 30 June, O'Callaghan Westopp wrote:

> Commandant de Valera is a man to be reckoned with, he stands for the purest nationality unsullied by class hatred uncorrupted by appeals to greed, and while every word he utters is a cause of

> howling and offence to West Britons, may not we Irish hope so great a fire may light us on the road to nobler things rather than conceive the land we all love in a senseless conflagration.[46]

The 'greening' of County Clare

Shortly after the election victory, de Valera made a triumphal tour of the county and the people rejoiced again. Mass meetings were held in many towns and villages around the county, and republican flags were prominently displayed. Sinn Féin was quick to harness this republican fervour and, as County Inspector Gelston predicted, Sinn Féin branches sprouted all over the county, especially in the rural parishes. Old branches were revived, and many new ones were established between August and December 1917. The *Clare Champion* recorded only five clubs on 11 August, but by 8 December there were fifty-five Sinn Féin clubs in the county – at least one in every parish. Significantly, of the fifty-five clubs formed during that time, twenty-two of them had a priest as president – three parish priests and nineteen curates. With 40 per cent of the clubs having their local priest as president, the influential role of the Catholic clergy in Sinn Féin at that time is clear. The Irish Volunteers were also increasing their strength during this period. Gelston reported in June that there were thirty-nine branches of the Irish Volunteers in the county with a membership of 2,095 men.

Besides Sinn Féin, many further branches of Conradh na Gaeilge and Cumann na mBan were set up in the county by the end of the year. By December 1917 a total of twenty-two branches of Conradh na Gaeilge were established. The chief organisers were Sean O'Muirthile and Éamon de Bhaldraithe. The republican women of the county also participated in the revolution, and by December 1917 a total of twenty-two branches of Cumann na mBan had also been established in Clare. There were close links between these political and cultural movements. Naturally, the Gaelic Athletic Association (GAA) had many close links with the republicans too. This national sporting organisation had been set up in 1884 to promote Gaelic games such as Gaelic football and hurling in opposition to British games such as rugby, soccer and cricket. The Clare footballers had a banner reading 'Up de Valera!', and members of Clarecastle GAA club, contrary to the rules of the association, had even organised a fund-raising sports day for the de Valera election fund.[47]

Defiance and hunger strike

Emboldened by the heady political atmosphere just before the election, some of the local Irish Volunteer leaders began to plan a revival of public drilling in the county. This was in defiance of the law, which had banned public drilling after the Easter Rising. Michael Brennan recorded how his brother Patrick, now commandant of the Clare Brigade, outlined a new three-point strategy for the Volunteers: they would drill in public to provoke the British authorities; if they were arrested and charged, then they would refuse to recognise the courts; if they were sentenced to a term in prison, then they would go on hunger strike to seek political prisoner status. This three-part plan of action was accepted by the Volunteers in Clare, though it was not yet sanctioned by Sinn Féin or the Volunteer leadership.

This aggressive plan of action was brazenly implemented during the East Clare by-election, when the Volunteers drilled openly for a few days leading up to the event on Wednesday, 11 July. The police took no action in response. Encouraged by this defiance, public drilling was ordered for every branch of the Volunteers in Clare for Sunday, 15 July. On that Sunday, Michael Brennan led a parade of a hundred Volunteers in Tulla, Patrick Brennan led a parade of hundreds in Ennis, and Austin Brennan led a parade in Meelick. Other parades took place around the county on the same day, and on subsequent Sundays in July and August. The parades were closely watched by the RIC.[48]

The RIC responded sharply to these provocations by arresting the leaders. County Inspector Gelston favoured strict enforcement of the law, describing the challenges in July and August as follows:

> A great wave of Sinn Féinism has passed over the county in consequence of the East Clare election and the county is seething with it […] there is growing disrespect for the law […] Drilling has been revived and is taking place extensively in all parts of the county and if not checked with a firm hand, will no doubt, become a serious problem […] The arrest of some of the leaders which have taken place will probably have a good effect if the

> courts martial give a substantial sentence and if these sentences are not remitted.[49]

On 26 July four of the most prominent leaders – Austin, Michael and Patrick Brennan of Meelick, and Peadar O'Loughin of Liscannor – were arrested. They were court-martialled in Co. Cork and sentenced to between one and two years of jail for illegal drilling. The Brennan brothers and O'Loughlin then began a hunger strike. It lasted about a week, but they were ordered by Michael Collins, the head of the IRB, to suspend it until a larger body of prisoners joined them. Over the next few weeks at least twelve other Clare republicans were arrested and sentenced for illegal drilling. By the end of August more than thirty-eight Irishmen were imprisoned in Mountjoy Jail for illegal drilling, of whom sixteen were from Clare.

The hunger strike at Mountjoy Jail was led by the Clare Volunteers on 20 September 1917 when Sean Liddy of Cooraclare (subsequently commandant of the West Clare Brigade) delivered an ultimatum to the prison governor demanding political prisoner status for the thirty-eight prisoners. This was rejected, and by 22 September force-feeding had begun. This had tragic consequences: on 25 September, the Kerry republican Thomas Ashe died because of this force-feeding. The death of Thomas Ashe had a profound impact on Irish nationalism and reinvigorated the spirit of 1916. Although the hunger strike continued until 30 September, the death and martyrdom of Thomas Ashe caused a national outcry and ensured that the hunger strikers had won this heroic battle. All sixteen Clare prisoners had been forcibly fed at least thirteen times between 20 and 30 September. The hunger strikers were granted 'political prisoner' privileges on 30 September 1917. They could wear their own clothes, did not have to do prison work and could freely associate within the prison.[50]

Bishop Fogarty and the *Clare Champion* had publicly supported the hunger strikers despite threats of censorship. Dr Fogarty wrote a powerful letter condemning the treatment of the hunger strikers at Mountjoy Jail and the death of Thomas Ashe. He labelled those who force-fed the hunger strikers as 'brutal tyrants'. Despite strict censorship laws and instructions banning such publicity, this letter was published in both the *Freeman's Journal* and the *Clare Champion* on 27 September 1917. The editor of the *Clare Champion* also called for a mass meeting in Ennis on Sunday, 30 September in support of the hunger strikers. For publishing Dr Fogarty's letter and other articles that the chief censor of Ireland considered seditious, such as descriptions of Volunteer parades and motions in support of the hunger strikers at Sinn Féin meetings, the *Clare Champion* was nearly suppressed during October and November 1917. [51]

In the letter, Dr Fogarty wrote:

> It is horrible that the country has to stand silently by listening to the moans of the decent young Irish boys who are being slowly done to death behind the walls of Mountjoy Prison by brutal tyrants; or to see them thrown in their last gasp out to die like dogs outside the jail door. They may die as poor Thomas Ashe has died, but with other results than Dublin Castle has dreamed of. Their deaths will sanctify them in the memory of Ireland and surround their heartless torturers with inextinguishable hatred and ignominy. This is the sort of cruelty we were accustomed to hear of as possible only in the ancient Bastille, or the dungeons of Naples, or the black prisons of Russia; but as altogether impossible under English rule. We have no need to wait for the future to inform us; the world sees in these hideous atrocities what the triumph of English culture means for small nationalities.[52]

'Sinn Féin is the law of the land'

Most of the sixteen Clare men who took part in the Mountjoy hunger strike were released on 15 November 1917, and they arrived home to a tremendous reception from thousands of supporters in Ennis on Tuesday, 20 November. Through their sacrifice they had won a great victory, and their hunger strike inspired many other Clare men and some Clare women to follow their example over the next few months and years. At least nine other Clare men and one woman went on hunger strike between October and December 1917, and all were released within days of their actions.[53]

Over the next few months thousands of Volunteers openly defied the law by publicly drilling in many centres in Clare and other parts of Ireland. Though they were closely watched by the RIC, no action was taken against them. County Inspector Gelston was furious with Dr Fogarty's letter and the Volunteers' public defiance of the law. In September, Gelston wrote:

> The spread of Sinn Féinism has caused open defiance of the law and strong hostility to the police [...] The death of Thomas Ashe has caused a bitter feeling [...] this has been intensified by the letter, what I must call the most ill-advised and inappropriate letter of the Bishop of Killaloe [...] also a subject in the Clare Champion. Sinn Féin will be strengthened thereby, and the enforcement of the law made more difficult.

In October he wrote:

> The state of the county is serious due to Sinn Féin [...] illegal drilling is universally carried out [...] a strong spirit of disloyalty exists [...] the law is openly defied [...] Sinn Féin is the law of the land!

In November he wrote:

> Sinn Féin holds sway [...] drilling is carried out generally throughout the county, principally on Sundays [...] arrests for illegal drilling were doing well until the release of prisoners due to hunger-striking [...] arrests are now no punishment and they do more harm than good.

And in December he had the following words:

> There is a slight fall-off in drilling. The ceasing of arrests for drilling and its apparent ignoring of it by the police caused many to give it up, in many places it is only bravado.[54]

In October 1917 Bishop Fogarty published a leaflet entitled *The Sinn Féin Banner of Irish Independence, a letter from the Bishop of Killaloe*, which included the following words, 'We had almost ceased to be Irish until Sinn Féin arose and struck the English rust from the soul of Ireland. Unfortunately, that rust had eaten deep and spoiled many a good Irish heart.' Dr Fogarty later sent a letter to Edward MacLysaght of Raheen in which he expressed his fear 'that Home Rule would only be a sham'.

Though he openly supported Sinn Féin after publishing his leaflet on 6 October 1917, there is some evidence that Dr Fogarty was moving towards supporting Sinn Féin policies – including abstention from Westminster – as early as May 1917. In a letter to Bishop O'Dwyer on 5 May, he stated:

> The older folks, especially the older clergy, are not prepared to contemplate abstention yet. The Irish Parliamentary Party is contemptible. The country would gladly give an independent party a new flag. The best course for Plunkett [Count Plunkett, father of the 1916 patriot Joseph Plunkett] and Sinn Féin would be to form such a party, and having got it, then retire from the House of Commons, if they didn't get what they wanted.[55]

Clare Volunteers in the vanguard

Following the success of the hunger strike, public drilling by the Volunteers continued throughout the county and the rest of Ireland. The RIC published monthly reports on the state of the country. A survey of police reports for Clare shows that the Volunteers paraded in forty-one separate locations in the county between November and December 1917. A total of 1,127 men drilled at twenty-two venues around the county on 18 November; a total of 1,230 men drilled at twenty-seven venues on 9 December. On 25 November 1917 there was a national day of parading to commemorate the memory of Tomas Ashe and the hunger strikers of Mountjoy; a total of 2,655 Clare men paraded and drilled at twenty-six venues throughout the county, with the largest crowds – totalling between 400 and 500 men each – assembled at Ennis and Kilrush.

The police reports between October 1917 and February 1918 show that the Irish Volunteers of Clare were in the vanguard of republican agitation in Ireland. Reports from Inspector General Byrne highlight the leading role taken by Clare Volunteers between October 1917 and January 1918:

> Of the 140 cases of illegal drilling reported nationally for October, 50 of them took place in County Clare [...] There was a total of 334 cases in Ireland in November, with 114 occurring in County Clare alone [...] There were 386 cases of illegal drilling in Ireland by Irish Volunteers in January 1918, compared with 293 in December of 1917, an increase of 98; 311 of the total drills took place in Munster, the county of Clare where a released prisoner [Patrick Brennan] is in command, being most affected. Of the remaining 77 cases, rather more than half occurred in Connaught.

In February 1918, Inspector General Byrne noted:

> Illegal drilling by Sinn Féiners was extensively carried on in Munster; to a lesser extent in Connaught and here and there in other provinces. 70% of the cases occurred in Munster and 24% of the cases were in the county of Clare alone [...] Although probably unimportant from a military point of view, this drilling has very mischievous results. Sunday after Sunday, bands of young impressionable men march about the roads carrying hurleys or imitation rifles and practising martial exercises [...] Notwithstanding the presence of large numbers of troops in Clare, drilling is still carried on in out of the way places for bravado by small parties, who disperse on the approach of soldiers or police.

Some local police urged that strong action should be taken against the illegal drilling by the Volunteers. The sergeant at Bodyke stated, 'It [drilling] should be nipped in the bud.' In Feakle the drill instructor, Joseph Tuohy, was described as 'an extreme Sinn Féiner'. In Quilty the RIC report stated, 'Since drilling began here on 25 November, the majority of men do not speak to or recognise the police at all.' In Kilkishen, John Dwyer and thirty young men shouted, 'Up the rebels of Easter Week!' William Darcy of Ballina, when challenged by the police, stated, 'I am drill instructor Darcy of the Ballina Republican Army, I'll drill the Volunteers whenever and wherever I like!' In Clarecastle the police report noted, 'James O'Reilly appeared to be their leader [...] [O'Reilly] will, sooner or later, have to be arrested. He is a very disturbing element at Clare Castle.'

Few of those who turned out for drilling carried weapons. Many had wooden 'dummy' rifles while others carried hurleys or blackthorn sticks. Some had Sinn Féin badges or emblems. Most of them drilled in their 'Sunday best' after Mass [surely not the most suitable clothing for training]. They carried out military manoeuvres such as 'fall in, forming fours, wheeling, marching'. Some of the leaders had military-style uniforms. Edward Casey of Ruan had an air pistol; Daniel Fitzpatrick, a carpenter from Kilmihil, carried a double-barrelled gun.[56]

A socio-economic study of the Volunteer leaders who conducted illegal drilling in Clare between October and December 1917 shows that most of them were from rural areas in the county. Of the fifty-one leaders identified at that time there were twenty farmers' sons, three farmers, nine farm labourers, five carpenters, five shop assistants, three publicans' sons, two teachers, one blacksmith, one clerk, one stonemason and one railway signalman. The farmers alone made up over 44 per cent of the total. It is significant, and was remarked upon critically at the time, that the farming community provided very few volunteers for the British forces during the First World War.[57]

Sinn Féin had won a stunning victory with the election of Éamon de Valera in the East Clare by-election of July 1917. The Clare Volunteers were quick to follow this success with public drilling that openly defied the law. For about a month they were almost alone in defying the law on drilling – only in September did open drilling become more general throughout Ireland. Their prominence in the Mountjoy hunger strike and the tragic death of Thomas Ashe culminated in a victory for the prisoners after a heroic struggle. Undoubtedly the pioneering role of the courageous and determined Clare Volunteers, 'soldiers of the Clare Brigade', in defying the law on public drilling, contributed enormously to the revival of the national spirit in 1917.[58]

Cattle drives in 1918

Ironically inspired by government advertising in the local press urging more tillage with slogans such as 'Why Grassland Must Be Broken', cattle drives became common in Clare during the spring of 1918. The men who drove the cattle from large ranches may have also been spurred into this illegal activity by the words of Bishop Fogarty in his Lenten pastoral letter of February 1917 – a letter, published in the papers, in which he attacked the 'lifeless' ranches. Another factor was the price of basic provisions. Prices had increased significantly since German submarines began sinking British merchant vessels in 1914. The harvests of 1917 had also been poor due to heavy rains during the harvesting season, and Sinn Féin had organised the distribution of cheap food in Ennis in December 1917 because of the high price of food. There may have also been other reasons for the new agrarian conflict, such as 'land hunger' and ancient disputes over land holdings. Whatever the reasons, large groups of small tenant farmers and labourers invaded several estates; they drove the cattle off the lands and began to plough up large areas in order to grow crops such as oats and potatoes as soon as possible. This agrarian revolution started in north Clare and spread throughout the county.

The Irish Volunteers had a prominent role in this land agitation. Sinn Féin men and women turned out in large numbers – sometimes hundreds of people; almost whole communities – armed only with hurleys and sticks, and drove the cattle from the graziers' farms. Clare was becoming ungovernable as the people brazenly defied the RIC and openly ignored the law. The public drilling by Volunteers made it easy to organise cattle drives, as they gave leadership to their communities. The testimony of leading IRA members in the county clearly indicates that local Irish Volunteers and Sinn Féin leaders were very active in the agitation. Some Volunteers wanted to manipulate the acquisition and division of the large ranches and tried to ensure that local Sinn Féin members would get preference.

Michael Brennan, in his memoir, states, 'There was much agrarian discontent in Clare and we decided to "cash-in" on this. Cattle drives became popular and all over the county Volunteers took part in them as organised units.' Brennan's opinions were corroborated by other Volunteers in their witness statements for the Bureau of Military History, including that of Andrew O'Donoghue, Joe Barrett, Peter O'Loughlin and Thomas MacNamara. There was some concern in Sinn Féin headquarters that the cattle-driving might distract members from political action; the *ard comhairle* (executive council) of East Clare Sinn Féin issued a directive on 9 February stating that Volunteers should not take part in cattle drives without permission from the *comhairle ceanntair* (the district executive).

There were cattle drives in many parts of the county. The RIC, though armed, were almost powerless to stop the land agitation and other lawlessness such as arms raids. Two policemen were beaten up and their rifles stolen during a Scariff cattle drive on 20 February 1918; two more rifles were stolen from the RIC at Inch, and a shot was fired into the police hut there on 16 January. There were arms raids in Ennis and Kilrush on 18 January, and another in Kilrush a week later. The most serious incident occurred on 24 February at Manusmore, where cattle were driven from the McInerney farm by a crowd of over three hundred. The police, who stated that they were under attack, fired on the crowd, wounding three men – one of whom, John Ryan of Newmarket-on-Fergus, died from his injuries. That was probably the final straw for the authorities. The police needed help to keep the peace, so Clare was declared a special military area and large numbers of soldiers were drafted into the county.[59]

Special military area

Major General Burnett, the competent military authority in Clare, issued a communiqué on Tuesday, 26 February 1918:

> The outbreak of lawlessness which has occurred in County Clare rendered it necessary on Sunday to send additional troops into the county to assist the police. The county has been declared a special military area within the meaning of the realm regulation 29B, and all the powers hereby conferred on the commandant will be enforced so long as it is necessary for the restoration of order.

Burnett issued orders proclaiming special measures for the preservation of law and order in Clare. Restrictions were placed on entrance into, and movements within, the county. Drilling and the wearing of paramilitary uniforms was prohibited, along with all meetings, parades and processions; stricter censorship was also imposed. Burnett ordered the surrender of all legally-held weapons; although a large number of weapons were handed up, practically all of them were the property of 'loyal people'.

Naturally, these new rules had an impact on cattle drives and public drilling by the Volunteers. Commandant Michael Brennan had led a parade of about two hundred Irish Volunteers through the streets of Ennis on Tuesday, 26 February. He was reported to have said to the Volunteers, 'We could only die once and that we could not die in a better cause than for Ireland.' He was arrested the next day and spent most of the rest of the year in jail. Other Volunteer leaders arrested included Art O'Donnell of Tullycrine and Peter O'Loughlin of Liscannor. Though public drilling by Volunteers ceased, some drilling took place in 'out of the way places for bravado'. However, the small parties quickly dispersed on the approach of the police or military. Clare remained a special military area until the end of the First World War on 11 December 1918.[60]

Censorship of the *Clare Champion*

The *Clare Champion*, which had barely escaped being seized in October and November 1917 for breaching the censorship laws, was closed without any warning on 2 April 1918. The paper did not reappear until 28 September 1918. Military authorities seized the printing press on the orders of the chief censor, Lord Decies, who had warned the editor on several occasions between October and December 1917 that some of the articles, such as giving notice of Volunteer parades were, seditious and breached the censorship regulations. Ironically, County Inspector Gelston's reports had consistently described the tone of the *Clare Champion*'s articles throughout 1917 and early 1918 as 'moderate'.

The closure of the *Clare Champion* was a big loss for Sinn Féin and the Irish Volunteers, as it was the leading nationalist newspaper in the county – the *Saturday Record* followed a pro-government line. The *Clare Champion* proprietors (the Galvin family) and the editor, Sarsfield Maguire, had converted to Sinn Féin policies prior to the East Clare by-election of 1917. The newspaper had given wide publicity to nationalist policies in the county. It gave prominence to Sinn Féin activities and club meetings, as well as other Irish cultural organisations such as Conradh na Gaeilge and the GAA. The paper also supported the hunger strikers, and its closure was a big propaganda loss to the nationalists of Clare.[61]

'England has no moral right to impose conscription'

The conscription issue united all nationalists in Ireland in a determined campaign to resist the British government's attempt to impose compulsory recruitment in Ireland. The matter came to a head in the spring of 1918 after the collapse of Russian armies on the Eastern Front and a major German advance in the Western Front, just before the American forces began to arrive in large numbers. There was a fear that the Germans would break through and force the British and French to surrender. During this military crisis there was a huge demand for extra troops. The leaders of the

Irish Parliamentary Party and Sinn Féin united in a pan-nationalist coalition, which was strongly supported by the Catholic Church. Together they successfully resisted the British plans to impose conscription. Members of Cumann na mBan were prominent in organising processions in Clare, and they held a separate petition for women to oppose conscription. Bishop Fogarty gave powerful moral leadership to the campaign. On 5 April, Dr Fogarty sent a letter to the Ennis Sinn Féin club in which he said, 'England has no moral right to impose conscription!'

A national anti-conscription day was held after Mass on 21 April 1918. In a powerful speech in Ennis cathedral, Bishop Fogarty denounced the 'brutal exercise of tyranny [...] the Conscription Act was oppressive and unjust, and the organisers called on the people to resist it by every means at their disposal [...] should they attempt to enforce it, the people would have the right to resist this atrocious act of tyranny.' Though all public parades were banned from 4 April, religious processions were not. In places such as Ennis and Miltown Malbay, members of Cumann na mBan took part in religious processions to oppose conscription. Faith and fatherland were united in a powerful political gesture.

Bishop Fogarty had, by now, become an open and passionate supporter of Sinn Féin. In the letter to the Ennis Sinn Féin club on 5 April, he had stated:

> We had almost ceased to be Irish until Sinn Féin arose and struck the English rust from the soul of Ireland [...] Martial Law has not shaken the hand of Clare, which still holds in firm grasp the Sinn Féin banner of Irish independence and will continue to hold it until that independence is fully realised.[62]

Gaelic Sunday

In July, because of the unrest in the country, the authorities in Dublin Castle, the centre of British rule in Ireland, prohibited the holding of any public meeting, including sports events, without a special permit. This outraged the GAA, and as an act of defiance, the Central Council instructed all county boards to organise as many matches as possible on Sunday, 4 August at 3 p.m. More than 1,800 games were organised throughout Ireland on this day in a national protest that they called 'Gaelic Sunday'. The GAA publicly challenged the government, and when tens of thousands of Gaels – men, women and children – turned out to play and watch Gaelic games, the government was unable to do much about the massive public opposition to the unpopular law.

Undoubtedly, many GAA games took place around the county on Gaelic Sunday, but perhaps because of the absence of the *Clare Champion*, there was only one report of this public defiance in Clare – in the *Saturday Record*. The paper reported that visitors and locals celebrated Gaelic Sunday at Kilkee:

> It was truly a Gaelic revival. Instead of the usual cricket, tennis, golf, etc., a splendid and keenly contested game of hurling was enjoyed on the strand. The competing teams were made up of visiting clergy, the Priests vs the Brothers. After a well-fought contest, the former were declared winners by 11 goals 3 points to 3 goals 2 points. The enthusiasm of the hundreds of spectators as either side scored gave much evidence that the 'game of the Gael' is, notwithstanding trying times, holding its own.[63]

Though the county remained under martial law and seemed outwardly peaceable, underneath it was seething with discontent encouraged by Sinn Féin, which was becoming the main political power in the country. In September, County Inspector Gelston reported, 'A disloyal rebellious spirit prevails [...] the power of Sinn Féin is paramount.' In October he prophetically stated, 'The National Party have been thrown over by a large majority of people.'[64]

Towards the end of the year some local Sinn Féin leaders who had been arrested during the year were released. According to the police reports, they returned home quietly with few demonstrations in their favour. They were also in poor health after extended incarceration. County Inspector Gelston wrote:

> On 14th November two prisoners returned to Lisdoonvarna, Peter O'Loughlin and Austin Geraghty. Their return caused little excitement, only four or five of their Sinn Féin friends met them. They are remaining quiet, but we are informed, holding secret meetings in connection with the election. They both continue as commanders and drill instructors of the Irish Volunteers. No drilling took place in the county except marching in pairs at funerals [...] An interned Sinn Féiner, Arthur O'Donnell, was released on account of ill-health. He arrived in Ennis on the night

> of 30 December though some rejoicings were evident [...] the crowd went home quietly and on his arrival at Kilrush the following day no one met him at all [...] Michael Brennan, another prisoner released for ill-health arrived in Ennis last night, he was not met, and no demonstration was made.[65]

Bishop Fogarty was not alone in publicly endorsing Sinn Féin; he and many other Catholic clergy in Clare proposed and endorsed de Valera for re-election in the general election of 1918, which took place shortly after the First World War ended. In fact, five parish priests and twenty curates supported de Valera's candidature. With such powerful ecclesiastical and clerical backing, combined with the support of the *Clare Champion*, the Irish Parliamentary Party did not stand a chance in Clare; they didn't put up any fight this time or even nominate any candidates. De Valera was elected MP for East Clare while Brian O'Higgins, a Gaelic League teacher at Carrigaholt, was elected MP for West Clare.

Fr Pat Gaynor, then a member of Sinn Féin's national executive, explained why Brian O'Higgins was chosen to stand in the West Clare constituency in the 1918 general election:

> Brian O'Higgins would be the more popular choice; he was well-liked in West Clare for his charm of manner and his sincerity [...] I was afraid that many of the older voters would hesitate to support Paddy Brennan, who was regarded as a firebrand at the time. Brian O'Higgins, on the other hand, was regarded as a moderate and level-headed; he was styled the gentle poet of the Sinn Féin movement. I ought to have known that a gentle poet can prove more extreme than a fighting man.[66]

The success of Sinn Féin candidates in Clare was mirrored in many other Irish constituencies in the 1918 election. Out of 105 seats, Sinn Féin won 73, the Unionists won 26 and the Irish Parliamentary Party only won 6 seats. Clearly Sinn Féin was now the representative voice of most nationalists in Ireland. The electors of East Clare had signalled a transformation in Irish politics in July 1917. Following this stunning electoral victory, the Irish Volunteers of Clare had played a significant and pioneering role in the ascendancy of Sinn Féin, especially when considering their defiance of the law on public drilling and their advocacy of hunger strikes. Sinn Féin also received much propaganda support from the *Clare Champion* after 1916. Credit for the 1918 electoral rout must also be given to the members of Cumann na mBan, to the powerful ecclesiastical support of Bishop Fogarty in favour of the hunger strikers of 1917, and to the involvement of many Catholic priests in Clare politics. In 1918, Mr Charles E. Glynn, a prominent merchant and industrialist from Kilrush, referred to Dr Fogarty as 'the recognised head of the Sinn Féiners in Clare'.[67]

Though Sinn Féin had won the political battle, the Volunteers were seeking a military victory. The county seemed to be peaceful and the Volunteer prisoners had returned quietly to their homes, but the IRA, as the Volunteers were now openly describing themselves, were quietly preparing for another war with the British forces. In a letter to the *Clare Champion*, all the Clare hunger strikers at Mountjoy described themselves as members of the IRA. The major problem was that they had too few arms for a major conflict. During the year, they acquired some weapons through robbery. In January they robbed Todd's gun shop in Ennis and several houses in the Kilrush district, acquiring at least six shotguns, several revolvers and some ammunition. The IRA also attacked the RIC and stole some weapons. On 20 February two constables on 'protection duty' at Inch were attacked and robbed of their carbines. A similar attack took place near Kilrush on 15 April when two constables on 'protection duty' were 'rushed' and overpowered by a mob of about twenty men and robbed of their carbines. Finally, in August two rifles were stolen from the army barracks at Killaloe. Through these acts they acquired a total of about fifteen weapons: six shotguns, several revolvers, four police carbines and two army rifles, as well as some ammunition to add to their limited arsenal.

In November 1918, County Inspector Gelston observed, 'The Volunteers are insufficiently armed and equipped for conflict with soldiers and fears of the consequences restrains them from rebellion.' Little did Gelston imagine that the IRA would indeed start a rebellion in the middle of July 1919, with most of their energies being devoted to attacking the RIC, not the British army.[68]

2
PREPARING FOR WAR

Following the election of Sinn Féin MPs in the East and West Clare constituencies in December 1918, the year 1919 witnessed the growth and consolidation of Sinn Féin and the Irish Volunteers, also known as the IRA, in Clare. The county gradually drifted into a state of war fomented by the IRA, who openly defied the police. The RIC found themselves in a very difficult position; calls were made for them to resign their positions in the national interest, and they were ostracised and boycotted by a majority nationalist community. One serious handicap facing the IRA was a shortage of weapons. To prepare for war, they embarked on a campaign to acquire more weapons through persuasion or force. They persuaded sympathetic farmers to voluntarily hand over their shotguns, and they stole weapons from members of the unionist community as well as from the RIC.

In the middle of summer, the IRA began a guerrilla war and went on the offensive against the RIC, who were deemed to be 'enemies of the people'. The campaign became more vicious, culminating in the killing of two policemen on 4 August 1919. Because of increasing lawlessness, the county was proclaimed a special military area on 7 August. In the second half of the year, the IRA attempted to enforce the boycott of the RIC by attacking and intimidating people who were deemed to be collaborating with the police or the army, and they continued with the attacks on police and arms raids. Throughout the year, Bishop Fogarty made several statements that gave strong moral support to Sinn Féin and the cause of Irish independence.

'Release the prisoners!' was the cry heard at several public meetings held around the county in January, especially in towns such as Ennis, Killaloe and Kilrush, highlighting the case of many nationalists still held in prison. Several Catholic clergymen took a prominent part in these meetings. At the Ennis meeting, a letter from Bishop Fogarty was read out in which the bishop defended the prisoners. Dr Fogarty stated, 'the prisoners were not criminals, but upright men and women, who were incarcerated under an oppressive regime under Dublin Castle.' Later in the year Dr Fogarty stated that 'our public men were worthy representatives of the Irish nation; they were ardent patriots, fiercely determined to establish our country's freedom; that spirit is their glory and not a crime!'[69]

Sinn Féin held *comhairle ceanntair* meetings for East and West Clare in January 1919. These gatherings were attended by delegates from all parts of Clare, representing nearly every parish. The Catholic clergy were prominent at these meetings. Fr William O'Kennedy of St Flannan's College was treasurer and vice-president of the Ennis branch of Sinn Féin. Of the forty-seven delegates in attendance, a total of eight were Catholic clergymen. Besides Fr O'Kennedy there was also Fr M. Breen, Fr A. Clancy, Fr C. Culligan, Fr Crowe and Fr Roche. However, while Sinn Féin focused on the political struggle, the IRA prepared for the forthcoming military struggle against the British government.[70]

Although Sinn Féin had banned members of the party from cattle driving in 1918 as it was distracting from the national struggle, a significant cattle drive took place after Sunday Mass in Miltown Malbay on 12 January 1919. The lands had been held by James Kenny, a barrister and president of the local Sinn Féin club, who was then serving eighteen months in prison for offences under DORA; Kenny had previously been evicted from the lands due to a family dispute. Nine young men, including some, such as Ignatius O'Neill, who were to become prominent in the War of Independence, were subsequently arrested for the offence, but they refused to recognise the court. Another cattle drive took place in the Moy district, and the cattle were driven towards Inagh. In October eight men from Carrigaholt were arrested for cattle driving at Kilballyowen.[71]

Besides cattle drives, there were several other reported agrarian disputes in the county during the year in which people were shot at or badly wounded over land. For instance, on 18 January three men were arrested for a shooting outrage at Cregboy, Tubber. On 3

August a man was badly wounded by gunshots at Lisdoonvarna; on the same day another man was seriously wounded at Ennistymon by gunshot fire. On 1 October a man was wounded by gunshot pellets at Corofin. On 23 October a family was badly beaten up at Kinlea, near Kilrush, resulting in the death of a man a few weeks later. Early in December, shots were fired at a farmer in Bearnageeha near Darragh. All these outrages were related to disputes over land, a very divisive issue in Clare then and, indeed, for decades.[72]

The Clare brigades

The IRA set up a new military structure in Clare. Originally, up to 1916, the Volunteers in the county were under the control of the commandant in Limerick. However, after the confusion of the Easter Rising and dissatisfaction with this structure, the Clare Volunteers wanted their own division. This was established in 1917 with Paddy Brennan of Meelick as commandant, but it also proved to be unsatisfactory, apparently due to rivalry between some leading republican families in the county. Ernie O'Malley, a prominent IRA organiser and commandant of the 2nd Southern Brigade during the war who later wrote a celebrated book about his experiences during the War of Independence, *On Another Man's Wound*, recalled an IRA meeting at HQ in Dublin in early 1919 in which Cathal Brugha (minister for defence), Michael Collins (director of operations and intelligence) and Richard Mulcahy (chief of staff) were in attendance and the three new brigades were established:

> There had been a brigade in Clare; headquarters was at Meelick, a few miles from Limerick City, although Carrigaholt on the Shannon was more than sixty miles away. Control was, as a result, uneven. The county had gained strength in recruiting, and the staff had divided it into three brigades: East, Mid and West Clare Brigades. The Brennan brothers, Padraig, Michael and Austin, had helped to build the Irish Volunteers in the county. Padraig and Michael resented the formation of three independent brigades, they wanted to form a division to control the three brigades. The Brennans had minds of their own, but they were not sufficiently impersonal. Padraig Brennan had been dismissed. Michael Brennan was now in charge of East Clare. Collins during a pause said, 'the bloody bowseys!' Mulcahy did not speak. He was always calmer than Cathal Brugha, less taut and more

> impersonal […] 'You will have difficulty and opposition,' Cathal Brugha said, 'but you know how to manage situations by this.'

Under the new military structure in the county, Art O'Donnell of Tullycrine was appointed commandant of West Clare; Frank Barrett of Bearnageeha, Darragh became commandant of Mid-Clare; and Michael Brennan of Meelick became commandant of East Clare.[73]

Some of the leading IRA members in the county who had been arrested early in 1918, such as Art O'Donnell of Tullycrine and Michael Brennan of Meelick, were released from Belfast prison on Christmas Eve and returned to Clare early in the new year. They were determined to carry on the fight and quickly resumed their organisational and drilling operations in west and east Clare. The RIC tried to keep a close eye on the leaders. In January the county inspector noted:

> Sinn Féin has not been very openly active during the month, but the leaders, including Michael Brennan and Arthur O'Donnell, both released prisoners have been moving about a good deal. It looks as if they are marking time to see what may come of the Peace Conference or to what extent Dáil Éireann will be allowed to go.[74]

Ostracising the RIC

Relations between the police and the people of the county had been difficult, especially since the hunger strikes of 1917 and the shooting dead of John Ryan following the Manusmore cattle drive in February 1918. The police had been unpopular in several parts of the county for many years due to their role in preventing cattle drives and protecting landlords and large farmers who were opposed to land division. In January, County Inspector Gelston noted, 'The police are boycotted in some portions of the county and cannot in most places get supplies. This is arranged by Sinn Féin […] and it is desired to cause disaffection amongst them if possible […] Relations between the police and people are strained.'[75]

The first attack on the RIC in 1919 occurred on 4 January near Carrigaholt. Constable Reynolds was cycling home from duty at Kilrush when he was attacked by a gang of four men armed with sticks. He was overpowered, beaten with his own baton, tied up with hay-ropes and thrown into the marsh. His assailants took his revolver and bicycle, as well as a sum of £4–£5. He had severe head wounds and his wrist was broken. This attack was only a prelude to far more serious and numerous attacks upon the police in the county, which occurred throughout the year. It is not clear whether the attack on the constable was politically motivated and authorised by the IRA, or whether it was plain robbery and assault for agrarian or criminal purposes, but the local IRA acquired a revolver and several young men went 'on the run' afterwards.[76]

By March, relations between the RIC and the public had deteriorated further. They were not helped by Sinn Féin propaganda against the police, which was even used in the Catholic churches at Mass. Inspector Gelston's report for March noted:

> In nearly all the chapels in the county documents were read, received from the Lord Mayor of Dublin, dealing with the alleged ill-treatment of Sinn Féin prisoners in Belfast jail [...] The speeches made recently by Sinn Féin speakers has intensified the feelings of Sinn Féiners who regard the police as their greatest enemies [...] Consequently, they will use all their efforts to oppose the police, driving them into disrepute with the people in the hope, no doubt of causing disaffection and perhaps resignations.[77]

Sinn Féin MPs denounced the RIC at the first public session of the Dáil on 10 April 1919. President de Valera and other Sinn Féin MPs vilified the RIC, calling them agents of the British government, 'Janissaries of England', who should be ostracised by the people of Ireland and boycotted. Éamon de Valera made a long and impassioned speech denouncing them:

> They are spies in our midst. They are England's Janissaries. They are the eyes and ears of the enemy. The RIC is a military body, armed with rifle and bayonet, revolver and baton [...] Their history is one of brutal treason against their own people. They must be shunned and socially ostracised to show them how the Irish people loathe them and their calling.[78]

Shortly after returning home, Art O'Donnell began organising and training the IRA in the Tullycrine area. The local IRA members – a group of between forty and fifty young men – decided to disarm three local RIC men – a sergeant and two constables – who were observing a group of men publicly drilling outside Knockerra church after Mass on Sunday, 13 April. They managed to overpower the two constables and take their carbines. A revolver shot was fired at Sergeant O'Donohue, but the sergeant returned fire upon them and the men scattered. The two carbines were hidden in a local house. Art O'Donnell, who had not directly participated in the operation, was arrested along with five other locals, and the guns were retrieved. O'Donnell was court-martialled in Cork on 8 May; he was sentenced to two years in jail for illegal drilling, and aiding and abetting an assault upon the police, but he was released shortly afterwards, on 18 June, due to ill-health. This debacle weakened the IRA movement in west Clare for a few months.

County Inspector Gelston blamed the attack at Knockerra on a visit from Michael Brennan and Ernie O'Malley:

> The south of the county including the whole Kilrush district has become disturbed and active [...] this change is directly attributable to the visits of Michael Brennan of Meelick and a man named O'Malley from Dublin, both are organizers and visited Kilrush district resulting in the occurrence of 13 April where three policemen encountered a party of men drilling, they were attacked and rifles taken, these, however were recovered and six persons secured and marched four miles through a hostile neighbourhood to Kilrush barracks.

In fact, Ernie O'Malley had stayed at Art O'Donnell's house in Tullycrine in March, and he spent some time giving lectures on military tactics to the IRA leaders in west Clare. In his book, *On Another Man's Wound*, O'Malley states that he suggested that the local RIC at Knockerra should be disarmed after Mass on Palm Sunday. Two policemen were 'jumped' and two rifles taken, while O'Malley stated that he had a gun battle with the sergeant. O'Malley directed that Art O'Donnell should not take part in the affair.[79]

A shocking incident occurred on Sunday, 29 June when a 55-year-old farmer-fisherman named Patrick Studdert from Kilkee was shot dead by a soldier of the Scottish Horse Regiment on guard duty at the sports field in Kilkee, the regiment's base. Studdert left a widow and a large family. The soldier who fired the fatal shot was exonerated after an inquiry. The death of Patrick Studdert, who, it seems, was not a member of Sinn Féin, angered the west Clare community, just as they had been outraged after the death of Thomas Russell, a Gaelic teacher in Carrigaholt, who was bayonetted by the military in March 1918.[80]

Arms and the IRA

While Sinn Féin was the dominant political force in Ireland and had, following the general election of December 1918, declared an Irish republic at the Dáil in January 1919, it could not achieve Irish independence by words alone. They had a strong following of IRA men throughout the country, but they were an army in military structure only. The IRA were poorly armed. Many of the officers may have had revolvers, but rifles and ammunition were scarce for most of the members on a national level.

This was also the case in Clare. Though about three hundred Volunteers had turned out for manoeuvres during Easter 1916, their main weapons were shotguns, with limited ammunition, and a few rifles and revolvers. They had publicly drilled in late 1917 with sticks and hurleys. Although the number of IRA members in Clare had increased significantly, to about 1,200 by December 1917, their arsenal had not improved much, even during the conscription crisis of 1918 when many blacksmiths around the county were busy making pikes sold to the IRA for 2*s* 6*d* each (about €10 in today's currency).

Michael Brennan, commandant of the East Clare Brigade in 1919, highlighted the arms shortage in 1919:

> It was difficult to hold the Volunteers together after the end of the 'conscription crisis' and of the First World War in 1918. There was a large number enrolled, but rarely more than 25% turned up for parades [...] With the exception of a few revolvers and some shotguns, arms were practically non-existent in my brigade and I gave instruction that all privately held arms were to be collected. Most of these were in unionist hands and their collection involved widespread raids. Except for a few shots which hit nobody, they were carried out quietly and with success.

Brennan also recorded how he had planned an operation in the summer to seize arms from the RIC. He suggested 'a general onslaught on the RIC all over the Brigade area for one night'. However, two days before the planned onslaught, General Richard Mulcahy heard about the plan and Brennan was ordered to call off the operation. Ernie O'Malley, who was organising in Clare at the time, countermanded all operations. General Mulcahy argued that 'the people had to be educated and led gently into open war.' O'Malley added, 'We had thought in terms of a general, simultaneous, rebellion throughout the country, now headquarters endeavoured to teach us to train, arm and equip and to carry out minor operations for the seizure of arms.'

In west Clare, Martin Chambers, the captain of B Company, 3rd Battalion, West Clare Brigade, relates how a planned attack on a British military truck at McGrath's Cross, Moyasta, on 15 August was called off because Commandant Sean Liddy claimed that there were not enough rifles to cover a retreat. Chambers states that about forty IRA members were assembled, and that their arsenal consisted of nine rifles, five revolvers and about twenty-six shotguns. John Flanagan, also of the West Clare Brigade, corroborated this, 'Our brigade, with 8–10 rifles and 25–30 shotguns, could not hope to deliver a serious attack on the enemy.'

There was a similar situation in the Mid-Clare Brigade. The testimony of several IRA members suggested that they had few weapons in the middle of 1919. Sean McNamara of Muckinish Ballyvaughan stated, 'We had no guns till the end of 1919.' Pat Kerin of Miltown Malbay stated, 'Up to the middle of 1919 we had little arms.' Joe Barrett stated, 'The Volunteers took up the shotguns from a number of farmers.' Incidentally, the IRA had to pay for the ammunition that they were using to fight the Crown forces! For instance in August 1919, Frank Barrett, commandant of the Mid-Clare Brigade, sent a sum of £16 to Michael Collins at general headquarters (GHQ) for the purchase of grenades at 6*s* 6*d*, or 7*s* each (about €30 today). One of Frank Barrett's sisters was used to collect grenades in Dublin for the Mid-Clare Brigade in November 1919.[81]

Clearly the IRA had inadequate weapons in the face of the heavily armed Crown forces – the army, the marines and the RIC. The IRA arsenal in Clare had not increased much since 1916. In January 1919 each brigade had only a few rifles, a couple of dozen shotguns, some revolvers and limited stocks of ammunition. This limited arsenal would not last long against the heavily armed military forces concentrated in barracks in Ennis, Ennistymon, Kilrush and Killaloe. At the end of February 1918 the Crown forces were increased in Clare when, after widespread land agitation, the county was proclaimed a special military area; hundreds of extra troops were drafted into the county until the end of the year. Thus, there were about six hundred heavily armed troops stationed here at the beginning of 1919 – a formidable opposition for the IRA.

On the other hand, the RIC presented a softer target for the IRA. There were dozens of barracks scattered around the county – located in every village – with many police huts in the countryside protecting people under threat due to land agitation. While barracks in large towns such as Ennis and Kilrush had a police force of more than ten policemen, many smaller barracks in the villages had only a few constables. Although the police were armed with revolvers, carbine rifles and batons, they usually patrolled in relatively small groups. The policemen were lightly armed and could be ambushed and overwhelmed by large IRA forces, armed mainly with shotguns. Clare, because of land agitation, was heavily policed, with over 480 policemen based there in 1914. According to Jim Herlihy, who wrote extensively about the history of the RIC, 'the RIC was the primary target of the IRA at the start of the War of Independence, as the police barracks was the most convenient symbol of British imperialism in Ireland. The police force was not equipped to fight a guerrilla war.' Despite the vast inequality in their arsenals, the IRA, in a David versus Goliath conflict, decided to go to war with the British forces in Ireland.[82]

One difficult factor in targeting the RIC was the fact that they were a police force largely composed of Irish Catholics. Most of the rank-and-file constabulary had come from small farms; thus, they came from a broadly similar background and culture to most of the IRA and, indeed, the population of Ireland at that time. In peaceful times the police would be regarded as decent respectable people, but since 1916, relations between the police and the people had deteriorated, and by 1919 many people regarded them as an alien force. Sinn Féin had orchestrated a highly successful propaganda campaign to blacken their character, encouraging people to boycott them. The morale of the police must have been low, and faced with such pressure from de Valera, the leader of Sinn Féin, many of the police resigned early in 1919 and in 1920. In January County Inspector Gelston reported, 'The police are boycotted in some portions of the county and cannot in most places get supplies. This is arranged by Sinn Féin, because the police are government servants and it is desired to cause disaffection amongst them if possible [...] Relations between the police and people are strained.'[83]

However, while it may have been easy to boycott a policeman, it was another matter to shoot one. Most Irish people were genuinely shocked by the attacks on the police at the beginning of the War of Independence. The attacks were considered as 'murderous outrages' and were widely condemned by the Catholic church, moderate politicians, the press and the public. Over the next couple of years, as the war intensified and as the RIC was strengthened by the Black and Tans and Auxiliaries, who were mainly English Protestants from urban areas, there was less sympathy for members of the Crown forces killed by the IRA. This was especially the case during the 'reign of terror' (in 1920 and 1921 when the Crown forces, especially the Black and Tans, carried out terrorist reprisals in response to IRA attacks).

The war begins

The War of Independence in Clare may be said to have begun early in July 1919 when several assaults were made on police patrols and upon police huts and barracks around the county. According to Piaras Béaslaí, a TD, the editor of *An tÓglach* and the director of publicity for the IRA, 'It was really in County Clare that the guerrilla warfare may be said to have started.'[84] A wave of assaults on the police began in July, with attacks occurring throughout the county. The first attack began on Sunday, 7 July, at about midnight. Constables Hanrahan and O'Connor were on protection duty, guarding a boycotted farm belonging to the O'Dwyers, which was about one and a half miles from Kilfenora on the Kilshanny Road. They were fired on by a group of three or four men lying in ambush, and both constables were hit with buckshot; Hanrahan received about a hundred grains in the right thigh while O'Connor was hit by about forty pellets in the right arm. Constable Hanrahan's carbine was stolen during the attack.

Andrew O'Donoghue, an officer of the Mid-Clare Brigade IRA, stated that the decision to begin the war against the police in Clare was taken some time in June:

> In June 1919 at the first meeting of the Mid Clare Brigade Council regarding operations, it was decided that police patrols in each area should be attacked. The first attack took place on a patrol of four RIC men between Kilfenora and Kilshanny with shotguns. Two policemen were wounded, and one rifle captured.

Martin Chambers of the West Clare Brigade recorded, 'Around 18 June we received orders from HQ to attack police patrols whenever they appeared.' The East Clare Brigade began their operations in early August. The first attack in east Clare occurred around 2 a.m. on Sunday, 3 August when the RIC barracks at Broadford, occupied by a sergeant and five constables, was attacked by a large number of armed IRA men from the East Clare Brigade, who made use of shotguns and a few rifles. The IRA maintained a brisk fusillade of gunfire for about an hour; they fired at the barracks from the direction of the church field, and the police returned fire on the assailants. More than two hundred shots were fired at the building and much damage was done. One constable was slightly injured, but the police did not surrender, and the attack was called off. The telegraph wires were cut to isolate the barracks.[85]

The IRA assault on the constables guarding the O'Dwyer farm provoked an angry response from the shocked community of Kilfenora. A public meeting was held in the village on the following Thursday night to protest the assault. At the meeting the local parish priest, Fr P. Cassidy, proposed the resolution, 'That we condemn in the strongest manner the cowardly and murderous attack which took place outside Kilfenora on Sunday night, by which two constables nearly lost their lives.' He stated:

> I know no reason why two courteous and inoffensive police should be attacked [...] the miscreants who planned this foul outrage must have come from outside the parish [...] The people of Kilfenora, in common with Clare people generally, believe in

> fair play. They do not think that the right of Ireland to self-determination can be helped by midnight assassins. The true friends of Ireland prize the honour of their native land too highly to have it stained by abominable crime.

At the Grand Jury of County Clare, Colonel Tottenham of Mount Callan proposed, and William A. Fitzgerald seconded, the following proposal, 'That the High Sheriff and the Grand Jury of the County Clare desire to express their admiration of the splendid conduct of the Royal Irish Constabulary in the discharge of their duties in the present trying and disturbed times.'[86]

Though the culprits were called 'cowardly midnight assassins' and their actions deemed 'abominable, murderous assaults', the IRA in Clare seemed to be immune to the harsh criticism. On the night of Wednesday, 9 July, two RIC constables, Mannion and Creaghan, were fired on while on night patrol at Danganelly near Cooraclare. Three shots were fired at the policemen, but they were not injured. Apparently, threatening notices were posted in the district warning people not to associate with the military or police. This attack was considered 'the first outrage of this type in West Clare'.[87]

The Mid-Clare Brigade decided to attack the RIC huts at Inch and Connolly in late July. Ernie O'Malley, who had been sent by HQ to organise Clare between March and May 1919, stated that he had arranged for the Mid-Clare Brigade to attack some police patrols, posts and huts. The police huts were a legacy of the land struggles, as they were protecting people who were involved in agrarian disputes. The Inch police hut was attacked early morning on Sunday, 20 July by a group of men armed with shotguns and revolvers. At about 3.30 a.m. a sergeant and four constables were woken by an explosion from a bomb that had been thrown in through the front window of the hut. Two more bombs were thrown in through a back window, but they only caused slight damage. The police returned fire with their rifles and revolvers. The fight continued for about three-quarters of an hour, after which the attacking party withdrew. None of the policemen were injured, but at least one of the IRA men was injured; the police noticed a considerable amount of blood around where spent cartridges were strewn by the attacking party.

Around the same time on Sunday morning, another party of men from the Mid-Clare Brigade attacked the Connolly police hut. Four sleeping policemen were awoken by the sound of a loud crash at the front door. They discovered that men armed with guns had succeeded in bursting the lock but could not force their way in because the door was still held by a chain. The police were called upon to surrender and shots were fired through the windows where the shutters were smashed. The police returned fire, and after a sharp but brief encounter, lasting about an hour, the armed raiders withdrew. No bombs were used in this attack, and neither were any of the police or any of the attacking party injured. No arrests were made at Inch or Connolly, as the raiders escaped under cover of darkness.[88]

To raise money for arms purchases, Michael Brennan led a raid on the main post office in Limerick in November 1919, which netted £1,500 for the republican cause. Brennan was removed from his position as commandant of the East Clare Brigade by General Mulcahy, as the robbery was an embarrassment to the republican cause; his brother Austin was appointed as commandant in his place. Michael Brennan was restored as commandant early in the new year. The East Clare Brigade were, however, allowed to keep the money for arms purchases.[89]

The attacks on the police were condemned by the Church of Ireland bishop of Kilfenora and Killaloe. At the annual meeting of the Kilfenora and Killaloe Diocesan Synod, Bishop Sterling Berry admitted that the policies pursued by the British government in its treatment of Ireland had been disastrous to the peace of the country but that the recent attacks were indefensible:

> The policy has been one of vacillation and irritation […] But no policy, however misguided, could justify crimes, which make all true lovers of Ireland hang their heads in sorrow and shame. I refer specifically to the murders or attempted murders of officers and men of the police force. We, as a Synod of Irish churchmen, cannot hesitate in our expression of horror at these crimes and we tender to our police our sympathy with them in their extremely hazardous life and our assurance of the appreciation, which we have for their courage and their devotion to duty […] no cause can ever really prosper if it is stained with heartless

> crimes. The greatest enemies of Ireland at this juncture are those who shed innocent blood.[90]

Murder at Illaunbaun

The most shocking incident of 1919 occurred at Ballyvraneen, about 4 miles from Ennistymon on the Inagh Road. On the night of 4 August, two RIC men, Sergeant Riordan and Constable Murphy, were shot by armed assailants. The constable died at the scene; the sergeant died the following day. The injured sergeant attracted the attention of a local farmer by blowing his whistle and calling for help. While wounded at the scene, the sergeant wrote a few words on his prayerbook, 'shot by three assailants, wounded them [...] a repeater did for us.'

The next day, about four hours before he died, Sergeant Riordan made a dying declaration:

> When Constable Murphy and I got near 81 Cross, cycling abreast, three fellows jumped out from behind the bushes at the cross on the right-hand side. They shouted: 'hands up!', at the same time firing at us. One fellow had what I thought was a Winchester repeating rifle, I don't know what the others had. Myself and the young fellow [Constable Murphy] fired. They all fell, I hit my man twice. They ran a bit then and fired at us. I was shot first and then I saw the young fellow fall.
>
> I fired the five rounds of the revolver, the fellow who fired and hit me also shot the young fellow was about 25 years old, had a small black moustache, brown clothes and was about 5 feet 8 or 9 inches. I don't know the others description as it was dark at the time. The fellow who shot me said he would shoot me if I did not put up my hands. I then threw my revolver to him and was shot lying on the ground. The men took Constable Murphy's bicycle and then went away.

Constable Murphy, 20 years old, was from Co. Leitrim; Sergeant Riordan, about 44 years old, was from Macroom, Co. Cork. They were returning to the police hut at Illaunbaun, where they were on protection duty. They left Ennistymon police station at 8 p.m. and were discovered by a farmer at around 10 p.m. They were armed only with revolvers.

The death of the two policemen caused shock and outrage throughout the county, and indeed further afield. The killings were publicly condemned by Dr Thomas O'Dea, the Bishop of Galway, as Ennistymon and much of north Clare was part of Kilfenora diocese, which, along with the diocese of Kilmacduagh, was under the ecclesiastical jurisdiction of the Bishop of Galway. Dr O'Dea wrote a letter to Very Rev. Fr Nestor, the parish priest of Ennistymon:

> I am pained and shocked by the two most recent murders in your parish [...] it is appalling that the Law of God should be thus outraged. No amount of government provocation can justify such a deed. It is wilful murder and as such a grievous sin against God. As Christians and as Irishmen we denounce this awful deed against the most sacred rights of God and man, a sin so grievous as to draw down the curse of God on the perpetrator. 'Now therefore, cursed shalt be upon the earth', said God to Cain [Genesis, 4,11]. You will, of course denounce the crime at all Masses on Sunday next.

Fr Nestor read out Dr O'Dea's letter and condemned the killing at Mass the following Sunday at Kilfenora. He expressed horror at this 'shocking crime, which has cast a gloom over the parish, a crime against our dear country and a grave sin against almighty God'. At Sunday Mass in Lahinch, Fr Mullins denounced the 'abominable, fiendish crime [...] which brings the curse of God upon them'. The killings were also denounced at Kilrush church by Fr O'Gorman 'as a grave violation of the law of God'.

A meeting of some locals was held at Kilfenora on the Sunday night following the deadly attack. Those attending condemned the murders and sent a resolution to the county inspector of the RIC. One of those who attended the meeting was William Cahir, who farmed 144 acres at Knockroe, Kilfenora. For his role in this meeting, Cahir was threatened, his house was raided and he had to leave his home and live in Corofin until March 1924.[91]

'The Stain of Blood', 'Drawing Down God's Curse' – these were the headlines in the *Irish Catholic* denouncing the killing of the policemen at Illaunbaun. The report in this paper read:

> Again, we grieve to say it, has the soil of Ireland been reddened by the blood of a murdered policeman. On Wednesday, Constable Murphy and Sergeant Riordan, returning off patrol to

> a police hut at Illaunbaun were murdered. This hut owes its existence to a murder a few years ago of a labourer named Kildea; it was erected for the protection of a family, the members of which were witnesses for the Crown against two men charged with the murder, but whom the Crown failed to convict. Horrible deeds like the killing of this poor young constable, which are enough to bring down on the country and on the County Clare in particular, the vengeance of God, should evoke not only shame and indignation, but stern determination to root out the vile assassins and hand them over to justice.

The ambush at Illaunbaun was also condemned in the national and local press, and was widely denounced in the county. In the words of the editor of the *Clare Journal*, 'the murderous assault sent a thrill of horror throughout Clare. Taken in conjunction with other local occurrences lately, it has caused deep seated alarm and uneasiness in the community and the future action of the authorities is the subject of much speculation.'[92]

A meeting of Ennis Urban Council passed a resolution condemning the crime and outrages occurring throughout the county. Mr Moroney, presiding, denounced the 'senseless and futile outrages which had eventually culminated in the callous murders of innocent persons.' He said that a wave of insanity was pervading the county, bringing in its train a reign of terror and lawlessness. He called upon 'all who valued their country's welfare and who had the courage of their convictions to denounce such dastardly and fiendish outrages [...] which were disgracing the good name of our county.'

Remarkably, Bishop Fogarty of Killaloe did not publicly condemn the shooting of the policemen at Illaunbaun. A special correspondent of the *Daily Mail* interviewed the bishop, noting that thirty years previously Dr Fogarty was known as a powerful enemy of the 'moonlighters' (as people involved in agrarian crimes were called in the 1880s). Time and again, Fr Michael Fogarty (as he was then known) had denounced the cowardly policy of shooting land agents from behind hedges. However, when asked if he would condemn the recent outrages in Clare from the pulpit, Dr Fogarty allegedly replied, 'Why should I? Why should bishops be asked to become police agents? I will not permit myself to become a tool of any political agitator.'[93]

Three IRA members were involved in the Illaunbaun attack: Seamus Connolly, Martin Devitt and John Joe Neylon. Martin Devitt was wounded in the attack. John Joe Neylon claimed that the ambushing party had three guns – a Martini rifle, a carbine and a revolver. After the ambush, the IRA men took the two revolvers and ammunition from the police.

Frank Barrett, commandant of the Mid-Clare Brigade, corresponded with Michael Collins on the matter of the Illaunbaun attack:

> Illaunbaun is in my area. I didn't consider it prudent to risk a report through the post under the circumstances, but will be glad to comply with the order at the earliest convenient moment that I can get a reliable person going up to Dublin. You will be pleased to know however that our men engaged upheld in the most gallant manner the tradition of the Irish Volunteers.

Collins replied that 'Cathal Brugha would be visiting Ennis shortly and is conscious to have a conversation with you on the subject of Illaunbaun.'[94]

Arms raid

On the day after the killings at Illaunbaun, a sensational and successful arms raid took place at the RIC barracks in Newmarket-on-Fergus on the night of Tuesday, 5 August. Michael Brennan, commandant of the East Clare Brigade, led a group of about six or seven armed and masked men in the attack, which was facilitated by one of the RIC men, Constable Buckley, who was in sympathy with the republicans. The IRA men entered the barracks via the back door while a sergeant and five constables were asleep in their beds. The police were handcuffed and tied to their beds, and the raiders then ransacked the barracks for about an hour and a half, carrying off six rifles, five revolvers, a sword, some bayonets and a quantity of ammunition. After the raid, Sergeant Porter, distraught by the incident, allegedly attempted to commit suicide by cutting his throat. He was removed to the county infirmary in Ennis for treatment.[95]

The raid on the local barracks was mentioned by Sir Lucius O'Brien, Lord Inchiquin, of Dromoland Castle, a Representative Peer for Ireland in the House of Lords, in a letter to his son

Donough, then in India as *aide-de-camp* to the Governor General and Viceroy of India, Lord Chelmsford:

> The county is getting into a hopeless state. Last night at 3 am some men broke into the barracks at Newmarket, pointed pistols at Sergeant Porter and the other sergeants' heads. They seized them, bound and gagged them and they took all their rifles and ammunition and departed! The barracks at [...] was also fired into for over an hour the other night and a sergeant at Ennistymon has been shot dead. No one has been charged.[96]

Proclamation of the county

Following the attack at Illaunbaun and the arms raid at the Newmarket RIC barracks, Sir John Byrne, the inspector general of the police, requested that the government reimpose military regulations in the county. Byrne, accompanied by Assistant Inspector General Flower, had visited Clare on Tuesday, 7 August to attend the funerals of the slain policemen and to assess the security situation in the county. The county was proclaimed a special military area the same day as their visit. All public assemblies (except religious services), including fairs and markets as well as sports events, were prohibited. In addition, political organisations such as Sinn Féin, the IRA, Cumann na mBan and the Gaelic League were all suppressed in the county by order of Alfred Cope, under secretary at Dublin Castle.[97]

Undeterred by widespread condemnations for their actions and by the proclamation of the county (in which an army officer was put in charge of law and order, not the RIC), the IRA carried on with their campaign against the police. On the night of 8 August, a police hut at Moyne near Scariff was hit by gunfire. The attack lasted about an hour; the police returned fire and one assailant was wounded. The West Clare Brigade first went into action in mid-August with an ambush. On the night of 14 August, a sergeant and three constables on patrol at Labasheeda were fired on; the police returned fire and claimed that one assailant was wounded in the attack.[98]

Undaunted by the proclamation of the county by the Dublin Castle authorities, the Mid-Clare Brigade cheekily posted a republican proclamation in reply simply entitled 'Proclamation!!'; it was a warning against any collaboration with the police or military. It was posted up in several districts around the county towards the middle of August 1919:

> *Proclamation!!*
>
> Under the Irish Republic – Mid Clare, a Special Military Area
>
> To all whom it may concern, a list of offences punishable of High Treason under proclamation:
>
> 1 Displaying either publicly or privately, friendship towards enemy military or police.
>
> 2 Supplying the enemy military or police with information calculated at some time to be useful to the enemy and dangerous to the interests of the Irish Republic or any of its loyal subjects.
>
> 3 Selling to or otherwise furnishing the enemy with supplies.
>
> 4 Aiding the enemy, military or police in their investigative searches.
>
> 5 Attempting in any way to disrupt the organised forces of the Republic in the area.
>
> 6 Spreading slanders on the character of any officials of the Republic.
>
> 7 Committing an offense of any kind against loyal subjects of the Republic.
>
> The natives of Mid-Clare are further warned that it is their duty to report to the nearest military authority any person whom they know to be guilty of any obvious offences. And further that they are to have a careful look-out for crime manufactured by the enemy, especially where enemy police have been compelled to evacuate. Until further notice all minor disputes are to be referred to the competent military authority. The Republic demands and are confident that all loyal subjects of the Republic will act in a noble manner. You have only one enemy.
>
> By order,
>
> The Competent Military Authority[99]

Intimidation

The boycott of the RIC continued and intensified, and in a new departure, people who had various kinds of dealings with the police were threatened and intimidated, sometimes violently, as the following incidents based on police reports show: On 27 July John McNamara's house in Ballyvaughan was fired on because he had associated with police. On 7 August Thomas Madigan, a car driver, was fired at because he had carried the police at Doolin. On the night of 11 August, a draper named M. Casey received a letter threatening that his house in Miltown would be burnt down unless he evicted one of his tenants, a constable. On the night of 15 August, threatening notices were sent to persons who dealt with P. Duggan, Kilrush, who had supplied the police with straw. On 20 August in Cooraclare, five masked men attacked two brothers named Donnelly, and a revolver shot was fired; one of the party accused the brothers of giving information to both the parish priest and the police. On the night of 15 August, the houses of Austin and Michael Mescal were fired on because they had dealings with a publican named Murphy, who had billeted and received soldiers at his house; Fr J. Considine of Mullagh stated that two men were flogged for ignoring the boycott of Murphy's pub.

Police reports indicate that threatening notices were received by people who had worked for and supplied police in Corofin and Crusheen in September. A man who allowed the sergeant at Doolin into his seat in chapel on Sunday was threatened in November. Around the same time, shots were fired at a farmer named Whelan, from Shragh, because he allegedly sold turf to the local resident magistrate; his house was attacked, and his wife was beaten. Shots were also fired into the home of Mr Slattery, a workman employed by W.J. Studdert, a justice of the peace (JP) living in Kilballyowen, Carrigaholt. A very distressing attack occurred at Kildysart in late December when the home of Mary Scanlan, who was employed at the RIC barracks as a 'barrack servant', was raided by a party of men in disguise. They seized the unfortunate woman and humiliated her by cutting off her hair and otherwise maltreating her because, they said, she worked for the RIC.

To be accused of being a spy was an extremely dangerous charge;

it was very damaging to a person's reputation, and possibly life-threatening. Few people were more cursed in Ireland than an informer – the person who betrayed his friends or a cause, especially the Irish republican cause – to the British. For those who betrayed their comrades or their country, the penalty, if they were caught in a time of war, was usually death. In classic Irish literature, the informer is portrayed as a dark-souled figure who is detested by the peasantry. In Gerald Griffin's celebrated novel *The Collegians* (1829), Danny Mann, who murdered 'the Cailín Bawn', could not bear the thought of being branded as an informer who 'is despised and detested by the Irish peasantry beyond all social sins'. For the republican Liam O'Flaherty, in his famous novel *The Informer* (1925), the word 'informer' was 'whispered with fear and hatred'. An informer was 'an outcast, who had to be wiped out like the first sign of a plague [...] a viper that must be crushed.'

One man was falsely accused of being a spy during the summer of 1919, and the accuser was forced to make a public apology in the *Saturday Record* for slandering the accused:

> I Michael Meehan of Cloontybonniv, Connolly, County Clare, farmer, hereby publicly apologise to Mr Michael Kearney of the same place, for having on 27th August last on the public road at Cloontybonniv, called the said Michael Kearney a spy. I admit there is no foundation for such a slander and I express my regret for same. I agree to pay the costs of the said Michael Kearney, including the costs of preparing and publishing this apology. Dated this day, 3 September 1919, Michael Meehan, witness, James Lynch, solicitor for Michael Kearney, Ennis.[100]

Meanwhile the Volunteers of the various Clare brigades, ignoring their critics and the military proclamation, carried on ambushing the police, whether in barracks, in police huts or on patrol. Around 1.30 a.m. on Saturday, 16 August the police barracks at Tubber was attacked by several armed men. The barracks came under fire for about a quarter of an hour before the attackers withdrew; there were no reported casualties on either side. Another attack took place at Moyadda in the parish of Coolmeen on Thursday, 21 August. The police had been withdrawn from the nearby Labasheeda barracks the previous week. On Saturday, 27 September two RIC men, constables Henehan and McCarthy, were fired at from both sides of the road as they returned from Scariff to the Moynoe protection hut. That same night the Moynoe protection hut was attacked by a large party of men but 'vigorously defended by the police'. The hut had been erected some years ago for the protection of Dr Sampson and his properties against agrarian agitation; he was a prominent landlord in the county and a brother-in-law of RIC Inspector General Byrne. A shooting incident occurred on Monday, 24 September at about 10.30 p.m. when a party of three RIC constables was ambushed at Cahercannivan in the parish of Kilmihil. They were attacked with shotguns and revolvers from behind hedges on both sides of the road. The police were uninjured, but one of the attackers was injured. On Sunday, 11 October at around 9.30 p.m. a party of six police patrolling near Quin, led by District Inspector McMahon, were fired upon but not injured. On Sunday, 7 December at about 9.30 p.m. the police barracks in Kilfenora was attacked by a party of armed men and the windows of the building were shattered. The police returned fire and refused to surrender, and the attackers withdrew after a short while.[101]

The police response

These attacks on the police undermined their morale but also forced them to take steps to protect themselves. Patrols were curtailed, the number of protection huts was reduced, some small barracks were closed, police armaments were increased, barracks defences were reinforced and the police began to rely on the military for some of their operations. The following extracts from police reports for August and September show how they reacted to the crisis:

> It has been necessary to concentrate the police; some outlying barracks have been vacated and the remainder fortified for defence; and in a few cases protection afforded to persons in consequence of agrarian intimidation has had to be withdrawn.
>
> It is impossible to carry out protection duty and eight persons are no longer receiving protection by police.
>
> Police are being encouraged to keep dogs to give warning of any approach by night and to accompany patrols.
>
> A survey of barracks with respect to fitting steel shutters are not

> yet to hand. Bombs have been issued and are carried out on patrol.
>
> Action in the way of intimidation of those working for the police has increased. On 10 August notices declaring policemen to be spies and informers and warning persons to have no intercourse with them were posted up in certain districts and it is practically impossible to induce civilians to give evidence.

The county inspector's reports for October, November and December 1919 indicate the growing isolation of the police and their dependence on military assistance:

> The general state of the county has been unsatisfactory during the month. A spirit of unrest and fear prevails which prevents any person of high standing from giving the police any information or assistance. The police are being steadily isolated and even parties friendly or supplying goods to men on leave have been intimidated.
>
> In the more disturbed areas it has been necessary to close isolated barracks and to reduce the number of patrols in order that each patrol may be of sufficient strength to repel attack, and the police are largely dependent on military aid in the performance of their duties.
>
> The county continues to be in a disturbed state, especially in the western portion. The extremists, though they cannot be said to consist of large numbers have succeeded in terrorising the more respectable people to an extent that they are practically afraid to open their mouths regarding the situation. Police information is now reduced to what they can observe.[102]

When the RIC closed some of their smaller barracks, the IRA responded by burning them in case they were to be reoccupied by the Crown forces. At Cooraclare on Tuesday, 11 November, an RIC patrol – consisting of Sergeant O'Reilly and constables Gleeson and Horan – came upon a group of fourteen men marching in military formation at Dromelihy near Cree. The RIC called upon the group to halt, and two of the men, Michael Fitzmaurice and Michael Pender, were apprehended, as they refused to give their names. Later, a crowd gathered around the police patrol demanding that the men be released. For safety, the police went to the RIC barracks at Cooraclare, which had been closed a few weeks before. Upon the patrol's arrival in the village, the crowd got increasingly hostile in demanding the release of the prisoners. The police took shelter in the now-disused barracks along with their prisoners. Some members of the crowd outside were armed and commenced firing on the barracks. The police returned fire and refused to surrender. Police reinforcements arrived from Kilrush and the attackers withdrew. After the police withdrew from the former barracks that same night, an angry mob bombed and burnt down the former barracks.[103]

There were further incendiary incidents in west Clare when two police huts were maliciously burnt down – one in Quilty village and the other at Inagh. Both were burnt down overnight on Tuesday, 2 December; they had been vacated by the police shortly before the incidents took place. Lissycasey police hut was also burnt down by armed raiders on Saturday, 28 December. Though the police had vacated the hut several months before, it was then occupied by Mrs W. Mullan, wife of Sergeant Mullan, who had been transferred to Kildysart. Mrs Mullan was given only five minutes to get out before the hut was burnt down around midnight; there was no sympathy or shelter for her in the neighbourhood, and she had to flee to Ennis for safety.[104]

Propaganda

While the police were being ostracised, ambushed and blackened as traitors, there was an attack on a farmhouse at Glan near Ennistymon. On 13 August, at around midnight, a dozen shots were fired into the home. It resulted in the tragic death of a young boy named Francis Murphy, causing outrage in the district and damaging the reputation of the military, who were widely suspected of the deed. The parish priest denounced the shocking death as 'a foul, brutal and savage murder'. Some witnesses said that the attackers were dressed like soldiers, and the jury at the inquest returned a verdict of 'wilful murder against soldiers unknown'. Naturally, this allegation and verdict against the military caused an upsurge of feeling against the Crown forces in the district. In a confidential police report, County Inspector Gelston stated that the boy's father had assisted a boycotted neighbour, Michael Neylon of Caherfeenick, and that the assassins had disguised themselves to throw suspicion on the soldiers of the local garrison. No one was held responsible for this appalling tragedy and loss of young life. After a military inquiry, the commander-in-chief of the British army in Ireland found that the murder could not have been committed by any serving soldier in the county at the time. However, few local people would have accepted this verdict. Naturally, Sinn Féin and the IRA rejected it as propaganda at the inquest and still blamed the military for the death of young Francis Murphy.[105]

Meanwhile, in the propaganda war across the Channel, the security situation in Clare was being misrepresented in sections of the British media, which alleged that some clergymen were being intimidated by the IRA and were afraid to condemn the outrages against the police. Fr M.J. Hehir, the parish priest of Cooraclare, wrote a letter to the press to highlight some inaccuracies written about him in the English press. He asserted that he did publicly condemn outrages from the pulpit. He denied that he had gotten any information from the Donnelly brothers, who were accused of giving information to him and the police, or anybody else. He denied that he had a rifle or needed one to protect himself from certain individuals or organisations; he stated that he did not call upon the people to protect him. Finally, he denied that a military lorry was needed to protect him as he moved around the parish on his parochial duties.[106]

Economic and social impact of the war

The proclamation of the county and the introduction of military regulations on 7 July had a huge economic and social impact upon Clare, and the collective punishment of the people for the actions of a militant minority was greatly resented by the law-abiding general public. Events such as the County Agricultural Show, Lahinch Races and Kilkee Races were postponed or abandoned. Hurling and football matches were also banned, along with all political meetings, as the following *Clare Champion* report shows:

> The Ennis butter and pig markets were banned on Wednesday as large numbers of military took up positions around the town to prevent the farmers from entering the town with their produce such as butter, milk or eggs for sale. A hurling match between

> Scariff and Newmarket was banned, and the military prevented this match taking place on Sunday 28 September at Tulla. The military also prevented the Michaelmas Fair from taking place in Tulla.[107]

The police and military were also active in searching the homes and offices of known members of Sinn Féin. For example, there was a major raid in Ennis on Friday, 12 September. On Sunday, 8 November the police and military raided a dance being held at Knockerra School at around midnight. The dancing was in full swing when the school was surrounded by police and military. The women were ordered to leave; all of the men were searched and their names were taken. In all, ten policemen and fifty soldiers, who had travelled quietly on bicycles, were involved in the search; a military lorry was parked about half a mile away. Such actions by the police and military were deeply resented by the populace.[108]

An editorial in the *Clare Champion* of 23 August highlighted the desperate economic state of the county:

> A government which is a tyranny and a country driven beyond the border line of exasperation. On Sunday night last, every road and path from Ennis was guarded by military and people returning home from football matches were searched for arms, such conduct is indefensible. The cruelty and repression are fast driving the people to desperation. There is only one cure [...] grant the people the right of self-determination. It will be a trying time for the county [...] the situation is desperately serious; the people are being provoked to breaking point, but we hope they will not lose their heads [...] we are passing through a grave crisis. Restraint, discipline and determination must be our watchwords. We now have an opportunity of showing that we are a Christian people, who if given freedom, could live together respecting not alone each other's rights and interests, but the laws of God and man.

Around the middle of August, the RIC decided to close many of the outlying small barracks and police protection huts dotted around the county. This was done in an effort to concentrate their men around the larger towns and villages, but it left an increased risk of crime in the areas that they moved away from. In response, some rural communities set up vigilance committees. One such parish was the community in Kilmurry McMahon, which decided to set up a vigilance committee to uphold law and order in their own district. Fr Glynn, chairman of the committee, also announced at Sunday Mass that the licensed premises in the village agreed to close early during the week and to strictly observe Sunday closing by not opening for the sale of alcohol on Sundays.[109]

Meanwhile, trade restrictions and other limits imposed by the proclamation of 7 August were having a serious effect upon the economy of Clare, which was largely based upon farming activities. Farmers, traders, merchants, councillors and even unionists such as Colonel George O'Callaghan Westropp of Lismehane made representations to have the restrictions on fairs and markets lifted. O'Callaghan Westropp, then High Sheriff of Clare, wrote a letter of complaint to Lord French, the Lord Lieutenant of Ireland (the representative of George King V in Ireland), in October 1919:

> The prohibition of fairs and markets is under a military proclamation against assemblies. But, persons attending these fairs are really too busy to be agitators. The prohibition of fairs and markets, therefore appears to the public as vindictive and disproportionate; and anger caused by the application of this provision to peaceful and lawful districts alike, outweighs any conceivable advantage from it and invest the procedures with an aspect of injustice. I see no reason why the farming class should be singled out of the entire community [...] I earnestly appeal with respect to your excellency. I know that grave harm has been done and how quiet and loyal persons are becoming desperate [...] the ban on assemblies was contrary to the good government and the peace of County Clare and was fast alienating hitherto well-disposed persons of the community.

Early in December, O'Callaghan Westropp wrote to the editor of the *Morning Post*. He stated, 'The restrictions are penal not precautionary, one class carrying on the dominant industry of the county is selected for punishment, without proof of guilt.' With the support of Richard John Stacpoole of Eden Vale, foreman of the Grand Jury of County Clare, O'Callaghan Westropp requested Sir Michael O'Loghlen, Lieutenant of Clare, to convene a general meeting of the justices of the peace of Clare 'to consider the situation created by these prohibitions and to take such actions as may be in the interests of the peace of County Clare.' Because of all these appeals, the government allowed the Fair of Clare, by special permit, to take place at Clarecastle on Tuesday, 9 November for the sale of cattle, sheep, pigs and horses. The Fair of Clare was traditionally held on 30 May and 11 November each year. One report of the fair was positive, 'The Fair of Clare held this year was one of the largest ever held in the village, attracting animals from all over the county and buyers from far and wide.'[110]

Further arms raids

The IRA could also get weapons by purchasing them or raiding private houses around the county. Many of these raids were on the homes of the gentry, as they were more likely to have weapons for sporting or, as ex-army officers, for personal use. Most of these raids took place towards the end of the year, but the first raid took place in January. A party of disguised men entered the home of Frank Martyn, JP, in the Ballyvaughan district and took a Webley Revolver, two pistols, a sword and a dagger, along with a few cartridges and binocular glasses.[111]

Several arms raids took place in September. The home of Mrs Blake Foster, Kilfenora was raided on 5 September and two guns were stolen – a shotgun and a blunderbuss. On 8 September Canon King, the rector of Kilkishen, was knocked off his bike and his shotgun was stolen. On 14 September, the house of George Blood of Ennistymon was raided and a gun was taken after a struggle. On 21 September, the home of James Blackwell, Inchiquin was robbed and a double-barrel gun was stolen. In October, several masked and armed young men raided the house of George Pilkington of Tarmon, Kilkee, and they took four guns and one revolver. They then cycled to Querrin and raided the home of a Dr Counihan but came away empty-handed.

The raiders were not always successful, as some of their victims put up a stout resistance. One such instance was the raid on the home of Denis Lynch, a well-known fowler and an elderly man from Doonmore, Doonbeg, whose home was raided during the night of Saturday, 4 October. About five armed and disguised men raided the home, but Lynch, his brother and sister resisted them with chairs and the legs of a table, holding off the raiders, who fired some shots. When Lynch went for his fowling piece, the attackers ran off and he fired a few shots after them. The attack on the Lynch family home was strongly condemned by Rev. Fr O'Donoghue at Doonbeg chapel during Sunday Mass. In November there was a successful arms raid at Hazelwood, Quin; it took place at the residence of Francis William Gore Hickman, a leading loyalist in the county. The attack occurred in broad daylight at around 10 a.m. when ten armed and masked men entered the house, locking up Mrs Hickman and the servants for several hours. The raiders stole three shotguns, two rifles, two revolvers, two bayonets and a small quantity of ammunition.[112]

At 8 p.m. on 21 November, nine or ten armed and masked men raided the home of another leading Protestant unionist, Colonel Tottenham of Mount Callan. They were armed with pistols and sticks. The colonel put up a fight but was beaten about the head; he suffered two black eyes and was overpowered. He was forced to hand over his weapons under threat of further violence and destruction of his house. The colonel handed over two double-barrel guns, two revolvers and a rifle, as well as a quantity of ammunition. Anthony Malone, vice-commandant of the 4th Battalion, Mid-Clare Brigade, from Miltown Malbay, stated that the raid on Colonel Tottenham's was organised by Ignatius O'Neill of the Glendine Company. He said that 'the colonel put up a fierce resistance, but he was overpowered, and we captured some sporting rifles, two or three revolvers and some shotguns.' Colonel Tottenham wrote a letter to the *Irish Times* about the raid. He stated that he was 69 years old and was crippled with arthritis. He lived with an aged cook and two servant girls. His home at Mount Callan was rather isolated; the nearest police hut was about 10 miles away, while Ennis was 13 miles away and Ennistymon was 12 miles.[113]

More arms raids on private houses occurred early in December. Two armed men raided the house of an ex-RIC man named Brady and forced a young girl to hand over his revolver. On the same night, Bank House in Scariff was raided and a gun and a revolver were stolen.[114] Overall, there were twelve reported raids on private houses in which the IRA acquired a total of twenty-seven weapons and a small quantity of ammunition. Through these raids, some of which were carried out with violence, the IRA spread terror among many people in the community, especially those who had guns. Because of attacks on the police and house raids, the IRA's arsenal in Clare had grown by a total of at least forty-two weapons. This cache included sixteen revolvers, fifteen shotguns, seven police carbines, two rifles, two pistols and several hundred rounds of ammunition.

Skirmish at Shessymore

One sensational attack that attracted some national and foreign attention was the attempt to hold up Henry Vincent MacNamara's grouse-shooting party at Shessymore, near Carran, on 6 December. MacNamara, DL (deputy lieutenant), of Ennistymon House, a leading Protestant, landlord and unionist in the county, had organised a shooting party on his estate. There were two cars in the party: in the first was MacNamara, a Mr Manning, Orlando Osborne the gamekeeper and John Smith the chauffeur; the second car was driven by the Hon. Edward O'Brien of Roslevan House, and he was accompanied by his wife, Lady Beatrice O'Brien, and W.H. Ball, DL, of Fortfergus. At Shessymore Cross the cars were forced to stop, as boulders and rocks were placed on the road. Then the attackers appeared and ordered the party to put their hands up and surrender their weapons. The party were fired upon, and though each of them was wounded by gunfire, they managed to return fire and refused to surrender their weapons. They then sought refuge in a nearby herdsman's hut. Apparently two of the assailants were injured. The assailants did not get any weapons, but they managed to steal some wraps, some rugs and a luncheon basket – to dine in style with a champagne picnic after their morning's shooting. The attack on MacNamara's shooting party, and especially the injuries sustained by all of them, including Lady Beatrice O'Brien, attracted notice in the national and foreign press. The *Irish Independent* report stated that the attack caused a profound sensation in north Clare.[115]

Lord Inchiquin described this attack in some detail to his son Donough O'Brien:

> You may have heard about the attack by Sinn Féiners on Uncle Eddie, Aunt Bea and a party who were going shooting woodcock

> about three miles from Lemanagh, on the road to Ballyvaughan. They were in two cars and when they came around a corner they saw a heap of stones across the road. Mr McNamara's car was leading, directly they pulled up, fire was opened on them, mostly with shotguns and one or two revolvers. They were almost all of them hit at once, but Mr Ball and Aunt Bea, who were sitting in front were protected by the windscreen which was entirely shattered. Bea dropped to the bottom of the car where she was fairly safe; Eddie jumped out of the car and with his gun went to the wall and saw a man behind it firing a revolver; the man saw him and put up his hand and arm to protect his head, but Eddie gave it to him under the arm at a distance of under three yards, and of course he dropped. Then Eddie heard another man shouting: 'Surrender! You are surrounded!' But Eddie couldn't see him for a minute or two, then he saw him looking through a hole in the wall across the road and he fired point-blank in his face and he didn't trouble them again. Then he fired another shot at a man running away but this was at some distance, though he is sure he hit him. The men in MacNamara's car also fired six or seven shots when the Sinn Féiners all bolted.
>
> All seven of the party were hit, Eddie three times, once on each side of the face and once on the right shoulder; Aunt Bea was hit on the face; Ball in the back of the head; MacNamara in both arms by a revolver bullet; another man, (I forget his name), also in the arm by a bullet; and MacNamara's keeper had the front of his scalp shot off by a shotgun, a very near shave [...] the Sinn Féiners had looted all boots and bags out of the cars and cut the high-tension wires, so as to render them useless. They also had removed all their dead and wounded. They think that two of them were dead and four or five were wounded. So, I think the Sinn Féiners came off second-best in the scrap! [...] by the way, Eddie's party were attacked at about 10.20 on their way to the shoot.[116]

Two of the IRA men involved in the attack gave some details of the ambush. They claimed the intention was to capture the weapons of the shooting party, although MacNamara later claimed that it was an assassination attempt on him. Andrew O'Donoghue, commandant of the 5th Battalion, Mid-Clare Brigade, from Kilfenora, stated:

> There were seven men in the ambush party and that everything was done to prevent injury to civilians. The occupants were

> ordered to surrender their weapons, but the reply was a volley of shots for about twenty minutes. MacNamara and company barricaded themselves in a vacant house, every member of their party was wounded.[117]

Another IRA man, Thomas Shalloo, vice-commandant of the 5th Battalion, Mid-Clare Brigade, gave a similar account, in his witness statement, to that of Andrew O'Donoghue:

> Six men attacked, armed with one rifle, two revolvers and three shotguns. The shooting party arrived at about 9 am. It included four or five military officers, along with Lady Beatrice O'Brien, HV MacNamara and his gamekeeper, Osborne. O'Loughlin shouted: 'Hands Up! Surrender weapons!' They replied with a volley of shots for about a quarter of an hour. MacNamara and company managed to get to a herdsman's house and barricaded themselves. Every member of the shooting party was injured including Lady Beatrice. She took an active part in the fighting and had to be treated as a dangerous combatant. On our side, O'Loughlin and Geraty were wounded.[118]

Shortly before this attack, Lord Inchiquin was warned of a possible arms raid on Dromoland Castle and sent his weapons to Newmarket-on-Fergus RIC barracks for safekeeping:

> I sent every gun, rifle, revolver, sword, pistols, spears, crossbows, even the old Dublin Castle flintlock muskets, up to the police in Newmarket, where there are now ten police and two sergeants. We were going to have our shoot next week, but I have postponed it as Eddie could not come and they might attack any other guns that we had on their way home after the shoot.[119]

Summary

Early in the year the IRA had set up a new military structure in the county with three brigades for west, mid- and east Clare. The War of Independence in Clare officially began in July 1919 when the IRA received orders from GHQ to attack the police wherever they met them. The IRA in Clare were in the vanguard of the War of Independence with their guerrilla war tactics. From a military perspective the IRA had achieved some success through guerrilla warfare with an extremely limited arsenal, mainly consisting of shotguns at the start of the war. Perhaps their greatest success was psychological, as the morale of the RIC was badly affected by the guerrilla war – which was mainly directed against them. The police were ostracised and boycotted and denounced as traitors, while people who assisted them in any way were threatened and intimidated. In about six ambushes the IRA had killed two policemen and wounded several others; they had attacked a dozen police huts and barracks and had burnt down four of the huts. They had acquired fourteen weapons from the RIC, six rifles and eight revolvers, as well as about three hundred rounds of ammunition, with the bulk of these taken during the nocturnal raid on Newmarket-on-Fergus barracks.

The military operations of the IRA were mainly carried out under cover of darkness. Initially their weapons largely consisted of shotguns, which were supplied by sympathetic farmers, along with a handful of rifles and revolvers; these were later supplemented by weapons stolen from Big Houses, unionists and policemen. Their attacks on police patrols, RIC barracks and police protection huts took place mainly in the rural areas and smaller villages of the county. The attacking parties ranged from three men, at Illaunbaun, to about fifteen men in the attacks on the Inch and Connolly protection huts. The 'battles' with the police stationed in barracks, such as at Broadford, usually lasted for about an hour. Ambushes on police patrols occurred in places such as Moynoe, Tubber, Moyadda, Labasheeda, Kilmihil, Kilfenora and Quin. The IRA burnt down some abandoned protection huts. At least one IRA man was wounded in the attack at the Inch hut, and three or four of the IRA men involved in the attacks on the barracks were wounded by the police. Two RIC men were killed at Illaunbaun on 4 August, and several other policemen were injured by gunshots. These 'hit and run' attacks were typical of guerrilla warfare. The IRA's actions had compelled the RIC to retrench and concentrate their forces in larger barracks. By the end of the year the police were better armed to face the military challenge from the IRA; they occupied more fortified barracks and operated joint patrols with the military.

In response to the killing of the two policemen and the arms raid on Newmarket-on-Fergus RIC barracks, the county was proclaimed a special military area on 7 August. Normal social and economic life was greatly interrupted by this. The County Agricultural Show on 15 August was banned along with several other agricultural shows and race meetings. All GAA hurling and football matches were also prohibited. Under military regulations all fairs were banned in the county for several months, which caused severe hardship on the farming community. Many gentry homes were raided for arms, and the Protestant community was terrified. Since the war began in July, the actions of the IRA had been condemned in many quarters, especially after the attacks on the police and the killing of two RIC men. The Bishop of Galway, Dr Thomas O'Dea, wrote that the 'murder' of the policemen 'would draw down the curse of God on the perpetrators'. There were other denunciations in the *Irish Catholic* and by the local clergy, but these condemnations did not deter the IRA.

Towards the end of the year, comments by the Lord Chief Justice, Thomas Molony, on the state of criminality in Clare, which he said 'was much worse than any other county in Munster', incensed Bishop Fogarty. Addressing the Grand Jury at the winter assizes, which were periodic courts held in various counties – this time in Cork – Justice Molony condemned and lamented 'the moral degradation to which Clare has fallen'. 'What is wrong with Clare?' the judge asked.

In a robust reply Bishop Fogarty, who was receiving communications from Michael Collins in October 1919, asserted:

> to vilify a whole community of Christian people is neither just nor judicial, but a mean and cowardly crime. When I think of the people of Clare and see them defamed before the world by the hirelings of British tyranny as a race of moral degenerates, I am filled with indignation and cannot restrain my anger. It is an infamous falsehood.

In this reply, which must have boosted the morale of Sinn Féin and the IRA, both locally and nationally, Bishop Fogarty concluded, 'I will tell the world what is wrong with Clare, it is that they have the manliness to stand up against tyranny and to flourish the flag of Irish independence in the face of castle hacks, whether on or off the bench!'[120]

3
ACTIVE AND OPEN REBELLION

The war intensified in 1920 as the various Clare brigades geared up for the conflict. After suppressing a mutiny among some sections of the Mid-Clare Brigade over its leadership, the most urgent issue the IRA had to face was a shortage of weapons. The IRA acquired some more weapons through arms raids on unionists' homes – though they only secured a few guns and little ammunition. They had more success in disarming a platoon of British soldiers in Ennis in June, and in a raid on Ruan RIC barracks in October; these actions yielded more than twenty rifles and over three thousand rounds of ammunition for the Mid-Clare Brigade. The IRA carried out many more attacks on the police this year, and in a spectacular gesture to mark the fourth anniversary of the Easter Rising, they burnt down more than thirty former police barracks and protection huts around the county that had been abandoned by the RIC.

During the summer and autumn, the IRA formed flying columns. These mobile units carried out many ambushes on police barracks and patrols. As the IRA continued their attacks, especially on the police, the attitude of the Crown forces hardened, and in the Canada Cross killings at Miltown Malbay in April, three unarmed people were killed. The Crown forces, under the guise of an 'Anti-Sinn Féin gang', carried out reprisals against IRA and Sinn Féin supporters after the IRA killed policemen or other members of the Crown forces. The worst atrocities committed by the Anti-Sinn Féin gang during this year occurred after the Rineen ambush on 22 September (in which six policemen were killed) when the Black and Tans and Auxiliaries destroyed more than twenty houses and killed six people – four people were killed during the attacks while two others subsequently died from their wounds. Other victims of this reprisal policy during the reign of terror were men such as Peadar Clancy and Conor Clune, who were murdered after Bloody Sunday in Dublin; Michael Egan, Martin Gildea, Michael McMahon and Alfred Rodgers, who were murdered at Killaloe bridge on 16 November; and the Doonbeg Volunteers, Michael McNamara and Willie Shanahan, who were murdered while in police custody in late December in Ennis.

Besides boycotting the RIC and intimidating those who associated with the police, the IRA undermined the legal system by setting up Sinn Féin courts and forcing many justices of the peace to resign. Shots were fired at people supplying the Crown forces, and women who associated with the police, soldiers or even members of the coastguard were humiliated by having their hair cropped. The IRA burnt down houses belonging to unionists – for example, Kiltannon House, Tulla, owned by Major Molony, a Protestant, which was the first 'Big House' burnt by the IRA. Some IRA supporters also carried out sectarian attacks by burning Protestant churches in Clarecastle and O'Briensbridge. Many Protestants and unionists experienced a 'reign of terror' during the year, with armed attacks on their homes, sometimes accompanied by violence. One man, Martin Counihan, was executed by the IRA for being a spy.

As the war progressed, the attitude of the Catholic Church towards the armed campaign by the IRA began to change. The character of the RIC also changed; there were many resignations and early retirements due to the IRA boycott. The vacancies in the force were mainly filled by English Protestant recruits from urban areas, who were called Black and Tans because of their uniforms – because of a shortage, they wore black jackets and beige trousers. By the end of the year more than half of the RIC were composed of Black and Tans. Unlike the former members of the RIC, who were mainly of Irish Catholic farming stock, the Black and Tans had little respect for the Catholic clergy, whom they suspected of collusion with Sinn Féin. Priests were threatened and physically abused, and several priests' homes were raided. During the reign of terror, there were fewer denunciations of IRA attacks from the Catholic clergy. There was even a plot to murder Bishop Fogarty, the leading Sinn Féin supporter among the Catholic hierarchy. Towards the end of the year, a Clare-born prelate, Dr Patrick Clune, the Archbishop of

Perth, made significant efforts to secure a truce between the British and Irish combatants. But his peace efforts failed because of British insistence that the IRA surrender their weapons as a prelude to talks.

Mutiny in the Mid-Clare Brigade

The restructuring of the Clare Brigade into three separate brigades in January 1919 was not accepted by every IRA member in the Mid-Clare Brigade area. Apparently, some members in the 1st, 2nd and 3rd battalion areas objected to the leadership of Frank Barret, and they attempted to form their own independent brigade for a time. This mutinous disaffection festered for some time and caused problems for the IRA until it was openly dealt with in February 1920, when the dissidents were disarmed and suppressed by the Mid-Clare Brigade.

Peter O'Loughlin of Ennis, captain of the 1st Battalion, Mid-Clare Brigade, recalled:

> After the creation of three brigades in Clare, exception was taken in certain quarters to the appointment of members of the Barrett family to the higher posts in the brigade staff, Frank as OC and Joe as adjutant [...] An attempt was made to form an Independent rival brigade in Mid Clare. The adherents of the Independent Brigade were mainly from the Kilmaley district, where most Volunteers joined the Independent Brigade and they refused to recognise the central authority. Land trouble was rife in the area and land agitation was stirred up against any farmer who had not the goodwill of the 'Independent' Volunteers.[121]

William McNamara, from Quin and a member of the IRA, stated that many members of the 1st and 2nd battalions, and a good part of the 3rd Battalion, supported the Independent Brigade for a few months, while the new commandant of the Mid-Clare Brigade, Frank Barrett, was regarded by many of the men under him as unsuitable.[122]

On the other hand, Andrew O'Donoghue, commandant of the 5th Battalion, Mid-Clare Brigade, wrote that some prominent officers in the Kilmaley–Connolly areas caused the problem, 'There was some trouble in the 1st, 2nd and 3rd Battalions, but very little support for an independent Brigade in the 4th or 5th Battalions.'[123]

Patrick Devitt, from Kilnaboy and vice-commandant of the 5th Battalion, Mid-Clare Brigade, said, 'There was a split in the 1st, 2nd and 3rd Battalions, they refused to recognise the officers, they attempted to set up their own Independent Brigade, which would be harmful to the movement. The split was fomented by land agitation and disputes.'[124] Another IRA member, Seamus McMahon from Ennistymon, captain of the 4th Battalion, Mid-Clare Brigade, also stated that the problem was caused by land disputes in the Connolly district, 'I was one of a party of 30 or 40 men from the 4th and 5th Battalions who were sent into the Connolly district to quieten some people, who were causing some difficulty over land.'[125]

The Mid-Clare Brigade council decided to end the rebellion. A column from the 4th and 5th battalions, under Martin Devitt, was ordered to disarm the dissidents. This column of thirty-five men, armed with rifles, revolvers and shotguns, went to the district on 14 February 1920; they seized about eight or nine men and ended the rebellion. However, on the return journey on 17 February they lost two rifles and two or three shotguns when they encountered a British army officer, Colonel Cotton, and his driver.[126]

County Inspector Gelston became aware of the row within the brigade:

> A serous split of Sinn Féiners in Inagh district […] One of the principals was kidnapped […] A large party of Volunteers from Connolly and Inagh districts visited Inch in connection with this. Colonel Cotton, who was travelling in a military motor car ran into a party of armed republicans beyond Inagh. They left two cars, a rifle and five shotguns in their haste to avoid what they thought was a military raiding party. The colonel secured the weapons and the arms were brought to Ennis.[127]

Pádraig Óg Ó Ruairc, a historian, states that the Independent Brigade had not been active in attacking the RIC or British army. The breakaway group had become involved in land disputes.[128]

The mutiny within the ranks of the IRA was also noted in the local press, and some of the dissidents were named:

> Sensational events near Ennis. On Tuesday 17 February, a large body of men called at several homes in Bearnageeha and Inch districts and commandeered some horses and carts and

> practically made prisoners of some men named Collins, O'Keefe, Devaney, Freeman and Gregan, whom they compelled to go with them on the Miltown Road. They were overtaken by Colonel Cotton an officer commanding troops in Clare who was motoring from Ennis to the west of the county. The colonel passed some side cars and two common cars, with some guns lying against the side of the ditch, one rifle, three single barrel-breech loaders, and two double-barrelled breech loaders. He took the guns and went back to Ennis on the Inagh Road.[129]

Vice-commandant Patrick Devitt wrote that his brother Martin led the party to suppress the mutiny:

> A party of 34–40 armed men from 3rd and 4th Battalions under Martin Devitt, marched into the Kilmaley–Connolly district to impose discipline in January 1920. Five or six shotguns were seized. Later at Crowe's Bridge while going home they encountered Col. Cotton, O/C for Clare, and some of our shotguns were lost.[130]

Seamus McMahon, from Ennistymon and captain of A Company, 4th Battalion, Mid-Clare Brigade, corroborated Devitt's account:

> I was one of a party of thirty or forty men from the 4th and 5th Battalions who were sent into the Connolly district to quieten some people, who were causing some difficulty over land. The Vice OC, Martin Devitt was in charge. While returning in horses and traps, we ran into a British patrol and lost some weapons.[131]

Incidentally, there was also some dissension in the West Clare Brigade, which resulted in the resignation of Commandant Art O'Donnell of Tullycrine; he was replaced by Sean Liddy of Cooraclare. Among the Michael Collins Papers there are several communications between Michael Collins and Art O'Donnell. Collins, as director of organization and intelligence, complained several times that O'Donnell had failed to send in reports for brigade activities during June and July. These reports were finally received on 11 September 1919. There were also charges and complaints against O'Donnell, from west Clare, relating to boycotting. These complaints resulted in O'Donnell and four officers of the brigade being called to a disciplinary meeting at GHQ in Dublin, which was held on 1–3 December 1919. There were other allegations against O'Donnell relating to land and boycotting in the new year, which resulted in his replacement as commandant of the West Clare Brigade. These dissensions over its leadership weakened the brigade's activities.

Art O'Donnell, in his witness statement, outlines the reasons why he was removed from office. He states that in his role as a judge of the Sinn Féin Land Court he helped solve some boycotting problems relating to a publican in Danganelly and a farmer in Shragh. However, he alleged that the boycotting of two business people in Carrigaholt, early in February 1920, was the cause of his removal as commandant of the West Clare Brigade. O'Donnell investigated the boycott at Carrigaholt and advised the local IRA to call it off. Two of the local officers, Edmond Fennell and Thomas Haier, objected to O'Donnell's action and reported him to GHQ, demanding that he be court-martialled. O'Donnell was called to Dublin and met the adjutant general, Gearóid O'Sullivan, who demanded that O'Donnell resign his position immediately, which he did. He returned to Clare shortly after that with Peadar Clancy, and they brought about a dozen revolvers and ammunition with them. Peadar Clancy presided over the meeting in which Sean Liddy was elected commandant in May 1920.[132]

Arms raids

During 1920 the IRA carried out at least sixteen arms raids on private homes, mainly those of the Protestant gentry, but the armed and masked raiders got very few weapons because the owners had been advised to hand them to the police for safety. The attackers encountered some resistance; the victims fought back in some cases, and several people were injured during the raids.

The Mid-Clare Brigade carried out a few raids but stole only one weapon. They raided the homes of Michael Shea and William Neylon, Duogh, Lahinch; John St George Lucas, Knocknaraha, Ennistymon; and J. Miller, Ballyvaughan. Most of these raids took place in January and February. On 3 February, 'a large body of men some masked and armed, raided the coastguard at Ballyvaughan, but they found only one small weapon, they took away binoculars, a miniature rifle, two telescopes and two signal books.' Some other raids took place later in the year. The home of Colonel Tottenham,

DL, of Mountcallan, was raided for arms a second time on 27 June; this time no guns were found, but a field glass was taken.

The West Clare Brigade raided some loyalist homes in the Kildysart area towards the end of January, but they got no weapons. There was a raid on Fortfergus House, the residence of Captain W.H. Ball, DL, during the night of Sunday, 25 January, but all of his weapons had previously been handed over to the police. On the same night, Paradise House, the home of Mrs Henn, widow of F.B. Henn, was also raided, but no arms were found. A Protestant woman from Ennis, Helen Keane of Beech Park, recorded an anecdote on the raid on Paradise House in which one of the raiders apologised for the raid:

> Old Mrs Henn was alone in the house sitting by her drawing room fire when a gang of masked and armed men burst into the room demanding arms [...] They left a masked and armed man to guard her while the others searched the house. After an awkward silence for some time he said to her, 'Begging your pardon, Ma'am, but them's terrible times we're livin in.'

The House of Rev. Canon Waugh of Cappaghaverogue, Kildysart was also raided that night, and shots were fired into the rectory, but no guns were retrieved there either. The home of Mrs A. Vandeleur, Cahercon, was also raided in vain.

The East Clare Brigade acquired only a few weapons through arms raids. A large party of armed men raided Woodpark House, Scariff, the home of Captain R.F. Hibbert, JP, during the night of Monday, 5 January. Several shots were fired, and a lady's maid was wounded. Hibbert returned fire and, apparently, he shot one of the attackers and no arms were taken. The home of Major F.G. Cullinan of Feighmore, near Quin, sub-sheriff of Clare, was raided for arms on the night of Saturday, 31 January by two armed men, but his gun had been handed over to the police. Cullinan's house was raided a second time some weeks later, and shots were fired; Cullinan was hit in the face with pellets on the second occasion but was not seriously injured. The homes of Samuel G. Thompson of Carrowmore, Scariff and J.H.K. Dobbyn of Kilkishen were also raided in February, but no weapons were found. On the night of 6 January, eight armed and disguised men entered Colonel

O'Callaghan Westropp's house in Lismehane, Tulla. They held up the maidservants and began to search the house. The colonel and one of the raiders fired at each other, but there were no injuries. The raiders then 'rushed' the colonel and another military officer, his guest, whom they tied up, and they made off with some rifles, revolvers, swords and ammunition. In a letter to a friend, O'Callaghan Westropp stated, 'we were raided on 6 January [...] after the scuffle, the raiders behaved with courtesy, did no mischief and even expressed regret for having to do what they did.' The colonel's home was raided a second time on 8 August, but no guns were taken on this occasion. Finally, in August the home of Captain Beresford Molony, Kiltannon House in Tulla, was raided by masked and armed men, but no arms were found there.[133]

The total number of weapons stolen from private houses by the three Clare brigades during this year was quite small – only two rifles, two revolvers, one shotgun and one miniature rifle. Commenting on the number of raids, Judge O'Connor, addressing the Grand Jury of County Clare in March, stated:

> this county is in a grave condition, the main source of the trouble seems to be the desire to get arms and to stop at nothing – whether it is raiding of barracks or private houses for the purpose, the vast majority of the people do not approve of the crime but do nothing to stop it.[134]

The arms raids on the homes caused fear and alarm among the gentry, and even their sporting habits, such as fowling, were affected by the 'troubles'. Lady Inchiquin described how a pheasant shoot at Dromoland in January 1920 was affected; they had to get armed assistance from the military and police, and had to take other precautions:

> Our shoot passed off safely, no contretemps. We had an armoured car outside Andrew's house during lunchtime and a patrol on the roads. At dinner, dad and Phaedrig and the other men all had revolvers in their pockets. And everyone took their guns up to their rooms at night. It was not pleasant having two guns, Fionn's small gun and a revolver. They all stayed the night. The three ladies, Mrs Stackpoole and Dorothy Stackpoole, Eden Vale and Mrs MacDonnell, New Hall, came over in a separate car together, so that they would not have any guns on them, in

> case they would be held up at the point of a revolver and then they would smash the engine of their cars [...] The general commanding in Cork was to have come to our shoot, but he was detained in Cork and the colonel in Ennis could only come one day, as he was wired for to Cork. I am afraid this is all about troubles. What is Lloyd George doing? A hopeless person![135]

One victim of the arms raids, Captain Robert F. Hibbert of Woodpark, Scariff, described an experience close to a reign of terror for the Protestants of east Clare around this time, and he stated that he and his family had to leave the county after their lives were threatened in April 1920:

> The condition of affairs in my neighbourhood in Co. Clare is beyond description; there is no protection whatever for life and property. Recently an attempt was made by some forty masked men, armed with rifles, revolvers, and axes, to raid my house. They got in by rushing the back premises of the house. They reduced the servants to a state of panic by threatening to shoot them, they seized the steward's gun and tried to gag him with a rifle butt. I immediately armed myself with a repeating rifle and fired on the raiders from the lobby forcing them to retire, one of their number being wounded. I have since been warned repeatedly that my life is in danger.
>
> The houses of most of the respectable people in the neighbourhood have been raided, but such is the terrorism that exists that many who have suffered in this way are afraid to report what has occurred to the authorities, lest worse befall them. I reported the raid on my house to the authorities, who sent down a small detachment of infantry, but recalled them after about three weeks. The police were then withdrawn from Scarriff, and the barracks closed, leaving no police at all for a distance of over 15 miles. Two nights after the closing of the barracks the Petty Sessions Court, opposite the barracks, was broken into, and everything in it destroyed. A week afterwards about two hundred men pulled down the barracks with pickaxes and crowbars.
>
> As far as personal property goes, last week my boathouse, and other outhouses were raided, while timber is constantly stolen, fences and walls thrown down [...] every night gangs of armed men assemble in different houses and walk the countryside terrorising the respectable inhabitants [...] They collect

> subscriptions in this way as everyone is afraid to refuse to subscribe. From dawn to dark law-aiding people scarcely dare to sleep. Owing to the withdrawal of police all regulations are disregarded, and the public houses remain open night and day. Consequently, as may be imagined, the state of drunkenness and robbery is appalling. Even the farmer's crops are stolen out of the ground to buy drink [...]
>
> The state of the country is such that I and my family must leave and shut up the house. I have little doubt that when we are gone, and there is a caretaker in charge of the house, it will be broken into and destroyed. Others in the same position as myself agree with me that we will find great difficulty in procuring caretakers who will undertake to look after houses which have had to be abandoned in this way.[136]

Lenten pastorals

The Lenten pastorals of Bishop Fogarty and Bishop O'Dea were published in local newspapers in late February, and there was a marked difference between them. The tone of Dr Fogarty's pastoral could be interpreted as giving tacit support to Sinn Féin and the IRA campaign, whereas Dr O'Dea's pastoral urged his flock to reject violence as a means of achieving Irish independence.

In his pastoral letter, Bishop Fogarty of Killaloe wrote:

> Ireland has the spirit to stand up against this national plunder, what wrongs, what outrages are heaped upon her, her homes broken into and her liberties trampled under military rule, her towns and cities sacked, her young men and women either shot or hauled off to prison without trial or charge and more hideously done to death in the name of law and order. I sympathise profoundly with my suffering countrymen and pray almighty God to fortify their hearts with the patience and strength that will enable them to uphold the assertion of their national rights and the observance of God's Holy Law.

By contrast, Dr O'Dea, the Bishop of Galway, Kilfenora and Kilmacduagh, stated in his pastoral letter:

> I desire the freedom of Ireland as ardently as most Irishmen and I abhor the hypocrisy and injustice and cruel tyranny to which Ireland is now subjected. Yet not even for Ireland would I have any of my own people turn against the Law of God. We appeal

> to our people to exercise patience under the terrible provocations to which they are subjected, to remember the law of God, to combine amongst ourselves to prevent crime, to restrain the promptings of revenge and abstain from deeds of bloodshed and outrage calculated to bring shame upon themselves and their country and the anger of Heaven.[137]

Death in action

On 19 January, the police at Cooraclare were attacked by members of the West Clare Brigade. Shortly after the police barracks at Cooraclare and Doonbeg were closed, they were burnt to the ground by the IRA. Following the evacuation, one policeman named Costigan left his wife and family and rented a house in Cooraclare. His wife and children were ordered to leave by the landlord and were relocating to Knock when a police motor lorry removing Constable Costigan's furniture was attacked about a mile outside Cooraclare. The lorry was accompanied by four police on bicycles. They were fired upon from both sides of the road by a party of men. The lorry was riddled with bullets. The police returned fire, and the attackers fled. One young IRA man, Michael Darcy from Cooraclare, jumped into the local river and was drowned. Several witnesses testified that the police prevented people from attempting to rescue Darcy. At an inquest held at Cooraclare National School on 21 January, the jury returned the verdict, 'That the body of Michael Darcy was found drowned and we unanimously condemn the heartless action of the police in preventing his rescue.' He was the first member of the IRA to die in the War of Independence in Clare.[138]

Several days after the embarrassing debacle in which the Mid-Clare Brigade lost about five weapons to Colonel Cotton and his driver on 17 February, the brigade ambushed a police patrol in the southern portion of the Inagh district. A party of four RIC men, Sergeant Giles accompanied by constables Glynn, Hughes and O'Connell of Maurice's Mills RIC barracks, were attacked while returning to the barracks at Formoyle Cross at around 1.45 p.m. on 23 February. There were between sixteen and twenty IRA men involved in the ambush, which went on for nearly two hours. The IRA suffered a major blow when Martin Devitt, vice-commandant of the Mid-Clare Brigade, was fatally wounded and died the next day. His body was buried secretly in a bog in Clooney South for about a week before the police discovered it. On his breastplate was written, 'Martin Devitt died 24 February 1920.' His brother, Patrick Devitt, stated that his body was discovered by spies. Patrick Devitt also stated, 'I regret to say that the Parish Priest of Ennistymon refused to allow the remains into the parish church, so it was taken to the church in the local workhouse. There was a military funeral the next day, with hundreds of men from all over the county.' The death of Martin Devitt, whom one colleague called 'fearless and resourceful', and the serious wounding of Ignatius O'Neill in an IRA ambush in September were a big blow to the Mid-Clare Brigade, and their activities were curtailed for some months after these events.[139]

Following an inquest into the death of Martin Devitt, the jury at Ennistymon returned the following verdict, 'That Martin Devitt, died on 24 February 1920 from a bullet wound received while fighting for the freedom of his country, which freedom is prevented by mis-government; and we tender our sympathy to his relatives.' The Ennistymon branch of the National Union of Railwaymen passed a motion of sympathy to Devitt's family and Devitt himself, 'who died fighting for his country'.[140]

A bonfire of barracks

On 30 March the IRA issued a warning to people to treat the RIC as spies and traitors:

> Whereas the spies and traitors known as the RIC are holding this country for the enemy and whereas said spies and bloodhounds are conspiring with the enemy to bomb and bayonet the otherwise, peaceful, law-abiding and liberty-loving people; that we proclaim and suppress the said spies and traitors, and so hereby solemnly warn prospective recruits that they join the RIC at their peril. All nations are agreed as to the fate of traitors. It has the sanction of God and man.[141]

A few days later, on the fourth anniversary of the Easter Rising, there were extraordinary scenes in many parishes around Clare when, on Saturday, 3 April at around 10.30 p.m., about thirty police barracks and huts, which had been evacuated by the RIC over the previous few months for security reasons, were burnt or destroyed. All the barracks and huts had been unoccupied for some time. They were located in the following: Ardnacrusha, Ballydoorus, Ballykelly, Ballynacally, Bodyke, Bunratty, Caher, Caherfeenick, Carrahan, Carran, Castlefergus, Crusheen, Doolin, Fanore, Inch, Kilfenora, Kilkishen, Kilmore, Knock, Labasheeda, Lahinch, Liscannor, Lough Graney, Maurice's Mills, Moynoe, O'Callaghan's Mills, Ogonelloe, Tuamgraney and Whitegate. The Miltown Malbay revenue offices were also destroyed, along with the courthouses at Mountshannon and Tuamgraney. Also, the Mullagh RIC barracks was demolished on the night of Sunday, 11 April.[142] Earlier, in March, the Connolly police hut was burnt down. The IRA was making it clear that the RIC would not be reoccupying these abandoned barracks.

The decision by the police authorities to close many small police barracks and protection huts around the county was condemned by the Grand Jury of County Clare at the spring assizes of 1920. The Grand Jury passed a resolution in which they deplored the condition into which the county has been permitted to drift:

> We regard as regrettable the closure of many police posts, which should have been adequately strengthened by reinforcements and by elementary defences. As a result of this policy of abandonment, the county has been left at the mercy of lawless and violent persons particularly after nightfall [...] while the peaceable population exists in hourly terror of outrage. With the abandonment of these police posts the unfortunate rate payers will suffer a double-blow for withdrawal of protection to which the civilians of a civilised society are entitled.[143]

Murder at Canada Cross

Early in February, the British authorities arrested and deported sixty prominent Sinn Féin prisoners. Among them were several Clare men: Councillor Michael Quinn, chairman of the Ennis Rural District Council; Frank Gallagher, Kilkishen; J. Clancy, Kilkishen; M. McNamara, Kilkishen; Thomas Dillon, Broadford; Thomas Wall, Scariff; and M. Reidy, Inagh. After some months in English prisons, the Clare prisoners were released. Meanwhile, other Clare prisoners who were arrested and incarcerated in Mountjoy Jail under DORA demanded political prisoner status. Peadar Clancy from Cranny, the vice-commandant of the Dublin Brigade, played a prominent part in organising a hunger strike that involved about ninety other republicans at Mountjoy. It lasted from 5 April until 14 April, when the British gave in, not wishing to have more republican martyrs. The prisoners were released. As the historian Charles Townshend observed, 'It was a republican triumph and a staggering blow to the morale of the forces of law and order.'[144]

On Wednesday, 14 April at around 9.30 p.m., a meeting to celebrate the victory of another group of hunger strikers led by Commandant Peadar Clancy was held in Miltown Malbay. There was a bonfire on Main Street, and a large crowd of men, women and children was gathered around. The police and military ordered the people to disperse, and as they were doing so, shots were fired into the crowd without any warning. Three people, Tom O'Leary, Jack O'Loughlin and Pat Hennessy, were killed at the scene, and eleven others were injured. This tragedy caused 'wild excitement' in the town and district. After the shooting, the people remained up all night in terror.

An inquest was held at Miltown Malbay, and the local parish priest, Canon Hannon, testified that only a couple dozen people were gathered around a lighted tar barrel and that it was a peaceful meeting; the police and military called on the people to disperse, and as they were doing so, without any time to disperse, shots rang out. Canon Hannon stated that the IRA did not organise the meeting, and that there was no procession, no bands or banners – no provocation whatsoever. He denied that shots were fired from the crowd at the police or military.

The jury at the inquest found a verdict of 'wilful murder' against Sergeant James Hampson, constables Thomas O'Connor and Thomas Keenan, Lance-Corporal Kenneth McLeod, and privates William Kilgear, James McEwan, Patrick McLoughlin, Robert Bunting and Richard Adams. After the inquest, Sergeant Hampson and constables Keenan and O'Connor were removed, under military escort, from Miltown Malbay to an unknown destination. The military authorities refused to state if any action would be taken against the soldiers.

At the House of Commons, in a reply to a question from the veteran Irish Parliamentary Party member Thomas Patrick O'Connor, a government spokesman, Mitchell Henry, MP, stated that there were about 150 people in the town square and that shots were first fired at the police and military. Henry added that, according to Inspector Tyrrell, the coroner acted illegally in convening the inquest.

Speaking at Mass in Miltown Malbay on the following Sunday, Bishop Fogarty stated that

> the dead men had been the victims of a barbarous and inhuman outrage, which filled the town with grief and sent a thrill of horror through all classes in the county. Those who ruled in the name of law and order had made a Calvary of the town square, but it was consecrated ground to the innocent blood of Irish martyrs.

He hoped that those responsible for 'this infamous slaughter would be brought to justice'. He appealed to the people 'to exercise Christian fortitude and restraint, that wild retaliation would be useless and a pretext for further massacres'.[145]

The Battle of Kilmihil

On Sunday, 18 April the West Clare Brigade decided to ambush a party of soldiers returning from Mass in the local chapel. The *Irish Times* described the attack as follows:

> Head Constable Hoare, with five men, went to attend Divine Service at Kilmihil parish church on Sunday morning [...] After Mass, the party returned to the barracks, which is about 100 yards from the church [...] when suddenly shots rang out, killing Sergeant Patrick Carroll and severely wounding Constable Collins. One civilian named Breen [in fact, a member of the IRA] was also shot in the face by a revolver and died, while two others, named Higgins and McMahon were wounded.

Inquests were held on the two dead men, the RIC sergeant and the IRA Volunteer. At the inquest on Sergeant Carroll in Kilmihil, the local jury found 'that Sgt Carroll died from shock and a haemorrhage as a result of a bullet wound inflicted by some person or persons unknown whilst bearing arms on behalf of an alien and enemy government.' The jury also returned a verdict on the death of John Breen, 'We find a verdict that John Breen died from shock and haemorrhage caused by a bullet wound inflicted by Constable Martin, while John Breen was fighting for the freedom of his country.'[146] Bill Haugh, from Kilkee and adjutant of the West Clare Brigade, explained, in his witness statement, why the decision was taken to attack the police while returning from Mass, 'The policy now was to attack the RIC in the village streets, e.g., the attack at Kilmihil on RIC returning from Mass. The sergeant was killed, and a constable was crippled, Volunteer John Breen was killed.'[147]

There was some clerical uneasiness at the attack on the Catholic RIC men after attending Sunday Mass. Fr Patrick Gaynor, who was then a curate in Mullagh, and was the West Clare representative on the Sinn Féin national executive, gave a clerical insight into the attack on the police in Kilmihil, which he labelled the Battle of Kilmihil:

> In West Clare, so far as I know, apart from Michael Brennan's attack on Kilrush barracks, there was no clash of arms between the Volunteers and the British army except alone in Kilmihil village after Mass on Sunday 18 April 1920. Four policemen were at Mass, they had moved down the street and were able to run to the barracks. The attack was made by three Volunteers, Martin Melican, John O'Dea and Peter McMahon on three armed police who were on guard duty. Sergeant Carroll, a native of Wexford, who had only been two weeks in Kilmhil, was killed along with John Breen, a native of Kilmihil.
>
> For months the Tans had played havoc with the people constantly looting shops, raiding houses and taking away farmers' wooden gates for firewood. I have heard too that Fr Culligan CC Kilmihil had rashly urged the people to defend themselves against the Tans and police. Even so, I doubt if Fr Culligan had been consulted and had given sanction for the attack on the street after Mass; he had discouraged other assaults on the enemy, which were planned by the local Volunteers. It is regrettable that the Kilmihil attack took place after Mass [...] Moreover, the attack had a good result, the British forces were withdrawn from Kilmihil two weeks later and there was an end to looting and terrorism in the parish.[148]

Other police deaths

Two other RIC men were killed in Clare during the summer: Constable Duffy in Boston, Tubber and Constable Hanlon in

Kilrush. In Boston on 19 August, a patrol of six police marching in twos fired on a car being driven without lights. Constable Duffy was shot dead by 'friendly fire' in this incident. Only two out of thirteen jurors turned up for the inquest. He was a native of Mayo. Ironically, he had applied to resign from the police force at the request of his two sisters, both nuns, and the papers accepting his resignation arrived on the day after he was shot dead.

During the evening of Saturday, 21 August at about 5 p.m., Constable John Hanlon was shot dead in Walsh's public house on Moore Street in Kilrush. He was followed into the pub by his assailant, who shot him through the right eye, and the bullet went through his skull. Constable Hanlon, a native of Kerry, was a married man with two children. His death caused terrible excitement in the town. The crowds on market day were dispersed by armed police. That evening, heavily armed police and military patrolled the streets, discharging rifle shots into the air, terrorising the local people. At Mass on Sunday, the murder was strongly condemned by the parish priest Dean McInerney and the curate Fr Molony. Dean McInerney said that it was a sad consolation that the assassin, from all accounts, did not belong to the town or parish of Kilrush.

Bill Haugh of the West Clare Brigade, who carried out the killing of Constable John Hanlon at Kilrush, described why and how the operation was carried out (referring to himself in the third person):

> It was, however, known that there could be only one person responsible for the organisation of enemy intelligence, the local R.I.C. detective at Kilrush. It was decided that immediate action should be taken towards the disposal of this official. He was seldom or never out of town on duty. The Kilrush Volunteers proved a squeamish lot; it was therefore necessary that a party should enter the town and in daylight at that […] On the third Saturday in August a lone Volunteer entered the town on a bicycle […] when the detective turned into a licensed premises two doors away. He was followed in shortly afterwards, lured to the kitchen and done to death, while police and military mingled in the streets outside. No suspicions were aroused, and escape was a matter of moments.[149]

While RIC men were killed by the IRA at Kilmihil and Kilrush, many Clare-born policemen were also shot dead by the IRA during the year – RIC men could not serve in the county from which they came. One of them was a policeman named Neenan, who was killed in mid-February. At the end of February, Mr Nagle, one of the Kilrush magistrates, proposed a motion offering sympathy with the family of Constable Neenan, a native of Kilmihil who was shot dead in Cork. Two other Clare-born policemen named Haugh and McNamara were killed in August. Constable Matthew Haugh was shot dead at about 2 p.m. on Wednesday, 25 August in Bantry, Cork; he was a native of Ballyea. Constable John McNamara, 25 years old and a native of Crusheen, was shot dead in Glengariff on Tuesday, 24 August by four masked and armed men. Other Clare-born RIC men killed by the IRA in 1920 included: Sergeant John Flynn, from Kildysart, who was killed on 10 May at Timoleague, Cork; Constable John Crawford, from Miltown Malbay, who was killed in Co. Roscommon on 12 October; Constable Michael Kenny, who was shot dead in Roscommon on 12 October; Constable Martin McCarthy, who was shot dead in Roscommon on 1 September; Detective Sergeant Denis Moroney, from Tulla, who was shot dead in Derry on 15 May; and Constable George Roche, who was killed in Dingle on 6 October. The Clare-born RIC men were buried privately.

On the other hand, a Clare-born IRA member named Joe McMahon, a native of Kilmaley who died in Co. Cavan, apparently due to an explosion, was given a massive public funeral when his body was returned to Clare. There was a huge attendance at the funeral Mass in Ennis Cathedral followed by interment at Kilmaley. All the shops in Ennis were closed, and IRA lined the streets, with thirteen clergymen in the cortège. The coffin was draped in the tricolour, and IRA men marched the 5 miles to Kilmaley in procession and fired three volleys over the grave. There were no police or military present during the funeral.[150]

Sectarian attacks

A shocking development occurred on 17 April when the Protestant church at Clarecastle was maliciously destroyed in an arson attack. This was a sinister and unwelcome development in the struggle for independence. This sectarian outrage was not sanctioned by Sinn

Féin or the IRA but was carried out by some local disaffected republicans. Another sectarian attack of this kind occurred in east Clare when an attempt was made to burn the Protestant church at O'Briensbridge in June.

The *Saturday Record* described the malicious burning at Clarecastle as follows:

> This dastardly outrage condemned alike by Catholics and Protestants was perpetrated on Sunday morning when the Protestant church at Clare Castle was burnt to the ground. A police patrol at midnight noticed nothing but at 2 am word was brought to the police by a woman that the building was in flames. On their arrival at the church the police found that the building was falling in and in a short time the building was completely gutted allowing no opportunity of saving any of the valuable church property; silver communion vessels, dating from the mid-seventeenth century, and mural tablets belonging to the Keane family, were all destroyed. Up to within the last few months the church was in constant use, but of late, Divine Service had only been held there occasionally and no service was in contemplation for that Sunday. It is impossible at present to estimate the total cost of the damage done. This is, so far as we know, the first occasion on which a Church has been maliciously destroyed. A two-gallon can containing a little paraffin oil was found nearby.

At a meeting of Clarecastle parishioners chaired by Very Rev. Canon Bourke, PP, with Mr B. Mescall, a district councillor and member of Sinn Féin acting as secretary, the following resolution was unanimously passed:

> That we, the heads of the families of this parish of Clare Castle, in public meeting assembled desire to place on record our deep sense of horror of the dastardly deed of the night of Saturday 17 April, which resulted in the destruction by fire of the Protestant church in the village.
>
> We beg to assure the little Protestant community in our midst that the occurrence has aroused the deepest indignation of all classes. Whatever may have been the underlying motive of the deed, it cannot be attributed to any change in kindly feelings and relations between Catholics and their Protestant neighbours in this parish. This deeply regrettable occurrence cannot, therefore, have any religious significance; nor can we see any political

> motive whatsoever for it. We are, therefore, at a loss how anyone in our community could have been guilty of such a criminal folly. We can assure our Protestant fellow-townsmen that the dreadful occurrence has caused us the deepest pain, and we take this, the earliest possible opportunity of offering our sympathy to them in the destruction of their place of worship.

The Select Vestry of Drumcliff parish met and a resolution was unanimously adopted:

> That we desire to place on record our sense of deep gratitude towards the people of Clare Castle parish, who under chairmanship of Canon Bourke called a public meeting to denounce the recent burning of our church. The kindly sympathy extended to us by our fellow countrymen of a different religious persuasion has done much to lessen the sorrow caused to us by the wanton destruction of our place of worship, and we earnestly hope that the widespread sympathy so generously extended to us on this occasion will only tend to further increase the kindly relations that have existed in the past between Irishmen of different religious denominations in this parish.

The case of the Clarecastle Protestant church was heard at the Ennis quarter sessions, and a claim for £3,000 was submitted. Canon Griffin said that services were held at Clarecastle once a month for the few people who attended there regularly. Not only was the church set on fire: all its contents were destroyed, including the silver communion chalice. Canon Griffin recommended that the church not be rebuilt. Judge Bodkin allowed compensation of £1,000, plus £28 expenses. This compensation was later increased to £1,665.[151]

On 29 June the Protestant church at O'Briensbridge was set on fire and considerably damaged in what the Inspector General Bryne stated was 'an attempt to introduce religious strife into the conflict'. However, local members of Sinn Féin and the IRA helped to quench the flames. These outrageous acts were undeniably sectarian and were probably carried out by some disaffected IRA men or people without the sanction of local IRA commandants or Sinn Féin. Nevertheless, these were isolated incidents and not supported by Sinn Féin or the IRA leadership.

The small Protestant community of Ennis and its hinterland were naturally concerned about these sectarian attacks and condemned the religious bigotry, outrages and reprisals taking place in Northern Ireland at this time. At a meeting in Ennis on Sunday, 20 September, with Richard J. Stacpoole, JP, DL, of Eden Vale in the chair, they passed the following resolution:

> That we, the Protestant residents in the parish of Drumcliffe, Co Clare, view with the gravest concern, the outrages and reprisals which are taking place in Ireland, and deeply regret that while we in our churches are praying for the peace and welfare of our country, our co-nationalists should commit such outrages which are in direct contravention to our prayers. We desire to record the fact that we live in peace and good will with our Catholic fellow-countrymen, that religious intolerance does not exist in our county; and we sincerely hope that nothing has been done that will disturb the harmony which has always existed in this parish.

Sir Michael O'Loghlen of Drumconora, Lieutenant of County Clare, sent a copy of the resolution to the Lord Lieutenant of Ireland.[152]

Intimidation

With Sinn Féin and the IRA publicly branding the RIC as spies and traitors, people who had any dealings with the RIC or other British forces were threatened and intimidated, often violently, to stop them co-operating. Both men and women were intimidated, and there were many instances where women and young girls were publicly shamed – their hair cropped by the IRA – as a punishment.

The first reported instance of this practice occurred in Miltown Malbay; a *Clare Champion* report stated that a number of young men visited the railway station house on Saturday, 10 April and cut the hair of two young girls who had been 'keeping company' with soldiers. The girls had been given repeated warnings to avoid soldiers, which they failed to heed. Afterwards, they had to wear wigs. At 1.30 a.m. on 12 June, a party of eight masked men entered the house of a man named Sullivan, a fisherman from Kilrush, and forcibly removed his daughter, Kathleen. They took her outside and cut off some portions of her hair. One report stated, 'The Sullivan family have been friendly towards the police.' In October, a party of armed men visited the home of Ann Hogan from Miltown Malbay. They forced the door open, stole some goods and cut off part of Miss Hogan's hair as a punishment for associating with the police. Threatening letters were sent to Mary Burns and Bridget Burns in Kilrush, ordering them to leave their employment as domestic servants of an English lady, the wife of an excise officer, on 3 December. On 8 December two girls, Minnie Kane and Annie O'Shea of Kilrush, had their hair cut off by members of Sinn Féin for being friendly to the police. Twelve masked men visited their houses and warned them that they were lucky they were not shot. O'Shea sought compensation in the courts and was awarded £100. She stated that her marriage was called off because of her treatment by the IRA. On 8 December Margaret Nash, a domestic servant, was held up by three men when returning from her home in Kildysart; they threw her on the road and cut her hair. The police report noted, 'The motive is definitely intimidation, as this girl was on friendly terms with Constable Flynn of Kildysart.'

In his memoir, Fr Pat Gaynor reflected on the practice of cropping women's hair, which he found to be distasteful. He recalled one instance of this in Quilty:

> British soldiers and Tans had no trouble finding girls in Irish towns during the Sinn Féin war [...] Their preference for the aliens and their lack of patriotic principles annoyed some of the Volunteers, with the result that girls were sentenced to the penalty of having their hair clipped for associating with the enemy. The abuse did not occur in rural areas, but we had an unfortunate incident in the fishing village of Quilty.
>
> There were coastguards beyond the village, who had no part in the conflict and were quite harmless; a few Quilty girls walked towards the station perhaps more than once and stood chatting with the local coastguards on the public road. The local Volunteers, whether through jealousy or outrage principles, brought this trivial occurrence before the battalion council and, very unwisely, Fr McKenna CC Mullagh, allowed the council to impose sentences of hair clipping on the Quilty girls. The Quilty boys, with their moonlighting instincts, would drag the girls from their homes after dark and subject them to worse insults than hair clipping. I do not know whether the hair clipping was initiated at Volunteer HQ or by the ladies who controlled Cumann na mBan. It was carried out rarely and was regarded with distaste by all decent-minded folk. Genuine Volunteers who

> were occupied in fighting the Tans took no part in this paltry campaign against foolish young women.

There were other women who were intimidated and who claimed compensation from the Irish Distress Committee. Nora Logan of Main Street, Lahinch was, in her own words, 'friendly with the RIC'. She claimed that her hair was cut several times between 1919 and 1921. Katie McNamara of Bogberry, Ennistymon, was a mother of eleven children and worked as a laundress and cook for the military in Ennistymon. She opened a tearoom, which was frequented by the army and the RIC. She was ordered to stop by the IRA, but she refused to do so. She then claims that she was kidnapped and was held a prisoner in 'wild mountainous country, where she was ill-treated shamefully'. Because of this treatment 'she miscarried and spent six weeks in hospital'. Her husband was an ex-employee of Henry Vincent MacNamara. Susan O'Loughlin, of Chapel Road, Ennistymon, was warned that she was going to be tarred for working in the RIC barracks. She stated that she had to leave the country until 1926.

Despite threats and intimidation from the IRA, there were still some women who associated with the Crown forces – even some who had been in Cumann na mBan. Kitty Shinnors, secretary of the Ennis Battalion, Mid-Clare Brigade, wrote in her witness statement to the Bureau of Military History, 'There were only ten girls [out of more than one hundred] in our Cumann na mBan branch who could be accused of going with British soldiers and they aren't claiming pensions!'[153]

There were several instances of intimidation in which shots were fired at people to warn them against working for, or even speaking with, the RIC. On 11 January shots were fired outside the house of a man named Keane, living near Kilrush, who had been seen speaking to the police the previous day. On 20 April a shot was fired into Mr O'Keefe's house in Broadford. Mrs O'Keefe was a servant at the local RIC barracks and Mr O'Keefe had recently carried potatoes for the police.[154]

In other cases, threatening letters were sent. For example, the house of James Cleary, living in Knock, was visited by a party of men who kidnapped him. Cleary was a witness in a police prosecution arising out of a labour dispute at Gore Hickman's estate. Mr Martin, the steward of Gore Hickman of Kilmore, was fired upon and seriously wounded. On 19 August John Hynes, a farmer from Ballyvaughan, received a letter warning him that if he continued to supply the British army with milk, he would be shot dead. His sister received a similar letter. One police report noted, 'He has been supplying the police for some years and states that he will continue to do so.'

Peter Blake of the Bridge, Ennistymon was a blacksmith and ran a coach-building business while his wife managed his pub beside the bridge. He worked for the military and the RIC, repairing their cars; the officers also visited his public house. He was threatened for this association but continued working for them until they left after the Anglo-Irish Treaty. He was also threatened for attending the funerals of RIC men. Thus, he was boycotted, and he claimed that his business and his health was ruined. Another blacksmith that had assisted the Crown forces was Michael Garrahy of the Square, Ennistymon. The IRA punished him by cutting his bellows to pieces.[155]

Johanna Slattery, Fr Hayes's housekeeper at his home in Feakle, was kidnapped on 23 October by armed and disguised men. The police report stated, 'Fr Hayes is very unpopular in the district owing to the condemning of attacks on police, murders etc. Miss Slattery was accused of being a spy.' A young man named Cunningham, a farmer living at New Hall, was 'arrested' on Friday, 28 June by a party of armed and disguised men who took him away to 'parts unknown'. He was returned to his home the following Tuesday morning. He did not disclose where he was detained, or by whom.[156]

Threatening notices were also posted to individual policemen around the county. In April, a letter was sent to the RIC at Ennistymon stating, 'Your days are numbered. Your life is that of a dog, so say your prayers.' One policeman stationed in Ennistymon, Constable Cooper, received the following letter, 'Citizens of the republic have been murdered by police at Miltown; unless you clear out of Ennistymon before midnight on Saturday 24 April a similar fate is in store for you and any Peelers left behind.' On 28 June, a threatening notice was sent to Constable John Gleeson at Broadford,

'Prepare to meet thy doom!' Publicans were also warned not to serve policemen.

On 13 April a notice was posted in O'Briensbridge, 'Take notice of IRA – keep policemen out of public houses. Are you supporting the police?' Due to the ostracization of the police by the nationalist community and the threats to their lives, many RIC men resigned between 1919 and 1921, including several members from Clare. Notices of several resignations were put in the local papers, naming two of them: Constable F. Crowe of Carbane, Knock, who had twelve years' service, and Constable J. O'Brien, a native of Doonbeg, who had spent more than seven years in the force.[157]

Sinn Féin courts

Besides paralysing the police, the IRA also succeeded in undermining the legal system in the county. Court houses were burnt, justices of the peace were pressured into resignation, witnesses were intimidated, and people were urged to boycott the official courts and present their cases to Sinn Féin courts instead. Sinn Féin courts were pioneered in west Clare and were operating unofficially for a few months before they became a model for a national courts system. The judges were appointed by Sinn Féin and usually included prominent Sinn Féiners, businesspeople, Catholic parish clergy and members of the IRA. The courts mainly dealt with local issues such as land disputes, cases of trespassing, assaults and burglaries.

Several courthouses were wrecked in April, around the time of the mass arson attacks on the former RIC barracks. On 3 April the courthouse in Tuamgraney was burnt down and all records destroyed, and on 4 April the magistrate's rooms at Killaloe were burnt. In June the Quin courthouse was raided by a gang of sixteen men, who wrecked the building: doors and chairs were smashed, statutes were broken and volumes of court files were set on fire in a field. The *Dublin Gazette* announced in October that all quarter sessions were to be held in the Ennis courthouse, as the courthouses in Ennistymon, Killaloe, Kilrush and Tulla had been wholly destroyed or rendered unfit for the holding of quarter sessions. By September the boycott of the British legal system seemed complete, and one newspaper reported that, at the petty sessions in Kilrush on Monday, 20 September, there were no cases before Captain Lendrum, the newly appointed resident magistrate, 'as the litigants were appearing before the Sinn Féin Courts instead.'[158]

In August, County Inspector Gelston summarised the overthrowing of the official legal system by the Sinn Féin courts:

> All ordinary administrative work in the county is suspended. Courts of law are avoided by the general public; cases being taken through fear to the Sinn Féin courts. The courts of law are practically neglected by the general public. Disputes are settled by the SF arbitration courts. Sinn Féin magistrates have been selected throughout the county. In the case of officials this will be enforced by refusing to pay their salaries. All public bodies have sworn allegiance to Dáil Éireann. Clare County Council passed a resolution calling on all deputy lieutenants and justices of the peace to resign their commissions. Those who refuse to do so will be compelled to resign. The county was in a state of active and open rebellion. The forces of law and order were utterly inadequate, and protection could not be afforded to loyal subjects.[159]

Lord Inchiquin of Dromoland Castle gave his opinion of the legal transformation:

> The Assizes have been on for the past month, but there have been very few cases at them as nobody will give evidence in the case of outrages, and all civilians are taken before Sinn Féin courts which are sitting daily! And the Government apparently take no notice of them. Orders are issued from them in the name of the Irish Republic! The Dáil Éireann, or Irish parliament are sitting in Dublin. Sinn Féin flags are flown on courthouses, harbours and on every public building in Ireland, except, of course, in Ulster.[160]

As the War of Independence gathered momentum, pressure mounted on the people who were appointed justices of the peace to resign their commissions. The resignation of justices of the peace helped to undermine the legal system, as there would be a shortage of them to try petty offences. Ennis Urban Council and Clare County Council made calls for the justices to resign their commissions. Justices of the peace were requested by the IRA to resign; they were also threatened and boycotted to induce them to resign. Some of the justices of the peace who resigned included: C.W. Healy, Manusmore, Clarecastle; Dan O'Brien, Thornville, Ruan; Stephen Honan, Ennis; M.F. Nagle, Doolin; Dr Hillery, Spanish Point; and Michael Griffin, Kildysart. Economic pressure was also used to prompt magistrates to resign. Kilrush District Council passed a resolution that no employee of the council who was a magistrate would be paid in future. In response to this resolution, in September 1920 Dr Studdert stated that he had resigned as a peace commissioner and that he had not attended the petty sessions for twelve months.[161]

However, some justices stubbornly refused to resign, despite intense intimidation. Among them were: Joseph Browne, Knockerra, Killimer; Bartholemew Culligan, Kilrush; Dr Peter O'Dwyer, Ennistymon; William James Corbett, Wilbrook, Corofin; William Charles Doherty, Kilkee; Mr Hogan, Main Street, Ennistymon; Joseph McInerney, Ennistymon; and James Wakely, Mountshannon. The IRA put them under enormous pressure to resign their positions as part of their campaign to undermine the British justice system and replace it with the Sinn Féin courts. Because of the boycotting, intimidation and economic losses, these justices of the peace sought compensation from the Irish Distress Committee and the Irish Grants Committee. These committees were established by the British government in the years after the Treaty to compensate loyalists who had suffered because of the War of Independence.

One justice of the peace, Christopher Kelly of Craggaknock, Kilmurry Ibrickane, defiantly refused to resign as a peace commissioner at first, but following intense intimidation from the IRA – he received threatening letters, he was boycotted, his house was raided by armed men and his only son was kidnapped – Kelly reluctantly resigned. The kidnapping of his only son was probably the final straw. The police report for June noted, 'Mr Christopher Kelly has been subjected to a degree of terrorism because he has refused to resign his commission and submit to Sinn Féin jurisdiction.' In August, his resignation was announced in the local press. He was forced by Sinn Féin and the IRA to write a message in the papers indicating that his resignation was 'to express his abhorrence of the entire brutal regime carried on in Ireland and of the campaign of assassination pursued by military agents of the British government against his fellow-countrymen.' They were publicly mocking Kelly, who was a well-known loyalist.[162]

Fr Pat Gaynor, curate at Mullagh, a Clare delegate on the Sinn Féin executive council, and also chief of police in the West Clare Brigade, gives some insight into the background of the case against Christopher Kelly. He states that Kelly accused the local IRA of stealing £60 when they seized his gun during the conscription menace in 1918. He was summoned to attend a Sinn Féin court-martial, which he ignored. He evaded arrest by the IRA and demanded police protection. A party of twenty soldiers from Kilrush protected him. His son was kidnapped by the IRA, and Kelly was told that he would be shot. Fr Gaynor acted as an intermediary between Sean Liddy, commandant of the West Clare Brigade, and Kelly. Kelly was to renounce British army protection, resign as justice of the peace and submit to the Sinn Féin court. Fr Gaynor witnessed a statement signed by Kelly stating, 'Sir, in view of the campaign of murder, which is being pursued by the British Government against my fellow countrymen, I hereby renounce my commission as Justice of the Peace.' After Kelly signed the letter, Fr Gaynor posted it, but Kelly later wrote a letter retracting the resignation, stating that he was forced to resign under duress. In his memoir, Fr Gaynor concludes, 'Christy, treacherous as usual, succeeded in retaining his little honour.'[163]

Joseph Daly, from Kilmurry Ibrickane and the commandant of the 4th Battalion, West Clare Brigade, gave more details of how Kelly was coerced into resigning his commission:

> We induced Justices of the Peace to resign from their posts, though generally speaking, these people were not in sympathy with Sinn Féin, most of them resigned as time went on [...] In my area, there was only one person to deal with, a gentleman farmer named Mr Christopher Kelly of Craggaknock; he was asked to resign several times, but he refused. To compel Mr Kelly to resign the brigade HQ decided to kidnap his only son, Joseph, aged about 20. He was captured by Volunteers under Patrick Clancy. He was kept a prisoner for nine or ten days. I met the brigade OC, Sean Liddy, at Fr McKenna's house, Mullagh and a

> message was sent to Mr Kelly, that if he resigned as a JP, then his son would be released. After the kidnapping, a party of about twenty soldiers guarded Mr Kelly's house. Mrs Kelly was hysterical. Mr Kelly gave an undertaking to resign from his post and his son was released next day.[164]

In January 1921, Kelly, 'a broken man', who along with his family had paid a huge price for his loyalty to the British system of justice, described his experiences at a court in Ennis: He had been a justice for thirteen years, and he had refused to resign. He had a large farm at Craggaknock, and on 29 June seven 'boys' came to his house and said they wanted him. Shots were fired as the family were saying the rosary. The next day the military came, staying in his house on protection duty until 14 July. On 9 July he told his son Joseph to bring butter to a neighbour and his son was kidnapped and kept for several days. Kelly added, 'my cows remained un-milked and my horse died, my servants went away.' Kelly's health was affected, and Dr Hillery and Dr Hickey attended him. Dr Counihan, from Ennis, corroborated the medical evidence, stating, 'he was in terror and in poor health, as was his wife and son.'[165]

Meanwhile, the Sinn Féin courts were generally being supported in west Clare. Charles Townshend, citing the witness statement of Kevin O'Sheil, Bachelor of Laws, Commissioner of the Dáil Land Commission between 1920 and 1921, states that Brian O'Higgins, the MP for west Clare, called a conference in January in which a district arbitration court was set up in west Clare. A constitution was drawn up with the aid of local lawyers, judge-arbitrators and registrars were appointed, and a scale of court fees and fines was settled. The establishment of arbitration courts in west Clare was the template on which a national legal system was modelled. This was perhaps the greatest legacy of the IRA and Sinn Féin of west Clare during the War of Independence.[166]

However, in his witness statement Art O'Donnell, then the commandant of the West Clare Brigade, states that he was the person who founded the Sinn Féin courts of west Clare:

> I had been appointed Secretary of the West Clare Sinn Féin Executive and I called a meeting on 1 November 1919 at Sean Cunningham's, Cree, to deal with the vexatious matter of land

> disputes. More than 100 delegates turned up at this meeting and I proposed that we set up a Land Court to settle disputes and to keep peace among the Volunteers. I said that I would back up the decisions of the court. My proposal was approved by the delegates, including Fr C Culligan, CC; Mr Brian O'Higgins, TD, and others. I was appointed first secretary of the Land Court.
>
> The very first Land Court in Ireland was held in Tullycrine. It was necessary to devise rules and regulations and a special meeting was held in Moyasta on New Year's Day for this purpose. The rules which were drafted at Moyasta were submitted to the Minister for Justice, Austin Stack, TD, and approved. They were sanctioned by the Government and became the template for a national scheme of Land Courts. Due to my work as commandant of the West Clare brigade, I had to resign as court registrar and from my position on the Sinn Féin Executive.[167]

The *Clare Champion* records that the first official west Clare Sinn Féin courts were set up at a meeting in Mullagh in July. Fr Charles Culligan, CC, from Kilmihil, was chairman. Éamon Waldron represented the Dáil. Judges were to be selected by ballot. The first judges elected were Fr C. Culligan, Peadar O'Loughlin, J. O'Dwyer, W. Carroll and P.M. Kelly. There were many newspaper reports of Sinn Féin arbitration courts in different parts of the county from May onwards – for example, in Ennis, Ennistymon, Cooraclare, Liscannor, Flagmount, Feakle and Miltown Malbay. The judges at the Sinn Féin court in Ennis in June were James McParland, B. Mescall and Fr J. Considine. The court dealt successfully with thirty-five cases involving land disputes from the Newmarket-on-Fergus, Lisdoonvarna and Ennis areas.[168]

Arbitration courts dealing mainly with land disputes were the first to be set up; later, district and parish courts were established. The IRA policed the courts, enforcing decisions, imposing fines and detaining prisoners. Prominent Sinn Féin clergymen such as Fr Culligan, CC, Kilmihil, Fr Clancy, PP, Kildysart, and Fr Hamilton, St Flannan's College, Ennis, acted as judges. IRA members who acted as judges included Art O'Donnell, Tullycrine, commandant of the West Clare Brigade; Conor Whelan, Doonbeg, vice-commandant of the West Clare Brigade; Hugh Hehir, Ballynacally; Thomas

McNamara, Mountshannon; Thomas Shalloo, Ennistymon; Peadar O'Loughlin, Ennis; Andrew O'Donoghue, Kilfenora; Patrick Kerins, Miltown Mabay; Seamus Connolly, Ennistymon; and Éamon Fennell, Carrigaholt.[169]

Fr Pat Gaynor gives a colourful insight into the workings of the Sinn Féin courts in west Clare during 1920. People flocked to these district courts to solve ancient disputes over land, including trespassing cases, turbary rights or land claims. The disputes often related to small holdings – even as little as an acre of cut-away bog. These few acres were as passionately disputed as anything described in John B. Keane's magnificent work of fiction, *The Field*. Fr Gaynor outlined the difficulties of enforcing decisions of the courts when dealing with some recalcitrant characters. In one instance a man named Connors, reminiscent of the character 'Bull McCabe' in *The Field*, defiantly refused to accept the verdict of the Sinn Féin court after being sentenced to one month's imprisonment on Mutton Island. Fr Gaynor called a joint meeting of the West Clare Brigade staff officers, the Sinn Féin executive and judges of the Sinn Féin district courts to enforce the court decision. Eventually, Fr Gaynor, who was the 4th Battalion chief of police, threatened to shoot Connors just before he fled from the disputed farmstead.[170]

Daring disarmament of a military party in Ennis

While the IRA only gained a few weapons and little ammunition through their raids on private homes during 1920, the Mid-Clare Brigade had a spectacular coup when they boldly disarmed a military party in Ennis on 23 June, securing seven Lee–Enfield rifles and some ammunition from the soldiers. The spectacular and bloodless disarmament was successfully organised by Joe Barrett, adjutant of the Mid-Clare Brigade. In his witness statement, he wrote:

> On Wednesday, 23 June, on the eve of the Fair of Spancilhill, a military party consisting of a corporal and six soldiers of the Highland Light Infantry were proceeding from the Butter Market, where they were guarding military transport, to the Home barracks at Jail Road at about half past six on Wednesday evening. The military party was ambushed at the upper end of O'Connell Street where they were 'rushed' by a large group of men with revolvers. The soldiers were forced into Jack D'Arcy's

> yard and disarmed. Seven rifles were taken, and the captured rifles were taken away in motor cars to Michael Keane's in Ivy Hill Inch. The sensational affair lasted only a few minutes. The attacking party were not disguised and went about their work most methodically.[171]

The eve of Spancilhill Fair was chosen because many strangers would be in Ennis for the fair and the IRA men could easily mingle in with the crowd. The military detail – three pairs of soldiers and a corporal – had been observed marching in formation for a couple of weeks. At least twenty-two IRA men were directly involved in the operation; seventeen others were there as back-up. The twenty-two men who were directly involved came from the IRA companies in Barefield, Crusheen, Kilnamona and Ruan; they would be strangers in Ennis. The back-up group came from the Ballyea, Clooney and Ennis companies.

Four members of the military detail had turned into O'Connell Street from Carmody Street when the attack began. At that point, Joe Barrett blew a whistle and the IRA men attacked the soldiers:

> Panther-like, the attackers sprang into action. Each soldier was held up, gripped by the throttle and disarmed in a series of movements carried out almost simultaneously. The corporal alone showed fight, but his resistance was quickly overcome with a few well-directed punches by Sean O'Keefe. Within the space of two minutes the operation was over.

The guns were taken to Kilmorane in a car driven by John Joe Neylon and subsequently hidden in an arms dump in Darragh.[172]

In July and August the IRA arsenal was augmented by attacks upon the police and military. On 17 July a soldier on sentry duty at Ennistymon bridge was 'rushed' by a group of men, and his rifle and bayonet, along with some ammunition, was stolen by Michael Nestor. On 20 July four rifles were stolen from a police lorry in Ennistymon. On 27 August, RIC Sergeant Fitzgerald was assaulted at Kildysart and his revolver was stolen. While attempting to disarm a pair of officers at Ennistymon on 22 July, Michael Conway, a member of the IRA, was shot dead by one of the officers.[173]

The Connaught Rangers mutiny, June 1920

Many Irishmen who had served in the British army during the First World War continued their service in the army or re-enlisted following demobilisation after the war ended. Among them was Joe Hawes from Kilkeedy, Tubber, who took part in the Connaught Rangers mutiny in June 1920. He had served in the British army from January 1916 until the end of the war in conflict zones such as the Middle East, the Mediterranean and on the Western Front. He was demobilised on 18 February 1919. However, he re-enlisted the next day and was sent to the Punjab in India.

While home on leave in Clare in June 1920, Hawes had heard about and witnessed the activities of the British army and the atrocities committed, in Clare and elsewhere, by the Crown forces. Back in India, at the Jullunder barracks on the night of 27 June, Hawes and a few army friends in C Company of the Connaught Rangers were chatting about the political situation in Ireland. The group, consisting of five men, decided to make a protest. The following morning, the mutiny began when the men went to the guard room and declared that 'they would no longer serve the king as a protest against the atrocities of the British army in Ireland.' At the barracks, they raised a tricolour instead of the Union Jack. Hawes was elected as one of seven spokesmen for the mutineers. The mutiny spread to other members of C Company at a barracks in Solon, where the 'rebels', led by James Daly of Tyrrelspass, Co. Westmeath, attacked an army magazine to get weapons, which resulted in the death of two soldiers.

Joe Hawes and sixty other mutineers were court-martialled at Dhagsai Jail on 23 August 1920. For his actions as one of the ringleaders, Hawes, along with thirteen other Irish soldiers, was sentenced to death at a military court-martial on 4 September 1920; but only one Irish man, James Daly, was executed for the mutiny. On the day before Daly's execution by firing squad, Hawes sent him a letter of comfort:

> Dearest comrade, Fr Baker was here speaking to me today, he says you are a man and you will be in Heaven tomorrow, you will be better-off, Jim. I will pray night and day for you, for you are sure to go straight to Heaven and join the lord mayor

> [Terence MacSwiney, who died on hunger strike on 25 October and was buried on 31 October]. From a fellow mutineer, Joe Hawes, Irish R.A., 1 November 1920.

Hawes's death sentence, along with that of twelve others, was later commuted to life imprisonment. He and other mutineers spent some time in solitary confinement in jails in India and in British prisons such as Maidstone, Portland and Shrewsbury; they went on hunger strike for eleven days in Portland Jail, in protest against their harsh treatment. Under an amnesty agreement negotiated by the Irish government after the Anglo-Irish Treaty, Joe Hawes was released on 4 January 1923. The next day he returned to Ireland as a hero and settled in Kilrush for the rest of his life. He died on 29 November 1972 while on holiday in Birmingham and was buried in Shanakyle, Kilrush on 6 December. His tombstone has the following inscription, 'Joseph Hawes, leader of the Connaught Rangers Mutiny, India 1920.'[174]

Rineen ambush and reprisals

Late in August, County Inspector Gelston wrote the following report, forecasting more determined action by the IRA:

> The situation is becoming more dangerous in the county and may at any moment result in more determined attacks on military and police; to cope with which a much larger force of military and police will be required. The death of the Lord Mayor of Cork will be likely to precipitate this state of affairs. So far, the county police force has been comparatively successful in repelling attacks and as regard casualties.[175]

The fears of the county inspector were realised a few weeks later when the IRA launched its most ambitious ambush yet at a site known as Rineen, located on the coast road from Lahinch to Miltown Malbay. The Rineen ambush took place on Wednesday, 22 September. It was wholly organised by the 4th Battalion of the Mid-Clare Brigade under Commandant Ignatius O'Neill, an ex-Guardsman of the First World War. More than sixty IRA members took part in the operation, belonging to seven companies in the region – from Ennistymon, Glendine, Inagh, Lahinch, Letterkelly, Miltown Malbay and Moy. About twenty-five of them were armed, the rest were scouts. Their weapons consisted of eight or nine rifles, two revolvers, sixteen shotguns and two bombs. They had about sixty rounds of ammunition as well as cartridges.

Their target was a police Crossley Tender motor truck that travelled from Ennistymon to Miltown Malbay each Wednesday. The IRA members marched through the night from various locations and arrived at Rineen early in the morning; they waited in hiding for hours for the arrival of the police tender. Due to a misunderstanding, they did not attack the police tender coming from Ennistymon at around noon, but they did strike the motor truck on the return journey from Miltown Malbay at around 2.30 p.m. Within a matter of minutes, six policemen were fatally wounded; one of them had apparently run for his life for several hundred yards, but he was chased and gunned down by the IRA men.

The IRA searched the Crossley Tender and recovered six Lee–Enfield rifles, six .45 Webley revolvers, several 'Mills bomb' hand grenades and about a thousand rounds of .303 ammunition. After the weapons and ammunition were recovered, the Crossley Tender was set on fire. Shortly afterwards the IRA were surprised by the sudden arrival of several trucks of British soldiers, and further soldiers on bikes, totalling about one hundred and fifty troops. A running battle ensued, and the IRA men retreated safely into the countryside behind Dromin Hill. Two of the IRA party, Ignatius O'Neill and Michael Curtin, were wounded, and several British troops were also injured. The attacking party then dispersed to safe houses, and the wounded IRA men were taken to be treated by Dr Hillery.[176]

In reprisals two nights later, on 24 September, parties of drunken and enraged police and Black and Tans took revenge on the people of Ennistymon, Lahinch and Miltown Malbay for the deaths of their comrades. The local and national newspapers carried sensational reports of the shocking reprisals in west Clare:

> Fearful occurrence in West Clare, police party ambushed, and six lives lost. Awful sequel, three towns were attacked with major loss of property and three civilians were shot dead. On Wednesday six constables were shot dead, Constables Hardman, Hodnett, Kelly and Maguire, Constable Harte was missing but

> was found dead next morning. Sgt. J. Hynes died from wounds next day. Forty men were arrested in round-ups afterwards.
>
> Parties of uniformed men turned out in a series of raids on Friday night in Miltown Malbay, Lahinch and Ennistymon. In a night of terror, groups of men ran amok and roamed the streets shouting, shooting, smashing windows and doors, they set fire to several premises and shot three people in Miltown Malbay around 11.30 pm. The business premises and homes of Messrs O'Neill, Roche, Collins, Hayes, Jones, Marrinan and Casey, were destroyed. Petrol was doused into buildings, while other houses, especially pubs were looted. People fled in terror. Several soldiers and officers in the town tried to put out the blazes. The uniformed men did not leave the town till about 5 am. The garage of Dr Hillery, who had recently resigned from the Peace Commission, was entered and his car was burnt.
>
> While this orgy of destruction was taking place in Miltown Malbay, similar scenes were taking place in Lahinch, where parties of uniformed men in lorries set fire to several premises. The homes of O'Dwyer, Flanagan, Vaughan, Howard, Walsh, Reynolds were burnt, along with the town hall. People fled in terror to the sand hills and stayed up all night. Three motor cars went up and down the streets firing indiscriminately; the house of Dan Lehane, Moy, was burnt and he was wounded in the throat [he died from his wounds a few weeks later]. A farmhouse was set on fire. The body of a young man named Pakie Lehane of Moy, who was one of the Volunteers at the Rineen ambush, was discovered in the burnt ruins of Flanagan's house. At Lahinch, a young man, a visitor named Joseph Sammon from Killanena, was shot dead.
>
> Another party descended on Ennistymon around the same time burning, looting and shooting. The town hall, along with the houses and business premises of Messrs Whelan, Claire, Callinan, Devitt and Connole were set on fire; the public house of Mr Madigan was looted. To add to the horror, two young men named PJ Linnane and Thomas Connole were shot dead and Thomas Connole's body was thrown into the flames.

More than two weeks later, John Keane, a 69-year-old farmer, died of gangrene. He was wounded by machine gun fire during the attack at Rineen.[177]

The funerals of the policemen who died following the attack at Rineen – constables Hodnett (Cork), Hardman (London; a Black and Tan), Kelly (Roscommon), Maguire (Mayo), Harte (Sligo) and Sergeant Hynes (Sligo) – took place in their respective towns. When the funeral cortège passed through Ennis, the RIC requested that business premises be closed. There was a solemn 'pathetic spectacle' in procession from the RIC barracks at 11 a.m. It was led by a sergeant, who was followed by a dozen members of the 10th Hussars carrying rifles. Next, the band of the Hussars, about thirty of them, played the 'Dead March' and funeral dirges. They were followed by another military party, about forty of them; they, in turn, were followed by motor lorries carrying the coffins. After that came the men of the local constabulary, military officers and about fifty men of the Royal Scots Regiment. County Inspector Moore, District Inspector Monroe and Head Constable Crowley marched at the head of the police; they were followed by Major Kershaw, commanding officer at Ennis, Major W. Williams, Captain Gosling and Lieutenant Clinch of the 10th Hussars, and Captain Henderson of the Royal Scots Regiment.[178]

The funerals of those murdered during the reprisals at Lahinch and Ennistymon – Tom Connole, Patrick Lehane, P.J. Linnane, and Joseph Sammon – were attended by huge crowds in Lahinch, Ennistymon, Killanena and Moy. Bishop Fogarty, in a sermon in Ennis, offered sympathy for the families and appealed to the people to be calm:

> May God have mercy on the souls of those killed in that series of horrible mishaps, uprisings, reprisals, devastations and slaughter without mercy. I appeal to the people to be patient and firm, revenge is useless. Recklessness is not patriotism but madness. Hot-headed actions on behalf of irresponsible individuals is wholly to be deprecated as most injurious to the national cause and gives only a pretext for brutally victimising innocent people.[179]

Bishop O'Dea deplored the ambush and the reprisals. He denounced the ambush as 'unwise and a grave breach of the law of God, except, of course, if it occurred in lawful self-defence, which we have no means of ascertaining at this moment.' The bishop appealed to the people not to give any provocation or pretext for a recurrence of violence on the part of the British forces.[180]

Dublin Castle authorities issued an official statement on the ambush at Rineen that attempted to blacken the character of the IRA, accusing them of using dum-dum bullets (expanding bullets that cause terrible injuries) and sadistically murdering an injured policeman:

> On September 22, a party of five constables of the RIC and a driver were fired upon and five constables were killed or died shortly afterwards. All the fatal wounds were caused by expanding bullets, but one constable, whose body was found some distance away next day, had been finished off, as he lay in agony on the ground, by firing into his body with shotguns at close range. It is one of the most terrible stories of brutality in the long annals of Irish criminal practice.

The statement added that in the morning post, the police at Ennistymon received an anonymous letter, which read as follows:

> Dear Sir, I am giving you a warning to make your men look out for themselves for the SF is going to make a raid on them some day. Let your men look out and the two officers that is going by themselves in the black car. They will give them a downfall as sure as you are reading this. They would want to look out for themselves.

Dublin Castle also stated:

> At 11 o'clock in the morning a non-commissioned officer in Ennistymon was given a hint that a police car was to be ambushed, whereby a party of troops was despatched on the Miltown Malbay Road. Shots were fired, and a driver was injured. A Lewis gun was brought into action. The rebels took skilful advantage of cover behind banks, whins and hedges. The original wounds caused by the dum-dum bullets were bad enough, but the bodies showed that after the men had fallen, the criminals had further fired at their victims at close range with shotguns. The evidence of this bestiality was indisputable, one wounded man had managed to crawl 400 yards, but, as the tracks showed, he had been hunted down and butchered in cold blood. Certain individuals must have known of the ambush and refused to give information.[181]

Sir Hamar Greenwood, the Chief Secretary for Ireland, justified the reprisals by stating in the House of Commons:

> The police lost their heads. They went to the villages of Ennistymon and Lahinch. It is true that reprisals followed the murder of these gallant men. Sixteen houses and shops were destroyed, houses that were considered to be occupied or owned by notorious Sinn Féiners […] Here, I am again convinced that the people of these two villages knew of this ambush […] I am putting to you the provocation that comes to brave men. I hope I have shown that the ambush must have been apparent to many people in the vicinity. The Irish Republican Army is very strong in that area. We have lists of the numbers. We know exactly, so far as is humanly possible to know, the persons who connived at and helped in that ambush.[182]

However, Rev. Fr A.J. Nestor, PP, Ennistymon, denounced Greenwood's statement that the people of these towns knew in advance of the ambushes as 'an outrageous falsehood'. Also, at a meeting in the Mansion House in Dublin, Bishop Fogarty stated, 'We have read the speeches made in the House of Commons in the past few days. If the Italian poet, Dante, lived now, he would write across the door of the House of Commons: "All you that enter here, abandon truth."'[183]

Ernie O'Malley commented on the reprisals:

> After ample drink for their incendiary thirst […] The RIC had prepared lists of houses to be burnt, the burning was seldom carried out in daylight. The intention was to crush a town. Forays were seldom made in hot blood – there was often a day's space, but more usually it took place on the night ending a day attack […] The people did not blame the IRA for the destruction, or for the terror, neither did they withdraw sympathy or support from the IRA; indiscriminate destruction backfired on the British.[184]

County Inspector Gelston's report on the ambush and aftermath, dated 3 October, blamed the reprisals on a party of 'unknown men' whom he called an 'anti-Sinn Féin gang', 'In Ennistymon, Lahinch and Miltown Malbay twenty-seven houses were burnt following the murder of six policemen at Rineen. A party of unknown men, an anti-Sinn Féin gang, invaded the towns after Rineen and burnt houses, fired shots etc.' The county inspector made no attempt to find out who the members of this 'anti-Sinn Féin gang' were. In a police report towards the end of the month, Major Davin, acting as temporary county inspector, recorded some benefits in the policy of reprisals:

> The occurrences of Ennistymon, Lahinch and Miltown Malbay, following the ambush of police at Miltown Malbay, has had a most salutary effect on the whole county. Practically no Sinn Féiner now sleeps in his own bed. The boycott of police may be said to exist except in so far as talking or associating with them and even this is improving. There is no difficulty in getting provisions etc., simply because the police do not obtain them on credit. The death of the Lord Mayor of Cork has aroused very little interest in the county and the most of what has been aroused is purely artificial on the part of a few agitators. The tone of the local press has been moderate. The Clare Champion even has a leading article asking for moderation and restraint.[185]

The drunken rampage of the 'anti-Sinn Féin gang' in west Clare on 24 September marked a new hard-line policy on the part of the British government in their fight against the IRA. These and subsequent reprisals mainly involved the destruction of houses belonging to people known or suspected of being members of Sinn Féin and the IRA; they were officially sanctioned by General Nevil Macready, commander-in-chief of the British army in Ireland, in martial law areas such as Clare. This policy was supported by General Tudor, the chief of police in Ireland. Other reprisals occurred in Balbriggan on 23 September and in Cork city, with the destruction of the city centre, in December 1920. Another aspect of the reprisals strategy was a policy of 'gunning' or 'shooting-to-kill' known IRA men, which was supported by Lloyd George, the Prime Minister of the United Kingdom.[186]

Charles Townshend states that the government defended these reprisals on military grounds. The chief of police in Ireland, Major General H.H. Tudor, supported the system of unauthorised retaliation or reprisal, which was to become largely associated with the Black and Tans and Auxiliaries in Ireland. Also, Prime Minister Lloyd George supported the policy of counter-terrorism in Ireland in 1920. He had a private meeting with General Tudor on 6 June and he assured him of his full support. Speaking at the Mansion House in London in November 1920, Lloyd George stated, 'We have murder by the throat. We had to re-organise the police. When the

Government was ready we struck the terrorists and now the terrorists are complaining of terror.'[187]

Another consequence of the Rineen ambush was the resignation of Ignatius O'Neill as commandant of the 4th Battalion. Anthony Malone noted that Commandant Ignatius O'Neill, who was wounded during the Rineen ambush and incapacitated for some time, resigned from his post in December 1920 'due to some differences with the brigade staff'. He was replaced by Seamus Hennessy. The resignation of Commandant Ignatius O'Neill was corroborated by Patrick Kerin from Miltown Malbay, captain of the 4th Battalion, Mid-Clare Brigade:

> After the Rineen ambush Ignatius O'Neill resented being reprimanded by the Brigade HQ for his failure to send official reports of the ambush. At a meeting on 12 December 1920 chaired by Frank Barrett, commandant of the Mid Clare Brigade, O'Neill resigned as OC 4th Battalion, stating: 'I am not a paper soldier!' Most of the officers sympathised with O'Neill after a very heated debate. Some of those supporting O'Neill never fought again.

John Joe Neylon, Kilfenora, captain of the Ennistymon Company, 4th Battalion, Mid-Clare Brigade, also wrote about the falling out between O'Neill and Barrett. Recalling the planning before the Moanreel ambush on 18 December, Neylon states:

> I heard Ignatius O'Neill say that if an attack was not made immediately on a convoy which had been travelling between Ennistymon and Ennis, he would start a column of his own. O'Neill then held no rank at all, but he was recognised throughout Clare as one of its most daring Volunteers and he was highly popular among the men who wished to inflict the maximum damage on the British forces. He always regarded the Barretts, Joe and Frank, the Brigade 0/C, as men who wanted to be officers without having to do any fighting, though in fairness to the two men in question, I must say that they had a very high opinion of O'Neill's soldierly qualities and overlooked his shortcomings.[188]

Ernie O'Malley, who had spent some time training the Clare IRA in guerrilla tactics, gives a colourful pen picture of Ignatius O'Neill:

> Ignatius O'Neill. A fair-haired ex Guardsman, who had a way

> with him, was in charge [...] when O'Neill inspected single and double-barrelled shotguns, his language was redder than the rust that pitted some of them! [...] O'Neill a tall, fair-haired officer had served in the Irish Guards in WW1 and he bore himself with an ease, which had not been blotted out of him by his rigorous training. He had a way with him, I could see he was as wild as a March hare! There was an amount of rashness in O'Neill, but he had a fair quantity of ease, combined with a surging gaiety, which made him popular with his men.[189]

Death of Captain Lendrum

On 22 September 1920, the morning of the Rineen ambush, Captain Alan Cane Lendrum, who had been appointed resident magistrate for Co. Clare in July 1920, was travelling unaccompanied by car from Kilkee to Ennistymon to preside at a petty sessions court when, at Caherfeenick railway junction near Doonbeg, he was stopped by an IRA ambush. Captain Lendrum was shot by the IRA party and his two-seater Ford car was stolen. There was no trace of Captain Lendrum, and it was rumoured that he was kidnapped. The truth is that he was mortally wounded, and his body was dumped in a lake, Lough Donnell, near Doughmore Strand in Doonbeg. The body was not discovered until nine days later. In the meantime, the community of west Clare was terrorised by the police and army. After the body was returned, the death of Captain Lendrum was used by the police to discredit the IRA by accusing them of sadistically murdering him.

Incidentally, this was the second time that Captain Lendrum had been fired on since his arrival in Clare in July. In August, while driving from Ennis to Kilrush with RIC district inspector George H. Noblett, he was ambushed at Tullycrine; the road was trenched, but he escaped unhurt, although the car was perforated with bullets. About twenty armed men were involved in that ambush.[190]

Captain Lendrum was a courageous officer who had experienced the horrors of trench warfare on the Western Front, and a few bullets in west Clare would hardly have deterred or frightened him. He had served with distinction with the Royal Inniskilling Fusiliers during the First World War. According to the *Irish Times*, he had served in France with the Ulster Division and was wounded four times during the war. He was also an honourable man: he was court-martialled on 24 July 1917 and demoted to the rank of lieutenant for refusing to take charge of a firing squad set to shoot a soldier who had been sentenced to death for desertion, because the soldier and his family were personally known to him. The demotion was subsequently commuted by the army council to a 'reprimand' on 14 June 1918. Four months later, Captain Lendrum displayed 'conspicuous courage and excellent leadership during the attack at Gullegem on 15 October 1918', for which he was awarded the Military Cross.[191]

Though, in his role as a resident magistrate, Captain Lendrum was travelling to attend a petty sessions court at Ennistymon, it appears that it would have been a waste of time due to the rise of the Sinn Féin courts and the boycotting of the local courts by Sinn Féin and the IRA. For instance, at the petty sessions court in Kilrush on Monday, 20 September, there were no cases before Captain Lendrum in court. The *Saturday Record* added, 'For some time past this has been an ordinary occurrence in West Clare as the litigants appear before the Sinn Féin courts.'[192]

Captain Lendrum had left his home in Kilkee at 10 a.m.; when he had not arrived at Ennistymon by 1 p.m., the police and army were alerted, and search parties set out to look for him. Several lorries travelled the roads of west Clare looking for him. By coincidence, the Rineen ambush was taking place around this time – the large party of soldiers that arrived at Rineen shortly after the ambush had taken place was accidental; they were a search party looking for the captain. The police and military found no trace of Captain Lendrum that day.

The deaths of the six RIC men at Rineen and the disappearance of Captain Lendrum led to a reign of terror along the west coast of Clare, especially after the reprisals on Friday, 24 September. Over the next week, the police and military terrorised many communities in towns and countryside around west Clare. National and local newspapers reported the outrages. The *Clare Champion* reported:

> Excitement in the West following shooting of police and kidnapping of Capt. Lendrum [...] a reign of terror prevailed all along the western seaboard between Miltown and Kilkee [...] many trams and ricks of hay were burnt as well as cabins on the road between Cree and Kilkee. Soldiers arrived in Doonbeg around 2 a.m. and began firing wildly then left in the Kilrush direction [...] a house was burnt at Lisdeen [...] The police in

> Kilkee fired shots up Curry's Lane and searched the Victoria Hotel and the Concert Hall where a cinema was showing.
>
> There were sensational scenes in Kilkee on Sunday when people and homes were searched. Written notices were posted in the town warning that if Capt. Lendrum was not back in Kilkee within 48 hours from 12 o'clock on Monday, certain towns in west Clare would be destroyed, namely Kilkee, Kilrush, Carrigaholt, Doonbeg and Kilmihil. Copies of the notice were put on the back of two men who were paraded in the streets. The notices caused great alarm and many families and visitors prepared to leave Kilkee, a number of shots were fired in Kilkee [...] The residents of Kilkee had a dreadful experience at about 2 am on Monday 11 October when bodies of uniformed men appeared in the town and started firing in all directions. Two houses were attacked, Talty's newsagency in O'Connell Street and Mr Marrinan's in Albert Road; they were riddled with bullets. Messrs Talty junior and Marrinan are identified with the Volunteers. It is believed that this is the motive for their houses being picked on. Several auxiliary police arrived in the town also. Canon Glynn pleaded with the police to keep the peace as the people were panic-stricken.

The *Saturday Record* reported that there was also 'wild excitement' in the village of Kilfenora on Monday, 26 September, at around midnight, when about twenty military men entered several premises and stole drink and tobacco; they then fired shots up and down the street, killing two cows. [193]

The shooting of Captain Lendrum at Doonbeg nearly caused Kilkee to be burnt down by the Black and Tans. The local parish priest, Canon Glynn, negotiated with the IRA for the return of the body; following these representations, the body of Captain Lendrum, 35 years old, was found in a coffin on the West Clare railway track between Cragganock and Kilmurry at 11 a.m. on Friday, 1 October. The coffin was found near Clonadrum with a label attached to the coffin, 'For Kilkee'. Inside the coffin was a hand-written note in blue pencil, 'Capt. Lendrum represented a foreign Hunnish government, his body was given up regardless of threatened reprisals.' There were two bullet wounds to his head. The body showed evidence of having been submerged in water for some days.[194]

Bill Haugh, vice-commandant of the West Clare Brigade, wrote an account of the killing of Captain Lendrum. Although the dates are wrong, it is the only IRA account of the tragedy, and it is credible. In this account, Haugh states that the object of the attack was to steal his car and not to kill Captain Lendrum:

> Captain Lendrum, an ex-British army officer and a native of Co. Tyrone, was at this time acting R.M. He attended all petty sessions courts on due dates, but his duties were severely nil; police summons had become things of the past. He sometimes travelled on police tenders, but usually went about in his own car unaccompanied. The car was a Ford two-seater and looked good in the eyes of some Volunteer officers. The tacit consent of the brigade commander was given for its seizure when opportunity favoured with the understanding that its owner was not to be injured. How this was to be achieved in the event of his offering resistance was not made clear. It became known that he was to travel from Kilkee to Miltown-Malbay on September 6th. Two Volunteers lay in wait at a level crossing at Caherfeenick, two miles north of Doonbeg. The railway gates had been closed across the road and an officer who was supposed to be present had not yet arrived when Captain Lendrum drove up.
>
> According to the account afterwards given [by the IRA men involved], he whipped out an automatic when challenged. Before he had a chance to use it, he was fired on and mortally wounded. The Volunteer officer concerned now came up. The car was taken a mile further on and the wounded man was taken to an outhouse in a field nearby, where he died that evening. In the meantime, the car was secreted eight miles further on. The body was weighted down and sunk off low-water mark the same night.
>
> The Rineen ambush, in which several of the enemy were killed and wounded, took place eleven miles further away, on the same road and date. The double event occasioned an immense concentration of police and military in all West Clare. Savage reprisals were carried out in Lahinch and Miltown-Malbay and were carried on in lesser form all along the coast road to Kilkee. Over twenty miles of countryside smoked and smouldered for days afterwards; dwellings and business premises in the above-mentioned towns, and almost the entire hay and corn harvest thence to Kilkee.

> The police were now clamouring for the return of Captain Lendrum's body. The parish priest of Kilkee acting as an intermediary approached the Volunteers with an enemy ultimatum that unless the remains were delivered up by 12 noon on September 11th, the villages of Mullagh, Dunbeg [*sic*] and Cooraclare would be burnt out. The West Clare Brigade decided to call this bluff. Parties were posted in the threatened villages on the night of September 11th and again on the night of September 12th. Fr Michael McKenna was commandant of the IRA company at Mullagh!
>
> The roads in the vicinity were blocked and snipers posted in the event of a daylight descent. But the enemy remained in barracks and the threat was not carried out. Captain Lendrum's brother now arrived on the scene and requested the return of the remains. His request was granted. Exhumation, if it could be called so, accordingly took place. The body was placed in a rudely constructed coffin and placed, labelled 'For Kilkee' on the railroad track near Craggaknock railway station at night. It was picked up by the crew of the down train the following morning and conveyed to Kilkee. The terror engendered among the people by this affair was indescribable. In addition to the threatened villages being almost entirely evacuated, by their inhabitants, few people in the Third Battalion area remained in their homes.[195]

Fr Pat Gaynor, referring to the death of Captain Lendrum, states that after the shooting:

> the car was driven to the seashore and Major Lindrum [*sic*] was buried in the sand close to the incoming tide. After a subsequent autopsy, the police claimed that he had been buried while still alive, and that his death was due to drowning. It is a pity, since he was shot in panic, that the Volunteers had not the good sense and humanity to leave him in the car and let the station master phone for medical help. The incident is not to our credit.

Fr Gaynor stated that he was unsure of the details of Captain Lendrum's death while he was attending a Sinn Féin executive council meeting in Dublin the next day. He added that he later heard that Willie Shanahan, chief of police of the West Clare Brigade, had no part in the attack but drove the car away. Information to that effect was given to the police by some local spy, and Willie was arrested and murdered in reprisal. Meanwhile, in fear of reprisals, Fr McKenna, commandant of the IRA company at Mullagh, 'mobilised his battalion and kept watch in the village of Mullagh all night, but there was no attack. That was the only military operation in the parish during the Sinn Féin war!'[196]

While there was evidence that the body had been in water, Fr Gaynor denies the police claim that Captain Lendrum was buried alive in a lake or in the sea. This was undoubtedly used as black propaganda to discredit the IRA at this time; it was first written about in May 1921, and was accepted by many historians and writers up to as recently as 2009. One writer, Rex Taylor in *Assassination: The Death of Sir Henry Wilson and the Tragedy of Ireland* (1961), describes the alleged burying alive of Captain Lendrum as follows, 'In all the history of Irish sadistic violence, there is nothing to equal this atrocity committed against a gallant and decent man.'

During 2010 Eoin Shanahan, a nephew of Willie Shanahan, discovered the death certificate of Captain Lendrum in the Irish National Archives. On 5 October 1920, at Kilrush, a military court of inquiry was held into the death of Captain Lendrum. The death certificate from that inquiry clearly stated that death resulted from 'murder by shooting by persons unknown'. Thus, the black propaganda about the death of the unfortunate Captain Lendrum, which was used to malign the IRA in the west Clare area, was exposed as total lies. The mortally wounded Captain Lendrum was not murdered in a cruel sadistic way by drowning. Eoin Shanahan also records that Willie Shanahan drove Captain Lendrum's car from the scene and that a local IRA man named Joe Daly had 'executed' the badly wounded officer. However, the lack of compassion for the badly wounded officer in not seeking medical help for him, and the disposal of the body by the IRA, was not honourable, as indicated by Fr Gaynor.[197]

The 'anti-Sinn Féin gang'

By the summer of 1920 there was a shortage of manpower in the police force. There had been many resignations and retirements in the RIC because of the IRA campaign and the Sinn Féin policy of ostracising the police. The traditional source of recruiting among the Catholic farming classes had almost dried up. The government launched a recruitment campaign in the spring of 1920, and this led to the enlistment of a new cadre of police recruits – mainly English, Protestant and urban young men – who were totally different to most of the old RIC who had come from Catholic farming backgrounds. Townshend states:

> Law and order had broken down. The British were taking into the RIC an increasing number of British ex-soldiers with no mental habitation to the methods and restraints of a civil police force and no affinity with the local population in the re-building of the RIC's shaken morale [...] The Black and Tans were mainly urban, non-Catholic, a sharp contrast to the old RIC ranks. The Black and Tans neither looked like nor behaved like the old RIC.[198]

These new policemen only received about six weeks' training, unlike the old RIC recruits who received six months' training. They were paid 10 shillings a day and had little empathy with the local population. A shortage of police uniforms meant that the new recruits had khaki trousers and black jackets, which earned them the nickname 'Black and Tans'. They were heavily armed; they quickly earned a reputation as a tough fighting force, and they were hated by the people. By the spring of 1921, more than half of the membership of the RIC was composed of Black and Tans. Thus, the new RIC was totally different to the old RIC. They became a heavily militarised police force, a gendarmerie, and they terrorised the community. In addition, the police and military began to operate joint patrols, with the police acting as guides for the military, who would not have been familiar with the county or its people.

In addition to the Black and Tans, a new force known as the Auxiliaries was formed to back up the police. This body of men was recruited from ex-army officers who were demobilised after the First World War. They were temporary cadets who were paid the sum of £1 a day. They too were regarded as tough fighters in combatting the IRA, and they were also heavily armed. The Auxiliaries and the Black and Tans were an essential part of a new, tough government policy, a policy which included reprisals. There were about 1,500 Auxiliaries in Ireland by February 1921. The Auxiliaries in Clare established bases at Lakeside Hotel Killaloe in November 1920 and at the workhouse in Corofin in April 1921. They were a highly mobile and heavily armed force, who were feared by the community. The Black and Tans and the Auxiliaries stationed in the county from October 1920 were associated with the new policy of reprisals sanctioned by the British government. They introduced the 'reign of terror' into the county, especially after the Rineen ambush and the death of Captain Lendrum.

By late spring of 1920, many police barracks and huts had been closed by the authorities and destroyed by the IRA. The RIC was now more concentrated in large fortified barracks, mainly in the principal towns around the county. Windows were barricaded with steel shutters, and the doors were reinforced. Barbed wire and mesh wire fences were erected around the barracks as an extra defence. Foot patrols were now largely abandoned, as the police and the Auxiliaries now travelled around the county in Crossley Tender trucks. The police also carried grenades and Verey lights (flare guns) to deal with attacks by night. Many barracks kept dogs to act as watchdogs.

The British navy base in Clare was also reinforced in June. Early on Monday, 8 June, a destroyer landed fifty Royal Marine light infantrymen, with equipment and ammunition, at Kilrush. So between the British army, the Auxiliaries and the Black and Tans, the IRA faced formidable forces, which were heavily armed. Historian John Borgovono states that 'due to lack of arms, the IRA were so out-gunned that they could only engage Crown forces when they enjoyed clear advantages in firepower, terrain and an element of surprise.'[199]

Between August and December 1920, Captain R.C. Grey, a retired English civil servant who had moved to east Clare, witnessed the behaviour of the Black and Tans and Auxiliaries first-hand. Reacting to a letter to the press by Major General H.H. Tudor on 6 December 1920 in which Tudor praised the 'magnificent service which is being rendered to the Empire by the Auxiliary division of the RIC, who with their comrades in the RIC proper, are lifting the terror of the pistol from the people of Ireland', Grey wrote an article drawing attention to the thuggish way the RIC and the Auxiliaries had behaved in the district around Killaloe:

In August or September last, some recruits from England – Black and Tans – were drafted into the police force in the district and it was not long before they set out to alter the complexion of affairs. They made tours of the town at night, threatening people with their revolvers. They visited small public houses, commandeering drink and cigarettes, for which they did not always pay. Sometimes, they fired shots when leaving, by way, it is supposed, of lifting the terror. They always had the excuse that they were searching for someone who was not there [...] They constantly insulted and abused people [...] The people remained quiet. They did not even complain, though they related their troubles when they thought they had sympathetic listeners.

A little later a considerable body of the new Auxiliary Police the force to which General Tudor refers in his letter as a 'corps d'elite', was sent down to be quartered in a hotel called Lakeside Hotel, which is situated at Ballina, the village across the bridge from Killaloe. The people were inclined to welcome the arrival of these men, who were known to be officers and expected to be gentlemen. It was freely stated that they would keep the Black and Tans in order.

On the night after the murders of the officers in Dublin in the morning, followed by the murders of men, women and children at Croke Park in the afternoon [Bloody Sunday], it looked as though on receipt of the news from Dublin these members of the Auxiliary Police, or perhaps their C/O were seeing red. That night there was a good deal of shooting in Killaloe; on the following night machine-guns were brought out and a demonstration made which continued for many hours and which was highly successful in terrifying nervous people and disturbing the old, and the sick. I am told that nobody went to bed that night.

The colonel of these Auxiliary Police himself went through the town on the Monday night, pushing his revolver against men whom he met, threatening to shoot, and insisting that all shops would be closed at seven o'clock. He gave out that if a shot was fired in Killaloe he would have the whole place burned down [...] Danger to the lives of the inhabitants continues, a friend of mine, walking down the street to his house after dark some days ago, had four shots fired in front of him. This was done by some Black and Tans, but though these men go through the town at night singing Irish songs, jeering and shouting: 'God Save Ireland', and doing all they can to excite the people to retaliation, there is no response [...] General Tudor, in the letter from which I have

> quoted, claims that his force is unique [...] A short time ago I should have refused to believe that such a force could exist anywhere in the world that calls itself civilised.[200]

Judge Bodkin

The state of Clare was such that Judge Bodkin, at the Clare assizes in October, refused a pair of white gloves that were presented to him by Sub-Sheriff Major Cullinan as a sign that law and order in the county was excellent, as no cases were presented before the judge. This was largely due to the Sinn Féin boycott of the official courts. The judge stated that crime was rampant in the county, but he was also highly critical of the reprisals committed by the forces of law and order, which he described as 'arson and murder'. He stated:

> I regret that I cannot accept the white gloves, they are in no way symbolic of the condition of Clare, while crime is rampant in the county. It is a matter of regret that there are no criminal cases to be tried in a properly constituted court of justice. Within the past few months, crimes have been committed in the county which shame our common humanity, police constables have been ambushed and shot down with explosive bullets and a Resident Magistrate [Captain Lendrum] has been cruelly murdered. From a long experience of the people of Clare I am convinced that these outrages are regarded with abhorrence by the vast majority of the people of Clare, whatever may be their political convictions.
>
> But I would be false to my position if I did not at the same time condemn the outrages committed at Lahinch, Ennistymon and elsewhere by the servants of the government, the appointed guardians of law and order. These outrages are called 'reprisals'. Their true legal names are arson and murder. It is madness to suggest that by arson and murder law and order can be maintained or restored. And if these outrages by the servants of the Government, whose duty it is to restrain them, are allowed to continue, sheer anarchy must be the inevitable result of this competition in crime.[201]

Raid on Ruan RIC barracks

The most successful and sensational arms raid carried out in Clare occurred in Ruan on Monday, 18 October when a party of IRA men from the Mid-Clare Brigade raided the heavily fortified barracks, which was occupied by a sergeant and thirteen constables; they stole a large quantity of weapons and ammunition. The arms raid was carefully planned and carried out efficiently. In the operation, one constable who resisted arrest was shot dead. Two of the constables were 'kidnapped' and taken by the IRA as a guarantee that there would be no reprisals by the Black and Tans or Auxiliaries after the raid.

The barracks was heavily fortified. It was surrounded by a high stone wall and a dense network of barbed wire; all the windows had steel shutters and sandbags, and the doors were heavily strengthened. It would have been quite difficult for the IRA to launch a frontal assault on the barracks and capture it. However, one of the constables attached to the barracks, Bill Carroll from Roscommon, was sympathetic to the IRA and he made approaches to some local IRA people indicating how the barracks could be taken. The Achilles heel of the fortifications at Ruan barracks was the fact that every morning at around 7.30 a.m. a constable opened the back door to fetch some milk from Callanan's, a neighbouring house about 100 yards away.

Once Constable Carroll's bona fides were accepted by the IRA (lest it be a trap), the daring plan was put into action. A huge IRA operation was organised involving between fifty-five and sixty men. On the night before the raid, all roads around Ruan were obstructed by roadblocks. At around 7.30 a.m. Constable Wilmott opened a gap in the barbed wire fence and went to fetch the milk. Within seconds he was overpowered by the IRA. Seeing this, Constable Carroll opened the back door and allowed a party of IRA men armed with revolvers to surprise the sleeping RIC men and Black and Tans, capturing the barracks. Several of the RIC men attempted to resist arrest, but they were quickly overpowered. Constable John Lougheed put up some resistance and was shot; he was mortally wounded and died shortly afterwards. At least two other policemen were wounded.

The IRA men then raided the armoury and captured a substantial haul of weapons and ammunition: fourteen Lee–Enfield rifles, fourteen .45 Webley revolvers, two shotguns, one automatic pistol, two Verey lights, twenty-four Mills bombs (hand grenades), more than one thousand rounds of .303 ammunition and around seven hundred rounds of .45 ammunition. The IRA also took fourteen bicycles belonging to the police. After the weapons were secured, the police, including the wounded and dying policeman, were taken out onto the road and then the barracks was set on fire. Then, according to John Joe 'Tosser' Neylon, Ignatius O'Neill ordered the hapless policemen to 'fall in', and he paraded them up and down the road for about ten minutes:

> Ignatius blew his whistle and he blew it loud and shrill,
> You'll love to see those Peelers and they all lined up for drill,
> To obey a rebel captain, the Peelers, they said no!
> But Ignatius said he'd send them, where the Blarney roses grow.

Following this humiliating parade, the IRA took two of the constables, Carroll and Wilmott, as 'hostages' and warned Sergeant McCarthy and the other RIC members that the hostages would be shot if the Black and Tans carried out any reprisals in the area. Constables Carroll and Wilmott were then taken to Carron. Wilmott was released the next day and was found alive and well in Boston. Bill Carroll joined the 6th Battalion of the Mid-Clare Brigade in the Ballyvaughan area. Despite the warning from the IRA, public notices were posted in Ennis stating that if the constables were not returned by midnight, the persons already warned should be prepared for death. The notices were typewritten and signed 'Black and Tan'. However, no reprisals took place.[202]

County Inspector Gelston mentioned the raid in his monthly report, rightly surmising that Constable Carroll was a traitor:

> On 18 October an attack was made by Sinn Féin on Ruan RIC barracks; the barracks was captured and burned; all the arms being taken away. The police were surprised. Constable Lougheed was shot dead and Constables Varley and Ruddy were wounded. Constables Carroll and Wilmott were kidnapped. Subsequently notices were posted that if these two constables were not released forthwith, severe measures would be taken. Constable Wilmott was then released. Constable Carroll sent a wire from Kinvara, Co Galway, to say that he was fine. No trace has since been found of the latter, there is little doubt that he, who was one of the two barrack orderlies, was in league with the Sinn Féiners and admitted them [...] Constable Carroll was probably a traitor and he has not since re-joined.

In September 1921, the county inspector mentioned in his report that ex-constable W. Carroll and ex-sergeant T. Harrison (both RIC 'traitors') were awarded £300 each after a meeting in Ennis courthouse chaired by Michael Brennan, commandant of the East Clare Brigade.[203]

Capture of Brigadier-General Lucas

The highest-ranking British officer to be captured by the IRA was Brigadier-General Cuthbert Lucas, who was captured on 26 June by Commandant Liam Lynch. Lucas was captured while fishing with some other officers on the River Blackwater about 4 miles from Fermoy, Co. Cork. There was a massive manhunt for the general; for operational reasons, he was moved to Clare, where he was kept for a few weeks as a prisoner under Commandant Michael Brennan. The duty of care towards the high-ranking officer was a significant burden on Michael Brennan and his men. Minding their prisoner seriously curtailed the activities of the East Clare Brigade for most of July and was a drain on their finances. Brennan and Lucas respected each other, and they got on well together, though Brennan hated Lucas's drinking. They even brought the general on a fishing trip at Doonass, where they went poaching for salmon. Eventually, after about a month's incarceration, Brennan received orders from HQ in Dublin to release General Lucas; he allowed his prisoner to escape from confinement on 30 July.

Brennan's memoir describes his role in the affair:

> Early in July, Seán Finn and some of his men crossed the Shannon near Bunratty and handed over Lucas to me for 'safe keeping'. This was a frightful imposition, but they promised it was only for a few days, so I couldn't refuse. We kept Lucas for some weeks: at Ernest Corbett's in Cratloe; at Brennan's in Clonmoney; at Hasting's in Tullyvarriga, and Hartigan's in Doonass. His presence completely immobilised us as we daren't do anything which would involve raiding by the British. In addition, he was an expensive luxury as he drank a bottle of whiskey every day which I hated like Hell to pay for [...] I even arranged for General Lucas to send and receive letters from his wife in England, which greatly impressed the general.

Lucas was keen on exercise and he spent most of his day

> saving hay, while he played bridge every night until about 2 a.m. [...] I kept appealing to G.H.Q. to get rid of our prisoner but all I got was news that East Limerick would take him over soon. In Doonass the same routine held, and the hold-up of the Brigade continued. Hartigan's house was on the bank of the Shannon and the local men offered to take Lucas 'stroke-hauling' for salmon some night if he wished [...] Every now and then he expressed anxiety as to the possibility of the river bailiffs discovering us, but Carroll reassured him this wouldn't happen [...] in fact Seán Carroll was the Head Bailiff!
>
> We had brought Lucas to Doonass on a promise to have him taken over by the East Limerick Brigade. After another week's appeals they asked us to bring him to Caherconlish which would be more convenient for them. We took the road again one night in a horse and trap escorted by cyclists, but when we reached Caherconlish no arrangements had been made. The local Commandant, Dick O'Connell, put us into the doctor's house near the village as the family were away in Kilkee and asked us to stay.
>
> We had realised by now, of course, that nobody wanted Lucas, as his presence held up all activities. We also knew that G.H.Q. and the Dáil Government were very embarrassed by him [...] We spent three days in Caherconlish and then moved to a vacant house near Herbertstown, Bruff [...] Up to this we had always left a man on duty outside his bedroom window at night. Now when the room was on the ground floor we withdrew this man. At first nothing happened, he may have suspected a trap, but when we got up on the second morning our prisoner was gone.

Following his 'escape' from capture, General Lucas was asked by an English journalist how he was treated by the Irish rebels. He replied that he was 'treated as a gentleman by gentlemen'.[204]

Actions of the East Clare Brigade

Relieved of the burden of minding General Lucas at the end of July, Michael Brennan and his officers in East Clare began planning more operations against the British forces in the district and resumed their operations in September. Incidentally, Michael Brennan had taken part in the successful attack on Kilmallock RIC barracks, Co. Limerick, in May 1920 with members of the Limerick brigades. In the attack, two RIC men were killed and ten others surrendered; the barracks was burnt down afterwards. J.M. McCarthy, adjutant of the East Limerick Brigade, recalled Michael Brennan's role in that successful attack:

> I believe two or three members of brigades outside our area joined our attacking party at Kilmallock. The only one in that category of whose participation I was personally aware, however, was Michael Brennan of Co. Clare. He was under some form of suspension from his appointment as Brigade Commander at this time. How he came to be present at Kilmallock I do not know, but when we were assembling to open the attack he was on the spot and I was asked to include him in my section with which I was to occupy Herlihy's house opposite the barracks. I treated him as an ordinary Volunteer, to which unaccustomed role he readily adapted himself, apart from a tendency to be prolific in suggesting alternative courses of action. This irritated me – perhaps unduly so – to the point of stubborn adherence to my way of doing things and the delivery of a sharp reminder as to who was in command. Actually, he was fully co-operative and held on manfully through the long engagement at the post to which I assigned him. This was at a window next to the one where I was posted. Both these windows faced the front of the barracks across the street and so shared with those of our two adjoining posts – the bank building and Clery's Hotel – the full volume of the police defensive fire.

Perhaps inspired by his experience at Kilmallock, Michael Brennan led the East Clare Brigade in several operations against police barracks in the areas of Broadford, Feakle, O'Briensbridge and Scariff during the autumn. These ambushes occurred between 18 September and 20 October and resulted in the deaths of five policemen; no IRA men died, although some, including Michael Brennan, were injured.

The first operation occurred at Scariff RIC barracks on 18 September following an order from Brennan. The barracks had a garrison of fourteen men, two sergeants and twelve constables. The fighting lasted about two hours; the IRA used grenades, which had been sent from Dublin, but they did not explode. Two policemen were wounded, but the RIC garrison did not surrender. In response to this attack, the RIC attempted to burn the town hall in Scariff on the following night, but they were fired upon by the IRA. Brennan, in his memoir, states that they had to spare the ammunition in this attack, as it was scarce. Thomas McNamara, lieutenant of the Mountshannon Company, East Clare Brigade, stated that the IRA group attacking the barracks consisted of twelve men armed with one rifle and eleven shotguns. About a week after the attack, the barracks was closed.[205]

The next attack occurred in Broadford, where a party of about twenty IRA men attacked a patrol of five policemen on Saturday, 25 September at around 9.15 p.m. Constable Michael Brogan was killed in the operation, and Constable Brown was wounded. The third attack occurred four days later on the night of Wednesday, 29 September when two constables named Downey and O'Keefe were shot dead in O'Briensbridge. The police report noted that they were shot dead in O'Brien's public house in the village. Miss A. Ryan, the daughter of the publican, was wounded in the attack. Michael Brennan was also badly wounded in his right arm by friendly fire during the attack.[206]

A few weeks after the killing of the two policemen in O'Briensbridge, a party of Auxiliaries burnt a few houses in the village. The *Clare Champion* reported:

> At 11 30 pm on 1 November, two lorries containing masked and armed men terrorised the community. After warning people to clear out, they set fire to several premises in the village. In all, a total of six houses were destroyed. The homes of Michael Power and James Crotty were burnt, while the pub of Mr Kelly was damaged; also, the houses of two men named Kelleher and Fitzgerald were bombed and wrecked. The house of Pat Crotty a district councillor was bombed and wrecked. The people of the village fled in terror. In a court case in February, Mrs Mary Crotty stated that armed and masked men entered her house on 1 November and ordered them to leave; then they drenched the rooms with petrol and burnt the house. Also, masked and armed men in uniform called to the house of Edmund Power and burnt his house. Mr Fitzgerald stated that about thirty armed and masked men, ordered the family out of the house and burnt it. He was put up against a wall, petrol was doused, and the house was burnt. James Kelly stated that he was ordered out of his house under threat and put up against a wall with other men who were ordered to put their hands up, then the house was burnt.[207]

Shortly after the attack in O'Briensbridge, the East Clare Brigade attacked a party comprised of a sergeant and five constables on patrol in Feakle. They were ambushed on Thursday, 5 October at about 11 a.m. The police patrol had left the safety of the barracks in groups of two at intervals of about twenty yards, and when they were near the post office, they were ambushed and caught in a triangle of fire from the IRA. In a matter of minutes, two of the police were mortally wounded and another was seriously injured. Constable Stanley was shot dead at the scene, while Sergeant Doherty was badly wounded and died within an hour; Constable Murphy was wounded with what the police claimed were 'expanding bullets'. The rest of the police party retreated to the relative safety of the barracks. The rifles and ammunition of the two dead policemen were stolen. At an official inquiry, it was stated that Constable Stanley was married with four children. The authorities, in order to blacken the reputation of the IRA, alleged that they used dum-dum bullets. They also stated that the two policemen were only about six yards from the attackers when they were shot and mortally wounded. One report stated that the ambush party consisted of about fifty men.[208]

Following the ambush, there were scenes of terror in the village of Feakle on the nights of Thursday, 5 October and Friday, 6 October. Gangs of uniformed men, Black and Tans, came to the village and burnt the homes of Mrs Moloney and Mr Nugent, both of which were adjacent to Feakle Post Office, as the police suspected that they were collaborating with the IRA. They also burnt the home of T. Kelly, a county councillor, and Mr O'Brien's cottage. The residence of the local curate, Fr Nugent, was also attacked; shots were fired, and the priest's furniture was taken out of his home and burnt. People fled from their homes in terror. The police report stated that more than one hundred IRA men had taken part in the ambush and that the 'whole male population of Feakle had fled to the hills'. A few nights later, the home of Mrs Brennan in Meelick was also burnt down in reprisal. She was the mother of the three Brennan brothers, Austin, Michael and Patrick – prominent republicans in the East Clare Brigade. The raiders were described as wearing long coats and soft hats.[209]

Tom Tuohy, vice-commandant of the 6th Battalion, East Clare Brigade, recalled that after the Feakle ambush the local parish priest, Fr Hayes, 'a violent imperialist' who regularly entertained members of the enemy forces, strongly denounced the IRA from the pulpit. He referred to them as a 'murder gang' and declared that any information he got would be sent to the British authorities, and that he would not desist until the last of the 'murderers' was swung by the neck. This denunciation led to unpleasant consequences, and for some time afterwards, services that he attended were boycotted by most of the congregation.[210]

Murder on the bridge at Killaloe

Following these operations in the region, some members of the East Clare Brigade flying column were staying in safe houses in the Killaloe district. One such house was Williamstown House, a mansion on the shore of Lough Derg about 4 kilometres east of Whitegate, which was then unoccupied except for a caretaker. The IRA felt safe there, but on the night of Tuesday, 16 November, a party of Auxiliaries from G Company, based at Ballina, secretly arrived at the house by boat into Williamstown harbour. They surrounded the house and arrested the caretaker, Michael Egan. They discovered three IRA men hiding in the house. The three men were Martin Gildea, Michael McMahon and Alfred Rodgers from Scariff.

All four men were beaten up, shackled and taken across the lake to the Lakeside Hotel in Ballina, which was then being used by the Auxiliaries. The men were tortured for hours before being taken to the centre of the bridge at Killaloe, both ends of which were guarded by the Crown forces; after being beaten up again, the men were shot dead by the Auxiliaries and the Black and Tans at around midnight. Their deaths were clearly part of the British government's policy of reprisals at the time. The next day the families of the deceased men received telegrams informing them that the deceased had been 'shot dead, when escaping from custody last night'. The telegram was signed by Mr Gwynn, district inspector of the RIC. One newspaper account stated that between fifteen and twenty shots were fired that night between 11 p.m. and 1 a.m.

The bodies were released to their respective families on Thursday and brought to Scarriff church until the funerals on Saturday. After Requiem Mass in Scarriff on Saturday, four lorries of Crown forces arrived in the town and compelled everybody attending the Mass to pass by the church gates, where they were closely scrutinised. Some of the Crown forces entered the church. The authorities did not allow an inquest, but an autopsy carried out by Dr Holmes on the dead men revealed that two of them had been shot at point blank range and that some of the men had been hit at least seventeen times. The presence of such large numbers of police, Auxiliaries and British army in Scariff prevented the IRA from giving a military style funeral to their dead comrades, who were buried together in the local graveyard. However, the manner of their deaths ensured that they were honoured as martyrs by their community.[211]

Of the four men murdered at Killaloe, three of them, Martin Kildea, Michael 'Brud' McMahon and Alfie Rodgers, had been involved in the attack on Scarriff barracks and in other operations in east Clare. Michael Brennan, commandant of the East Clare Brigade, recalled the circumstances of their deaths:

> On November 16th three of the men who were with me when I was wounded were murdered by Auxiliaries on the bridge at Killaloe. This Auxiliary Company had recently occupied the Lakeside Hotel on the Tipperary side of Lough Derg, just across from Killaloe. They had gone up the lake in a boat and surprised Alphie Rogers, Brud McMahon, Martin Kildea and another Volunteer [Michael Egan] in a house near Mountshannon on the edge of the lake. They took the prisoners to the Lakeside Hotel and that night took them out on Killaloe Bridge with their hands tied behind their backs and riddled them with bullets. The British issued a statement that the four men were 'shot trying to escape', though their hands were still tied behind their backs when the bodies were found.[212]

Thomas McNamara, another comrade of the murdered men, believed that the men had been betrayed by spies, 'There is no doubt whatsoever that these unfortunate men were betrayed to the enemy by someone living in the locality.' Harry O'Mara recalled that the people of east Clare were proud of the young martyrs:

> Four Volunteers were arrested at Williamstown House on Tuesday, 16 November and martyred at Killaloe [...] In the midst

> of the anguish and sorrow, there was deep down in everyone's heart, a sense of pride that young men of their generation were prepared to make the supreme sacrifice for faith and fatherland.

O'Mara also mentioned that an ex-British army officer, Captain Grey, had denounced the murders, 'Captain Grey of Ballycuggeran House Killaloe organised a petition protesting against the murder of the four men and he printed a pamphlet of atrocities. He had to leave Killaloe in a hurry.'[213]

Flying Columns

East Clare

The response of the temporary county inspector, Major Davin, to the Rineen ambush and reprisals in his September report has already been noted, 'The occurrences of Ennistymon, Lahinch and Miltown Malbay, following the ambush of police at Miltown Malbay, has had a most salutary effect on the whole county. Practically no Sinn Féiner now sleeps in his own bed.' In fact, many IRA men had already been on the run for months by this time, finding shelter in hay barns and isolated huts as well as being welcomed in safe houses around the county. Groups of IRA men on the run joined together to form flying columns – it seems that three separate flying columns were formed in the county between late summer and late autumn of 1920. These columns consisted of between twenty and thirty men who shared a life on the run. Michael Brennan suggests that the development of the flying column in east Clare was a spontaneous natural event in response to the evolving military situation in the county. In his witness statement he stated:

> We had more than enough of prison, after going on the run flying columns were formed spontaneously. No instruction of any sort to form a flying column reached us and in fact we ourselves did not consciously form a column, it was purely a spontaneous development, which arose directly from the prevailing conditions. In the early part of 1920 three quarters of us were 'on the run', wandering about individually. As the year went on we drifted together, partly for company. There were fewer 'safe' areas, but the local Volunteers always posted a watch at night to protect us and to warn of raids. We were billeted in barns, empty houses and haysheds.

When we billeted in empty houses, barns or hay-sheds, one of the party could remain awake on guard, whereas alone one was liable to be surprised asleep. As far as we were concerned, the trend towards the column was interrupted, when I was wounded and during the months of October, November and December the increasing number of men 'on the run' moved around near their own districts in small groups.

After he was injured in the attack at Broadford, Michael Brennan had to lie low and live in rough conditions for a couple of months, as he described in his witness statement:

> When the daily papers arrived, we learned that two R.I.C. men fired at in O'Brien's Bridge the previous night had been killed. Hogan's house, in Moyhill, Cratloe, was dangerous, but they insisted on my staying there, and extensive precautions were taken by the Volunteers. All roads for miles were made impassable for motor transport and guards were posted in every direction [...] In about 10 days I could move around again with some help and, as everybody for miles knew I was wounded and at Hogan's, I insisted on changing to another house in the district. About two hours after I left, a strong party of troops, which must have come on bicycles or on foot, raided Hogan's. I wandered round now from place to place in East Clare for some weeks, always having to be transported in a pony trap, as cycling or walking was too much for me. Because of my slow and difficult movements, I never undressed and except for two or three nights, I always slept in a hayshed or barn. Late in October I arrived at the house of some cousins in Smithstown near Newmarket-on-Fergus [...]
>
> When I returned to active duty after the injury to my hand, three or four men always remained with me. Moving about in a group gave us greater security; other men joined us, and our numbers grew, many whose houses had been burnt in reprisals. All the best men were certain of being shot by the Black and Tans, so they preferred to be always armed and, in a position, to fight back. The column was the only place in which they found these conditions. Ammunition was our most serious problem and I don't think we ever possessed more than an average of 30 rounds per rifle, which was captured ammunition, the be all and end all of every operation was arms and ammunition, particularly ammunition. The problem of food, drink and billeting was difficult; therefore, it was necessary to keep the regular column of men down to about twenty. When a large operation was planned, extra men joined us from local units,

> e.g., ten men from Newmarket-on-Fergus joined us for the Glenwood attack. Our strength rarely exceeded thirty men, each man was armed with a rifle, a revolver and a haversack, with socks, shirt and shaving equipment.[214]

Michael O'Dea of Tulla, commandant of the 5th Battalion, East Clare Brigade, said that members of the Active Service Unit were not paid, 'we were supplied with the best quilts, clothes, trench coats, riding breeches, leggings and boots and daily rations of cigarettes.' Thomas McNamara described how the men were treated by the country people, 'After every engagement we broke up into smaller groups and were billeted in mountainy parts [...] the country people were very good to us they gave us the best food they had and watched while we slept.' The IRA also provided their own secret accommodation for men on the run in what were known as 'dug-outs'. Harry O'Mara, commandant of the 6th Battalion, East Clare Brigade, described one of these dug-outs, 'There was a dug-out in Mountshannon in a limekiln in Pat Noonan's farm, its dimensions were eleven feet square and six and a half feet high. It was equipped with mattresses and bed clothes.'[215]

Michael Brennan, as commandant of the East Clare Brigade, was concerned about the moral and spiritual welfare of his men and felt strongly about drinking:

> I held strong views on the question of drink, mainly based on bitter experience. Several of our men had been captured and killed under conditions which left little doubt that their carelessness had resulted from too much drink [...] It seemed likely that a little might ease the longing for a lot and I introduced a scheme which permitted every man two drinks before we dispersed into billets. Tom McGrath, who was my second in command, stood by, saw that each man got two drinks (if he wanted them) and then paid the bill. Most of the men took 'soft' drinks, but the thirsty ones had their 'two pints' or whatever it was, and they were satisfied for the night. The scheme created a lot of amusement, but it worked, and we had no more trouble from drink.

Commandant Brennan and the men of his flying column rarely missed Mass on Sundays or on Holy Days:

> Attendance at Mass was of course dangerous, but I doubt if we ever missed Mass on a Sunday from the time the column was

formed. As we might have to fight our way out, we always attended fully armed while all the local Volunteers covered the surrounding country. As far as possible, we attended churches where Mass was said quickly, but sometimes we slipped up. Once in Bodyke, we attended the parish priest's Mass at 11 and he finished at 1.30. After that we avoided Bodyke on Sundays!

Confessions were a simple matter as the priests everywhere were most helpful. On one occasion the curate of Broadford heard our confessions in a field on the mountainside. It must have been a curious sight – a large body of heavily armed men stood at one side of a field while a priest sat on a low wall some distance away. One by one the armed men walked over to the priest, removed their hats and knelt down. But next morning witnessed a still more striking scene. We had marched across the mountains and we were billeted in Cooleen Bridge a few miles north of Scariff. I met there a well-known priest, Dr. Clune, who was home on a holiday. As an operation was on next day's programme we were starting early, and he offered to say Mass for us before we marched away. His offer was, of course, gratefully accepted and at 4 a.m. he said Mass at an improvised altar in the kitchen of his home. It was long before dawn and the kitchen was lighted by an oil lamp and the candles on the altar. The whole column crowded in and most of us received Holy Communion, it was the most impressive Mass I have ever attended.[216]

Mid-Clare

The Mid-Clare Brigade flying column seems to have been formally organised by the officers of that brigade some time in November, although Joe Barrett, in his witness statement, wrote that the Mid-Clare Brigade flying column was formed at the end of August 1920, and that he was placed in command. However, both Peter O'Loughlin and Andrew O'Donoghue state that the Mid-Clare Brigade decided to form a flying column in late November with Joe Barrett in charge. John Joe Neylon disagreed and stated that the flying column was formed about a week before the Moanreel ambush on 18 December.

Initially, each battalion in the brigade was to supply nine or ten men to form the column, but a column of fifty to sixty men was considered too large, as there would be difficulties with billeting and provisions. O'Loughlin and Neylon stated that only the 4th and 5th battalions met their full quota, with only a total of twelve men from the 1st, 2nd and 3rd battalions. In all about thirty-five men attended a training course near Kilfenora, and they were billeted at Lickeen and Tullaha. The men were trained by Ignatius O'Neill and Martin Slattery, both ex-British army, having served in the First World War. The column was equipped with thirty-five rifles, fifteen shotguns and a good supply of .303 ammunition, cartridges and Mills bombs, which were captured at Ruan.[217]

William McNamara from Quin, a member of the Mid-Clare Brigade, had reservations about the size of the flying column:

> About 60 men joined initially, and each man got a rifle and 50 rounds of ammunition, plus a daily ration of cigarettes. The food was given free by people where we were billeted. We had an arms dump in John McMahon's sand pit, lined with timber [...] The Brigade Flying Column was not a success, it was too big and unwieldy and though the people in rural parts gave what they had, with the best of goodwill, their resources were sorely taxed, when 60 or 70 men arrived to be housed and fed. The Flying Column was later reduced in size.[218]

Joe Barrett, the operations officer of the Mid-Clare Brigade in charge of the flying column, recalled that after the Moanreel ambush on 18 December, the Mid-Clare Brigade reviewed the whole question of one large brigade column of upwards of fifty men, deciding that three flying columns would be more appropriate:

> It was felt that a smaller column could be better handled and more easily fed and billeted. It was decided that, instead, the brigade column should consist of not more than thirty men, all of whom would be drawn from 1st, 2nd and 3rd Battalions, and that the 4th and 5th Battalions should each form its own battalion column, each of which would consist of about fifteen riflemen and as many shotgun men.[219]

West Clare

Bill Haugh, vice-commandant of the West Clare Brigade, stated that a flying column was formed in west Clare sometime in July 1920. They were mobilised at O'Donnells' of Tullycrine for a few days' training, but the place was raided, and the IRA had to flee:

> Towards the end of July 1920, the Brigade Headquarters received, a circular from G.H.Q. to the effect that as far as means allowed, flying columns were to be formed in all brigade areas. It was decided that each company in the brigade would furnish one Volunteer, all to be mobilised at Simon O'Donnell's in Tullycrine for a short training period. This was a new departure necessitated by a change of tactics on the enemy's part. The first mobilisation took place on the first Sunday in August. The men were lectured on the rudiments of flying column tactics and put through a course of practice with a miniature rifle. This was repeated the following Monday and Tuesday.
>
> Some men dispersed to their homes at night; others, who lived a distance away, remained in the neighbourhood [...] on the forenoon of the fourth day, a large force of military and police from Kilrush swooped down on O'Donnell's. About ten of the column who had remained in neighbouring houses over-night easily escaped. The remainder were not due to assemble before four o'clock, thus there were no arrests. The enemy concentrated on a thorough search for arms. Forty-three trams of hay were thrown down. O'Donnell's garden, house and out-offices were tapped, sounded and partly dug up, but the raiding force drew a complete blank. Only the miniature arm and one Lee-Enfield rifle were being used for demonstration purposes; these were removed at night.
>
> The temporary disbandment of the column was now decided upon, and the Volunteer Intelligence concentrated on an effort to discover whence the leakage of information. There was suspicion cast on a number, but the effort failed for that time. It was, however, known that there could be only one person responsible for the organisation of enemy intelligence – the local R.I.C. detective at Kilrush. It was decided that immediate action should be taken towards the disposal of this official.

Constable John Hanlon, the detective that Bill Haugh referred to, was killed by Haugh on Saturday, 21 August. Fr Pat Gaynor described the killing of constable Hanlon, 'Bill Hough, a returned exile [Bill Haugh had served in the US army during the First World War], beckoned an obnoxious policeman into a shop in Kilrush, shot him dead and walked calmly away, leaving the task of accounting for the corpse to the owner of the premises.'[220]

Art O'Donnell recalled that the selection of the men for the flying column in west Clare was unsatisfactory:

> When a flying column was proposed in West Clare, each company captain was supposed to select two of their best men for the column, but this did not happen, as many company commanders drew lots to select their men. As a result, many were selected who had no intention of going on Active Service Units. When the full column was mobilised, Sean Liddy asked me to take charge and I agreed. I found that only about a dozen of them would be suitable for the flying column. They were billeted locally and trained by Bill Haugh, an American ex-serviceman.[221]

Martin Chambers of Cooraclare, a member of the West Clare flying column, described how the men on the run built dug-outs as secret hiding places:

> Dug-outs were constructed at the beginning of 1921, two in Shragh Bog and one in Erinagh, Monmore. They were built on the side of turf banks, roofed with sally branches covered by rushes. The walls were lined with straw. The dimensions were 9 feet 6 inches by 6 feet. The dugouts were used in rotation and had two armed sentries when being occupied. News of the existence of dugouts reached the British in May 1921. From that time until the Truce in July 1921, I slept in the open under the cover of a piece of tarpaulin.

Historian Eoin Shanahan, in his book *The Hand that Held the Gun*, describes an IRA dug-out at Greygrove, Kilmihil, in some detail. Secret documents captured by the IRA in May 1921 show how the RIC were aware that some members of the IRA in the west Clare area were hiding out in dug-outs:

> Willie Haugh and 20 others are in a dugout in the Shragh district since October. They are armed with rifles […] John Liddy, Michael Honan and Michael Killoughrey have been living in a dug-out in the townland of Clonreddan, which was discovered on the 8 May. This was large enough to hold six men and apparently a tent had been erected, as a number of tent pegs were found.[222]

Debacle at Drumdigus

The West Clare flying column first took action on 4 September 1920 at Drumdigus, Kilmurry McMahon. A party of twenty IRA members under Commandant Sean Liddy dug a trench across the road to immobilise an army lorry that regularly commuted between Kilrush and Kilmihil. However, the truck arrived early that day and the IRA panicked and fled. Bill Haugh was disgusted by the behaviour of the IRA men in what he called a 'discreditable episode':

> Communication between Kilrush and Kilmihil was maintained by a single lorry. This ran a few times a week, but always on Mondays via the Knockerra–Kilmurry McMahon road. The column which had temporarily disbanded was called up again on September 4th. It may be remarked that column personnel changed from time to time, a rather doubtful arrangement. The few rifles remained the nucleus around which gathered a varied assortment of revolvers and shotguns. Altogether about twenty men mobilised on this occasion. The spot selected was at Kilmurry McMahon [Drumdigus], a poor position, but the best available.
>
> The lorry usually passed by from Kilmihil at 2 p.m. The column had not mobilised until 9 a.m., on the spot. Scouts were not effectively posted. Positions were allotted and [...] it was decided that the road, which was narrow at the point, should be entrenched. Preparations were scarcely half complete when, about 11 a.m., the lorry suddenly appeared over a rise three hundred yards away. A momentary pause occurred, when someone involuntarily shouted 'Run, lads'. The line of retreat was at angle of 135 degrees away from the lorry; about fifteen men were jammed together in a small gateway as the 'Tommies' [British soldiers] came into action. Severe casualties must have occurred at this point but for the presence of mind of two Volunteer officers who were on the opposite side of the road from the main party. Those were Lieut. Hassett of the Cooraclare Company and Captain Willie Shanahan. They opened rapid fire on the military and distracted their attention from the side on which the main rout was taking place. They now also retreated but could be considered as having done so honourably.
>
> In the meantime, the main body fled wildly through the country. Some flung away their arms and did not halt for miles. One, however, did not fly. Captain Martin Chambers of B/Coy. 3rd Batt. was posted on the roadside a short distance off and knew nothing of the retreat until the lorry drove up and halted on the road beside him. It was then too late to move. He lay on his rifle inside a bank, four feet high at the road, and two feet

> high inside, expecting discovery at any moment. He was obliged to remain in this nerve-wracking position for over an hour, while the enemy carried out searches locally, and closed the road. They drove off, leaving him undiscovered. Except for one prisoner, there was no casualty. The prisoner was Staff Captain William Shannon, who was down on a mission from G.H.Q. His home was within a half-mile of the scene. He was sentenced to a year's imprisonment.[223]

Martin Chambers, who was involved in the ambush at Drumdigus, largely corroborated Bill Haugh's recollections:

> The party consisted of about 20 men equipped with rifles, revolvers and shotguns and were assembled at Paddy Haugh's haggard. The trench was cut in the road between Drumdigis Cross and Haugh's house and was large enough to contain a lorry. Willie Shanahan and Paddy Hassett, also armed with rifles, were in positions in a field on the other side of the road almost opposite the main party. The lorry which was coming from Kilmihil appeared about 11 a.m., some time before it was expected to arrive. It contained 14 soldiers under an N.C.O. [...] As the lorry approached the crossroads before coming to the road trench, the occupants saw our men who had left their positions and opened fire. The lorry halted just outside where I was lying. Shanahan and Hassett were, as far as I know, the only two of the I.R.A. party who fired at the enemy [...] There was adequate cover in the vicinity, however, and they all made their escape. Unfortunately, Bill Shannon and the two men who had gone with him were all captured. I stayed in my position for about two hours after the firing began [...] None of our party was hit by enemy fire, and I cannot say if the few shots fired by Shanahan and Hassett inflicted any casualties. The engagement at Drumdigis did not help to boost the morale of the I.R.A. in West Clare, an area all over which the British forces soon after became very aggressive.[224]

Bloody Sunday

The term 'Bloody Sunday' marks a significant day in Irish history. It refers to an extraordinary sequence of events in Dublin on Sunday, 21 November 1920, when at least twenty-six people were killed and dozens injured by the actions of the IRA and the Crown forces. On the morning of Sunday, 21 November, twelve British agents and two

Auxiliaries were shot dead in Dublin by the IRA on the orders of Michael Collins. That afternoon the Auxiliaries reacted viciously to the deaths of some of their top detectives by firing into a crowd of about 5,000 GAA supporters attending a football match at Croke Park. A challenge match between Dublin and Tipperary was being played. The Crown forces entered the stadium and fired on the crowd from the Canal End for a couple of minutes, killing twelve people, one woman, two boys and nine men, while eleven were seriously injured. Two of the victims were crushed by the fleeing spectators.

The following day Dick McKee, who was commandant of the Dublin Brigade IRA, and Peadar Clancy, who had been vice-commandant and subsequently director of munitions for the Dublin Brigade, along with Conor Clune, a civilian, were shot dead. Clancy and Clune were from Clare: Peadar Clancy was from Cranny, Conor Clune was from Quin. Clancy was a 1916 veteran, and for his role in the rising he had initially been sentenced to death, but this was subsequently commuted to ten years' prison, of which he served some time in Portland Jail. Both Clancy and McKee had been involved in the planning of the operation to execute the British intelligence agents on Bloody Sunday. Clune was not in the IRA; he was in Dublin on commercial business for MacLysaght's of Raheen, but he was unfortunately in the wrong place at the wrong time and was arrested. The official statement alleged that he was a lieutenant in the Clare Brigade of the IRA and part of 'the murder gang'.

Dublin Castle authorities issued a statement claiming that the IRA were responsible for the Croke Park massacre and that 'unknown gunmen' had fired on the police at Croke Park. However, an official inquiry was held in secret by the British government, and the truth was so damaging that the findings were suppressed for eighty years. This inquiry asserted that at around 3.30 p.m., the firing was started by unknown civilians; it found that two hundred and twenty-eight rounds were fired into the crowd by the police and Auxiliaries, and that a further fifty rounds were fired from a machine gun mounted on an armoured car in the grounds. The most damaging finding of the inquiry under Major General G.F. Boyd, commanding officer of the British army in Dublin, was 'that the firing by the police and Auxiliaries was carried out without orders and that it was indiscriminate and unjustified'.

Peadar Clancy, Conor Clune and Dick McKee had been arrested on the night before Bloody Sunday. Clancy and McKee had been arrested at an IRA safe house, Fitzpatrick's of Gloucester Street, while Clune was arrested at Vaughan's Hotel on Parnell Square, another hotel frequented by the IRA. Clune was not registered to stay in the hotel and was found there after curfew. Apparently, he went to the hotel to meet a man named Michael O'Connell to discuss matters relating to the Gaelic League, of which Clune was an enthusiastic member.

The controversial deaths of the three men in custody occurred at around 11 a.m. on Monday, 22 November in the guardroom of Dublin Castle. An official inquiry headed by Sir Ormonde Winter, relying on an interview with the officer in charge of the guards, found that a sentry had been left in charge of the prisoners:

> The sentry then alleged that he was attacked by the prisoners and he fired a shot to alert the guard. The remainder of the guard then rushed into the room where one of the prisoners attacked an Auxiliary with a spade, while another prisoner fired a shot from the guard's rifle [...] The guard then opened fire and the three miscreants were shot dead.

This was the official British version of events at Dublin Castle that morning, but most people in Ireland did not accept that story, believing that the men were shot dead as a reprisal for the shooting of the British intelligence agents on Bloody Sunday.

Edward MacLysaght of Raheen, Tuamgraney stated that he travelled to Dublin with Conor Clune, who was employed as a clerk at MacLysaght's business in Raheen. They motored to Dublin on Saturday, 20 November. Clune was doing some accountancy business for MacLysaght in Dublin. Clune had lodgings on Haddington Road, and MacLysaght last saw him at around 3 p.m. on Saturday. They had arranged to meet outside Croke Park for the match on Sunday, but Clune never showed up. On Monday afternoon MacLysaght heard that three civilians had been shot dead in Dublin Castle. He located the bodies of the three men at King George V Hospital and saw the bodies in the morgue. He asserts that the faces of the men were not disfigured. Clune's body was taken to Westland Row church that evening. The following morning, Tuesday, 23 November, MacLysaght arranged for Dr William Pearson, an ex-colonel in the British army, to examine the body. Dr Pearson noted thirteen bullet wounds to Clune's chest. His report made it perfectly clear that the British claim that Clune was shot while trying to escape was a complete fabrication. The three men were clearly murdered as a reprisal.

Perhaps as a warning to MacLysaght and a punishment for his investigation into the death of Conor Clune in Dublin, his family home in Raheen was wrecked by the Auxiliaries on the day of Clune's funeral in Quin. MacLysaght was later awarded £1,000 compensation for the destruction. He also wrote to the *Times* of London, contradicting the official report from Dublin Castle about the deaths of the three men in custody, who were referred to as 'Murder Gang Members'. He was subsequently arrested by the authorities and spent a night in Dublin Castle in the same cell where the three men were murdered. Fortunately, he was freed the next day.[225]

Local government elections, 1920

Any doubts about the Clare community's support for Sinn Féin and the IRA were quashed by the overwhelming victories of Sinn Féin candidates in the local elections for the urban councils, which were held in January, and Clare County Council, which were held in June. Sinn Féin dominated the rural district councils and the county council in Clare. The results, which were published in the *Clare Champion* on 12 June 1920, clearly showed that Sinn Féin and the IRA had a democratic mandate from the people of Clare to fight for Irish freedom. In fact, there was a no-contest, as Sinn Féin candidates were returned unopposed in each electoral area. The local election mandate buttressed the national electoral mandate secured after the 1918 general election. These election results gave moral and psychological sanction to Sinn Féin and the IRA in carrying on the fight for Irish independence. The first resolution of the new council, after the election of Commandant Michael Brennan as chairman, was to give its allegiance to Dáil Éireann as the government of the Irish Republic.

Moanreel ambush

On the morning of Saturday, 18 December at around 10 a.m., the Mid-Clare Brigade planned a daring attack on a joint army and police convoy at Gallery's Cross, about 2 miles from Ennistymon. This was the first operation of the newly formed Mid-Clare flying column, and it later became known as the Moanreel ambush. More than fifty IRA men were involved; there were some casualties on both sides, but no loss of life occurred. Five soldiers, one policeman and five of the attackers were wounded. The IRA were expecting two lorries, but three lorries were in the convoy. The soldiers had a Lewis machine gun on one truck; faced with this superior weapon, the IRA made a strategic retreat. Reports of shots were heard in Corofin and Kilfenora, causing alarm. Traces of blood and a military rifle were found by the army in one of the fields beside the road. The rifle was one of the rifles taken from the military patrol that was attacked in Ennis in June. Military parties from Ennis were quickly on the scene, but the attackers had dispersed by then. Reprisals were carried out and hay was burnt in the district.[226]

John Joe Neylon had some reservations about the selection of the ambush site:

> Personally I took a poor view of the ambush position and made this known to the column commander, Joe Barrett, and to the Vice-Brigade OC Peadar O'Loughlin, who was also with us, as soon as they consulted me about it. In the interests of truth, I think I should say that in discussions which took place in McCormack's house in Tullaha on the day before the ambush between the prominent men of the column I heard Ignatius O'Neill say that if an attack was not made immediately on a convoy which had been travelling between Ennistymon and Ennis, he would start a column of his own. O'Neill then held no rank at all, but he was recognised throughout Clare as one of its most daring Volunteers and he was highly popular among the men who wished to inflict the maximum damage on the British forces.[227]

The leader of the flying column, Joe Barrett, gave some details of the Moanreel ambush:

> There were fifty-six men involved, thirty of the men had service rifles and the rest had shotguns. The plan was to attack two

> lorries, but three lorries showed up. There was a danger of being outflanked, so we took the strategic decision to retreat and a successful rear-guard action took place. Five Volunteers were wounded in the battle.

Joe Barrett claimed in his witness statement that the attacking party killed sixteen soldiers and wounded fourteen.[228]

County Inspector Gelston described the ambush at Moanreel as 'serious'. He denied that reprisals had taken place and stated that the IRA had set fire to the hay ricks to provide a smokescreen to cover their retreat:

> There was a serious ambush of police and military at Ennistymon–Ennis road at 10.30 am on the 18th. The raiders were repulsed with at least four of them being wounded, they left behind a service rifle and two coats. Five soldiers, Creighton, Campbell, Black, Chalmers and Bolger, of the Royal Scots Regiment and one policeman, Constable WJ McInerney, received slight wounds. Some houses and hay ricks were burnt around the scene of the ambush, they appear to have been ignited by rifle fire or by the raiders to form a smoke screen to cover their retreat.

Michael MacMahon from Kilrush, vice-commandant 2nd Battalion, West Clare Brigade, stated that the home of Peadar O'Loughlin of Tullagha, vice-commandant of the Mid-Clare Brigade, and the home of the Tarpey family of Tullagha were burnt in reprisals.[229]

Destruction of Kiltannon and other Big Houses

On 24–25 September, around the time of the Rineen ambush, there were also alarming scenes in the Tulla district. Black and Tans moved around the town of Tulla on Friday and Saturday night, holding up people with rifles, threatening them and accusing them of laying ambushes. The home of Mr O'Molony, Ballyoughtra, chairman of Tulla District Council, was burnt down, and he was arrested. The people of Tulla fled in terror and haystacks were burnt in the district. The reason for this terrorism was probably the destruction of Kiltannon House, the home of Colonel Molony, which was burnt to the ground by members of the East Clare Brigade on 23 September.

On Thursday, 23 September, six armed and masked men entered

Kiltannon House at 2 a.m. They ordered the butler out of the house and set the historic mansion on fire. The house and much of its contents, including a Louis XIV period card table that had been in the family for generations, was destroyed. Colonel Molony and his wife claimed damages of £100,000, but Judge Bodkin awarded £46,484 in compensation, which was put on the ratepayers of Clare. Bodkin said, 'six blackguards, six worthless blackguards burned down a residence, six irresponsible, worthless lunatics, criminal lunatics burnt this house with historical associations for some stupid reason or wantonness. It was a monstrous thing and very hard on the taxpayers.'

Evidence was given in court that a note addressed to Colonel Molony was found on the grounds. The note stated, 'We are sorry to do this, but you proved very disloyal to your country; first of all, you sheltered the soldiers, then you sheltered the Black and Tans, now you must look for shelter yourself.'

Colonel Molony was not in residence at the time, having been away on military duty, and the home had temporarily been let to Lord Ednam. He was one of the officers of the 10th Hussars stationed in Tulla and Ennis; he and his wife and family had stayed at Kiltannon House for a month, until mid-July. Then Colonel Molony offered shelter to a policeman in Tulla who had been evicted at short notice. He and his wife and child had nowhere to go, and he was accommodated by one of the servants. These were the facts of the case presented in court, which were put forward as the reasons why Kiltannon House was burnt.

Helen Keane's memoir corroborates the evidence presented in court. She was a niece of Colonel Moloney:

> The worst period of these years was towards the end of the Troubles when a new form of terrorism was introduced in the arrival of the Black and Tans. They were recruited from the toughest thugs of the British Army, at least that's what we all thought. They created havoc and fear wherever they went [...] I think our worst moment was one morning in September 1921 [*sic*] when word was brought to the house to say that the previous night both Doondahlin [the Keane family summer home in Kilbaha] and Kiltanon [*sic*] had been burnt. This was a truly great grief especially to my mother, the two places she loved so

> dearly were gone. Kiltanon was destroyed for the reason that uncle Willie had taken in as guests an officer and his wife stationed in Tulla. There was no doubt about this as a note was found on the lawn saying, 'Molony we are sorry to do this, but you have failed to be loyal to our country. You have sheltered British soldiers and now you have taken in Black and Tans, what more can you expect only this. You shall be looking for shelter yourselves now.' [...] The rebels had piled up the furniture in a great pyramid in the drawing room and poured petrol on it. At the bottom of the mound they had put the famous round table given by Louis XIV to Bishop Molony, one of our ancestors, with the playing cards let in on the top [...] Uncle Willie had already had warning notes informing him that unless he got rid of his English batman who served as butler, he must expect trouble. He did not heed these warnings. Several years later my uncle received compensation of £45,000.

Colonel Molony and his wife paid a big price for offering shelter to an officer and a policeman, but the ratepayers of Clare paid a huge bill for the destruction. It was the first of many landlord's houses in Clare to be burnt by the IRA as a reprisal. By coincidence, Doondahlin, belonging to Marcus Keane of Beech Park, Helen Keane's father, was also burnt around the same time. The Keane family, like many other gentry families of Clare, decided to sell their properties at the end of the troubles; they left Beech Park in 1925 and went to England.[230]

Doolin House, belonging to Henry Vincent MacNamara, was also destroyed around this time. It had been leased to the RIC, who were protecting his farm there. The barracks was vacated on 13 October, and it was wrecked on 3 November 1920. A historic coach used by Daniel O'Connell was destroyed in the fire. The fact that it had been used by the RIC made it a prime target for destruction. MacNamara put in a claim of £20,000 for damages, but Judge Bodkin awarded compensation of £5,000.[231]

Death of British soldiers

While there were several clashes with soldiers, who began to operate joint patrols with the police during the summer, there were only a few casualties. The first British soldier to be killed in Clare was Private George Robertson, who, along with another soldier named

Lance Corporal Alexander McPherson, was captured by the IRA towards the end of October. The soldiers claimed to be deserters from the 2nd Battalion, Royal Scots (Lothian) Regiment; however, it is alleged that McPherson had been involved in the killing of Charles Lynch of Breaffa North, a 70-year-old farmer, on 21 October. Both soldiers had been arrested by the IRA near Connolly, Clare, and they were kept under guard for about a week, until McPherson escaped. Fearing that McPherson would return with a search party of British soldiers, the IRA then killed Private Robertson, 18 years of age, on 11 November in Lisroe, Kilmaley and secretly buried his body in a bog belonging to Colonel Tottenham of Mountcallan.[232]

The first British soldiers to be killed in action were shot dead by members of the East Clare Brigade in an ambush in late November. An RAF plane crash-landed in Cratloe on Tuesday, 23 November. Soldiers were placed on guard-duty to protect the aircraft, and during the following night, at 2.30 a.m., they were fired upon. One soldier, Private Speckman of the Oxford Light Infantry, was killed, and Private Robbins, of the same regiment, was seriously wounded. Later, on 2 March 1921, he died of his wounds. In reprisal, on Wednesday, 24 November, the military rounded up several young men from Cratloe, marched them to Sixmilebridge and interrogated them in the presence of Fr Culhane. Fourteen men, mainly from the farming community, were sentenced to three months' prison in default of procuring bail.[233]

Murder of two west Clare IRA members

On 17 December Willie Shanahan and Michael McNamara, two prominent Doonbeg IRA members who were on the run, were captured at a safe house near Doonbeg. It was widely believed that they were betrayed by informers. Willie Shanahan was chief of police of the West Clare Brigade and Michael McNamara was captain of the Doonbeg Company. They were initially brought to Kilrush barracks and interrogated there, but they were then taken to Ennis on 22 December under a heavy military escort. They were accused of being involved in the death of Captain Lendrum and the attack on the British convoy at Drumdigus. Before reaching their destination, Michael McNamara was taken from the lorry and shot dead 'while trying to escape'. His body, badly mangled after being dragged for several yards by the lorry, bore the marks of three severe bayonet thrusts and one bullet wound. That night, Willie Shanahan was interrogated for some hours at Ennis barracks before being murdered around midnight, again 'while trying to escape'.

The *Clare Champion*, under heavy censorship, published the official reports on the circumstances of their deaths:

> Last Thursday one of the two men arrested in the round up in West Clare and confined to the military headquarters at the Reformatory, or the Old Jail, had been shot dead during the night and it was stated by the military that he had attempted to escape from custody during the night, and in a struggle with his captors he was shot dead. He was about 24 years of age. An inquiry was later held by military court. His name transpired to be Willie Shanahan, son of a well-known farmer of Doughmore, near Doonbeg. The remains were removed by motor on Friday to the home of the deceased.
>
> On Wednesday evening last the dead body of Michael McNamara, Doonbeg, was conveyed to the County Infirmary. It was stated that while he was being brought to Ennis from Kilrush he attempted to escape and was shot dead. An official report from Dublin Castle on the death of Willie Shanahan stated that at a military court of inquiry instead of an inquest, a military witness giving evidence under oath stated: 'Willie Shanahan requested to go to the toilet, while the soldier was closing the gate, the prisoner attacked him and tried to take his revolver, in the struggle, the soldier shot the prisoner.'

There is no doubt that the two IRA men, just like the Killaloe martyrs, were murdered as part of the British policy of reprisals against the IRA. The two men were murdered by members of the Royal Scots Regiment. The Doonbeg martyrs were buried side by side with full military honours in Doonbeg cemetery on Christmas Day.[234]

Execution of a spy

Martin Counihan from Feakle was the first alleged spy to be shot in the county and the first to be publicly named as a spy by the IRA. The inspector general's report on the case stated, 'On 26 October a man named Counihan was murdered near Feakle by armed and disguised men. He was friendly with the police and was suspected of giving them information.' Gelston's report gave a little more information, 'Martin Counihan, 53, civil bill officer, was kidnapped and murdered in the townland of Dromore when returning from the bog, accompanied by his daughter [...] Counihan staggered into a public house in Bodyke, bleeding and dying; he died shortly afterwards. Counihan was friendly towards the police.'

A report in the *Saturday Record* briefly stated that 'while working in a field with his daughter he [Counihan] was approached by several masked men who told him to say an Act of Contrition and then they shot him.' The *Clare Champion* had a slightly different version:

> Martin Counihan from Feakle a civil bill officer [process server] of Ennis Court was working in a local bog [Cooleigh] with his daughter a girl of about nine years. Three masked and armed men approached him and compelled him to go with them. Poor Counihan made a desperate struggle for his life, but one of the men fired a revolver shot at him and another sent a charge into his back. They then went away, and the injured man managed to struggle as far as Bodyke nearly a mile away and went into the house of a friend, where Very Rev Canon McNamara PP attended him, the unfortunate man dying that night.

Two IRA men mentioned this case in their witness statements. Tom Tuohy from Scariff, vice-commandant of the 6th Battalion, East Clare Brigade, stated:

> Martin Counihan was arrested at Annagh, Feakle and brought to Cooleigh Bog, where he was interrogated by several IRA officers [...] He defiantly admitted that he had given information to the police [...] He was sentenced to death and the sentence was carried out that night. Though he received the contents of two shotgun cartridges and five .45 revolver bullets, two of which were through the head, he managed to make his way to Bodyke three miles away where he died.

Another IRA member, Patrick McDonnell, spoke of the shooting as follows:

> He came into Cooleigh Bog on the next Monday and two lads shot him there, but didn't he keep his entrails inside and he

> walked in the two miles to Bodyke to report the affair and he died there as he dropped inside the door of the barracks. The lads told me that when they moved him out a bit to shoot him, it never took a shake out of him.

Clearly, there are many inconsistencies and contradictions in these six versions of the death of Martin Counihan. He was undoubtedly friendly with the police and probably gave them information, but the manner of his execution as a spy by members of the East Clare Brigade was botched and cruel.[235]

The Catholic Church and the national struggle

Members of Sinn Féin and the IRA in Clare were overwhelmingly Catholic, and they received much moral support from Bishop Fogarty and many members of the clergy throughout the county and the diocese of Killaloe (which encompassed most of Clare, as well as much of north Tipperary and Offaly, and small parts of Limerick). Dr Fogarty was the most outspoken supporter of Sinn Féin among the Irish Catholic hierarchy; he was one of the three trustees of Sinn Féin funds, along with Éamon de Valera and Stephen O'Mara of Limerick. Although he publicly regretted their 'brave but misguided actions', Dr Fogarty privately admired the leaders of the Easter Rising for their bravery, and he never publicly condemned the IRA for their actions during the War of Independence. In his witness statement, Dr Fogarty justified the military campaign, declaring:

> in the Anglo-Irish War the national interest would over-ride such unpleasant happenings as the shooting of policemen, provided it was carried through by authorisation of at least de facto government. Obviously, without some such authorisation, it would not be allowable. It would be in that sense that Dr O'Dwyer [Bishop of Limerick] and I would stand over the guerrilla struggle [...] after a few days, the whole nation mobilised behind the Easter Rising and made it justifiable as far as possible.[236]

On the other hand, Dr O'Dea, the Bishop of Galway, Kilfenora and Kilmacduagh, who held ecclesiastical jurisdiction over much of north Clare, was not a supporter of the campaign of violence by the IRA and denounced the murder of RIC men, except in self-defence, as 'drawing down the curse of God'.

At parish level, the clergy were also divided on the morality of violence, especially in the preliminary stages of the War of Independence. Several prominent local clergymen were not in favour of the campaign of violence – senior parish priests and older clergy, in particular. These included: Fr Hayes, PP, Feakle; Fr Andrew J. Nestor, PP, Ennistymon; Fr Cassidy, PP, Kilfenora; Dean McInerney, PP, Kilrush (who was a loyalist, according to Fr Pat Gaynor); Fr Slattery, PP, Quin; and Fr John Francis Maguire, Tulla.

However, several other clergymen publicly supported Sinn Féin. These included: Fr Andrew Clancy, PP, Kildysart; Fr James Clancy, PP, Kilballyowen; Fr Crowe, CC, Doora-Barefield; Fr William O'Kennedy, St Flannan's College, Ennis; Fr Charles Culligan, CC, Kilmihil; and two curates in the parish of Mullagh, Fr Pat Gaynor and Fr Michael McKenna. Fr Michael McKenna was actually commandant of the local IRA in Mullagh, and Fr Pat Gaynor was a member of the Sinn Féin national executive, representing west Clare. At least twenty-five priests endorsed de Valera's election in December 1918, and according to David Fitzpatrick, a historian, about half of the priests of Clare publicly associated themselves with the Sinn Féin cause.[237]

Many Sinn Féin priests gave support to the IRA during the military struggle. They condoned their activities, or at least did not condemn them, and gave them moral and psychological support. Many on-the-run IRA men found shelter in a friendly priest's house. Priests also administered the sacraments of holy communion and confession to IRA men while they were on the run or before they engaged the British forces in combat. Priests also gave spiritual consolation to IRA prisoners who were about to be executed as spies. Tom Tuohy recalled that Fr O'Reilly, curate of Feakle, sent word that he would like to meet all the men of the battalion who had participated in raids and ambushes to meet at O'Grady's of Rossanne for confession and communion before their next operation. John Ryan, from Broadford and the commandant of the 3rd Battalion, East Clare Brigade, stated that after the attack on Ryan's pub in O'Briensbridge, where two policemen were killed, some of the IRA stayed for some time at the house of the local curate, Fr Murray.[238]

The Catholic Church's main concern regarding the IRA campaign of violence related to the fifth commandment, 'thou shalt not kill'. The killing of Catholic RIC members in ambushes presented a major dilemma for the Church. There were frequent headlines in Catholic newspapers, such as the *Irish Catholic*, denouncing these attacks with such terms as 'Murder Most Foul', 'The Stain of Blood', 'Drawing Down God's Curse', 'The Curse of Cain' and 'Blood-Stained Clare'.[239]

Though the killing of Catholic RIC members was an awkward issue for the Catholic Church in the initial stages of the war, this moral dilemma was somewhat eased from about the middle of 1920 onwards. By this time, the old RIC had been greatly affected by resignations and early retirements. The arrival of new recruits – the Black and Tans and the Auxiliaries – completely changed the character of the police force. By late 1920 the new RIC was a heavily armed force whose membership was largely British and Protestant. These new recruits had little in common with the Irish people. It was easier to denounce them as being part of the alien Crown forces. This was reinforced when the British forces started a campaign of reprisals in the autumn of 1920.

Furthermore, the relationship between members of the RIC and the Catholic clergy was fundamentally altered in mid-1920. The former Catholic policemen would have had respect for the Catholic priests. This was not the case with the Black and Tans and the Auxiliaries. As Brian Heffernan, a historian, states, they regarded priests as 'hostile agitators'; Sinn Féin priests were particularly numerous in Clare and Galway, and this was likely to have prejudiced the Black and Tans and Auxiliaries against them. This was certainly the case in Clare, where several Catholic priests came under attack. Death threats were even made against Dr Fogarty and a well-known priest named Fr Charles Culligan. Heffernan adds, 'When the Crown forces acted against the clergy from the summer of 1920 onwards, the priests reduced their condemnations of IRA atrocities.' Tomás Ó Fiaich, another historian, and later a cardinal and the Catholic Primate of All of Ireland, observed:

> The depleted ranks of the RIC were now being filled with Black and Tans and Auxiliaries, many of whom proceeded to terrorise

> the civil population, and the struggle became more clearly a war of independence waged by Irishmen against British occupation forces in contradistinction to the earlier period when the brunt of the attacks had been borne by fellow Irishmen. In addition, the earlier pattern of barrack attacks was now giving way to open-air ambushes, as many of the small outlying barracks had been abandoned or destroyed.[240]

The first threat against a Catholic priest in Clare was made against Fr Charles Culligan, a prominent Sinn Féin advocate. He had achieved some notoriety in the parish of Carrigaholt during 1916 and in the years that followerd; by April 1920 he was a curate in Kilmihil in west Clare. In April 1920 he received an anonymous death threat in the post:

> To Rev Charles Culligan CC, from The Brotherhood of Irish Avengers. An eye for an eye and a tooth for a tooth. Take notice that you were tried at the court of this brotherhood for complicity in the murder of Patrick Blake and were condemned to death. It is not right that a man should meet his maker without preparing his soul – make ready. The arm of the brotherhood is long, remember Carey.[241]

In late December the home of Fr Charles Culligan, CC, of Kilmihil, was raided and searched by the Black and Tans. Some papers were taken and some items of furniture were broken. Fr Culligan was not injured.[242]

The Crown forces raided and searched the homes of several Catholic priests during August and September. The military raided the home of Fr Grace, CC, of Inagh, and removed a shotgun and cartridges. About a month later, the RIC raided the homes of several priests in the parish of Mullagh. They took a shotgun and cartridges from Fr Glynn, the parish priest, and a motorbike belonging to one of the curates, Fr Michael McKenna. In fact, the curates' house, where Fr Pat Gaynor and Fr Michael McKenna lived, was raided at least five times during 1920. The police probably had good reason to raid the house, as Ignatius O'Neill was a frequent guest. Fr Gaynor stated, 'O'Neill had been nursed in our house for two months after he had received a bad flesh wound above the knee.' On three occasions O'Neill narrowly evaded arrest when the police and military raided the house. After these raids, it was considered too dangerous for O'Neill to stay there, and he found shelter elsewhere, such as in a dug-out in Mountcallan.[243]

After the East Clare Brigade attacked the police patrol in Feakle on 5 October, killing two policemen, the police and military returned the following night and burnt several houses in the district. The residence of the curate, Fr Pat O'Reilly, was also attacked by the Black and Tans. Shots were fired, and his furniture was taken out of the house and burnt.[244]

Following several more operations by the East Clare Brigade between September and November of 1920, the home of Fr John Kennedy, CC, of Killanena, was attacked by uniformed men; they arrived at the village by motor lorry on 10 November. Fr Kennedy was subjected to a frightening experience. They visited his home around 7.30 a.m. and told him they were going to shoot him:

> Some went into the church, a rifle was put to my back and I was forced down the aisle. I received blows to my ear and face. They searched the house and left a bomb device in the kitchen. I rushed into the sacristy next door and retrieved some vestments from the sulphurous smoke [...] I was roughly searched and threatened to be shot [...] I was invited to fight, and my collar was torn off. I was subjected to rough handling and was threatened with a bayonet. I was then forced onto the lorry and again threatened with a bayonet. I was put off the lorry about 12 miles from home. My home was ransacked, some valuables were taken, vestments were thrown on the floor of the church and a pyx, some corporals and purifier were taken away.[245]

Another priest who was abused by the Crown forces was Monsignor J.T. McMahon, a native of Ennis; he was visiting Ireland in November 1920, accompanying Dr Patrick Clune, Archbishop of Perth. Monsignor McMahon was secretary to Dr Clune, and they travelled together on holiday from Perth to Ireland and back. While visiting his parents' home in Ennis, Monsignor McMahon experienced mistreatment at the hands of the Black and Tans:

> On the night before I left Ennis, the Black and Tans raided my home at 2 O'Connell St., Ennis, and dragged me out into the street, and what could have happened then Heaven knows, had not my mother followed them down the stairs and clung on to me despite their efforts to shake her off. The Tans were drunk,

> demanding money which she gave them, and they satisfied their anger by kicking me down the street.[246]

Early in December an extraordinary nocturnal raid on Bishop Fogarty's residence at Westbourne, Ennis revealed a plot by Auxiliaries to kidnap and kill the bishop. The bishop's home was raided by four masked men armed with revolvers on Saturday, 4 December. Miss Murray, the housekeeper, was awoken at 3 a.m. by loud knocking. They shouted, 'Where is the bishop?' Two men had blackened faces. They searched the premises and ransacked the drawers, desks and filing cabinets in the study, and some records were taken. Miss Murray and Frank O'Connor, another servant, were ordered upstairs. The intruders made several requests to know where the bishop had gone, but Miss Murray did not tell them. The raid lasted for over an hour, and the masked men stole two bottles of whiskey before departing.[247]

County Inspector Gelston mentioned the raid on Bishop Fogarty's house and made an outrageous suggestion – that some Sinn Féin members had carried out the raid:

> The residence of Bishop Fogarty was entered on the 4th of December at 3 am by four armed and masked men, they asked for the bishop who was in Dublin at the time, and then searched the house and took away some papers, a case of razors and two bottles of whiskey, there were no police or military on duty there that night. It is believed that the entry was carried out by some civilians carrying out an unexplained form of a joke. On the morning of 4th December two large cuttings were made on the Ennis–Limerick road between Bunratty and Newmarket-on-Fergus and at Latoon. It is probably the party who raided the bishop's house that caused the damage. It made the road impassable.[248]

The prime minister, Lloyd George, subsequently repeated the county inspector's opinion in a reply to a question on the subject in the House of Commons. However, Bishop Fogarty issued a statement to the press refuting Lloyd George:

> I have read Mr Lloyd George's speech in the House of Commons in which he insinuated that the nocturnal raid was due to Sinn Féiners. The premier must be an innocent man indeed if he believed that story or expects the world to believe it. The people

of Ireland, who are on the spot, and who, unfortunately, have only too many examples of such raids to guide them have no doubt about the matter – It was not Sinn Féiners that raided my house, nor was it merely documents that the raiders wanted![249]

General Crozier, who had been appointed head of the Auxiliaries but resigned over the policy of reprisals, corroborates the fact that the raid was meant as an assassination attempt. In his memoirs, he states:

At Killaloe, I received further evidence that the hidden hand of Providence was still at work and was told in confidence that instructions had been received to kill the Roman Catholic Bishop of Killaloe, Dr Fogarty, by drowning him in a sack from a bridge near the River Shannon, so as to run no further risk of detection by having his body found.[250]

In mid-December an excommunication decree was promulgated by Dr Cohalan, the Bishop of Cork, against IRA men:

In reference to ambushes, kidnapping and murder. Besides the guilt involved in these acts by reason of their opposition to the Law of God, anyone, who shall, within this diocese of Cork, organise or take part in an ambush or in kidnapping, or otherwise, shall be guilty of murder, or attempted murder, and shall incur, by the very fact, the censure of excommunication.[251]

Around the same time, Dr Finegan, the Bishop of Kilmore, strongly denounced the murder of policemen by the IRA:

crimes that cry out to Heaven for vengeance, wicked deeds for which God will punish them. What devil's doctrine has gripped your minds? The war you are engaged in is unlawful and it is murder. Deluded young men committed a murderous act [...] Where is the chivalry in shooting a policeman or soldier from a well-protected spot and then running away leaving a town or village exposed to burnings and reprisals? These too are terrible infamies and cruel murders.[252]

Bishop Fogarty did not share these episcopal beliefs and did not condemn the IRA actions against Crown forces. Heffernan claims that Dr Fogarty was upset by Bishop Cohalan's excommunication decree and wrote to Archbishop Hagan in Rome to complain about it.[253]

The plot to murder the bishop was eloquent testimony to the enormous moral and political support that Bishop Fogarty had given to Sinn Féin and, indeed, the Volunteers since 1916. He fully supported de Valera after the Clare by-election of 1917, and he publicly condemned the ill-treatment of the Mountjoy hunger strikers that same year. He also didn't publicly condemn IRA attacks on the Crown forces on the grounds that the election of 1918 and the declaration of independence by the Dáil in 1919 had given moral sanction to the army of the Irish republic. In December 1919 he denounced Justice Molony's castigation of the 'moral degradation of the people of Clare' by stating that the people have the 'manliness to stand up to tyranny'. His 1920 Lenten pastoral letter included the words, 'Ireland has the spirit to stand up against this national plunder'. Finally, Dr Fogarty was unhappy with Bishop Cohalan's decree threatening excommunication of the IRA in the Diocese of Cloyne. Clearly Dr Fogarty had been a brave and powerful propagandist for the IRA since the declaration of a republic. He was probably the most republican bishop in the Irish hierarchy following the death of Bishop O'Dwyer of Limerick in 1917. Besides all this, he was one of three trustees of the Sinn Féin funds. No wonder the powerful forces in Britain wanted to be rid of this 'turbulent priest'.

Meanwhile, towards the end of 1920, Bishop Fogarty had been privately sounding out influential Anglo-Irish contacts to find a way towards peace. He carried on a correspondence with Shane Leslie of Castle Leslie, Co. Monaghan, a first cousin of Sir Winston Churchill. Churchill was Secretary of State for War in 1920, and he was responsible for recruiting the Black and Tans and Auxiliaries. Dr Fogarty corresponded with Leslie as a conduit to sound out British opinions on the subject. Shane Leslie wrote to Dr Fogarty on 5 November:

> My dear lord, I do not know where to begin writing about Ireland [...] Churchill told me to send word to Sinn Féin to stop murdering and the government would begin to argue. The government takes the attitude that it is not responsible for any murders by its own. English friends of Ireland advise that the assassination of the police present a revulsion of feeling in England [...] The moral effect of the death of the mayor of Cork was marked in London, but the subsequent murders clouded the

> light from the martyr's grave [...] If Ireland could only adopt passive resistance [...] I got nothing out of Churchill except that if the murders stopped, argument would begin. Murders by Sinn Féin are playing into the government's hands. There is nothing to hope for save an armistice [...] I wish I could advise better. In great grief and despair. Your obedient servant, Shane Leslie, 5 November 1920, PS, Lloyd George is a crook.

About six months later, Leslie wrote to Bishop Fogarty again:

> My dear lord, Ireland will have to rely on herself [...] Yes I am certain that you have held up the peace of Clare on your shoulders and if you were not with the people there would be murder in every hedge. But, as you realise who are the murderers now [after the attempt to kill him] the world and the spirit will take the side of the peasant against the militariat. Your obedient servant, Shane Leslie, 30 April 1921.[254]

Clerical spies

While many clergy supported Sinn Féin and the IRA, some were opposed to the movement, and a small minority of the clergy were accused of being spies. However, perhaps because of 'respect for the cloth', they were not shot by the IRA; instead they were boycotted by the community. One of these priests was Fr Hayes, the parish priest of Feakle. Both he and his housekeeper, Johanna Slattery, were suspected by the local IRA of being spies. The priest was boycotted, and his housekeeper was kidnapped for a few days. Tom Hayes, an IRA man from Clonoher in Feakle, describes these events:

> After the Feakle ambush, the local PP, Fr Michael Hayes, a violent imperialist, who regularly entertained members of the enemy forces, strongly denounced the IRA from the pulpit. He referred to us as a 'murder gang' and declared that any information he got would be sent to the British authorities and he would not desist till the last of the 'murderers' was swung by the neck [...] This denunciation led to unpleasant consequences and for some time, services, at which he attended were boycotted by most of the congregation [...] The boycott of Fr Hayes's services grew to such an extent that when Bishop Fogarty visited the parish there were only six people attending Mass.
>
> He had in his employment a housekeeper, named Johanna Slattery from Tipperary [...] she was very curious about the IRA [...] a very dangerous person, who was watched closely by

Commandant Michael Brennan (National Library of Ireland)

Commandant Frank Barrett
(*Clare Champion*)

David Lloyd George

Éamon de Valera at Ennis, 1917 (National Library of Ireland)

Captain Alan Cane Lendrum (History Press)

Brigadier-General Cuthbert Lucas, centre, with some of his captors, including Commandant Michael Brennan, second to right. (BBC)

Judge Archibald Bodkin

Vice-Commandant Peadar Clancy

Bishop Michael Fogarty (Killaloe Diocesan Archives)

Private Joe Hawes (*Irish Independent*)

Commandant Art O'Donnell
(Clare County Archives)

Archbishop Patrick Clune (St Paul's Publishers)

William Shanahan, Brigade Chief of IRA Police West Clare Brigade. Murdered by British Forces December 22, 1920 (*The Banner*)

Michael McNamara Captain (Doonbeg Company), West Clare Brigade, Murdered by British Forces, December 22, 1920 (*The Banner*)

Map of Clare Brigade Zones

Officers of the Mid-Clare Brigade, IRA (Clare County Archives)

The Mid-Clare Brigade at a training camp in Kilfenora during the Truce fronted by their leaders. (L–R) seated: Lexie O'Neill, Brigade Police Officer; Frank Barrett, Commandant; JJ Clohessy, Brigade Adjutant; Peadar O'Loughlin, Brigade Vice-Commander. Second row (with hands behind their backs): Seamus Hennessy, O/C 4th Battalion; Andrew O'Donohue, O/C 5th Battalion (behind seated four); Sean McNamara, O/C 6th Battalion; man on right unknown. (Source: Joe O Muircheartaigh, © Clare County Library.)

Ernest Blythe (National Library of Ireland)

Ernie O'Malley

A British convoy at Limerick (National Library of Ireland)

The British army at Eden Vale, c.1920 (courtesy of George Stacpoole)

Conor Clune, who was murdered on Bloody Sunday. (Alchetron)

Patrick Darcy who was executed by the IRA in 1921. (Courtesy of the Daly family)

> Cumann na mBan [...] it was felt safer to deport her from the district [...] on 23 October 1920 as she was returning in a car from Limerick, the car was held up a few miles from Feakle by three or four Volunteers, who made her a prisoner and took her off towards Scariff. That night she was conveyed by boat across the Shannon and left in her native county with a warning never to return. The Black and Tans and RIC threatened several people in the district with death if she was not released immediately. A fortnight later she was brought back under a heavy escort of police and military and Auxiliaries and left with the parish priest. From that time onwards she gave no more trouble and was not interfered with.[255]

Tom Hayes's testimony about the kidnapping of Johanna Slattery was succinctly corroborated by a police report for October 1920, 'Johanna Slattery, laundress to Fr Hayes, of Feakle, who is strongly opposed to Sinn Féin, was kidnapped, but released three days later.'[256]

Fr Pat Gaynor, who was a curate in Mullagh between 1920 and 1922, was elected as one of the sixteen members of the Sinn Féin national executive between 1917 and 1922. He wrote a frank memoir about his life as a priest and a member of Sinn Féin in west Clare during the War of Independence. It was written in the four years leading up to his death in 1949 and published by his nephew in 2003. In this work, Fr Gaynor made some controversial and disparaging comment about the conduct of the war in the area, and he named a fellow diocesan priest, Fr John Francis Maguire, as a spy:

> One of those police inspectors had recently been transferred from Tulla to Ennistymon, he was on our track from the moment of our arrival having been sent against us, I think, by his friend Maguire, a priest of little repute and of little mental ballast, who used to go for joyrides in Black and Tan lorries [...] In my opinion, we owed our arrest to Christy Kelly, Justice of the Peace, and to his brother-in-law, Fr John Francis Maguire, then curate of Tulla, but formerly pastor in Flagmount, whence he had to run for his life on suspicion of being a spy for the police. Fr John Maguire was the only Killaloe priest who knew of our trial that morning. He was brought to the courtroom by his friends, the police from Tulla.

Fr Gaynor was also of the opinion that west Clare 'reeked with spies'.

Another Catholic priest, Fr James Russell, CC, applied to the Irish Grants Committee for compensation. He claimed that he had been boycotted for associating with the Auxiliaries. He was appointed as curate of Ballina and Killaloe in July 1920, around the same time as the Auxiliary police came to the parish. He stated that both he and his housekeeper were friendly with the Auxiliaries and entertained many of them frequently. Because of his friendship with the Auxiliaries, he was boycotted, the windows of his house were broken, his collections to raise funds for a curate's house were opposed, and dances, a bazaar and a draw for prizes had to be abandoned as a failure. This boycotting continued for eighteen months. In January 1922 his housekeeper was ordered to leave the place by the local IRA, and she lost her health. Fr Russell sought compensation of £200 for himself and £60 for his housekeeper, but no money was awarded to either of them by the committee.[257]

'The cream of their race'

Dr Patrick Clune, the Archbishop of Perth, western Australia, was born on a small farm in Ruan, Clare in 1864. He was a moderate nationalist – more a Home Ruler than a republican. Yet he attended a Mass in Dublin for the repose of the soul of Terence MacSwiney, who died on hunger strike at Brixton Prison in October 1920. He was in Ireland in the autumn of 1920 and was outraged by the reign of terror being carried out by the Crown forces. He wrote a letter to the *Times* of London on 30 November denouncing 'the thuggery of British forces in Ireland, which was as bad as that of the Germans in Belgium during the First Wold War.' In December, he was used as an intermediary by the British to negotiate a truce between the IRA and the British government. Following a meeting between Lloyd George and Joe Devlin (an Irish Parliamentary Party MP), Dr Clune was invited by Lloyd George to a meeting in London. Dr Clune met the prime minister on 1 December and described what had happened in Clare during his recent visit home, which was around the time of the Rineen ambush and the reprisals that followed. The prime minister asked Dr Clune to go to Dublin on a secret mission, to interview the Sinn Féin leaders with the intention of arranging a truce. Dr Clune, accepted by both sides as an honest broker, worked hard to secure a truce for nearly a month. The former prime minister, H.H. Asquith, described Dr Clune's peace mission as 'the most promising peace move up to the Truce on 11 July 1921.' And yet Dr Clune's effort in December 1920 was all in vain.

Archbishop Clune received a letter from Dr Mannix – the Archbishop of Melbourne, another influential figure – advising him on political matters. On 2 December, Dr Mannix sent a telegram to Bishop Fogarty requesting him to meet Dr Clune at the Gresham Hotel in Dublin on 3 December. Incidentally, according to Dr Fogarty, this telegram and his decision to meet Dr Clune probably saved his life; at around 3.30 a.m. on Monday, 4 December, while Dr Fogarty was in Dublin, four 'assassins' with blackened faces came to his residence 'with murderous intent'.

On Tuesday, 7 December, Archbishop Clune and Bishop Fogarty met Michael Collins at a secret rendezvous on Merrion Square in Dublin. Dr Fogarty had named Michael Collins as 'the only one with whom effective business could be done'. The next day, the bishops went to meet Arthur Griffith at Mountjoy Jail, where he was incarcerated, to discuss a proposed truce, 'which Griffith welcomed with enthusiasm'. Griffith was vice-president of Sinn Féin and had been arrested, like many other leaders of this banned organisation. They also met Eoin MacNeill, 'who was not so impressed, but was willing to accept it'. Incidentally, Éamon de Valera, president of the Irish Republic, was then in America. Then they met Alfred Cope, the Assistant Under-Secretary for Ireland. Cope 'impressed Dr Clune with his sincerity regarding a truce, but he was alone among the die-hards in Dublin Castle'. Cope asked Dr Clune to submit a preliminary draft for a truce to Dublin Castle. Dr Clune emphasised that the Irish side would not surrender their weapons as a preliminary to a truce. However, the next day, Cope informed Dr Clune that the proposals he had submitted received a hostile reception in Dublin Castle. The 'die-hards' in Dublin Castle sent a strong deputation to Lloyd George, insisting that the IRA surrender their weapons as a necessary precondition for a truce.

Archbishop Clune returned to London. When he met Lloyd

George after a few days, he found that the prime minister's attitude had changed – Lloyd George mentioned the surrender of rebel weapons as a preliminary to talks. However, Lloyd George requested that Dr Clune go back to Dublin to discuss matters with the Sinn Féin leaders. Dr Clune did not want to meet Michael Collins in case he was shadowed and Collins was captured, but Lloyd George gave him assurances that his movements would not be watched. During this visit, he also met Desmond Fitzgerald and Kevin O'Higgins. After these meetings, he returned to London and met Dr Mannix and Lloyd George on Saturday, 11 December. Lloyd George persuaded Dr Clune to return to Dublin that night to discuss matters again with the Sinn Féin leadership. Meanwhile, the truce terms brought by Dr Clune were rejected by the cabinet in London.

Archbishop Clune went back to Dublin, and after meeting Arthur Griffith, Michael Collins and others, he brought back another truce proposal drawn up by Arthur Griffith and ratified by Michael Collins. It is significant that de Valera was still in America during most of Dr Clune's shuttle diplomacy (he only returned to Ireland on 23 December), and he had not been directly consulted by Dr Clune on the truce proposals. On Tuesday, 21 December, Dr Clune met Lloyd George again at Downing Street; he urged the prime minister, as a statesman, to waiver his insistence on the surrender of arms by the rebels. Andrew Bonar Law, the leader of the Conservative Party, declared that public opinion in England would oppose a truce without the surrender of arms. But he stated that he would withdraw his opposition 'if General McCready and Sir John Anderton thought otherwise'. Winston Churchill, Secretary of State for War, who had sent the Black and Tans to Ireland in 1920, was also opposed to the Sinn Féin proposals.

Talks were suspended for a few days over Christmas; during this time, a special British Cabinet meeting was held to consider the proposals. On 28 December Dr Clune gave Lloyd George a written statement of proposals for a cessation of hostilities in the new year. However, after a cabinet meeting on Wednesday, 29 December, Lloyd George and the Tory-dominated British government rejected the Irish proposals, insisting upon a surrender of weapons, 'The cabinet, after long and careful consideration, concluded that the proposed terms gave no guarantee for a permanent settlement [...] the Sinn Féiners were to surrender their arms and publicly renounce violence [...] the new Home Rule Bill would bring harmony to Ireland.' These terms were not acceptable to the Sinn Féin leadership. Dr Clune told the cabinet secretary that 'the British would not crush the Irish people or frighten them by terror.'

Sadly, Archbishop Clune's mission had failed. It was, Dr Clune opined, a wonderful opportunity for peace that was spurned by the British. The rejection of the truce proposals convinced Dr Clune that a 'hidden hand' was at work among the military 'die-hards' in Dublin Castle and the Tory politicians in the Cabinet, who, he thought, were convinced that they could achieve a military solution to the Irish question by defeating the rebels in a reign of terror. Dr Clune stated publicly that he believed that Lloyd George 'sincerely yearned for peace'. Though disappointed with the failure of his mission, Dr Clune stated, 'I suppose the time was not ripe in the mysterious ways of Providence'.

According to Bishop Fogarty and others, two events occurred around this time that destroyed Dr Clune's peace mission. The first was a resolution passed by just six councillors of Galway County Council requesting that Dáil Éireann nominate three delegates to negotiate a truce with the British. The second was a telegram sent on 15 December from Fr Michael O'Flanagan, the Vice-President of Sinn Féin, to Lloyd George that stated, 'Ireland is willing to make peace'. The next day, however, de Valera repudiated Fr O'Flanagan's proposal to Lloyd George. These 'peace feelers' might have given Lloyd George and the British Cabinet the impression that Sinn Féin and the Irish people were weakening under British military terror tactics. Dr Fogarty concluded that Lloyd George was a shrewd, wily politician that was beholden to the Tory majority in cabinet for his power, and that he was only playing for time during these talks with Dr Clune.

Michael Brennan, in his witness statement, also shared this view:

> In December Galway County Council passed a resolution calling for peace and Father O'Flanagan made some advances to the British Government. As was inevitable, this foolish action gave the impression that we were being beaten and couldn't hold out

> much longer [...] I hurriedly summoned a meeting of Clare County Council. The resolution came up on the agenda and instead of considering it, the council ordered it to be burned.[258]

Ronan Fanning, a historian, states that 'peace-making was a casualty of the Ulster-oriented policy priorities' of the British government at this time. The unionists and their Tory friends wanted the Ulster question settled first, before any agreement was reached with the nationalists. The Government of Ireland Act, which partitioned Ireland, only received the royal assent on 23 December 1920. The copper-fastening of partition occurred on 22 June 1921 when King George V officially opened the parliament in Stormont and made a plea for peace in Ireland. Only then, when the unionists had secured their parliament, were the British really prepared to discuss peace with the nationalists. The truce came into effect nineteen days later on 11 July 1921.[259]

It was about six months after the failure of Archbishop Clune's peace mission that the British government agreed to a truce without the pre-condition of the surrender of weapons by the IRA. Those six months of terror had not broken the Irish spirit. However, if the terms brought by Dr Clune had been accepted by the British in late December 1920, the Irish people would have been spared six months of much bloodshed, terror and tragedy.

Disappointed by the outcome of his efforts in December, Dr Clune went back to Perth. While en route to Australia, he travelled to Paris. There, on 10 January, he was interviewed by a journalist who asked him what he thought of the Sinn Féiners. Dr Clune replied that he 'admired their courage'. The archbishop added that when Lloyd George referred to them as 'assassins', he had corrected him by stating 'No sir, they are not assassins, but the cream of their race!' That phrase, 'the cream of their race', received global publicity.

After visiting Paris, Archbishop Clune went on to Rome, where he met Pope Benedict XV. Dr Clune and his secretary, Monsignor McMahon, were granted a private audience with the pope. They told him of the true situation in Ireland: the British government's policy of reprisals and the Black and Tan terror after the Rineen ambush. They did invaluable work in countering British propaganda within the Vatican.

Dr Clune also wrote a letter to Bishop Fogarty stating that 'the mission had done some good [...] and it has saved your life [...] they have given me assurances that all necessary measures would be taken to safeguard your life.'

Incidentally, it appears that Dr Clune had met Michael Brennan and members of the East Clare flying column during his visit to Ireland and had said Mass for them before an ambush. Michael Brennan recalled:

> We had marched across the mountains and we were billeted in Cooleen Bridge a few miles north of Scariff. I met there a well-known priest, Dr. Clune, who was home on a holiday. As an operation was on next day's programme we were starting early and he offered to say Mass for us before we marched away. His offer was, of course, gratefully accepted and at 4 a.m. he said Mass at an improvised altar in the kitchen of his home. It was long before dawn and the kitchen was lighted by an oil lamp and the candles on the altar. The whole column crowded in and most of us received Holy Communion, it was the most impressive Mass I have ever attended.[260]

Summary

The IRA intensified their campaign in 1920, having secured dozens of rifles and about two thousand rounds of ammunition through arms raids on private houses and attacks on police and military. The West Clare Brigade were active in the early part of the year and killed two RIC men at Kilmihil and Kilrush. However, these successes cost the lives of two IRA men. The Mid-Clare Brigade had a significant achievement when they disarmed a party of seven police in Ennis in June, but the loss of Vice-Commandant Martin Devitt during an engagement with Crown forces was a huge blow. In July the Mid-Clare arsenal was augmented by the capture of ammunition and five rifles from British soldiers stationed at Ennistymon. They followed this with a spectacular raid on Ruan RIC barracks in October, where they managed a substantial haul of guns and ammunition and killed one RIC man. The most successful ambush in 1920 occurred at Rineen, where the 4th Battalion of the Mid-Clare Brigade, led by Ignatius O'Neill, killed six policemen on 22 September. Around this time the IRA also killed Captain Lendrum.

The East Clare Brigade began their campaign in earnest with attacks on police barracks in Broadford, Feakle, O'Briensbridge and Scariff, which resulted in the deaths of five RIC men. Flying columns were formed in all the brigade areas, and highly armed bands of dedicated revolutionaries roamed the countryside, attacking the enemy wherever and whenever they could. This year, the IRA in Clare killed at least fourteen RIC men, along with two soldiers and one resident magistrate.

The British responded to the IRA campaign by bringing in new recruits to replace the vacancies in the old RIC. These new policemen, largely made up of ex-soldiers and ex-officers of the British army, came in the summer and were known as the Black and Tans and Auxiliaries. Their mission was to suppress the rebels with maximum force and without mercy. The first civilian victims of Crown forces were the three killed at Canada Cross, Miltown Malbay on 14 April. Following the deaths of police or soldiers, the Crown forces initiated savage reprisals, targeting known Sinn Féin and IRA supporters. They initiated a 'reign of terror' against the republicans and the public. Examples of the new reprisal policy were seen on 24 September in the towns of Ennistymon, Lahinch and Miltown Malbay. The reprisals were in response to the Rineen ambush; four people were killed and two were seriously wounded and died within weeks. Twenty-seven houses were also burnt. The Black and Tans and Auxiliaries showed no mercy to captured rebels and others unfortunate to fall into their hands. Among those murdered by the Crown forces were Peadar Clancy of Cranny and Conor Clune of Quin, who were killed after Bloody Sunday; Michael Egan, Martin Gildea, Michael McMahon, and Alfred Rodgers, who were murdered at Killaloe on 16 November; and Michael McNamara and Willie Shanahan, who were murdered in Ennis in late December. In all, ten IRA men were killed by Crown forces in Clare in 1920. Besides these deaths, at least ten civilians were killed by Crown forces this year. The IRA killed Captain Lendrum, a resident magistrate, and Martin Counihan was executed by the IRA for spying. Overall, a total of thirty-five people were killed in Clare this year. Thirteen other Clare people were killed outside of the county, including two members of the IRA, one civilian and ten Clare-born members of the RIC who were killed while serving in different counties.

The war intensified and the character of the old RIC changed. They went from being mainly of Irish Catholic farming stock to being of Protestant, English, urban origin. This shift in identity, and the punitive reprisals launched on the community, influenced a change in the attitude of the Catholic Church towards the IRA; there were fewer denunciations of IRA ambushes and atrocities. There were many Sinn Féin priests in Clare, and the Black and Tans attacked several of them. Bishop O'Dea and other bishops denounced the IRA campaign, but Bishop Fogarty gave significant moral support to the IRA and Sinn Féin, of which he was one of the three national trustees. Dr Fogarty was also a target for the 'anti-Sinn Féin gang', and he was lucky that he was not killed by Auxiliary or Black and Tan forces. There were some isolated instances of sectarianism in the county, such as when the Protestant church at Clarecastle was maliciously burnt in April and when there was an arson attempt on the Protestant church at O'Briensbridge in June.

In December 1920, Sean Liddy, commandant of the West Clare Brigade, sent a report to GHQ that was captured by Crown forces. The report is quite revealing with regards to the morale of the local population around this time, which, he wrote, was affecting his operations:

> The civil population, especially the farmers in a great many districts have become, in fact I may put it, hostile to the Volunteers. I find of late in a great many companies that the Volunteers themselves are rather inclined to fall in with the views of the old people to remain quiet. For instance, in one particular place where an ambush had been planned, the Volunteers in the vicinity refused to take any part whatever in it.

There may have been some truth in this report. In October 1920, Gelston noted:

> It is believed that the great majority of people are wholly tired of this state of affairs [...] undoubtedly more information is given to the police; and farmers, traders, gentry etc., are all heartily sick of Sinn Féin and but for terrorism would have nothing to do with it. On 25 October Sinn Féin began to tear up the roads near

> Knock to hamper police and military transport. The local farmers assembled and told them that if they did so they would tell the police. The Sinn Féiners desisted and withdrew.[261]

Towards the end of the year, Archbishop Clune, along with Bishop Fogarty, made a significant effort to negotiate a truce between the British government and the IRA, but Lloyd George and the British government, influenced by the militarists, die-hard Tories and unionists, pursued a military solution to the Irish problem at this time. However, the spirit of the Easter Rising, which had been rekindled in April, had not been quenched by reprisals and the reign of terror.

4
STALEMATE AND TRUCE

Following the failure of Archbishop Clune's peace initiative, the government, believing that they could defeat the IRA, pursued a military rather than a political strategy to end the war in Ireland. After the Christmas break, the East Clare Brigade carried out two successful ambushes at Cratloe and Glenwood, which resulted in the deaths of eight policemen. These attacks were followed by extensive reprisals in the district. However, in another ambush at Cratloe in June, two IRA men were killed. The West Clare Brigade were relatively quiet this year, but in a rare joint military operation among the Clare brigades, they were assisted by the East Clare Brigade in an attack on the Crown forces at Kilrush in April, where a policeman was killed. The Mid-Clare Brigade achieved a successful ambush at Ballyvaughan in which two marines were killed; they also killed an army sergeant in an attack on a pub in Ennis. All three brigades had opportunistic successes in killing individual policemen or soldiers. Several spies were also killed this year. The East Clare Brigade shot three soldiers and one policeman as spies. They also executed one civilian, John Reilly, for spying. The West Clare Brigade executed Patrick Darcy as an alleged spy.

The concentration of the Crown forces in towns and their use of heavily armed convoys made it difficult for the IRA to attack them. Despite this, the IRA frustrated and severely hampered the Crown forces through the extensive trenching of roads and destruction of bridges. The IRA also disrupted train services and the postal system through derailments and robberies, and they caused major damage to the telephonic and telegraphic communications in the county. Besides seriously damaging the county's infrastructure, the IRA also carried out an economic war by robbing rate collectors and refusing to put the costs of criminal injuries on the ratepayers by not striking a rate for the damages caused by Crown forces. Belatedly, in response to the Crown forces' acts of terrorism, the IRA also carried out reprisals in Clare and burnt several houses belonging to loyalists during May and June.

Besides engaging in terror tactics, the Crown forces also carried out an economic war by banning fairs and markets, and imposing curfews on inhabitants. They carried hostages on their trucks to deter IRA attacks on convoys, and they rounded up large numbers of men at gunpoint to repair damages to roads and bridges.

However, by the end of June there was a strong desire on both sides for an end to the conflict. The IRA had paralysed British law and administration, and seriously disrupted communications, but they could not defeat the vastly superior Crown forces. By early July the IRA were running short of ammunition, and they dared not risk any major military engagements with the Crown forces. The British were being damaged internationally by propaganda because of their reprisals policy; and the government acknowledged that the IRA could not be beaten except by a policy of total war, which the British were unwilling to pursue at this time. The British had also appeased the unionists of the north by opening a parliament at Stormont in June, and they were now anxious to settle with the nationalists. As in a game of chess there was a stalemate, the conditions for peace were ripe and a truce was declared on 11 July 1921.

Martial law

Early in January martial law was proclaimed in the most disturbed parts of Ireland, including Clare and the rest of Munster, and in counties Wexford and Kilkenny. General Nevil Macready signed another proclamation appointing military governors in each district. Martial law gave the British military forces extraordinary powers; more troops were brought into Clare, and the military governors had authority over the RIC and Auxiliaries. Under martial law the army had powers to search properties and arrest and detain suspects without trial. They imposed curfews, banned fairs and markets, and even imposed a ban on the use of bicycles from 1 July. The military authorities attempted to interfere with the courts to prevent people from making claims for compensation against the state. Innocent people could be shot for refusing to halt while fleeing from the military, and under army rule, reprisals continued and intensified. General Macready, commander-in-chief in Ireland, ordered that all arms and ammunition should be surrendered by 11 January. Any person found in possession of weapons after this date would be liable, on conviction, to the death penalty. With these draconian powers, the Crown forces terrorised the community and hoped to crush the IRA and re-establish law and order.[262]

Ambushes in East Clare: Cratloe and Glenwood

The introduction of martial law did not deter the East Clare Brigade; they went into action shortly after the Christmas break. They planned a series of ambushes in the Sixmilebridge-Cratloe region, which resulted in the deaths of eight policemen and the wounding of several others. These ambushes forced the British authorities to change their methods of transport; when carrying police or soldiers around the county or supplying RIC or army barracks, they started to make use of heavily armed convoys of more than two vehicles.

The first of these ambushes took place early in the morning on Thursday, 13 January. A Crossley Tender carrying seven policemen and travelling between Sixmilebridge and Limerick was ambushed at Cratloe, resulting in the deaths of two RIC sergeants and the wounding of four constables. Sergeant J. Curtin of Newmarket-on-Fergus and Sergeant S. Carty of Ruan were killed at the scene; two constables named Dempsey and McDermott were badly wounded. Two other constables suffered minor injuries. The driver, Sergeant Swain, was uninjured and drove to Limerick to get help. The police returned fire, but there were no reports of IRA men being injured. Another ambush took place at Clonolum Cross on a police tender travelling between Sixmilebridge and Broadford, and although shots were fired, there were no reports of injuries.[263] The IRA collected the weapons – four rifles and several pistols – as well as ammunition from the dead and wounded policemen following the Cratloe ambush.

The Glenwood ambush occurred a week after the Cratloe ambush, on Thursday, 20 January. On this occasion a group of nine RIC men, including four Black and Tans, were travelling on a

Crossley Tender between Sixmilebridge and Belvoir. A party of about thirty IRA men had been lying in wait at the ambush site of Glenwood, a thickly wooded area, for more than eight hours. The truck arrived at the scene at around 3.30 p.m., and Commandant Michael Brennan ordered 'Fire!' at very close range. Deadly fire was opened on the RIC from both sides of the road. Because of the suddenness of the attack, the police had little time to react and return fire. District Inspector Clarke, Sergeant M. Molloy and constables James Doogue, Michael Moran, F.G. Morris (Black and Tan) and W.J. Smyth (Black and Tan) were killed. Sergeant J. Egan was badly injured; Constable Selve (Black and Tan) was wounded in the fingers; two other Black and Tans, constables Seabright and Prior, were uninjured and fled the scene. The Crossley Tender was destroyed. County Inspector Gelston noted that 'this was a serious loss as it included an excellent officer and some of the best men in Sixmilebridge, with their arms.' Michael Brennan said that one of the IRA men was slightly wounded.

Although Michael Brennan, in his witness statement, claimed that they attacked a lorry of Black and Tans at Glenwood, four of the policemen killed were Irish – three of them Catholics – and only two of the men killed were Black and Tans. District Inspector Major W. Clarke was a Presbyterian from Lurgan, Co. Down; Sergeant Molloy, a Catholic, was a Mayo man who was married with three children; Constable Moran, a Catholic, was also a Mayo man; Constable Doogue, another Catholic, was from Queen's County (Co. Laois); Constable Smyth, a Protestant, was from Kent; and Constable F. Morris, also a Protestant, was from London. The *Irish Times* noted, 'Constable Moran was deeply religious and was a weekly communicant, he was found dead with his rosary beads across his face; DI Clarke, a Presbyterian, had a Sacred Heart badge sewn inside his jacket. Sgt. Molloy leaves a widow and 3 children.'

Michael Brennan stated that they had captured ten rifles, seven pistols and some ammunition, but other participants in the raid stated that they had captured eight rifles, five or six revolvers and about a thousand rounds of .303 and .45 bullets. This was a substantial haul of weapons and ammunition for the East Clare Brigade. Michael O'Dea recalled that after the successful ambush, the IRA moved off to Oatfield; they then dispersed to Kilmore, near Broadford, and stayed in a Mr Vaughan's hayshed. They remained together for about a week while the Tans and Auxiliaries scoured the countryside searching for them.[264]

Meanwhile, the Crown forces did not delay in exacting revenge on the local community. That evening, at about 7 p.m., large forces came from Limerick and Ennis to search the countryside around the ambush site in a dragnet sweeping movement, making their way across the mountains towards Limerick and the River Shannon. In the reprisals that evening, there was widespread destruction in Sixmilebridge and surrounding districts, and many houses were burnt.

The account in the *Clare Champion* conveys some of the terror experienced in the community that night:

> The people of Sixmilebridge and district spent a night of terror; hundreds fled from their homes, and at least a score of houses were burnt. Many farmhouses were burnt and Sixmilebridge was deserted. Outbursts of fire and explosions were heard; Casey's house; Moloney's butchers ; the National Bank; Fennessy's, a blacksmith; Pat Moore, a farmer, John Gilligan's Rossroe, the farm houses of Fitzgerald, McNamara, Dillon, and Duggan were burnt at Belvoir; also, Pat Herbert's Lisnagry; the villages of Kilkishen and Meelick also suffered [...] along the Broadford hills, several houses were in flames – John Ryan's, Hynes' and Donnellan's. The creamery at Bridgetown was also burnt.

According to the *Irish Independent*, a creamery and seventeen houses, including twelve belonging to farmers, were burnt that night.

Mrs Mary Molony, one of the victims of these reprisals, described how her house was burnt. She swore on oath that out of fear of the consequences of the ambush at Glenwood, she got her husband to take her little adopted daughter to Limerick while she remained alone in the house.

> Then about two dozen police came down the street and surrounded the house. I opened the door for them, they told me if I did not open it they would break it in. While I was opening the door they cried 'Murderers!', and I said, surely you don't think that I murdered your men. They told me to clear out or

> they would put a bullet through me. When I was about five yards from the house there was a shot fired. The house and furniture were then set on fire and completely destroyed.

In compensation, Judge Bodkin awarded a sum of £1,992 to the Molony family at the Ennis courthouse.[265]

The police reports stated, 'Reprisals indicated that Bridgetown Creamery and the houses of Martin Hayes and Edmond Hayes were burnt on the night of 20 January, the arson was by persons unknown.' Other reprisals occurred on 20 January, including malicious damage to the houses of Dan Keane, Dan Moloney, Martin Casey, Pat Moore and John Gilligan of Sixmilebridge, all of which were burnt. Michael Brennan recalled seeing thirty-six fires burning on the evening of the ambush. These significant and shocking reprisals seem to have had an impact on the operations of the East Clare Brigade. Joe Clancy, a member of the brigade, wrote, 'the scale of the reprisals after Glenwood and the widespread terrorism employed by the enemy on the civilian population did tend for a while to curb our activities in the brigade area.' Following the ambush and reprisals, a *Clare Champion* editorial appealed for an end to the violence:

> Last week was a truly tragic week in Clare and violence is intensifying. We have often appealed for a real truce. We have often expressed an opinion that violence would accomplish nothing and that coercive measures would settle nothing. It must be settled one day, it should be settled by some counsel on the principle of justice and without all this horrifying violence.[266]

After the Glenwood ambush, the authorities put an end to single-lorry transport. This meant that, from an IRA perspective, there were limited opportunities for attack. Joe Clancy, a member of the East Clare Brigade, recalled that the brigade had no rifles more powerful than Lee–Enfields – and that there were no more than twenty-five of them in the brigade. Another consideration, he said, was a scarcity of .303 ammo, as fewer than 1,000 rounds were captured at Glenwood. After the Glenwood ambush, police and army convoys consisted of two, three or more lorries, and these were equipped with Lewis machine guns. Such a concentration of military and police firepower was too much for the IRA's limited arsenal, as was exemplified in the Moanreel ambush in December 1920. In his report on a called-off ambush on the Tulla–Feakle road on 29 March, Michael Brennan stated, 'thirty two men were in position at 6am, twenty eight rifles and four shotguns, I could tackle anything up to three lorries, but I did not feel I could risk the men against anything more than that.'[267]

In January 1921, the East Clare Brigade's funds were almost exhausted and the supply of clothes, boots and occasionally food began to cause difficulties. Wounded men also caused the brigade some expense, although Michael Brennan never recalled any doctor, nurse or hospital ever charging for medical services. Commandant Brennan issued a letter appealing for funds, which was distributed all over east Clare. A public collection was organised through a church gate collection, and in just over a week an 'astonishing' total of about £1,500 was collected, three times what the IRA had expected. Clearly, many people in east Clare supported the IRA in their campaign. As Michael Brennan remarked:

> We had brought misery and terror on nearly every parish in East Clare and none of us had anticipated a vote of confidence of this nature. It made clear at once that the British reprisals instead of turning the people against us as the cause of their miseries had thrown them strongly behind us. We had always paid for anything we required and this was our first appeal to the people for financial help. That may have had some effect on the contributions, but I was certain that the real driving force was a determination to back us.

Early in February, Brennan received a letter from GHQ reporting that a certain traveller in east Clare told General Macready, commander-in-chief of the British army in Ireland, that he was 'much impressed by the spirit of the people in the face of hard times'.[268]

Round-ups and road trenching

The police and military began systematic searches around the county for men who were on the run. At a time when the rates of weekly Mass attendance were quite high, it was very convenient for them to surround a chapel during Mass on Sundays and search all the males leaving the chapel afterwards. This practice started towards the end of December 1920 and continued for several months. One early instance of this occurred at Ballycorick on Sunday, 19 December. All the men were searched, and five of them were arrested and lodged in Ennis Jail under DORA. On Little Christmas, 6 January, the Crown forces raided the village of Quin and searched all the men leaving the chapel after Mass. There were similar raids in the parishes of Corofin, Kilrush and Kildysart in the week before 22 January; more than two hundred prisoners were lodged in Ennis Jail at this time. Police and military searched large areas of the county for rebels during January.[269]

Tragedies sometimes occurred during these raids. At a raid in Mullagh during Sunday Mass, the church was surrounded by four military trucks; one man, James Downes of Ballymadra, was shot and wounded in the groin while running away.[270] Another tragedy occurred when a 22-year-old man named Gilloury was shot and killed near Moymore church; he was fleeing a round-up during Mass, and he was fired upon and subsequently died from his wounds. Another tragedy occurred when an aged man, Miko Russell of Corofin, was shot dead at Maurice's Mills. No soldier was held accountable for these deaths under the martial law regime. According to the police reports, 'these men ran away on the approach of the military, they refused to halt and were fired upon.'[271]

On Tuesday, 18 January at around 10 p.m., the authorities insensitively raided the home of Jane McNamara, proprietor of the Clare Hotel on Upper O'Connell Street, Ennis, where her daughter's body lay in repose after her death earlier that evening. The daughter was the wife of Patrick Brennan of Meelick, the former commandant of the Clare Brigade (before it was split into three brigades), who was then on the run. One of the raiders even thrust his bayonet under the bed in which the corpse was laid. There were thirty men in the house at the time, and all of them were searched. The police were hoping to catch the widower, Patrick Brennan, or one of his brothers, Michael or Austin, both of whom were well-known republicans that were also on the run. But the police were not successful in this aim.[272]

Large numbers of men were also rounded up from towns and

villages to repair roads and bridges, which were 'trenched' or damaged by the IRA in a strategy designed to frustrate communications and movement for the Crown forces. This tactic was introduced by the IRA from late 1920, and it lasted up to the truce in July 1921. The first reported trenching of roads occurred on 25 October 1920 at Knock, near Killimer. This was followed by two large trenches on the Ennis–Limerick road on 4 December 1920. On this occasion the police and military rounded up many civilians, compelling them to close the trenches. Latoon bridge was damaged for the first time on 15 December 1920, and locals in Clarecastle were rounded up to repair the bridge at gunpoint. Latoon bridge was damaged again at 3 a.m. on Saturday, 7 May 1921, and again the locals were rounded up at gunpoint to repair the damage.[273]

Bill Haugh of the West Clare Brigade stated that, at a brigade conference in February 1921, a decision was taken by the officers to make all roads impassable. On the other hand, Martin Chambers, also from the West Clare Brigade, recalled that they were busy trenching from October 1920, 'Late in October we were busy harassing the enemy, there was extensive cutting of trenches in roads with picks, shovels and spades by night. The enemy frequently commandeered locals to fill them in by day. There was considerable hardship for local people.' John Flanagan, commandant of the 2nd Battalion, West Clare Brigade, stated that the roads in rural areas were heavily entrenched, that stone barricades were erected and trees were felled to block the roads, and that the enemy used the roads as little as possible in the months preceding the truce. Anthony Malone of the Mid-Clare Brigade stated that, from March 1921 up to the truce, they were busy harassing the enemy by trenching roads, destroying bridges and disrupting the West Clare railway. Hugh Hehir of Ballynacally stated that a small number of the IRA were on the run, whereas the rest of the company remained as scouts; the activities of the latter included blocking roads and demolishing bridges. In east Clare, Commandant Michael Brennan recalled that a fight at Mountshannon on 5 April had seriously depleted their ammunition supply. In March Brennan was ordered by HQ to take members of his brigade into east Galway, where the local IRA men were lethargic. While there, his supply of ammunition was further depleted; this had brought it to a critical stage, 'We were down to about a dozen rounds per rifle and in the face of this, we daren't risk any operations, which didn't offer good prospects of capturing arms. We occupied ourselves in holding up trains and mail cars, road blocking and trenching and sniping.'[274]

Thus, from late 1920 until the truce in July 1921, the IRA were busy digging trenches, throwing rock barricades across roads, blowing up bridges and felling roadside trees to disrupt communications. Some of these trenches were quite deep. For example, according to an April police report, some trenches cut in the road near Kilrush on 12 April were four feet wide and two feet deep. Most of these activities occurred during the night. Following such nocturnal destruction, the Crown forces rounded up civilians at gunpoint during the daytime and forced them to repair the damage. There are reports of men being rounded up in Clarecastle, Cratloe, Ennis, Ennistymon, Feakle, Kildysart, Kilkishen, Kilrush, Lissycasey, Miltown Malbay and Sixmilebridge.

Some of the residents of these towns and villages, forced to repair damages, may have been busy both day and night. It was probably the case, however, that the destruction was done by IRA members from rural areas while the repairs were mainly carried out by men from the towns, who, although they may have sympathised with Sinn Féin, may not have been members of the IRA. Of course, these communication disruptions were co-ordinated by the brigade officers in the planning of some ambushes and to frustrate the enemy. Helen Keane of Beech Park recalled the felling of trees on her family demesne, 'we had trees cut down to fall across the road and so prevent any movement of traffic. Most of them fell over the demesne wall between the farm and the front lodge, a much-used road leading to Kilmaley and beyond.'[275]

At the end of March, the IRA chief of staff, General Richard Mulcahy, corresponded with Commandant Frank Barrett, officer commanding of the Mid-Clare Brigade, on the matter of road trenching. He wished to know the impact of this activity on the civilians. In reply, Barrett stated:

> people are generally able to carry on by using the by-roads, but these are, as a rule very badly made and have been neglected for

> the past six months. Of course, people have to travel considerably longer distances and at much trouble and disadvantage both to themselves and to their means of transport. However, as far as I can ascertain, they see the matter in the proper light and accept the consequences in a grand spirit.[276]

Some of the round-ups involved large numbers of Crown forces and civilians. For instance, during a round-up on Church Street and O'Connell Street in Ennis on Saturday, 12 March, between fifty and sixty men were rounded up to repair roads in the surrounding districts. A large force of police and military carried out the round-up, and clerks, shop assistants, ex-soldiers and labourers were taken to repair the Doora Road at Kilbricken. Other big round-ups occurred in Ennis during May. On Sunday, 14 May, the military commandeered men as they were going to second Mass; they were taken by lorry to Lissycasey to fill in trenches. Another round-up in Ennis occurred three days later, during the morning of Wednesday, 17 May. The police and military took men from shops and draperies. Three motor lorries were filled, and the men were driven to repair roads in Kildysart and Lissycasey. The men were brought back to Ennis at 9 p.m. that evening. Police also rounded up some men at the Fair of Kilkishen to repair the local roads, 'On Thursday morning 26 May, many roads were blocked in East Clare, particularly the main between Sixmilebridge and Limerick. The police and military rounded up a group of men at Kilkishen fair to clear the roads of felled trees and stones.'[277]

Judging by newspaper reports of these activities, May seems to have been the busiest month for damage to the road networks, and this tactic was quite effective from a military perspective. This fact is reflected in the police report for that month:

> On 7th May Latoon bridge was blown up by the IRA to prevent the police and military using the road. The county continues in a very disturbed state. Gangs of armed rebels still roam the county and commit outrages of various kinds. The present month has been especially marked by the destruction of property and the blocking and trenching of roads to prevent Crown forces from moving about. The people generally are terrorised, and even well-disposed persons are afraid to do anything likely to bring them into any sort of disharmony with the rebels.[278]

The Crown forces took other punitive actions besides rounding up civilians to repair damages. For instance, at Lissycasey the homes of two IRA members, that of Michael O'Rourke and Michael McMahon, were burnt as official reprisals for ambushes and the trenching of roads in the Lissycasey area on 19 January and 18–19 February. The most serious and punitive reprisal took place in the Ennis area on Monday, 18 April, when the great Ennis Easter Fair, due to be held on Tuesday, 19 April, was banned. Not only was the fair banned at short notice, all fairs within a 10-mile radius of Ennis were also banned. This collective punishment was described by the *Saturday Record* as 'a drastic measure, which would cause considerable losses to the farming and business communities.' In addition to the ban on all fairs, a military curfew was proclaimed in Ennis. In a proclamation signed by Colonel H.E.P. Nash, curfew was imposed between the hours of 10 p.m. and 5 a.m. In the proclamation, the new curfew was attributed 'to the recent cutting of bridges and damage to roads'. The banning of all fairs within a 10-mile radius of Ennis had serious economic consequences for the farmers and the business communities of mid-Clare. Fairs and markets at Corofin, Kilfenora and Kildysart were prohibited under this order. The great horse fair of Spancilhill, usually held on 23 June, was abandoned. The Fair of Clare, traditionally held on 30 May at Clarecastle each year, was also banned. The British authorities used economic war as a tactic against the IRA, punishing the whole community for the actions of the republican brigades.[279]

Tragically, some men were killed, either by the IRA or the Crown forces, because of trenching activities. One young victim was 20-year-old Joseph Falsey, a farmer's son from Kilmacduane, Cooraclare. Despite a warning notice put up in a trench, 'Don't fill this – IRA', Joseph Falsey, he and some others were apparently engaged in filling in the trench. While they were digging, they were fired upon. Six or seven shots were fired, probably by the IRA. Joseph Falsey was killed and others were wounded. At an inquest, the jury returned a verdict of 'wilful murder against persons unknown'. Bill Chambers stated, 'A young man named Falsey from Cooraclare was shot dead while closing in a trench, he was allegedly shot by the IRA.'[280]

At least four men were killed by Crown forces – 'shot while running away' in areas where roads were trenched. Two youths were shot at Lissycasey church on Sunday, 27 February. They fled from the church when several lorries approached during Mass time. John Connellan of Cahera was shot in the abdomen; another youth, a farmer from Lissycasey named Pat Conway, was injured. There were terrifying scenes in the village. John Connellan died from wounds on Monday, 28 February. The police claimed that the shootings occurred during a military operation where roads were trenched, 'The men ran away on the approach of the military, they refused to halt and were fired upon.'[281] In Tulla on Monday, 25 April, a farmer named John McGrath was shot dead by the military; an official report issued from Dublin Castle stated, 'At Tulla a road was trenched and a shot was fired at soldiers, who returned fire and John McGrath was killed.'[282] At Lissycasey an elderly man named Pat O'Rourke, between 60 and 69 years of age and living a short distance from the parish church, was shot dead by troops who were carrying out searches and rounding up men to repair roads. Some men were fleeing from the troops and were called on to halt. The police claimed that when Pat O'Rourke refused to halt, he was shot in the back and died. Another victim 'shot while running away' was James Grogan from Feakle. Dublin Castle issued the following report on his death, 'Feakle man shot dead, on Thursday 7 July, James Grogan, aged 30 of Feakle, ran from a place where a trench had been cut, he ignored warnings to halt and was shot.'[283]

In one of his reports to General Richard Mulcahy, Frank Barrett, commandant of the Mid-Clare Brigade, stated that his men were not inclined to fire on the enemy while civilians were at risk during road repairs. He said that the IRA fired over the heads of the workmen to deter them, 'On one occasion sections of the 2nd Active Service Unit waited for ten hours for a favourable opportunity to fire upon the enemy, but they were unable to do so as the enemy had with them the fathers, brothers and friends of the Volunteers.'[284]

One way in which the Crown forces tried to deter attacks on police or military trucks was to illegally seize hostages and carry them on the trucks. There are several reported instances of this practice being carried out in February and March 1921. In some cases, prominent members of Sinn Féin were kidnapped and brought on trucks. The IRA would not fire on the trucks for fear of injuring the hostages. In this way the police and army trucks got safe passage. Two well-known Sinn Féin members in Ennis, T.V. Honan and P. O'Grady, were seized and carried in police trucks from Ennis to Limerick and back. Two other men were carried separately in different trucks: Mr O'Grady, from Tubber, and Mr Cusack from Ballynacally, who was best man at a wedding on that same day. Two more men were picked up as hostages while standing in O'Connell Square in Ennis. In the Miltown area, Mr Finucane and two men named Neylon were rounded up and carried in police tenders to Quilty and Mullagh, guaranteeing that the police or military would not be attacked. John Burke, an IRA man, states that Malone, another IRA man, was carried as a hostage by the Crown forces. Bill Haugh of the West Clare Brigade corroborates this practice of seizing hostages, stating, 'the enemy retaliated to road trenching by carrying prominent Sinn Féin hostages on trucks.'[285]

Reporting to the chief of staff, General Richard Mulcahy, in April, Frank Barrett attested to

> a complete change in the enemy transport arrangements [...] For instance they used the roads from Ennis to Kildysart at irregular intervals on an average twice weekly prior to the road cutting and bridge destruction. Then they used two lorries as a rule, sometimes three [...] Now they run on average twice in three weeks and employs not less than five lorries and as many as nine altogether.

Barrett reported that one of the ambushes planned by the Mid-Clare Brigade had to be called off, as the IRA discovered that two priests, Fr Gaynor and Fr McKenna from Mullagh, were being transported as prisoners on a police lorry.[286]

With the closure and destruction of many police barracks in 1920, the police force in the county was concentrated in the main towns, a few villages, and in isolated rural barracks such as Tiermaclane. For instance, the Imperial Hotel in Lisdoonvarna was used as an RIC barracks from October 1920. This garrison consisted of a district inspector and an average of sixty policemen. Early in July, the Auxiliaries moved their base from the Lakeside Hotel in

Killaloe to the Corofin Workhouse; there were already sixty-seven RIC men based in Corofin.

The police needed more trucks and armoured vehicles so that they could travel around the county in larger convoys. The county inspector, William Attridge, requested more vehicles for this purpose in January, 'The main difficulty the police have is want of sufficient transport, we still require fifteen more effective cars to enable men to be moved about in sufficient strength to deal with ambushes etc. Representations to that effect have been made through the ordinary channels.' By the end of February, the police had extra vehicles and the county inspector confidently reported, 'The police and military are out in strong force and the rebels have little hope of attacking them. They seem to be a little down-hearted, owing to the police moving about in such strong force, and this can now be kept up as our transport has greatly increased.'[287]

However, despite extra police transport and official denials that the IRA were seriously disrupting the movement of Crown forces, the IRA tactic of damaging road infrastructure increasingly affected the mobility of the Crown forces. In March, the police report stated that 'the cutting of roads was seriously affecting the farmers.' In April, the police reported that there was 'exceptional IRA activity in cutting roads and bridges and erecting barriers along the main highways'. County Inspector Attridge stated that these cuttings 'delayed Crown forces to a slight extent' and that they managed to get through by means of bicycles, foot patrols and the utilisation of compulsory civilian labour. In May, County Inspector Attridge reported:

> The murder gang still terrorise the population and have resorted to the destruction of bridges and extensive cutting of roads to prevent Crown forces carrying out rapid pursuit. The destruction of roads is not seriously hampering Crown forces, but is causing serious economic loss to the residents of the county and is likely to ruin the tourist trade.

By the end of June 1921, however, the police authorities finally admitted that the IRA's destruction of the road network was seriously affecting them. Attridge reported, 'The present month has been marked by the destruction of property and the blocking and trenching of roads to prevent Crown forces from moving about. The blocking of roads seriously hampers Crown forces and causes much loss and inconvenience to the ordinary public.'[288]

Train robberies, boycotts, postal hold-ups and cutting wires

Besides disrupting road networks, the IRA also caused serious interference with other means of communication. Rail communications on the West Clare line and the Ennis to Limerick line were disrupted; the IRA tore up tracks, placed rocks on tracks, held up trains and raided railway stations. Besides these tactics, telegraph and telephone lines were cut, and post offices and postmen were robbed. There were several motives for robbing mail. One was to search for police and military correspondence to find out if people were informing the police about the IRA. Another was to disrupt supplies to the police and military. Lastly, it was to enforce the boycott of goods made in Belfast. This was a response to the pogroms in Belfast and other parts of Northern Ireland after the Government of Ireland Act 1920 divided the island into two territories.

The West Clare railway line was damaged on several occasions. In May some rails were torn up at Drumcliffe, and while a party of men were repairing the tracks, a number of men armed with revolvers ordered them to stop. The rail service was suspended until the track was repaired the next day. On Tuesday, 7 June, a train was derailed at Woodbrook. On Thursday, 9 June, the West Clare railway was held up by about one hundred armed men at Blackhill, about 2 miles from Miltown Malbay. A stone wall was placed across the tracks. When the train stopped, all the mail bags were stolen and official letters were taken. A train was held up again at Moy on Friday, 10 June by about one hundred armed men, and all mails and parcels were taken.

Ennis railway station was raided by the IRA on several occasions. In mid-February there was a raid that took place between 12 p.m. and 1 p.m. Parcels and letters for soldiers in Corofin, Miltown and Kilrush were removed by a party of four or five armed men. On Friday, 8 July, seven armed and masked men raided Ennis train station, destroyed stores and stole bicycles consigned to Auxiliary police at Corofin. Other raids on Ennis railway station were undertaken in order to enforce a boycott on goods made in Belfast – for example, cigarettes made by the Gallaher Company. In early March, parcels from Belfast were seized and taken away by armed men. On 7 March, property belonging to Gallaher's of Belfast was stolen – the IRA captured a huge consignment of cigarettes.

Fr Patrick Gaynor recalled how the *Clare Champion* was boycotted by Sinn Féin for carrying advertisements for Gallaher's tobacco products. His fellow curate in Mullagh, Fr Michael McKenna, had ordered the proprietors of the *Clare Champion* to cease advertising their products. When they refused, he persuaded the West Clare Sinn Féin Executive to order a boycott of the newspaper in west Clare. Fr Gaynor, as the chief of republican police in west Clare, then sanctioned the seizure of copies of the newspaper, and 'there was a merry bonfire at Kilmurry Ibricane station.' Following this incident, the proprietors dropped Gallaher's advertisements.[289]

Postmen and post offices were easy targets for armed raids, and the postman in Kilmaley was robbed on several occasions during February and March; military and police correspondence was removed from his bag. On the second occasion, ordinary mail was returned to him with a stamp reading, 'Censored by IRA'. The police reports show that only one post office, in Ennis, was robbed on 7 January. But according to the same source, there were six mail robberies (in which either post offices or postmen were robbed) in February, seventeen in March, seventeen in April, ten in May and fourteen in June.[290]

The IRA also cut telephone and telegraph wires. Of course, this tactic had been used previously, when the IRA attacked police barracks in places such as Feakle and Broadford during 1920 so that the besieged could not ring for assistance. The new policy, however, was to disrupt communications more generally. This seems to have been decided upon early in 1921. There were six cases in February, no reports in March and six cases in April. There was a huge increase in cases after this point: there were thirty-eight instances in May and twenty-nine in June. Cutting electronic communications caused considerable inconvenience to the authorities as well as the general public, especially business people. For instance, when the telegraph wires between Clarecastle railway station and Longpavement Station in Limerick were cut, trains were delayed for three hours.[291]

One of the many companies affected by the cutting of telephone and telegraph wires was that of Messrs Glynn and Sons, Kilrush. On 4 May, C.E. Glynn wrote to the chief secretary in Dublin Castle regarding the serious losses incurred by the firm due to the cutting of telephone and telegraph lines between Ennis and Kilrush since 13 April 1921:

> It is making it very difficult for us to carry on the flour milling business in Kilrush, we are placed at an unfair advantage against our competitors for nearly six months. We also have had a very poor mail service and we are losing hundreds of pounds every week. It is unfair and unreasonable that we should be cut off for six months.

The reply from Dublin Castle, about two months later, gives an indication of the disruption caused by the IRA and the inability of the government to repair the damage at that time. T. MacDonnell, acting for the chief secretary, replied that the government was not in a position to repair the lines on 30 June 1921:

> With respect to your letter of 4th May. The Limerick and Kilrush circuit [telegraph] and the Ennis-Kilrush trunk telephone lines have recently been maliciously damaged to such an extent that the Department is not at present prepared to incur the very considerable expense of repairing the lines. In the circumstances, while the inconvenience caused to you is regrettable, your request for the restoration of telegraphic and telephonic communication cannot be complied with.[292]

Economic war

Following the local elections of June 1920, Clare County Council, along with two urban councils – Ennis and Kilrush – and nine rural district councils, had transferred their allegiance from the Local Government Board to Dáil Éireann. Clare County Council was the first county council to take this action. Michael Brennan was elected chairman of the council. Many of the councillors were on the run, and Clare County Council was forced to hold clandestine meetings around the county. The meetings were held at various venues around the county, from an outhouse in Darragh to Lord Dunboyne's home, Knappogue Castle, near Quin and the County Clare Mental Hospital in Ennis.

In Clare the collection of rates was at a standstill as collectors were unable or unwilling to act in the face of conflicting orders from Dáil Éireann and the Local Government Board. In July 1920, the Dáil sent a memorandum indicating that county councils were not to strike a rate for criminal injuries. In October 1920 the lord justices in Ireland ordered that all government grants be withheld from county councils that refused to perform their duties regarding compensation for criminal injuries. Many people were unwilling to pay rates, and the rates due to the council amounted to over £20,000 by September 1920.

In July Clare County Council had refused to set a rate to cover awards for compensation to Crown servants and for malicious damage to property. As a result, British local government grants were withheld. Clearly Clare County Council was in a financial crisis. Michael Brennan, chairman of the council, complained that 'people were taking advantage of the troubled times and were refusing to pay rates.' Ironically, in February 1921 Michael Brennan urged injured parties to pursue their claims for criminal injuries in the British courts. This, of course, would mean that people would have to recognise the official courts, which the vast majority were boycotting at this time.[293]

Because of their financial difficulties, Clare County Council, which was dominated by Sinn Féin councillors, decided that the IRA would collect the rates to keep some of the services going. Almost simultaneously, in early February 1921, parties of armed and masked men visited the homes of rate collectors around the county and forced them to hand over their rate receipt books and monies collected. The rate collectors included C. Brennan, Smithstown, who handed over £1,400; M. McMahon, Ennis, who was deprived of over £1,013; M. O'Loughlin, Inagh, who was forced to hand over £500; P. Davoren, who was robbed of about £400; J. Hynes, Ballingaddy, who handed over £227; W. Halpin, who was forced to hand over more than £800; C. Kearney, who handed over more than £600; and Mr McClancy, who was robbed of £700. Other unnamed rate collectors were also robbed of substantial amounts of money. In some cases, collectors who had lodged the money in bank accounts were forced to write cheques for the sum of money lodged. David Fitzpatrick states that more than £8,013 was taken from the rate collectors. The police report for February indicates that twenty-three rate collectors were robbed. Another robbery of a rate collector occurred in April 1921.

Besides robbing rate collectors, the IRA stole the rate warrants for 1920–21 from Ennis courthouse; fifteen armed men entered the office of Francis Nathaniel Studdert, the county secretary, on Wednesday, 25 May, seizing the rate warrants, which authorised the rate collectors to collect the rates. Before the raid, the telephone wires to the courthouse were cut. Four clerical employees from Clare County Council and one employee from Ennis Urban Council were arrested on Friday, 22 May, but they were released without charge. The home of the assistant county secretary, Mr Carey, was extensively searched but nothing was found. In early July the Kilrush Board of Guardians was raided by two armed and masked men, who stole the books. Finally, the IRA attacked the local revenue offices and destroyed the offices and books.

The *Dublin Gazette* of 25 May 1921 carried a declaration from the government that read:

> No payments shall be made to the following local authorities out of the Local Authorities taxation account or out of any parliamentary grant, or out of any fund administered by any Government department or public body to the boards of guardians of the following Unions: Corofin, Ennis, Ennistymon, Gort, Kildysart, Kilrush, Limerick and Tulla, because the bodies named have failed to perform their duties.

Fr Pat Gaynor, chairman of the Clare County Council health committee from 1920 up to the time of his arrest on 1 April 1921, outlined the difficulties of administering the cut-backs in local health authorities during the War of Independence, 'We were deprived in Clare of the grant of £30,000 in aid of the local rates by the British Government and we had to effect an economy to the extent of £30,000.' Fr Gaynor outlined how the local authority was forced to rationalise the health services by closing down several workhouses around the county and opening a county home in Ennis; they also maintained district hospitals in Ennistymon, Kilrush and Raheen, and a county hospital in Ennis.[294]

Shortly after the robbery of the rate collectors, three IRA men were accosted by the police. They were found with stolen money and rate books and were arrested. John Joe Neylon and two others were accused of taking £227 and rate books from James Hynes, a rate collector. Neylon was convicted and sentenced to seven years of penal servitude, which he recalled in his witness statement:

> After Moanreel, I was not involved in any other action. I was arrested on 7 February 1921, I had seized rate books from Jim Hynes, rate collector, along with a sum of £207 at Kilshanny. I was arrested, maltreated at Ennistymon and Ennis by British Military intelligence officers, with fists, boots and rifle butts, they made a mess of my face, seeking information from me but they got nowhere. On 11 March I was sentenced to seven years in prison and was held in Cork, Kilkenny and Spike island until my release in December 1921.

Thomas McDonagh, one of the IRA men, who hid the rate books in Fr McGuane's house, was sentenced to six months.

Captured documents show that the police were aware of John Joe Neylon's role in the IRA, and that, despite brutal interrogation, he did not give them any information. The police euphemistically suggested that the prison authorities use their 'influence'(i.e., torture) on him to secure information:

> John Naylon of Kilfenora, who is serving a sentence for taking rates from a rate collector by threats, was in charge of all the administrative side of the IRA in North Clare. If the prison authorities, where he now is, use their influence he might supply some very useful information, although he did not do so when arrested.[295]

Michael Hayes of Kinvara, who joined the Mid-Clare Brigade in late February 1921, stated that his first job was to help collect the rates in the Kilfenora–Ballyvaughan district. He accompanied Pat Ward, Pat O'Loughlin and Sean McNamara, all of whom were armed with rifles, while collecting the rates. Hayes stated that the ratepayers willingly handed over the rates due, and that the funds were given to the brigade officers. Sean Murnane of Newmarket-on-Fergus stated that he collected over £2,813 and lodged the money with the trustees of the council. Anthony Malone was responsible for collecting rates in the Miltown, Inagh and Ennistymon districts. Assisted by local company officers, he collected a total of £4,800 and handed the money over to the brigade commandant, Frank Barrett. The testimonies of several IRA collectors indicate that there were few defaulters, that rates were handed over willingly, and that the amount of arrears was negligible.

However, Fitzpatrick records that these statements did not reflect the true state of affairs concerning rate collection in Clare – and that the financial state of Clare County Council grew steadily worse during 1921. He found that of the rates of £108,000 due in the first moiety of 1921, at least £26,000 was still outstanding in September 1921. He writes that the IRA collectors in the Mid-Clare Brigade area had only collected 51 per cent of the rates due by the end of the year. Michael Brennan, commandant of the new 1st Western Division (an amalgamation of the three Clare brigades and south Galway), complained that the truce 'prevented the IRA from taking the necessary action to enforce the collection of the rates!' Frank Barrett stated in April 1921 that a sum of roughly £28,000 in poor rates was collected by the Mid-Clare Brigade and lodged with the county council treasurers.[296]

John Quinn, from Lemanagh, who was clerk to the Ennis Rural District Council, gives some insight into the impact of the reduction in council income. With the British grants being withheld, the council was short of money to pay for its services. The inevitable result was cutbacks and curtailment of services provided. Some services were amalgamated – for example, the Poor Law services, such as workhouses and out-door relief for the poor. Several workhouses in the county were closed. Ennis workhouse was converted into a county home for aged and infirm people. The council stopped allocating monies to pay for the upkeep of the main roads in the county. This suited the aims of the IRA, who were regularly trenching many of the roads. The result was that many of the council's seasonal roadworkers were laid off. This caused hardship among the labouring poor. The local officials and employees of the council also went unpaid for months, and contractors received, after long delays, only a fraction of the monies due to them for supplying goods and services.

Council workers were, however, willing to make some sacrifices during the financial emergency. On 13 November 1920, the secretary of the Ennis branch of the Irish Transport and General Workers' Union (ITGWU) sent a letter to the council with the following proposal, 'In order to help the Guardians in their financial difficulties the members of the union are prepared to sacrifice for the present the following proportion of their salaries: 25% up to £150; 30% on salaries from £150 to £250; and 33% on salaries over £250 per annum.' The offer from the ITGWU may not have been enough to solve the financial crisis; on 28 February 1921, all the council roadworkers were dismissed. According to Fitzpatrick, the amount of money collected was greatly reduced, and road maintenance and other services provided by the council suffered. The quarrying of rocks and stones for road repairs was also curtailed by the ban on the use of explosives. A further indication of the financial crisis at Clare County Council was revealed in the half-yearly meeting of the council in July 1922, where it was stated that the council owed £138,000 for 1921 as a consequence of the unpaid rates during the second half of the year.

A September police report, following the truce, noted some local divisions in the council chamber, revealing friction between supporters of Michael Brennan and Frank Barrett:

> The Council had earlier had a heated dispute over the appointment of temporary rate collectors between the M. Brennan faction and that of F. Barrett. However, a compromise was reached, and forty one appointments were made to collect all the current rates and arrears, and rate collectors could use force if necessary. All the collectors were members of the IRA.

County Inspector Attridge also reported that, at 2.30 p.m. on 6 September, a county councillor was arrested by unknown men, driven away in a motor car and released the following day; his 'arrest' was the result of a factional dispute among the IRA parties in the county council.[297]

Cat and mouse

The Glenwood ambush was the most successful attack on the Crown forces in 1921. After this ambush, the IRA had limited opportunities to engage with the police or army and inflict significant losses. The RIC forces were mainly concentrated in large towns such as Ennis, Ennistymon, Killaloe and Kilrush. These towns were also the main bases for the British army in the county. Because the strength of the Crown forces in these towns was formidable – for example, in Ennis there were between forty and fifty RIC members in the RIC barracks, between three and four hundred infantry in the Home Barracks beside Station Road, and about two hundred cavalry in the Ordnance Survey House – the IRA could hardly attack them with their limited arsenal. The army and the police now usually travelled in convoys of three or more trucks, which were well armed with Lewis guns. These forces were too strong for the IRA, whose weapons and ammunition were limited. Nevertheless, the IRA still planned ambushes in various parts of the county, hoping to surprise the enemy and inflict casualties. The British authorities, meanwhile, carried out extensive searches throughout the county in search of IRA members, usually after an IRA operation.

Witness statements given by several prominent IRA men from all three Clare brigades highlight difficulties faced in attacking the Crown forces in early 1921. Sean O'Keefe (Mid-Clare Brigade) recalled:

> After the Caherea ambush [on 19 January] it became very difficult to get an opportunity to engage the British forces in the Mid Clare area. From thence onwards the enemy moved in large convoys varying from ten to twenty vehicles, generally accompanied by armoured cars. With the limited resources at the disposal of the brigade a total of about eighty rifles in an area constituting more than one third of the county, the job of successfully attacking these large convoys was beyond us. Besides, the area did not provide suitable country for engaging more than two or three lorries with a reasonable chance of victory.

Bill Haugh (West Clare Brigade) stated:

> There was a change in enemy tactics, there were no more single lorries, Lewis guns were mounted on trucks, and garrisons were fortified. Attack was beyond the scope of the Volunteers in

> daylight. Four fifths of the local terrain was level and open, except the one mile strip along the Shannon Estuary from Kilrush to Labasheeda, but the enemy did not use this road. Daylight attacks on the enemy were now out of the question except sniping. Ambushes were planned at night, but some prisoners were carried as hostages. The brigade had no explosives.

Tom Tuohy (East Clare Brigade) said, 'The enemy convoys were too large and the terrain was not suitable for engaging more than one or two lorries, they could only be sniped at.'

The ambush at Caherea on 19 January, which Sean O'Keefe refers to in his witness statement, involved between fifty and seventy men from the Mid-Clare Brigade. They were led by Commandant Frank Barrett; they trenched the road and lay in ambush. Once the attack was underway, the police returned fire and claimed to have wounded four or five IRA men. The IRA retreated into the surrounding hills, and there were no police casualties. William McNamara stated that the ambush party waited all day; once the enemy turned up, there was a running battle for about an hour, until the IRA retreated into the Kilmaley hills. Peter O'Loughlin stated that there were about seventy IRA men involved, and that they waited all day at Slaveen, from 8 a.m. until 4 p.m., for lorries expected from Kilrush. But two lorries suddenly came from Ennis, and after some shots were fired the IRA retreated towards Kilmaley at dusk.[298]

Despite the increased concentration of Crown forces in 1921, the IRA did carry out several ambushes and planned several more operations. An attack was carried out at Darragh Cross in June on a bicycle patrol of Black and Tans and Auxiliaries. Joe Barrett, adjutant of the Mid-Clare Brigade, stated that more than eighty RIC men were in the patrol:

> At short notice we mustered about twenty men, all armed with rifles. Five Auxiliaries were wounded, they used a machine gun, then RIC reinforcements arrived, with armoured cars from Ennis. There was a danger that we would be outflanked. We retreated towards Kilmaley, the battle lasted for one and a half hours. The IRA had no injuries but the British had eight wounded.

His brother Frank, commandant of the Mid-Clare Brigade, gave an official IRA account of the Darragh engagement:

> On 9 June fourteen rifles of the 2nd Batt. ASU were posted around Newhall and Buncraggy between Tiermaclane and Ennis in search of stragglers from the RIC barracks at Tiermaclane. Having remained in position from 9 am till 3 pm and no enemy appearance, the ASU moved to Bearnageeha, which place immediately joins Darragh to the north [...] At 6.20 pm [...] we observed a column of cyclists and horsemen at a distance of 500 yards in the direction of Ennis [...] The enemy consisted of Auxiliaries and RIC numbering between fifty and sixty, twenty rode horses and the balance cycled, they were stretched over about a mile of the road carrying rifles and two machine guns [...] All three sections opened fire on the enemy at 6.40 pm, two of them were hit, one seriously. They attempted to encircle us [...] we held him for close on an hour – fourteen men against fifty or sixty on a wide front. We decided to pull back, it would be a waste of ammunition and we were in danger from reinforcements. We withdrew quite easily. Not one of our men received a single bullet. Dublin Castle report of 'one unknown man left dead in the field' was false. The enemy shot a horse belonging to a local farmer and burned an outhouse belonging to the same man.[299]

Dublin Castle gave an official version of the 'Battle of Darragh', which was published in the local press:

> The Darragh ambush on the Kilrush Road. A cadet was wounded, official report: 'At 6.30pm on the 9th June a bicycle column of forty-three men were returning to Ennis from south west Clare, with pack horses, strung out over a mile. When the head of the column reached Darragh Post Office, two or three shots rang out from a hill to the south east, followed by heavy firing from hills to the north east. An Auxiliary division of RIC moving from Lissycasey to Ennis was fired at from the north side of the road about 400 yds range, just outside Darragh. The police quickly deployed, the main body attacking from the road and flanking movement up a lane running north. Two Lewis guns were brought into action and rapid exchanges of fire took place, the attackers retreated on the north side of the road, firing was kept up for about half an hour, after which the rebels retired, and were pursued for some distance, leaving one dead body behind. The Auxiliaries state that one man was killed and there was a large pool of blood, one cadet was wounded in the arm.' Information from a 'reliable' source in Ennis states that the attackers left three dead and five wounded.[300]

The British claims that between one and three IRA men were killed and five were wounded was mere propaganda, as no IRA men were killed in this ambush. The truth about this ambush probably lies somewhere between the IRA versions and the Dublin Castle version. It is also significant that the members of the Black and Tan and Auxiliary patrol were mounted on bicycles and horseback; this reflected the impact of the IRA's road-trenching tactics.

The Mid-Clare Brigade planned another ambush at Toonagh in late April; they hoped to attack the Auxiliaries, who had established a base in Corofin, having relocated from Killaloe. For the ambush, more than seventy IRA men were assembled at Hegarty's of Kilnamona; they gathered by night from all over the battalion area, and they marched the 4 miles to Toonagh. Most of them were armed with rifles, and they waited from about 7 a.m. until 4 p.m. But there was no sign of the enemy. Frank Barrett called off the operation after the accidental discharge of a bullet, which might have alerted the Crown forces.

Another ambush was organised on 16 May at Willbrook, 3 miles west of Corofin, where the Mid-Clare Brigade hoped to surprise a party of police collecting water at Patterson's Mill. More than sixty IRA men, mostly armed with rifles, were in position by 4 a.m., and they waited all day. The IRA were departing at around 7.30 p.m. when two lorries of Auxiliaries suddenly arrived. The IRA were exposed in a vulnerable position; they had to retreat hastily after a brief exchange of fire. There were no casualties on either side.

The local press reported another ambush near Corofin in July:

> Between 7.30 or 8 am on Monday 4 July, when a party of police from Corofin went to Riverston for water. They were fired upon and returned fire, and no injuries were reported. Eleven police in an armoured car and a Crossley were ambushed at Clifden, while proceeding to the Mills for water. Fire was opened from wooded crags, under the picturesque mountain overlooking Lake Inchiquin. One of the cars dashed through the ambush and summoned reinforcements from Corofin. The second car engaged the attackers for about a quarter of an hour, before they retreated through the woods. A large force of police and military raked the woods with rifle and machine gunfire. There are no reports of casualties.[301]

Trouble in the Mid-Clare and West Clare brigades

Frank Barrett, commandant of the Mid-Clare Brigade, had been suspended by General Richard Mulcahy in December 1920. There had been friction between the officers of the 4th Battalion and the brigade commandant since the Rineen ambush in September 1920, after which Ignatius O'Neill, commandant of the 4th Battalion, resigned. In early March, General Mulcahy, the IRA chief of staff, noted that Frank Barrett had written 'a Christmas letter' to the Auxiliaries which showed 'a want of judgement on his part. A considerable amount of information had been accumulated by GHQ with a view to tackling some of these people in their homes, when he thoughtlessly made manifest to the enemy the possibility of our doing such.' Mulcahy admitted that because of Barrett's suspension 'there was a want of equilibrium in the Brigade.' However, he was prepared to reinstate the former leader, as 'it was due to him in recognition of the work he had been carrying out.'

The activity reports of the Mid-Clare Brigade for the months of January and February 1921 are quite brief, indicating few ventures. In January, for instance, there was only a short paragraph indicating that the flying column had been reorganised on 6 January so that it now numbered sixty men. It mentioned that only two ambushes were planned, one at Corofin on 10 January and a second at Caherea on 19 January, but that the enemy did not show up on either occasion. It also mentions that road trenching was extensive. The February report was equally terse. It mentions that the county rate books and monies collected by rate collectors were stolen on 7 February. It also states that several ambushes were planned, but that they only came into contact with the enemy on one occasion, at Lissycasey on 19 February, claiming that a party of eighteen IRA men killed three enemy soldiers (which is not true). The February diary also justifies the brigade's inaction, stating that most of the officers and men of the flying columns got the 'flu' and consequently were inactive for much of the month.

About a month after Frank Barrett's reinstatement as commandant in March, General Mulcahy indicated in a letter to Barrett that he was very unhappy with the reports of operations carried out by the Mid-Clare Brigade. In response to Mulcahy,

Barrett admitted, 'I was not surprised at Mulcahy's disappointment over the bad results from my command [...] I must confess that I feel ashamed and have examined my own conscience in the matter. When I reviewed the work done for the month of March, I feel alarmed.' Barrett examined the situation, summoned the brigade council and the column officers, and declared his determination to improve the intelligence-gathering and efficiency of the brigade. He issued new orders:

> A, attack the enemy everywhere at all times.
>
> B, make every effort to destroy himself, his agents, his transport and his communications.
>
> C, armed or unarmed, on duty or off duty, he is not to be allowed escape.
>
> D, in no stronghold, in no post, in no street or road is he to pass unchallenged.

After receiving reports of brigade operations in April, General Richard Mulcahy again strongly criticised its activities. Mulcahy stated, 'The Volunteers had been watching constantly for the enemy in a district in which there is almost daily activity on the part of the enemy, yet contact with the enemy is only established on three days in the month.' Mulcahy warned, 'I am quite sure that you realise the extent of this failure [...] it would be a disastrous thing if there should be found in the heart of Clare anything like stagnation.'

General Mulcahy's conclusion indicates that Frank Barrett appears to have had difficulties with some of his subordinate officers:

> We cannot have inefficient officers blocking this way and we must get rid of them. You should communicate with GHQ staff officers, who will visit you shortly to discuss all your difficulties in this matter [...] We must now get away from the arrangement by which officers were placed in command by election. We must see that the best man for the job is in every case appointed to it. [See appendices one and two.]

There was concern at GHQ about these difficulties, but Frank Barrett wrote to the director of intelligence to inform him:

> all such differences have long ceased to exist at least as far as the

> three brigade commandants are concerned. Indeed to tolerate such differences in view of existing circumstances would be to my mind nothing short of treachery of the Republic and to our gallant comrades all over the country. For my part, I was ready to stand down if by my doing so harmony would be attained.

The West Clare Brigade also came under scrutiny from HQ. In his brief report at the end of June 1921, commandant Sean Liddy stated that

> re-organisation of the brigade was taking place, that the 5th Battalion was hitherto chaotic, but was being re-organised. All the companies were specialising on skirmishing details. The breaking of roads and bridges has been effectively systematised. Enemy repairs of same is rendered ineffective as soon as their back is turned […] The enemy barrack at Kildysart was sniped at on the night of June 29/30 […] During the first week of June a flying column of forty-two Auxiliaries entered the brigade area, they commandeered horses and bicycles and assisted the local garrison in carrying out searches in the Shragh area […] Activities of local enemy garrison have fallen off considerably owing to their inability to use lorries.

Following this report, the HQ sent an inspector into the West Clare Brigade area:

> The report shows the condition of the area to be very poor. I fear the OC of the brigade has been misleading us. In his report for April he reports that the organisation throughout the brigade is keeping up to a good standard and he positively refers to the 1st Battalion as being in good working form, whereas our inspector says that this battalion does not exist and the brigade OC told him that he had no hopes for the re-organisation of same. The matter is very serious and I am writing to the brigade OC for an immediate explanation of his report for April. It appears too from the inspector's report that the cause of inactivity in the brigade is owing to a scarcity of ammunition. Unfortunately, the inspector does not state what particular type of ammunition is required.

Concluding his report on the attack on the police, the army and the marines at Kilrush by a column from the East Clare Brigade on 23 April, Michael Brennan, commandant of the East Clare Brigade, made a few observations about the West Clare Brigade to GHQ:

> I found West Clare to be a district of great possibilities, there are fine men, very few capable officers and practically no arms. The OC would make a fine officer under supervision, so would his adjutant. The OC of the 1st Battalion is entirely inefficient and it should be scrapped immediately, the 1st Lieut., of Coolmeen Company would make a fine battalion commandant in his stead. The 5th Battalion should be wiped out and a few of the alleged officers shot if possible. These are the main points which struck me in the few days I was there. There are large numbers of men and fairly good local organisations, as proven by the splendid manner in which they have destroyed the roads. Our principal guide from Kilrush would make a very fine brigade officer and is worth keeping in mind [...] From my experience in West Clare, I have been absolutely impressed with the utter impossibility of campaigning under present circumstances on level country unless the roads are made impassable.[302]

It must also be remembered that Michael Brennan had temporarily been removed from his position as commandant of the East Clare Brigade after, in carly 1920, he lead a raid on the post office at Limerick and acquired more than £1,500 for the IRA – without sanction from GHQ. Also, Art O'Donnell, the first commandant of the West Clare Brigade, had been removed from his post in 1919.

Operations in East Clare

After the Glenwood operation in January, the East Clare Brigade lay low for a while. Once they renewed activity, they carried out some ambushes at Cratloe, Mountshannon, Newmarket-on-Fergus and Tulla. They had mixed fortunes in these raids. On 22 March, Commandant Brennan received an order from GHQ to carry out some operations in the east Galway area, which was relatively inactive. Taking thirty riflemen and four men with shotguns, the brigade marched to Derrybrien. After resting overnight, they then headed for Athenry, but en route he said that they 'met nothing but lies, inaccuracies, disappointments and incompetencies of the worst type' from the local IRA members. Brennan's experiences in east Galway prompted him to suggest that 'a wholesale wiping out policy for people associating with the enemy seems to me to be essential.' The party returned to east Clare to plan an ambush on the Auxiliaries at Killaloe on 3 April, but during the ambush seven

Crossley Tenders turned up and the flying column had to make a lucky escape.[303]

At Newmarket-on-Fergus on 17 June, at around midday, a group of between twenty and thirty IRA men ambushed a party of nine constables and a sergeant patrolling near Carrigoran Woods. While retreating, they were challenged at Craggalough by police reinforcements arriving from Sixmilebridge; these forces were led by the district inspector and consisted of about thirty constables. During this operation, one of the IRA party died of a heart attack: the brigade police officer, Tom Healy a 24-year-old native of Tralee. He was an ex-RIC constable and clerk at Ennis RIC barracks; he had supplied the IRA with valuable information before he resigned. The IRA group had marched about 10 miles during the retreat, 'on a roasting hot day', and it seems that Healy collapsed and died from exhaustion. His last reported words were, 'Boys, take my rifle and stuff and also empty my pockets and leave me, I am done.' It was his first IRA operation. His comrades brought him to a doctor, but he could not be saved. One policeman, Constable White, was wounded in the arm during the attack.[304]

The East Clare Brigade suffered the loss of three more IRA men in June. Captain Patrick White, a native of Meelick, who was arrested after the Glenwood ambush and interned at Spike Island in Cork Harbour, was shot dead in jail by a prison guard on 1 June while hurling.[305] About a fortnight later, on 16 June, two further members of the East Clare Brigade were killed during an ambush on a train at Cratloe that was travelling from Limerick to Ennis. Unknown to them, the train was carrying soldiers, who spotted the ambush party. The train reversed and the troops engaged the rebels, killing two of them. According to an official report from Dublin Castle:

> A fatal ambush near Cratloe occurred along the track of the railway about half a mile from the station where there were bushes on the track. Lieut Gordon and a party of Royal Scots were on the train. They encountered some rebels near Meelick, the train reversed about a half mile and in the exchanges of fire two civilians were killed and one soldier was wounded. Three rifles and a revolver were found by the troops and four prisoners were taken.

The two 'civilians' were actually IRA officers, both 22 years old, who were identified as Captain Christopher McCarthy of Coore, Miltown Malbay, formerly of the West Clare Brigade, and Captain Patrick Gleeson of Clondrinagh, Meelick. Michael Brennan reported that both IRA men were mercilessly killed after being wounded, and that Patrick Gleeson was killed while rescuing his wounded comrade:

> McCarthy and Gleeson got over the fence, but a little distance up the field McCarthy fell wounded. Gleeson had reached a place of safety, but finding that his comrade was down, he ran back down the field and helped him up, while firing back with his free hand at the pursuing soldiers. A little further on Gleeson got hit and fell, while McCarthy staggered on. The soldiers coming up on Gleeson finished him off and very soon after caught up on McCarthy and finished him off also.

Brennan also stated that the brigade lost three rifles and a revolver in the ambush, and that one soldier was badly wounded.

The deaths of Gleeson and McCarthy did cause some controversy, as Canon Patrick O'Dea, the parish priest of Newmarket-on-Fergus, allegedly refused to ask for prayers for the dead IRA men. In response to this, a motion was adopted at a Clare County Council meeting on 30 June that the name of the canon should be removed from all committees of the council.

There may have been other reasons for the canon's removal from the committees. Around this time, suspicions were rife that Canon O'Dea was collaborating with the Crown forces. At first Michael Collins, the IRA director of intelligence, communicated with Frank Barrett on the matter of Canon O'Dea, believing that Newmarket-on-Fergus was in the mid-Clare area, 'wrt to PP of Newmarket on Fergus, I suppose it would be possible for you to have his movements watched. It is a serious thing that he is actually giving information to the enemy and Kelly's remarks appear to indicate that this was quite definite.' (Kelly was a Black and Tan from Kilrush). In his initial reply to GHQ in March, Barrett, who had known the canon when he was administrator of Ennis parish, stated, 'All I can say about the canon is that I have always considered him a staunch supporter of ours and a thoroughly decent and straight man generally.' However, after making some enquiries about the canon, Barrett replied about a month later, 'On further enquiries I've found out that the canon has completely changed over and must be regarded in future as an enemy of ours.'

Michael Collins subsequently communicated with Michael Brennan about Canon O'Dea. Brennan replied on 26 April:

> I would like to point out to you that in one of my reports last December to the C.S. [chief of staff, Richard Mulcahy], referred to this priest as having interfered with one of our men who was watching enemy movements in the village of Newmarket on Fergus for the purpose of reporting of same to a body of armed men who were in the vicinity.

Collins suggested that the canon could be misled by false information about an ambush could lead the Crown forces into a trap, for which the canon could then be blamed. The canon was lucky that he, unlike another Newmarket-on-Fergus resident, John Reilly, was not shot as a spy. Perhaps his clerical status had saved him.[306]

A long march

During April the Crown forces were carrying out extensive searches for the rebels in isolated areas around the county, including Moneen Mountain, Ballyvaughan, Cahercon Woods, Kildysart and Bohatch near Mountshannon. On 5 April, while searching around Bohatch, they nearly succeeded in capturing Michael Brennan and about twenty-five members of the East Clare Brigade. However, the brigade's knowledge of the local terrain combined with their resilience and military tactics ensured their escape. They were pursued by police and military columns and withstood an exhausting journey, trudging for more than sixteen hours, for a distance of about 25 miles, over the bogs, moorlands and mountains of east Clare before they reached safety.

Michael Brennan recalled this extraordinary march and great escape. The East Clare flying column were based overnight at Bohatch and planning an ambush for the next day. At about 5.30 p.m., the men were aroused from their billets by scouts, who brought word that a military and police force, which had come in lorries from the

Tulla direction, was approaching Bohatch:

> I am not sure if it was immediately after the Kilrush attack, but one morning in Mountshannon we were roused before dawn with a report that one of the far away danger signals was burning. The houses in which the column men were billeted were very scattered and it was full daylight (about 5 a.m. I think) before they were all assembled. In the interval we had heard many lorries in the distance and we knew the British were getting into position for a 'round up'. Our situation was delicate as we were completely cut off on the south, east and north-east by the broad expanse of Lough Derg which curved round where we were. The British were in force on our west side and were moving towards the north so it looked like a race between us.
>
> After a mile or so the country was just completely open and bare moorland offering no cover of any sort. James Hogan and the missing men joined us and we accelerated our pace until we gained the top of an incline. A line of police and military in extended order had by now appeared moving after us about half a mile behind, but we were not worried about these. A much more serious matter was the appearance of troops along a line of hills to the north and north-west. This seemed to finish our last chance of escape and every man there saw that this looked like the end of the road.
>
> Out ammunition had gone very low and a long fight would have been suicidal for us […] I called up the local company captain Michael Clery and learned from him that this ravine remained hidden until one was beside it and very probably the troops were unaware of its existence. A shallow drain ran from our boghole to the far side of the hill and I saw that a man creeping along this would be covered from the view of our attackers. Once over the hill the way was open to the ravine and I decided at once to try this route. We were hampered by all the local scouts, numbering about fifteen, who had been driven in on us and were unarmed except for a few revolvers. They had to keep with us, as capture under the circumstances of that morning meant death for them.
>
> We were out of the trap but not yet 'out of the woods' and speed was essential, I estimated that we had about an hour before the trick was discovered and our route picked up. Our problem was to keep out of range of armoured cars and strong forces until it was dark when we could easily slip by. This, of course, meant continuous movement for about sixteen hours.

> We had a choice of going north-east towards Loughrea, north-west towards Derrybrien or west towards Lough Graney. In any one of these areas we could find food and a fairly safe billeting area, but no decision could be taken between them until we saw how the situation was developing. All through that beautiful sunny day we trudged through the bog and moorland. As there were no houses and breakfast had been scanty and hurried, food was badly missed in the mountain air.
>
> We had travelled mainly north, but late in the evening, we swung west and about 10 p.m. we marched down the side of Sliabh-an-Óir to the southern end of Lough Graney. When I measured our route on the map next day I found we had travelled over 25 miles since the fight at dawn. Despite their hunger most of the men fell asleep along the side of the road while the local guides to billets were being detailed. Some hours before, a boy had been sent ahead on a bicycle with a message and by the time we arrived all roads were completely blocked, protection arranged and billets selected.

Attridge's report for April corroborated Brennan's story:

> On 5th April a party of Tulla police and military came into conflict with rebels at Bohatch near Mountshannon. Firing at long range took place after which the rebels disappeared through the mountains, no police were injured, but reliable information has been received that several of the rebels were hit. The latter were under the command of Michael Brennan Commandant of the East Clare Brigade.[307]

Besides occasional ambushes, the IRA in mid- and east Clare also carried out some further attacks on police barracks during March and April. Feakle barracks was attacked on 3 March by a large number of men. The attack lasted for about an hour and a quarter, but there were no police casualties. On the night of Friday, 20 May, the police barracks at Tiermaclane was attacked by a party of men concealed by a hill behind the barracks. The police fired on the attackers, who were driven off after about a quarter of an hour; there were no injuries among the police or attackers. Joe Barrett stated that two attacks were made on Tiermaclane barracks, the first on 18 May and the second on 19 June. The barracks was heavily fortified, and the assaults were maintained for about an hour, until enemy reinforcements arrived. At midnight on 23 June, two bombs were thrown at Ennistymon barracks; no policemen were injured. At 10.40 p.m. on 31 March, three bombs were thrown at a police patrol in Clarecastle from over a garden wall. No police were injured in this attack.[308] These attacks were organised separately by each brigade; they rarely co-operated with each other during the war.

A raid on Kilrush

For most of the war, there was little co-ordination between the Clare brigades. GHQ, concerned about this, communicated with the three commandants to rectify the lack of co-operation. Frank Barrett replied to the director of intelligence with the following, 'As a result of your communication I have just sent notice to the O/Cs East and West Clare to meet me with a view to coordinating in all operations and a unified outlook generally. I will report the result to GHQ.'

Perhaps as a result of this meeting, the East and West Clare brigades, in a joint operation, launched an attack in the town of Kilrush on the night of Friday, 23 April. Kilrush was the headquarters of the Crown forces of west Clare, with a police barracks contingent of between forty and fifty Black and Tans, and a military barracks with more than one hundred troops; there was also a coastguard at Cappa consisting of between forty and fifty marines. The West Clare Brigade had been relatively quiet, as they had a limited supply of weapons (they had less than ten rifles). The commandant of the West Clare Brigade, Sean Liddy, requested assistance from Michael Brennan and the East Clare Brigade. Brennan brought a group of thirty-one men, all of whom were armed with rifles, and crossed the River Fergus from Clenagh to Kildysart, where, after attacking the local RIC barracks, they made their way to Tullycrine. There they were joined by a group of about eleven men from the West Clare Brigade led by Sean Liddy.

Under cover of darkness, the IRA party marched from Tullycrine to Kilrush. The attack began after 10.30 p.m. with a three-pronged attack on the RIC barracks, the army barracks and the marine base, which lasted up to two hours. After the successful operation, the Volunteers returned safely to their hideouts in west and east Clare. Michael Brennan stated, 'I shot and killed a police sergeant [...] We retreated towards Cree [...] after Sunday Mass we sang and danced until evening [...] then we made our way home via Lissycasey, Ballynacally Cross, and across the Fergus to Clenagh.' In his official report of the attack on Kilrush on 23 April 1921, Brennan claimed to have killed seven members of the Crown forces, which was untrue. He also again mentioned the problem of a shortage of ammunition, 'Might I again draw your attention to the lack of ammunition [...] and the danger of going on a dangerous operation which might entail a lot of fighting with only twenty rounds of ammunition per man.' Brennan also commented on the difficulty of conducting guerrilla warfare in west Clare, 'From my experience in West Clare, I have been absolutely impressed with the utter impossibility of campaigning under present circumstances in level country unless the roads are made impassable.'[309]

The local press reports convey some sense of the impact of the attack:

> There was a night of terror in Kilrush, a police sergeant was shot dead, and a Royal Scots sergeant was seriously wounded. There was terrible excitement on Friday night and in early hours of Saturday morning. Sergeant McFadden, a Catholic from Donegal, was killed and Sergeant Clapperton of the Royal Scots was badly wounded. There were attacks on the military, police and coastguard at Cappagh. Some unarmed marines were held up in town and later released, every house in Cappagh was riddled with bullets and windows were shattered. The residents fled through the fields in terror. All inhabitants were in a state of panic and people were up all night because of the machine gun and rifle fire. A private of the Royal Scots was also wounded. The killing of Sergeant McFadden [who was shot by Michael Brennan] was severely condemned by Very Rev Dean McInerney PP at Mass on Sunday. In reprisal for the killing of Sergeant McFadden and the attack on the Crown forces, the houses of John Liddy, Cooraclare and William Haugh, Monmore, Kilrush have been destroyed. The Market House Kilrush was burnt at 2 am on Friday.

Attridge's monthly police report briefly sums up the attack:

> On the night of 23rd they united at Kilrush with a party that came from Ennistymon and opened an attack on the police, military and marine barracks at Kilrush. Sergeant McFadden, RIC, who was on leave in the town, was shot dead. Two marines

> out walking were captured, but subsequently released; a soldier of the Royal Scots was captured, but escaped and was wounded when getting away. A sergeant of the Royal Scots in charge of a patrol was seriously wounded. The attack on any of the barracks was not pressed. It was more in the nature of sniping from points chosen in the day time and lasted for about two hours from 11.30 p.m. Crown forces from the three barracks replied to the fire. The enemy casualties are not known, but reliable information has been obtained that six coffins were ordered for secret burials of the rebels shot during the fight.

The British authorities imposed severe reprisals on the people of the town and district of Kilrush. The police report for April stated, 'Information received that the party attacking at Kilrush, were under the command of John Liddy Cooraclare and William Haugh of Monmore, whose houses were destroyed on 25th as a reprisal [...] On 29 April Kilrush Market House was burned down by unknown men [...] motive unknown.' Besides the destruction of the homes of Haugh and Liddy, and the burning of the Market House, other reprisals in the Kilrush district included the introduction of a curfew between the hours of 10 p.m. and 5 a.m., and the banning of all fairs and markets at Kilrush. About three weeks later, on the night of Tuesday, 14 June, the Manchester Martyrs' monument in Kilrush was torn down by the Black and Tans, and an arm of the statue was broken. At the quarter sessions in Kilrush, the trustees of the Market House, which belonged to the Vandeleur family, sought £7,000 in compensation for the burning of the premises; however, Judge Bodkin awarded only £700 in damages.[310]

More deaths

With the police and military concentrated in large garrisons and heavily fortified barracks in the main towns around the county, and travelling in heavily armed convoys of three or more vehicles, it became increasingly difficult for the lightly armed flying columns to carry out successful attacks or ambushes. There were, however, some successful attacks on police and military that occurred opportunistically and at random – cases where members of the Crown forces relaxed their guard and were shot and sometimes killed by the ever-vigilant IRA. These attacks, mainly on the police, occurred in both the towns and the countryside. When members of the police or military were killed by the IRA, the authorities usually carried out reprisals.

On 2 March, a Corofin policeman was wounded while cycling near the town; a revolver shot hit him in the leg. On 6 March, a policeman was fired at in Kilkee at about 9.30 p.m., and he was slightly wounded. On 8 March, Constable Sydenham was shot and injured at Kilkee. On 13 March, Constable W.J. Armstrong was shot and wounded by the IRA on the Ennis Road, 1 mile from Corofin. Constable Hogan was wounded as he was cycling home from Ennis to Corofin; he was found unconscious on the road. Police Sergeant Reilly was fired at while cycling on Mill Street in Ennis, near the Martryrs Memorial monument; he was fired at by two men but was not injured.[311]

Early in June 1921, a soldier was kidnapped, executed and buried in a bog near Moy. In May 2018, the body of a missing soldier who was shot and buried by the IRA was found in a bog near Miltown Malbay. The remains were identified as that of 18-year-old Private George Duff Chalmers of the Royal Scots Regiment, who was killed on 10–11 June 1921. He was captured at Lavoureen near Ennistymon by members of the Mid-Clare Brigade, and then executed and buried in Drumbaun bog. The body was exhumed and removed for reburial in Grangegorman cemetery in Dublin.[312]

At least four members of the Crown forces suspected of being spies were shot by members of the East Clare Brigade during the War of Independence – one member of the RIC and three soldiers. Constable Daniel Murphy of Broadford was killed on the evening of Friday, 12 March, because he was suspected of being on a reconnaissance mission in the Sixmilebridge region while disguised as a labourer. Joe Clancy from Killaloe, in his witness statement, gave a brief account of the reasons for, and the circumstances of, Constable Murphy's death:

> local Volunteers noticed an RIC man named Murphy had started to make visits to houses in the Oatfield, Belvoir and Broadford districts while dressed as an agricultural labourer and in that same disguise he frequently took despatches between the RIC stations at Broadford and Sixmilebridge. During his visits to

> houses in the vicinity he was always asking questions about the IRA. He was arrested by two men 'on the run' Martin McNamara and John Curley in the middle of the day while cycling from Broadford in the vicinity of the scene of the Glenwood ambush. On being searched he was found to be unarmed. He was taken to Enagh Wood and shot that night by McNamara and Curley. His body was buried in the vicinity.[313]

Sir Hamar Greenwood, the secretary of home affairs, was questioned in the House of Commons regarding Constable William Carroll, who had disappeared after the Ruan barracks attack and joined the IRA, and Constable Daniel Murphy of Broadford, who had disappeared after 12 March 1921. The mystery of Constable Murphy's whereabouts was solved about eight months after his disappearance, when his body was handed over by the IRA on 22 October 1921. A report in the *Saturday Record* stated:

> A coffin was found with a body at Sixmilebridge parish church on Saturday 22nd October. On the breastplate it stated that the coffin contained the body of Constable Murphy, who was kidnapped last March while conveying despatches between Broadford and Sixmilebridge, and who had not been heard of since. Constable Murphy, who was stationed in Broadford, left the station on 12 March in plain clothes and was cycling and was not seen again till his body was placed in Sixmilebridge church on 22 October.[314]

The *Saturday Record* recorded that 'on 19 February the dead bodies of three soldiers were found at Poolagoond, Loughgraney. They were murdered by rebels and a label tied around their necks with the word "spy." These soldiers were supposed to have been deserters from Galway.' Historian Pádraig Óg Ó Ruairc added some more information, giving their names and indicating that they were dressed as civilians:

> On 19 February 1921 members of the East Clare Brigade arrested three Englishmen wearing civilian clothing who were wandering in the countryside north of Feakle. The three men, D.J. Williams, W.S. Walker and H. Morgan, of the Oxford and Buckinghamshire Light Infantry, claimed that they were deserters from the British army. The three were court-martialled as spies and executed.

The *Saturday Record* mentioned the 'gruesome discovery of the bodies of three soldiers found dead near Woodford', who were described in an official report as being in uniform. The soldiers were killed by members of the East Clare Brigade. The British army HQ in Dublin issued a communiqué on Tuesday night:

> The bodies of three uniformed private soldiers of the Oxford and Buckinghamshire Light Infantry were found this morning near Woodford, Co. Galway, each of the murdered men had bullet wounds in the head and by their side was a note on which was written – Spies, tried by court martial and found guilty. All others beware.[315]

Members of the Mid-Clare Brigade shot and killed Constable Stanley L. Moore on Thursday, 7 April, at about 10.30 p.m., near the Central Hotel on Main Street in Miltown Malbay. According to one newspaper report, 'there was wild alarm in the town and a number of inhabitants were warned to flee; many fled to rural areas. The constable was a Black and Tan, a native of Bristol.' Canon Hannon, the local parish priest, denounced the killing:

> I hope that God would be more merciful to the victim than to the perpetrator of this terrible deed [...] it was a flagrant violation of the fifth commandment and more likely to bring a blight and a curse, it was a violation of the law of God, a cruel murder. Those responsible had small concern for the people of Miltown who endured distress and anxiety since the tragedy. Each night, most of the people fly from the town to seek shelter and refuge elsewhere. I beseech you to give no countenance to anyone who would violate God's Law.

In reprisal for the killing, O'Neill's store was burnt and two other houses were selected by the military authorities for destruction, J. Sullivan's drapery and M. Hayes's home; explosives were placed and the houses were blown-up, with considerable damage to other neighbouring houses.[316]

Terror in Ennis

On Saturday, 16 April at around 10.20 p.m., members of the IRA flung a bomb through the open door of Kate O'Shaughnessy's pub at 18 Market Street, Ennis. A party of military and police were inside, along with some civilians. Sergeant Rue, a 35-year-old soldier from London and a member of the Royal Scots Regiment, was killed; Constable Vanderbrugh was injured. O'Shaughnessy was wounded in the leg, and Mrs Danaher, a native of Ennis who was visiting from Limerick, had several minor injuries. The attack on Kate O'Shaughnessy's pub marked a new departure in the war. In any war, there are always innocent victims, but under standard rules of warfare, civilians are not deliberately targeted. This attack, in which Volunteers threw a Mills bomb and fired indiscriminately into the pub, was more akin to a terrorist-style outrage.

Peadar O'Loughlin, vice-commandant of the Mid-Clare Brigade, explained why and how this attack was carried out:

> All publicans were warned about serving drinks to enemy forces. The Black and Tans were received with a 'Cead Mile Failte' at O'Shaughnessy's, and also their lady friends. The IRA decided to attack and to kill as many as possible of the occupants. A party of eight or nine men attacked the pub at 10 pm on 16 April, under Paddy Con McMahon, with Aimee Barron, Jim Quin, Frank Butler, Joe Frawley, Paddy McCormack, Jack O'Grady and Peadar O'Loughlin, all armed with revolvers. Paddy 'Con', knocked at the door and as soon as it was opened, he hurled a Mills bomb into the bar, and the rest of us fired our revolvers. Sgt. Rew was killed, Constable Vanderburgh, Mrs Danaher, and Miss O'Shaughnessy were wounded.

At the quarter sessions in Ennis, Judge Bodkin awarded Kate O'Shaughnessy a sum of £1,317 as compensation for damage to her property; Sergeant Rue's fiancée, Miss Montgomery, was allowed £600.[317]

There were official reprisals in Ennis on Tuesday, 19 April. Around 2 p.m. many soldiers arrived at the home of Pat Considine, an Ennis urban councillor living in the turnpike area, and the contents of his home were burnt. That same night, the furniture in the Old Ground Hotel was taken out to the lawn and burnt, and the windows were smashed. The Clare Hotel on Upper O'Connell Street, belonging to Jane McNamara, was similarly wrecked; all the windows were smashed and the furniture was burnt. Both the Old Ground Hotel and the Clare Hotel were well-known Sinn Féin establishments. T.V. Honan's public house, on the town square at the junction of Brewer's Lane and Abbey Street, was visited next. He was chairman of Ennis Urban District Council and prominent in Sinn Féin. Honan was a widower with six children, and he was in hospital at the time of the killing of Sergeant Rue. The furniture was taken out and burnt, and four bombs were exploded around 7 p.m.; two more bombs totally destroyed the house, and several nearby houses were damaged. In addition to these reprisals, a curfew was imposed on the people of Ennis between 10 p.m. and 5 a.m.; the order was signed by Colonel H.E.P. Nash on 17 April, after the attack on O'Shaughnessy's pub.

The day after the slew of reprisals, on Wednesday, 20 April, the IRA retaliated by burning Mill View House, the residence of H.B. Mills, a leading loyalist in the town. He was the manager of Bannatyne's Mills. The house was burnt at about 9.15 p.m. Mrs Mills was accosted by four armed and masked men, who told her to remove the furniture because the house was to be burnt. Six tins of petrol were freely poured about the house. Most of the furniture was saved, but the police and military could not save the building. Ironically, H.B. Mills was only a tenant in the house; it belonged to the mill owners, Messrs Bannatyne. This was the first occasion in which the IRA retaliated in kind to the reprisal burning of a Sinn Féin supporter's house. Peter O'Loughlin regarded Mills as 'an Orange bigot, who detested Sinn Féin'.

That same night, an attempt was made to burn Westbourne, the home of Bishop Fogarty. The *Saturday Record* reported:

> At 11.15 pm, Miss Murray the housekeeper noticed a blaze through the windows, the front door was ablaze, and a petrol-saturated cloth was pushed through the letter box. Col. Swinton of the Royal Scots saw the blaze and rushed to help put it out. It is stated that five men were seen running from the scene.

It was assumed and widely believed then that the 'anti-Sinn Féin gang' were behind this arson at Westbourne. Bishop Fogarty appealed that there should be no retaliation for this outrage; he appealed for Christian restraint, 'I have been a sufferer myself, no one should be moved to retaliation for the attempted burning of my house, any such criminal madness would pain me.' In reply to a question in the House of Commons regarding the reprisals in Ennis, Chief Secretary Sir

Hamar Greenwood stated, 'the premises of Mr Honan and Mr Considine were selected for destruction, as the owners were known to be among the chief organisers of rebel activity in Ennis.'

One prominent member of the local Protestant and unionist community in Clare, Richard J. Stacpoole, DL, of Eden Vale, wrote a letter to Bishop Fogarty sympathising with him over the outrage:

> Dear Dr Fogarty, I was extremely sorry to hear of the outrage committed on you and write to offer you my very sincere sympathy [...] anybody with a sense of right and moderation must condemn these reprisals as they never turn wrong into right and only lead to bitterness and vengefulness. Personally, I have always condemned them and I would like you to know that, being aware of the efforts that have been made during the past two days to bring about a truce in Ennis and terminate the terrorism from which people have suffered. I shall only be too glad to do anything in my power to further this object [...] Please do not reply, I write simply to express my sympathy and condemn an outrage which everyone should deplore.

Another prominent Clare unionist who condemned the official reprisals was George O'Callaghan Westropp of Lismehane, Tulla, who was ostracised by his former unionist and loyalist supporters. Writing to one correspondent, he stated, 'The Crown forces were running wild and the shame of their behaviour just breaks my heart. Our men, that is the shame of it, were recruiting for Sinn Féin by their crimes and creating bitterness, which is the main cause of a difficulty in making a permanent settlement.' Some of this bitterness was vented on O'Callaghan Westropp in January 1921, when fires were lit in his cattle shed and hay barns. A warning was posted on the gamekeeper's door, 'Notice to O'Callaghan Westropp, commonly known as Mouse Trap. Our society has its eye on you, you are a double dealer and a twister. One more of your ruddy speeches or letters and you are doomed. There is no fool like an old fool. So beware, be wise. Anti Sinn Féin Gang.' In a letter to W.T. Cosgrave in December 1922, O'Callaghan Westropp wrote, 'Up to 1914, I was a unionist and a Die-Hard until I withdrew from party politics and got myself loathed by my former associates [...] and worse still when as a law and order man I condemned the unauthorised reprisals of 1920–1921, their hatred grew.'[318]

More killings

Two marines were killed in an ambush as they were proceeding to Ballyvaughan Post Office from the coastguard station just outside the village on the New Quay side. The ambush took place at about 10.30 a.m. on Friday, 20 April; a party of about twenty men, armed with rifles, shotguns and revolvers, fired on a party of marines. Before the assault, the telegraph wires were cut. The ambush party had stayed in the Corkscrew Hill area the night before the attack, and the marines were fired on from houses on both sides of the street. The attackers escaped with the weapons of the two dead marines – Private H. Chandler, 24 years old, from Kent, and Private J.J.R. Bolton, 19 years old, from Yarmouth – and the guns of two other marines who were badly wounded. After the ambush, 'there was wild alarm in the village and district all day as the people were expecting reprisals.' There were reprisals a few days later near Ballyvaughan, but no house in the village was burnt. On Sunday morning, some lorries appeared and burnt the house of Michael Kenny, who lived about a mile from the village; then they burnt the house of James Keane, and the house of Mr O'Donoghue of Auhhagliny about 2 miles from the village.[319]

While two off-duty policemen, Constable Budd and Constable Irvine, were cycling from Ennis to Kildysart on 26 May, they were attacked by six armed men from the 2nd Battalion, Mid-Clare Brigade, and Constable Budd was shot dead. Constable Irvine was chased across fields for about an hour; he was hotly pursued by the men, who fired at and wounded him at Cooga near Kildysart, but he escaped. In Kildysart, as reprisals for the killing of Constable Budd, three properties in the Kildysart district were damaged. The military visited the house of Mrs McNamara of Arnagla and burnt it. The house of Mr Cusack at Paradise was also burnt down, and the furniture of Mr Clancy from Glencunnane was also burnt.[320]

On 28 June there was an East Clare Brigade ambush on a military patrol – one officer and ten men – at Fortane Cross in the Tulla district. The officer was killed and three soldiers were wounded. Lieutenant Warren, of the Oxford and Buckinghamshire Light Infantry Battalion, was shot at about 2.30 a.m. and died from his injuries. Joe Clancy recalled that Lieutenant Warren was shot by

Mattie McGrath, commandant of the Feakle Battalion. In his report of this ambush, Michael Brennan stated with regard to Lieutenant Warren, 'I might add that on several occasions he, acted like a brute to unarmed civilians.'[321]

Two policemen were attacked at Roadford near Doolin on Friday, 8 July by members of the Mid-Clare Brigade. After they had finished bathing in Doolin, a party of men surprised them, stole their revolvers and shot them. Constable Hewitt, a Black and Tan, was shot dead and Constable Massey was badly wounded in the head. The police were in plain clothes, but they were armed with revolvers; they had cycled to Roadford and they were ambushed there. The revolvers were taken by the IRA. Perhaps because the attack occurred three days before the truce, the Crown forces did not carry out reprisals.

On the same day, another Black and Tan named Constable Needham was shot dead. Needham, who was from London and based in Tiermaclane barracks, was shot on O'Connell Street in Ennis by men from the Mid-Clare Brigade. He was on leave, and while talking to a Miss Corry from Tiermaclane, he was approached by two men who fired several shots over the girl's shoulders. He was hit by two bullets; one of them grazed his throat, the other hit him in the abdomen. He was brought to the county infirmary, where he died on Saturday, 9 July. The *Saturday Record* reported that

> A large force of Royal Scots Battalion took part in the funeral parade to the Railway station at Ennis, the band of the Royal Scots played the Dead March and the Last Post was sounded. A guard of honour from police at Clarecastle, Tiermaclane and Ennis escorted the remains to Ennis Station, with floral tributes from the RIC, Ennis, the Black and Tans and the Transport Division.

Constable Needham was the last member of the Crown forces to be killed in Clare before the truce on 11 July.[322]

Besides the police casualties that occurred in Clare, at least three Clare-born RIC men were killed this year before the truce in July. The first of these was Constable J. O'Regan, who was killed following an ambush in Ballinrobe, Co. Mayo. The Ennis-born RIC man, who was 25 years old, was killed on 3 May 1921. He was buried at Drumcliffe following a military funeral. The second Clare man killed was Sergeant Jeremiah Moroney, a native of Tulla who was shot and seriously wounded on 28 May; he died of his wounds in Limerick on Saturday, 4 June. He had 25 years' service and left a widow and a large family; he was interred in Tulla. The third Clare-born policeman to be killed was Constable James King, 'born in County Clare', who was killed in Roscommon on 11 July 1921, the day of the truce. He was probably one of the last RIC victims of the War of Independence.[323]

Mid-Clare diary of operations, March–June 1921

Following criticism from the chief of staff, General Richard Mulcahy, Frank Barrett, commandant of the Mid-Clare Brigade, sent a monthly diary of operations in his brigade area to GHQ. A synopsis of these diaries, which were sent between March and June, gives us a very good insight into the activities of this brigade towards the end of the conflict. According to these diaries, the Volunteers were inactive on thirty-two days between March and June; they set up ambushes on forty-seven occasions, but the enemy did not show up on most of them; they engaged with the enemy on fifteen occasions; they spent twenty-five days trenching or barricading roads; and they raided post offices on sixteen occasions and carried out three reprisals by burning houses. In these reports, Barrett claimed that the Volunteers killed a total of fourteen members of the Crown forces (four RIC members, eight marines and two soldiers). However, the actual number of enemy casualties in the Mid-Clare area during these four months was six (two RIC members, two marines and two soldiers). Frank Barrett also included separate diaries which consisted of the activities of the Crown forces for these four months. The information gathered by the IRA suggests that the British forces were inactive on thirty-six days, the combined police and military forces carried out searches on thirty-five occasions, and they rounded up civilians to repair roads on twenty-three occasions.

In his July report, after the truce, County Inspector Attridge noted, 'Since the Truce, the county has been in a comparatively quiet condition. Previous to that date, there was, evidently, an intention to murder as many police and the Crown forces as possible before the Truce came on.' There may have been truth in this statement, as Frank Barrett had issued orders in March 1921 'to attack the enemy everywhere at all times [...] armed or unarmed, on duty or off duty, he is not to be allowed to escape.' However, Michael Brennan stated that he was only informed of the impending truce on 9–10 July. Ernie O'Malley corroborates Brennan's statement, saying that he was informed by GHQ on 9 July that operations against the enemy were to cease at noon on Monday, 11 July. Historian Pádraig Óg Ó Ruairc, in a comprehensive analysis, refutes the county inspector's statement.[324]

Jailing of Catholic priests

While several Catholic clergy – such as Canon Hannon, the parish priest of Miltown Malbay; Fr Hayes, parish priest of Feakle; Fr A.J. Nestor, parish priest of Ennistymon; and Dean McInerney, parish priest of Kilrush – severely denounced IRA atrocities, other Catholic clergy were quite active in Sinn Féin and supportive of the IRA. Members of flying columns were sheltered in their homes, and some priests gave spiritual guidance and sacraments to IRA men before they went into ambushes. In 1921 five priests from the diocese of Killaloe were arrested and charged with possession of arms or with having seditious documents in their possession. The police suspected that the church authorities were harbouring men 'on the run'; St Flannnan's College was raided several times, and St Senan's College, Cahercon, a seminary for the Maynooth Mission to China, was also searched by Crown forces in late February. In 1921, three Catholic priests received prison sentences of up to six months for possession of illegal documents.

Andrew O'Donoghue mentioned in his witness statement that at the end of March or early April, the Auxiliaries came to Corofin and Frank Barrett planned to attack them in an ambush at Toonagh. O'Donoghue stated that before the planned ambush, the Volunteers received spiritual assistance, 'We assembled together between seventy and eighty men, nearly all with rifles. They were billeted at Kilfenora for the night and while there they received general absolution from Fr Hamilton of St Flannan's College before they marched off to the ambush site at Toonagh.'[325]

On Thursday, 6 January at 1 a.m., two priests, Fr James Greed and Fr P. Spain, were arrested in Killaloe. They were conveyed to Limerick and were tried by court-martial on Friday, 7 January. They were accused of having two sporting guns, some cartridges and a revolver, which were found in their home, along with a mass of documents. Fr Greed was declared not guilty, but Fr Spain was found guilty of having cartridges and fined £1; if he defaulted on this fine, he would have to spend one day in jail. Fr Spain paid the fine, which, according to Fr Gaynor, annoyed Bishop Fogarty.

Two prominent Sinn Féin clergymen, Fr M. McKenna and Fr P. Gaynor, both of whom were Catholic curates in Mullagh, were arrested on the morning of Friday, 1 April in Mullagh. Their house had been raided several times during 1920, and prominent IRA men such as Ignatius O'Neill had often stayed overnight; O'Neill was sheltered there for several weeks while recuperating from injuries following the Rineen ambush. In Limerick, the two priests appeared before a military court and were charged with having documents in their house on 1 April, 'the publication of which was likely to cause disaffection'. For example, one was a Sinn Féin document refusing to recognise the British government and recognising the Irish Republic, and there were other documents relating to Dáil Éireann. The accused priests refused to recognise the court. Fr McKenna said that the soldiers who arrested him were drunk and took up the sacred vessels disrespectfully. The priests were called 'murderers' and accused of being connected with the murder of Constable Moore in Miltown Malbay. Fr McKenna added, 'shots were fired over my head and I was struck with the butt of a rifle.' Fr Gaynor said that evidence was planted in the house, 'we were driven to Miltown and shown the dead body of a policeman and petty tyrannies were committed by the police and military.' The priests were found guilty, and both were sentenced to six months' imprisonment. They were released from Limerick Prison in October, after six months in jail.[326]

The last Sinn Féin priest to be arrested was Canon William O'Kennedy, President of St Flannan's College in Ennis. He was sent to Limerick on Wednesday, 6 July. His arrest led to a protest by his bishop, Dr Fogarty, 'His arrest during the annual retreat and Mass was uncalled for, a shameful outrage on religion and a lamentable exhibition of arbitrary rule.' Incidentally, Canon O'Kennedy was receiving communications from Michael Collins between February and May 1921. The letters to Canon O'Kennedy were delivered via the Mid-Clare Brigade. Canon O'Kennedy was sentenced to six months' jail and spent most of his incarceration at Spike Island in Cork Harbour. He was not released until after the treaty was signed; the date of his release was 10 December 1921.[327]

Hair cropping

Another new departure in the war occurred in a shocking reprisal against a woman in Kilmihil. Delia Browne, a 24-year-old dressmaker, lived in the village of Kilmihil. In the early morning of 25 January, her hair was cut off and she was handled violently by a gang of Black and Tans. A gang of eight or ten masked men entered her house and assaulted her. One masked man threatened her with a revolver, pointing it at her while another cut her hair with a scissors. They demanded money from her and threatened to burn the place. On leaving, they put a notice on the door, 'Anti-Sinn Féin gang; beware; your doom is sealed.' According to the police report, 'the motive for this attack was that the hair was cut off two other girls in same locality by the IRA and this, I am sure, was a reprisal as these two girls were on friendly terms with the RIC.' In reply to a question about this assault in the House of Commons, Mitchell Henry, MP, stated that there was a previous complaint – that Delia Browne earned between four and five pounds a week. But after this assault, she had to live with her father and she lost her business. Judge Bodkin awarded her £400 in compensation.[328]

IRA executions

In April the *Clare Champion* carried a report of the death of an alleged spy in Newmarket-on-Fergus under the headline, 'Spy executed by the IRA. We are getting them at last. Beware!' The second Clare civilian executed by the IRA for alleged spying, after Martin Counihan, was an ex-soldier living in Newmarket-on-Fergus. On 21 April 1921, John Reilly was executed in Newmarket-on-Fergus. He was found guilty of spying on the IRA. His death was mentioned in local papers, IRA witness statements and police reports. His 'treachery' was accidentally discovered among some letters intercepted by the IRA after a raid on a mail train. Following his 'trial', he was summarily executed after receiving spiritual assistance from the local curate.

The local papers briefly mentioned his tragic death:

> On 20 April John Reilly, an ex-soldier, was killed at Newmarket-on-Fergus. A card was attached to his body suggesting that he was a spy [...] Mrs O'Reilly stated that about 11 pm there was a knock at door by men claiming to be police. Six masked and armed men entered. Her husband was told to dress and bring some holy water. She was told that they would not harm him.

A second account gave a little more detail:

> Terrible Occurrence in Newmarket [...] Spy Shot Dead – John Reilly, an ex-soldier, 40 years old, 12 years in Royal Garrison Artillery, who served in the war, was discharged in 1919 on a pension of 10s. a week [...] He was working as a labourer in the Newmarket area for Lord Inchiquin and others [...] He was shot early on the morning of 21 April [...] he was blindfolded with a handkerchief [...] a notice was pinned to the shoulder of his suit: 'Spy, executed by the Irish Republican Army. We are getting them at last. Beware.' His widow was awarded £1,200 compensation.[329]

Three IRA men mentioned the execution of John Reilly in their witness statements. Seamus Connolly, of Cullinagh, Ennistymon, outlines how Reilly was discovered through the interception of a letter in the robbery of a mail train. Connolly was sympathetic to Reilly's fate and indeed stated his belief that Reilly was innocent – that he had been falsely accused by the real traitor, a postman:

> While holding up a train we discovered a letter addressed to John Reilly from the RIC. The contents suggested that O'Reilly was a spy. O'Reilly was tried by court martial and sentenced to death, I believe that he was innocent and that he was a victim of an unscrupulous villain who was employed as a postman, who was the actual spy. He used O'Reilly's name to shield his identity.[330]

Sean Murnane, from Stonehall, Newmarket-on-Fergus, who was commandant of the 1st Battalion, East Clare Brigade, briefly mentioned the execution of John Reilly in his witness statement, but strangely, given his rank in the battalion, he denied any knowledge of the circumstances leading to his death:

> Although I was OC of 1st Battalion I am not able to give details of the facts relating to the execution of Jim [*sic*] Reilly, Newmarket-on-Fergus, as a spy on 23/4/'21. The event happened when I was out of the district with the East Clare Volunteers who went to Kilrush. I do remember though that he was said to have been associated with the deaths of two volunteers in Galway named Loughnane. I also know that he was a man who mixed a good deal with the RIC.[331]

John Quinn, from Lemanagh, Newmarket-on-Fergus who was the adjutant of the 1st Battalion, East Clare Brigade, gave a detailed account of the execution of John Reilly:

> Before departing for west Clare Michael Brennan gave orders to Pat Reidy the adjutant of the First Battalion of the East Clare Brigade to execute John Reilly, an ex-British soldier living in Newmarket on Fergus. Reilly allegedly drank a good deal and had apparently ignored repeated warnings from the IRA to stop associating with Black and Tans and the RIC in local pubs. He came to the IRA's attention again after the murder of the Loughnane brothers in Gort on 6 December 1920. Both the murdered men's father and the IRA strongly suspected that Reilly had supplied the British with information that led to their capture and murder. This was confirmed when a letter bearing Reilly's name was found addressed to the RIC giving information about the IRA during a raid on the Limerick to Ennis train at Cratloe station.
>
> The day after receiving Michael Brennan's order to execute Reilly, Pat Reidy notified fifteen local IRA Volunteers to report for duty outside Newmarket at 9 a.m. and had Reilly's movements monitored during the day. James Quinn was one of the Volunteers who arrested John Reilly at 11 p.m. Reilly was taken under guard about a mile out the Ballycar Road and led into a by-road which runs to Monafola. About 300 yards or so down the by-road Fr William Kennedy, CC Newmarket-on-Fergus, was waiting to hear the prisoner's confession. Guards were posted around the spot while he was receiving spiritual attention which lasted fifteen or twenty minutes. When this was over a bandage was placed over the prisoner's eyes and he was ordered on his knees. The firing party, which so far as I can

> remember were all armed with revolvers, consisted of Jack Brennan, Clonmoney, Florence O'Neill, Rathfoland and myself. We stood about three yards away from our target and on orders from Paddy Maher, I think, we fired about three rounds per man. Reilly fell back dead and he was then anointed by the priest who witnessed the execution. A label bearing the words, 'Spy. Executed by the IRA' was then tied on his body which was left on the spot where he was shot until it was removed next day by the RIC and the Tans.

Michael Brennan did not mention, either in his witness statement or his memoir, the execution of John Reilly and Martin Counihan, the two spies shot dead in the East Clare Brigade area during the War of Independence. He did, however, correspond with the chief of staff, Richard Mulcahy, in April 1921 on the topic of women spies, and he sought advice on how to deal with them:

> Will you please instruct me as to what action I am to take towards women spies. I have one notoriously bad case in which the girl concerned has defied the Volunteers when she was warned, and another of a girl who has applied for a job as a woman searcher. There are also some notoriously bad cases of women associating with the enemy. Will I take action against these, or will I issue a public warning, (we have no proof of their giving information, only suspicion).

In reply, Richard Mulcahy stated:

> Let me have a statement of the circumstances of the women so charged. A copy of the summary of evidence which has been alleged against them and a note as to various ways in which from your knowledge of their circumstances, they can be punished. In one case of the kind formal authority has been given for the destruction of property belonging to a person so convicted.

Brennan, in his correspondence with the adjutant general at GHQ, Gearóid O'Sullivan, made some observations about the people of Killaloe, 'I find it impossible to get any information out of this town as all the inhabitants according to my information are dangerous and any man going in there from outside is liable to be arrested.' On another occasion, he wrote, 'The postmaster of Killaloe, Mr White has friends in Dublin […] he is a dangerous man.'[332]

'I forgive ye boys, ye are shooting me in the wrong.'

The third civilian executed by the IRA in Clare was Patrick Darcy, a 27-year-old teacher from Cooraclare. On 16 June 1921, he was shot dead on the street in Doonbeg by an IRA execution squad from the West Clare Brigade. He was accused of 'taking blood money' for betraying Michael McNamara and William Shanahan, IRA Volunteers from the parish of Doonbeg who were captured and murdered by British forces in late December 1920. Two of Patrick Darcy's brothers were in the IRA, and one of them, Michael, had drowned during an ambush in Cooraclare. His other brother, Jack, took the anti-Treaty side during the civil war yet to happen. Patrick Darcy was an assistant teacher in Doonbeg National School alongside Padraig Ashe, a cousin of Thomas Ashe, who had died on hunger strike in September 1917. The trial and execution of Patrick Darcy was controversial, and several inquiries were made over the years to establish his innocence or guilt.[333]

On 25 June the local newspapers carried the following headline, 'West Clare Sensation – a National Teacher was shot dead. Patrick Darcy about 27, who taught in Doonbeg.' The official report issued by the police stated:

> At 3 pm on Saturday 18 June 1920, a party of police found the dead body of Patrick Darcy a school teacher of Doonbeg, aged 27. Darcy had disappeared from his home at Cooraclare on Thursday night. A label bearing the words: 'Sooner or later we get them. Spy. Tried, convicted and executed by the IRA', was found on his body.'

About four months later, Patrick Darcy's mother sought compensation in the courts for the death of her son. The heading on the *Saturday Record* read, 'Mysterious death at Doonbeg'. In her application, Darcy's mother said that her son had a salary of £217 a year and earned a further £40 for teaching Irish. She had a farm of 13 acres. She stated that on 15 June five or six armed and masked men came to her house and they took away her son. She asked them what they wanted him for, and they replied that 'he took blood money'. The next she heard of him was when his dead body was found 3 miles from her house the following morning. She stated that she did not know any of the masked men. She denied that her son 'took blood money'. She said that a label was pinned to his body with the words, 'Spies Beware'. Judge Bodkin called it 'cold-blooded deliberate murder'. He awarded £600 to Darcy's mother and £100 to her daughter, who was training to be a teacher.[334]

These were the 'facts' of the case as reported in the local papers at the time. The witness statements of a couple of Volunteers throw further light on the execution of Patrick Darcy. Three West Clare IRA men, Martin Chambers, Bill Haugh and Michael Russell, gave statements relating to the execution of Patrick Darcy. Martin Chambers briefly mentioned the fact of the execution but gave little other information. Bill Haugh, who in the opinion of Michael Russell was centrally involved in the case, only made vague references to the execution of two spies in west Clare without naming either of them. On the other hand, the testimony of Michael Russell gives a comprehensive description of Patrick Darcy's trial and execution.

The following is Martin Chambers's account:

> Arrest of Willie Shanahan and Michael McNamara by Tans between 1am and 2am in Denis Reidy's house at Newtown, Doonbeg on 17 December. They were taken to Kilrush till 22 December then removed to Ennis. McNamara was bayonetted through the heart and Shanahan was shot dead in his cell at Ennis. Subsequently, a man named Patrick Darcy, a national teacher in Doonbeg was executed as a spy in June 1921 [...] I have no information to give concerning the guilt or innocence of Darcy, nor was I in any way connected with his execution.[335]

Bill Haugh's cryptic evidence suggests that the second enemy agent was Patrick Darcy, who, in his opinion, betrayed Shanahan and McNamara of Doonbeg:

> Michael McNamara and William Shanahan were betrayed and captured in Doonbeg on 13 December. While being brought to Ennis, McNamara was ordered out of the truck at Darragh and shot dead; Shanahan was shot dead in Ennis prison [...] Spy in the area! Towards the end of this month [December] the first enemy agent was executed in the area. To him was traced the betrayal of the second Burrane effort, also that of the Sinn Féin Court at Clohanes. Being closely related to some Volunteer officers, the execution was unofficial! [...] The NCO of Kilrush

> slipped information regarding the second enemy agent, to him was traced the betrayal of Shanahan and McNamara. He was executed, a brother of the scout drowned. The murder of this agent nullified enemy intelligence in the whole area.

Bill Haugh, acting as adjutant of the West Clare Brigade, justified the execution in a brief report sent to the adjutant general, Gearóid O'Sullivan, 'A publican named Sheehan of Kilrush was kidnapped. On statements taken from him under oath there was sufficient evidence for the execution of Patrick Darcy NT, Doonbeg as a spy.'[336]

To digress briefly, Ó Ruairc suggests that 'the first enemy agent executed' mentioned by Bill Haugh might have been Joe Greene, 'Though Haugh does not identify "the first enemy agent", he might be referring to Joe Greene of Toonavoher, who was shot by the IRA on 3 January 1921.' Ó Ruairc asks, 'was Greene killed for spying or was he murdered over some agrarian dispute?' However, County Inspector Attridge noted in February 1921, 'A man named Joseph Greene was murdered by Sinn Féin on 3 January, the reason given is that Greene did not obey litigation of the Sinn Féin court.' Historian Eoin Shanahan states that there were allegations that Greene was a spy, but he also mentions a land dispute and that Greene was shot by the IRA on Monday, 3 January 1921.

Another man murdered in west Clare in suspicious circumstances around this time was Thomas Shannon of Moyasta, who was killed on 13 March 1921. Attridge stated in his March report that Thomas Shannon was murdered at 10 p.m. on 13 March by unknown men. Attridge implied that members of Sinn Féin had killed him. He alleged that the motive for the killing was that 'Thomas Shannon had been a Sinn Féin magistrate and that some time previous to his being shot he had abandoned the organisation and condemned the shooting of police – hence the motive.' However, Shane Cahill, a historian, denounces the subsequent inquiry report into Thomas Shannon's death as 'black propaganda by the British' and asserts that Thomas Shannon's death was caused by Crown forces. This opinion is supported by Eoin Shanahan, who states, 'While it is not possible at this time to determine who was responsible for the shooting of Tom Shannon, there is little doubt that he was shot by British forces.'[337]

Michael Russell, a former battalion officer from Cree, gave a detailed account of the arrest, trial and execution of Patrick Darcy:

> Execution of Patrick Darcy a spy, a native of Cooraclare, a teacher at Doonbeg, aged 28/29 years. Two of his brothers were in the IRA. For a period, he was friendly with the brigade OC, Sean Liddy. During 1920 he was noticed frequenting Sheehan's Pub in Kilrush. He [Sheehan] was an ex-RIC man. The pub was a haunt of RIC and Black and Tans in Kilrush [...] information was being given to the British [...] any man known to be friendly with RIC or Military was regarded by the local IRA as dangerous and as a potential spy.
>
> As the year 1921 wore, Darcy's name was a by-word among all the IRA in West Clare as a British spy! He continued to frequent Sheehan's pub and to mix in the company of enemy forces. He also drank more. In the middle of June 1921 Sheehan was arrested while visiting a farm he held in Kilmihil. He was apprehended by the IRA led by Brigade OC Sean Liddy, along with Tom Martin, Myself, Tom Marrinan, Michael Melican and James Fitzmaurice. Sheehan, when accused of being a spy, denied it strongly and when threatened with execution said: 'It was not me who gave the information about Shanahan and McNamara, but it was Pa Darcy who gave it to the police in my house.' Sheehan was then released and went on his pony and trap to Kilrush.
>
> That night myself, Tom McNamara, James Fitzmaurice, Michael Cunningham, Michael Reidy and John Golden were sent to Darcy's house in Cooraclare to arrest him but he was absent, he had gone to see his brother Jack Darcy in Ennis. We called again and arrested him as he was leaving by the back door. I told him that Bill Haugh wanted to meet him. His reply was: 'What would Bill Haugh or anyone else want with me?' We met Bill Haugh near Cooraclare. In Cree, the brigade staff were holding a court-martial on Darcy in an outhouse owned by Tim O'Donnell. There was a guard of IRA men around the village. Half an hour later, Darcy and the members of the court were out of the building. The court consisted of Sean Liddy, OC, Bill Haugh, Conor Whelan, Tom Marrinan and Tom Martin.
>
> Darcy told John Cunningham that he was going to be shot and I was asked to intercede with Sean Liddy. We both went to Liddy and suggested before doing anything to Darcy, that he should be confronted with Sheehan the Kilrush publican. I felt

> that Sheehan was as much guilty as Darcy and that the latter, when confronted with Sheehan, might incriminate him also, and that between the pair of them a lot of useful information might be obtained. We volunteered to go to Kilrush and arrest Sheehan, but Sean Liddy told us he was finished with the case.
>
> Patrick Darcy was now in the hands of Bill Haugh. Haugh asked me if I had a bike, a whistle, and a gun [...] 'you are to be our number one scout in Doonbeg. Go to McNamara's house in Doonbeg.' The IRA party and the prisoner arrived in Doonbeg. The local parish priest, Fr McNamara, was asked to come and give spiritual aid to the prisoner. Fr McNamara did not come but sent word to carry on 'as the prisoner was all right.'
>
> Darcy was tied and blindfolded and was about to be shot in front of McNamara's house when the local company police officer said it would be unfair to shoot Darcy outside McNamara's house, which would have their home destroyed as a reprisal. The prisoner was marched to the other end of the village, blindfolded and tied. He was shot by a firing party of two members, Bill Haugh and Tom Marrinan. I heard Darcy say as he was being blindfolded: 'I forgive ye boys, ye are shooting me in the wrong.' After being shot, a label was pinned to the dead man's breast: 'Spies beware'. The body was left on the street. British troops came next day and brought the body to Kilrush. Widespread raids followed, but no one was arrested.

If the veracity of Russell's account is accepted, then it does raise a few questions as to the fairness of the 'trial', the kangaroo court, held in Cree, and the role of Michael Sheehan in the matter. Russell rightly suggested that both Darcy and Sheehan should have been questioned together, because Sheehan had named Darcy as the spy. Secondly, Patrick Darcy maintained his innocence to the end. Thirdly, it does seem remarkable that the local parish priest, when requested to give spiritual assistance to the condemned man, had, according to Michael Russell, declined to do so and told the IRA men to carry on 'as the prisoner was all right'. Does this mean that the parish priest agreed with the execution of the unfortunate Patrick Darcy? At the court of inquiry into the death of Patrick Darcy, his brother Martin stated that Patrick had gone to a priest, Fr Hehir, to ask his advice after Martin had told Patrick that several masked men had called to the Darcy home looking for him and accusing him of betraying Shanahan and McNamara. Martin stated that his brother Patrick denied this charge. On returning from the priest's house, he was arrested by the masked men and taken away.

Joe Barrett, adjutant of the Mid-Clare Brigade, wrote in a statement on 8 June 1947 that he believed that Patrick Darcy was innocent. He wrote that late in July 1921, General Eoin O'Duffy, the IRA deputy chief of staff, held an IRA inquiry at the courthouse in Ennis; the inquiry sought to address a number of matters that were causing controversy at the time, one of which was the shooting of Patrick Darcy. Barrett also recorded that Darcy, on hearing a rumour that his brother John had been killed in an ambush in Darragh in June 1921, travelled to Ennis by train to enquire of Major Kershaw, a British intelligence officer, where his brother's body was. Barrett noted that Patrick Darcy did not meet Major Kershaw but met Sylvester Barrett, Barrett's father, who informed Darcy that his brother John had not been shot. However, Darcy's enquiry at Ennis railway station about the whereabouts of Major Kershaw aroused suspicions among the IRA and was reported back to west Clare. This report may have sealed Darcy's doom.

Barrett stated that he had some confidential discussions with Francis William Gore Hickman, a solicitor based in Ennis who was a legal advisor to the British Army Southern Command during the years 1918–21. Barrett recalled that during a confidential discussion with Gore Hickman sometime in 1931–3, Gore Hickman informed him that Patrick Darcy was not a British spy and that it was very hard on his family to have him shot despite his innocence. Gore Hickman also told Barrett of his willingness to do his part to prove Darcy's innocence. Barrett informed the Darcy family of what Gore Hickman had to say.

Patrick Darcy's sister, Mary Daly, applied for a military pension in 1947 for her brother Patrick's IRA service. During a lengthy inquiry into this case, Sean Liddy, the former commandant of the West Clare Brigade, and other IRA men gave evidence. The intelligence officer of the West Clare Brigade stated that Patrick Darcy was not guilty of any connection with the British, while others questioned the fairness of the trial of Patrick Darcy. However, Sean Liddy still asserted that Patrick Darcy was a spy and deserved to be shot. The British War Office issued a statement on 31 July 1947 stating, 'It can be stated definitely that the above named [Patrick J. Darcy] is unknown to the department and has never acted as an agent or in any other capacity, on our behalf.'

Patrick Shanahan, a brother of Willie Shanahan, who was murdered by the British army in December 1920 and who Darcy was accused of betraying, stated in 1955, 'We have never believed that the man who was shot was guilty of spying and we have never been supplied with any information to connect him with it, although it was asked for.' Other members of the Shanahan family conveyed this strong belief to the Darcy family. The pension application was unsuccessful, but the inquiry raised serious questions about the role of the ex-RIC man Sheehan, the allegations against Darcy, his 'trial' and the justification for his execution.

Judge Seán Enright cites a convention, *nemo morituris praesumiter mentiri* ('truth sits on the lips of men about to die'), that a declaration made under an expectation of death has been admissible in courts as evidence for centuries, because it was recognised as being credible, 'Every sentient being faced with the inevitably of death has a moment of complete honesty and the law has recognised this for centuries.' Given that Patrick Darcy was about to be shot, his last reported words, 'I forgive ye boys, ye are shooting me in the wrong', must be acceptable as credible.[338]

General election

There was a general election on 20 May, and only four Sinn Féin candidates stood for election for the four seats. Two of them, John Joe Liddy and Patrick Brennan, were members of the IRA. The *Clare Champion* described it as, 'The most uneventful parliamentary election ever held in Clare. Four candidates were returned unopposed at election in Clare on Friday, Mr de Valera, Greystones, Mr B Higgins, Carrigaholt, Mr John Joe Liddy, Danganella Cooraclare [commandant of the West Clare Brigade] and Mr Patrick Brennan, Meelick [former commandant of the Clare Brigade], were elected.' County Inspector Attridge stated that the election was undemocratic due to intimidation from the IRA:

> Owing to the reign of terror no candidate dared to contest a seat

> for the elections to the Southern Parliament, with the result that the four Sinn Féin nominees were elected – Éamon de Valera, Brian O'Higgins, John Liddy and Patrick Brennan. The two latter are reputed to be two of the principal leaders of the murder gang in the county.[339]

Raids and reprisals

On 22 June 1921, GHQ of the IRA issued an order authorising reprisals against the enemy under certain conditions:

> On every occasion in which the enemy destroys house properties the IRA are authorised to destroy a similar number of the houses of the most active enemies of Ireland as a reprisal in the battalion area where the original destruction occurred [...] For the purposes of such reprisals, no persons shall be regarded as enemies of Ireland, whether they be described locally as Unionist, Orangemen etc., unless they are actively anti-Irish in their activities [...] No house shall be selected for destruction or destroyed without the personal approval of the brigade commandant.[340]

Several Clare mansions were destroyed this year. These houses belonged to the Protestant landed class, almost all of whom, in Clare, were unionists or loyalists. It is doubtful, however, if all the houses burnt in Clare belonged to people who were 'actively anti-Irish in their activities'. Several of the houses were owned by absentee landlords or non-residents who had fled their homes out of fear after the War of Independence began.

The first Clare mansion that was wrecked in 1921 was the historic Carrigaholt Castle, which was associated with the third Viscount Clare, who fled after the Battle of the Boyne in 1690. After he forfeited the property in 1691, the land passed to the Burton family. In 1920 the castle and estate belonged to Major Guillamore O'Grady of Limerick, who did not reside in the castle. The unoccupied house was vandalised in April 1921. Incidentally, the parish priest of Carrigaholt, Fr McMahon, had negotiated for the sale of the O'Grady estate on behalf of the tenants; the estate was sold in nine lots to forty-one locals for a sum of £2,600 on Monday, 7 February 1921.[341]

Kilmore House, located in Kilmurry McMahon, belonged to

Francis William Gore Hickman; it was damaged and windows were smashed by bullets on 8 May. Compensation of £70 was allowed. Ten days later, there was an attempted arson attack on Kilmore House, but it was saved on this occasion (is was, however, burnt down during the truce negotiations). The house had also been attacked in October 1920, and the steward, Alex R. Martin, was shot and severely wounded. Shots were fired and returned, and he was hit in the back. The wires were cut and no message was sent to the police or doctors. Bill Haugh stated, 'He was a well-known assistant to the sub-sheriff of Clare and superintendent of derelict farms in Clare.' Haugh also added that Martin was shot because he opposed the decisions of the Sinn Féin courts, 'The Féin courts were openly active and functioning and decisions of the courts were accepted by the mass of the people. They were resisted by Mr Martin, steward of Mr Gore Hickman at Kilmore House. He was wounded and bundled off to his Orange House in the North.'[342]

County Inspector Attridge noted in his June report, 'The residences of five county gentlemen were destroyed by fire during the month. These gentlemen are all loyalists.' The first of these was Williamstown House, Whitegate, which was destroyed by fire on 9 June. Williamstown was described in the *Saturday Record* as 'a beautiful and well-known landmark on Lough Derg'. Williamstown House was the location where the 'Killaloe martyrs' were hiding when they were captured by the Auxiliaries in October 1920. Frances Brooke Learoyd, the owner, who lived in England at the time, submitted a claim for £50,000. The house was attacked on 9 June by a large body of men, numbering about twenty; they told the caretaker, Mr Mullins, to get out because they were going to burn the house. Everything was burnt. Judge Bodkin allowed compensation of £14,650, plus £4,812 for furniture and fittings, as well as expenses.[343]

On 10 June, Woodpark House in Scariff, the residence of Mr William Hibbert and Mrs Hibbert, was forcibly entered by a number of armed men. Mr Hibbert, a unionist, had been elected as a member of Scariff Rural District Council for some years. The land attached to the residence was a 2,000-acre demesne and 3,000 acres of other mountainy land, which was good for shooting. At 2 a.m. on 10 June, a party of men ordered the caretaker out of the house (Mr and Mrs Hibbert were in England at the time). The house was burnt by 9 a.m. The property had belonged to Mrs Hibbert; Mrs Hibbert claimed £80,000 in compensation and Mr Hibbert claimed £10,000 for personal property. He believed that he was popular in the district, as he had been elected to the local council. He stated in his claim that he employed between thirty and forty men on the estate. Judge Bodkin allowed a claim of £58,206 for the house; also, £4,919 was allowed for furniture, plus about £1,000 for other costs. He stated that it was incredible that the ratepayers of the county would have to pay for this destruction.

Ironically, in April 1920 William Hibbert had written a letter to the government predicting the destruction of the house:

> The state of the country is such that I and my family have to leave and shut up the house. I have little doubt that when we are gone, and there is a caretaker in charge of the house, it will be broken into and destroyed. Others in the same position as myself agree with me that we will find great difficulty in procuring caretakers who will undertake to look after houses which have had to be abandoned in this way.[344]

Strasburgh House, located in Inch, was burnt down on 18 June 1921. The property belonged to Richard J. Stacpoole, DL, of Eden Vale House. Stacpoole was awarded £7,000 for the burning of Strasburgh House; he was also awarded a further £350 for the burning of a cottage at Rockmount on Sunday, 10 July.[345] Fortfergus House in Ballinacally, the residence of W.H. Ball, was burnt on the night of Monday, 27 June. Ball put in a claim of £50,000 for the destruction of Fortfergus House and its contents, but Judge Bodkin awarded a sum of £21,236. Frank Barrett, as commandant of the Mid-Clare Brigade, wrote to General Richard Mulcahy and justified the destruction of both Strasburgh House and Fortfergus House:

> On 17 June I received a report from the intelligence officer, 2nd Batt. that RIC and military officers had made a very careful inspection of Strasburgh House, it has been untenanted for about two years and would be a likely place to be occupied by the enemy. Having carefully considered the circumstances I decided on the destruction which was carried out by B Coy. 2nd Batt. on 18 June [...] On 25 June a party of RIC and military officers

> inspected and measured Fortfergus House, the enemy intended to occupy the house and I gave orders for its destruction, which were carried out by E Coy. 2nd Batt. on night of 27 June.

On 5 July General Mulcahy, the IRA chief of staff, replied to Barrett, 'regarding destruction of Strasburgh House and Fortfergus, the action in both cases is fully approved.'[346]

Another Clare mansion, Hazlewood House near Quin, the residence of Mr and Mrs Gore Hickman, was burnt down at about midnight on Monday, 4 July by a party of armed men. Mrs Gore Hickman was allowed to save a few cherished articles, but all the rest was destroyed and a valuable car was also burnt. The Gore Hickmans claimed £50,000 in damages. At a court in Ennis, Judge Bodkin allowed £14,996 for destruction of the house, £1,856 for Mr Gore Hickman's personal property, £470 for damage to the car and £880 for Mrs Gore Hickman's personal property, as well as expenses.[347]

Finally, the houses of two men in the Corofin district, one belonging to Francis Nathaniel Studdert, JP, and the other to William J. Corbett, JP, were burnt on the night of Saturday, 9 July. The *Saturday Record* noted, 'Mr Corbett is a well-known and popular resident of the county and is a familiar figure on the turf, he bred many good horses at Wilbrook including a runner-up at the Ascot Cup a few years ago. It is not believed the occurrence had a political origin.' However, Frank Barrett, in a letter to Richard Mulcahy, justified the destruction of both houses, 'The houses of two men, W. Corbett, JP and Mr Studdert, Corofin, were destroyed on 9 July, as it was reported on good authority that the enemy meant to occupy them.' Subsequently, Barrett wrote to Corbett, then residing at the Queen's Hotel in Ennis, after Corbett sought a reason for the burning of his home. Barrett told him, 'your home was burnt by the IRA as a result of information received to the effect that it was to be occupied by the Auxiliary RIC.' Barrett added that 'I am sorry for the loss and inconvenience.' Corbett replied and demanded to know the source of this information. However, Barrett refused; he stated that it would expose the IRA intelligence system.[348]

Apart from the burning and destruction of these houses, there were other occasions in 1921 in which the homes of several prominent Protestants were visited or raided by armed gangs. There was a shooting outrage at Eden Vale, the residence of Richard J. Stacpoole, in March. A party of five undisguised young men came to the front of the house on the night of Sunday, 20 March demanding that three men who had recently been sacked be reinstated. Stacpoole said 'the proper time to make such a request was in daylight', then two of the party fired upon him. Stacpoole responded by firing five revolver shots, and the party fled. He reported the matter to the police. According to the police report, the motive for the visit was that Stacpoole had recently dismissed a few of his employees over the larceny of milk. However, Frank Barrett's diary of IRA activities for March 1921 briefly mentions Stacpoole as a legitimate IRA target, 'Stacpoole DL, fired at in Edenvale.'[349]

The IRA entered Lord Inchiquin's residence at Dromoland Castle on 21 May, and a number of cross cuts (saws) and eight bicycles were taken away. An official report stated that Dromoland Castle was raided by sixteen armed and masked men who took eight bicycles and a quantity of tools.[350]

The residence of Edward O'Brien at Roslevin was raided on 31 May by a number of armed and masked men, who interrupted a tennis party. During the raid, they shouted, 'Hands Up!' A shot was fired and Captain William H. Ball, DL, of Fortfergus, was slightly wounded. The house was searched for arms, as O'Brien was a well-known shooting enthusiast. Ball's car was stolen and F.N. Studdert's car was burnt. Paddy Con McMahon, one of the armed raiders, recalled, 'We told them that if we wouldn't be allowed to ride bicycles, they wouldn't be allowed to use cars. We burnt two of them and we brought away one of them.' Frank Barrett justified the raid on O'Brien's tennis party as follows:

> While we had no definite idea as to who the party would be composed of, we took it for granted that amongst the number would be a few army officers. Even in the absence of enemy officers, the party would be composed of the county aristocracy, who are certainly associates of the enemy. In short all this class, in my opinion, must be made to realise that the country is at war, and that therefore amusements like tennis cannot be indulged in by them, while the ordinary people are denied the right of even attending fairs and markets [banned in the Ennis area since 18 April].

Nineteen members of the 1st Battalion (based in the Ennis area) armed with seven rifles and twelve shotguns raided O'Brien's house, and in the raid Captain W.H. Ball was wounded while attempting to escape. The raiders searched the house and found six shotgun cartridges. They burnt only one car because 'the mechanics of the second car was new to all the engineers in the force.' Barrett added:

> some Black and Tans dressed in mufti came on the scene after the IRA departed. The Tans were quickly followed by a military party, who opened fire on the Tans thinking that they were Volunteers, and injured seven of them. The IRA party escaped via Spancilhill, and the enemy were not able to pursue them as the road was blocked by trees knocked down after the Volunteers escaped. The pursuing enemy were fired upon by the seven riflemen.

Barrett's comment on the playing of tennis at Roslevan House must be seen in the context of the fact that the county hurling and football championships had been abandoned by the GAA in September 1920 because of the War of Independence. In fact, they did not resume until early 1922, and even then the championships that year were unfinished because of the civil war; they did not properly resume until 1924, when the civil war was over.[351]

The general order from the IRA leadership in Dublin that authorised reprisals on 'enemy' houses was not issued until very late in the war, on 22 June 1921. However, the destruction of most of the Big Houses by the IRA occurred before that date. Among them were: Dondahlin House and Kiltannon House on 23 September 1920; Doolin House on 3 November 1920; Mill View House in Ennis on 20 April; Williamstown House on 9 June; Woodpark House on 10 June; and Strasburg House on 18 June 1921. Only four of the Big Houses were burnt after the official sanction from the IRA leadership: Fortfergus on 27 June; Hazelwood on 4 July; and two houses at Corofin on 9 July.

In several cases the Big Houses that were destroyed in mid-1921 were unoccupied, as their owners had fled to England in 1920; these included Williamstown House, owned by Mrs Brooke Learoyd, Woodpark House, owned by the Hibbert family, and Strasburgh House, also owned by Richard J. Stacpoole of Eden Vale. Stacpoole was a well-known sportsman in the county, the president of Ennis Golf Club and a member of the Clare Hunt. He lived in Clare at the time, in Eden Vale House, and had chaired a meeting of the Protestants of the parish of Drumcliffe on 20 September 1920 that 'condemned the outrages and reprisals taking place in Ireland and expressed a desire to live in peace and harmony with their fellow countrymen'. Stacpoole was also a prominent promoter of the County Clare Farmers Association, which sought to establish a co-operative society in Ennis for the benefit of the farmers. He sympathised with Bishop Fogarty after the attack on his home on 20 April, and he condemned reprisals. Though he was a Protestant and a unionist, there is no evidence that he was one of the 'active enemies of Ireland' in 1921. The same case can be made for Mrs Brooke Learoyd and the Hibbert family.

Although the owners of Fortfergus, Hazelwood, Strasburgh, Williamstown, Wilbrook and Woodpark were Protestant and unionist in politics, there is no evidence, so far, to indicate that they were 'active enemies of Ireland' at the time of the burnings. However, it seems that the IRA believed that the RIC, the Auxiliaries or the British army intended to use these houses as billets and that this justified their destruction.

Nevertheless, while military factors may have been the decisive factor in their destruction, given the long history of land agitation against landlords in the county, there may also have been ulterior agrarian motives for the burning of the landlords' homes. Historian David Fitzpatrick writes:

> It is difficult to disentangle the economic, political and military strands in this campaign of violence, for the same assailant was often Volunteer, Sinn Féiner, and uneconomic land-holder or landless younger son. It is certain that the separatist movement gave guns and organisation to those with agrarian grievances and that Protestants were increasingly linked by separatists with their prime military and political targets, police, army and government.

Unfortunately, the cost of the destruction was imposed on the local ratepayers, as the chief secretary for Ireland, Sir Hamar Greenwood, prophetically observed, 'It will fall upon the local ratepayers for many years!'

Helen Keane, formerly of Beech Park House, recalled in her memoir that the homes of the 'gentry' were constantly under threat from republicans:

> The rebels or Sinn Féiners […] were constantly on the search for arms and used to raid homes to snatch or steal arms, so most people put their sporting guns into the police stations. Homes of the 'gentry' or Anglo Irish as we were known were constantly under threat and in many cases set on fire. Many of our friends and neighbours left the country and sought the safety of England […] one lived from day to day, not knowing when one's house would be raided or the occupants turned out to see their home going up in flames. We escaped at Beechpark, I'm not sure why.

George O'Callaghan Westropp was a former landlord whose campaign on behalf of the Clare Farmers Association, of which he was a founding member in 1918 and the chairman in 1921, meant that he was appointed to the Committee of Agriculture by the Sinn Féin-dominated county council in June 1921. But even though he was no longer a landlord, O'Callaghan stated that his demesne farm at Lismeahane, Tulla was targeted for division by land-hungry local Volunteers in 1921.[352]

Of course, any sympathy for the owners of the Big Houses belonging to loyalists in Clare that were destroyed by the IRA (of which there were at least nine) must be balanced against compassion for the owners of more than sixty houses destroyed by the Black and Tans and Auxiliaries during the 'reign of terror'. These houses, in places such as Ballyvaughan, Ballynacally, Cooraclare, Ennis, Ennistymon, Feakle, Lahinch, Lissycasey, Miltown Malbay, Moanreel, Moyasta, O'Briensbridge and Sixmilebridge, were razed in reprisals for ambushes during the seven months between the time of the Rineen ambush in September 1920 and the killing of two marines at Ballyvaughan in April 1921. Many of these houses probably didn't belong to the IRA members who had carried out the ambushes, and therefore many innocent Irish families were wrongly punished.

The Bodkin report

Up to 1921, the ratepayers of Clare were already overburdened with debt from previous criminal injury claims – a sum of over a quarter of a million pounds. Earlier in the year, on Saturday, 5 February, Judge Bodkin, the county court judge for Clare, read a report at the Ennis assize court that he subsequently sent to the chief secretary for Ireland, Sir Hamar Greenwood. In this report, he stated that at the Hilary sessions (from January to March) 356 claims for compensation were presented, amounting to claims of over £466,000. He stated that in 139 cases it was proven that the criminal injuries were committed by the Crown forces, largely in reprisals after the Rineen ambush, and that the awards in these cases amounted to £187,046. Judge Bodkin argued that in cases where the criminal injuries were carried out by the Crown forces in reprisals, then the Treasury, not the county ratepayers, should pay the compensation. Judge Bodkin agreed with Lord Justice O'Connor, who stated that to compel the ratepayers of a district to pay compensation for criminal injuries committed by the armed forces of the government would be 'a travesty of justice'.

Judge Bodkin's report was highlighted in the House of Commons, and in a speech on 21 February 1921, the former prime minister H.H. Asquith described it as 'the gravest indictment ever presented by a judicial officer against the Executive Government in a free country.' The government, however, ignored Judge Bodkin's and Asquith's comments; on the morning of 15 April, Judge Bodkin was served with a document addressed to him by County Inspector Attridge, 'To his honour Judge Bodkin. Sir, I have been directed by the commander of the forces to prohibit courts of justice dealing with claims for compensation involving allegations against the Crown forces or police in this area.' When Judge Bodkin took his place on the bench, he observed a large armed force in the courtroom, apparently for the purpose of enforcing this prohibition. Judge Bodkin then adjourned to the next session all cases in which it was alleged that the criminal injuries were committed by the Crown forces.[353]

Death and reprieve

Another tragic incident occurred in Ennis on 24 June when a 6-year-old boy, Patrick Morrissey, was shot dead. The young boy was killed during an operation in which two IRA men disarmed two Black and

Tans who were shopping in Duggan's Boot and Shoe Shop on O'Connell Street. The IRA failed to disarm the police, who then fired at them as they ran through the streets, seriously injuring one of the attackers, Pat O'Keefe, and wounding the other, Francis Keane. Two civilians, Patrick Morrissey and Miss Hewitt, were also hit by the police's gunfire. According to an official police report:

> At 3.45 pm, on 24 June, Patrick O'Keefe and Francis Keane from Kilnamona attempted to disarm two constables, who were shopping in O'Connell Street, Ennis. Although they knocked down the policemen they failed to disarm them; the men fled through streets and the police fired at them wounding both near Cooke's Lane. Unfortunately one woman, Miss Hewitt was wounded and a boy, Patrick Morrissey aged six years was killed by the police fire. The constables arrested Keane and O'Keefe.

The wounded men were brought to the county infirmary, but they were rescued by a party of IRA men led by Paddy Con McMahon.[354]

Although the IRA did not recognise the British courts, one Clare IRA man who benefitted from an appeal to the British legal system was John Joe Egan from Ennis, who was sentenced to death for being in possession of ammunition in a martial law area. Egan was a motor engineer employed by Clare County Council; he was found to be in possession of ninety-seven rounds of revolver ammunition and five rounds of service ammunition on 26 May near Quin. In the Chancery Court, the Master of the Rolls delivered a judgement on *John J Egan* vs *General Sir Neville McCready*. He was previously sentenced to death by a court-martial on June 11 in Limerick. The Master of the Rolls allowed a writ of *habeas corpus*, and the court ruled that the penalty given had no sanction under British law. *Habeas corpus* is a legal term for a writ requiring a person under arrest to be brought before a judge or into court – especially to secure the person's release – unless lawful grounds are shown for their detention. Egan was released from Limerick prison on the morning of Monday, 1 August and taken home to Ennis.[355]

The 1st Western Division

In May, GHQ reorganised the military structures throughout Ireland. The three brigades in Clare were amalgamated with part of

Galway to create the 1st Western Division. Michael Brennan was appointed as divisional commandant. The new structure and leadership created some controversy; it was not welcomed by Frank Barrett, commandant of the Mid-Clare Brigade, and many of the other officers of that brigade. Barrett's suspension in late 1920 and General Richard Mulcahy's harsh criticism of his leadership between March and May 1921 had damaged his military prospects. Fitzpatrick notes, 'The Irish Republican army was fragmented to an astonishing degree [...] tensions and rivalries between the commandants of Mid and East Clare Brigades was unsatisfactory and there was little or no co-ordination between their forces.'

The officers from all three brigades met at a conference held in Ennis on 2 September 1921 to establish the 1st Western Division. At the conference, the deputy chief of staff General Eoin O'Duffy stated, 'At a private meeting of the Mid-Clare Brigade, Commandant Frank Barrett explained the attitude of his command towards Commandant Brennan. He said that he had no personal objection to the selection of Commandant Brennan, but that the vast majority of his command would not work under him.' The staff of the Mid-Clare Brigade unanimously decided that Michael Brennan would not be their choice for the leadership of the 1st Western Division. At the conference on 2 September, Duffy told the officers that 'Commandant Brennan was the most efficient officer in the Division and for that reason alone he was nominating him.' He added that he would hold an inquiry and if any charges of dishonourable conduct against Commandant Michael Brennan were upheld, then he would not be appointed.

Michael Brennan recalled, 'There had been a certain amount of friction for years between the staff of the Mid-Clare Brigade and East Clare, and I was directed that for the present I was not to assume control over the Mid-Clare Brigade.' One possible cause for this friction, which went back a few years, was mentioned by Brennan in his memoir; it related to a plan to secure arms in mid-1919 in a widespread attack on RIC barracks in the East Clare Brigade area. It was arranged by Brennan but countermanded by General Richard Mulcahy, 'I had no idea of how he [General Richard Mulcahy] learnt of the intended attack. I learnt later that one of my battalion commandants had told Frank Barrett, OC Mid-Clare Brigade, who had promptly sent a messenger to Dick Mulcahy with the news.'

Following the truce on 11 July 1921, Brennan went to Dublin, and while recuperating from an injury due to a car accident, he met Cathal Brugha, the minister for defence. Brennan recalled the events from the time:

> Cathal Brugha came several times and we had long talks on the organisation and army of the 1st Western Division. He was amazed when he learned that the Mid-Clare Brigade was still not formally included in the Division under my orders, as he said he had given a direction for its inclusion some time previously.
>
> I returned to Clare and attended an inquiry held in Ennis by deputy chief of staff, General Eoin O'Duffy, into the objections raised by the Mid Clare Brigadier, Frank Barrett, to the inclusion of his brigade under my command. O'Duffy found that the differences were mostly imaginary and that many of his complaints were about men who wouldn't remain in Mid-Clare and had been allowed to serve with the East Clare column. As a result of his report, the Division was completed at once and Frank Barrett was appointed my second in command, Joe Barrett was Adjutant and James Hogan, Intelligence Officer.

An inquiry into certain allegations against Michael Brennan was held at Ennis courthouse on 27 October 1921, and these charges were proven to be unfounded. Following this decision, Frank Barrett spoke on behalf of the other officers of the Mid-West Brigade:

> We all feel now that the satisfactory result of the investigations today is the biggest blow ever struck at the enemy in County Clare. Now that Commandant Brennan has been cleared of any complicity in the nefarious work which has been going on in his name we are all prepared to give him our whole-hearted support and confidence.

Michael Brennan accepted his commission as officer commanding of the 1st Western Division with the rank of commandant-general on 15 November 1921.

Incidentally, another IRA inquiry was held the next day into the selection of rate collectors in Clare County Council. It was alleged that there was friction between the Mid- and East Clare brigades over these appointments. The Mid-Clare IRA members objected to the East Clare IRA men looking for positions in Mid-Clare. It must be remembered that Michael Brennan was then chairman of Clare County Council and that the Mid-Clare men resented the 'interference' by outsiders in these appointments.[356]

Boycott in Kilkee

On 29 April 1923, shots were fired into the home of a prominent merchant family, Michael Keane and Son of the Arcade in Kilkee; a bomb was also thrown into the business premises, causing substantial damage amounting to £207. The reason for this attack was an allegation that the Keane family were friendly with the RIC. It was alleged that they entertained the police in their home, and that they gave information to the police in the home of Joe Greene in early April 1921. Another allegation was that one member of the family, John J. Keane, assisted the police in the attempted murder of Tom Marrinan, an IRA man from Kilkee, on 23–24 February 1921. Because of these allegations, the family was boycotted for many months – even during the truce period, up to 16 November 1921.

In a letter to the *Saturday Record* in June 1921, John J. Keane strenuously denied these allegations and slanders, stating that 'his comrades of the past were now his worst enemies.' Keane also denied telling stories to the police and that he slept in the local barracks. Significantly, he stated that the only time that he was in the barracks was around Christmas time, when he said that there were ten or eleven other men from the town present. This was an unusual admission at a time when the police were supposed to be ostracised by the nationalist community. In the same issue of the *Saturday Record* there was a list of six people from Kilkee who were lodging malicious injury claims with the secretary of Clare County Council for the October quarter sessions. Among them were: Michael Keane, £220; Cornelius Fitzgerald, £250; James Leyden, £300; Stephen Duggan, £600; Peter Larkin, £300; and John Purtill, £350.

John J. Keane wrote several letters of complaint to the minister for defence, Cathal Brugha, and President de Valera, complaining that he and his family were being victimised and boycotted as if they were spies and informers. He denied the allegations against him and his family, stating that these rumours were maliciously spread by Tom Marrinan, whose family had been in a dispute with the Keanes for three or four years. He stated that his family was ruined, that his drapery shop and his meal-and-foodstuffs business had been closed down, that the losses amounted to between £1,500 and £1,600, and that his good name and reputation were destroyed. In his letter to Minister Brugha, Keane alleged that there were at least thirty other business families in Kilkee who were friendly with the police, and he asked why they were not boycotted.

Several enquiries were made into the case, and Michael Brennan, officer commanding of the 1st Western Division, interviewed the family in November. In his report on the case, Brennan stated:

> The Keanes admitted that they were in constant association with the enemy, but claimed that they were no worse than many others in Kilkee, as practically the whole population of Kilkee associated with the enemy [...] I pointed out that if a few of the worst offenders, like the Keane family had been executed, such a good example might have shown the others the errors of their ways [...] JJ Keane was a notoriously bad character, who constantly associated with the Black and Tans [...] A daughter of the older Keane married a Black and Tan last week.

Brennan told the family that if he were in charge of west Clare before the truce, John J. Keane would have been shot. The boycott was officially ended in November when the minister for defence ordered that it should cease. However, it would seem that the family were ostracised for many years after that.

In February 1927, John J. Keane, then 35 years old, applied to the Irish Grants Committee on behalf of his father Michael and himself trading as Michael Keane and Son for compensation. In their joint application, the Keanes stated that between June and December 1921, a strict boycott was imposed on them on account of their friendship with, and support of, the British police forces. The Keanes were tried by a republican military court on 16 September and 20 September 1921. The family were told that the boycott was ended, but that the boycott had not ceased, owing to the animosity against them. They said that they had suffered serious losses ever since 1921. They were frequently fired at, and the premises was maliciously damaged. The Keanes claimed that they suffered losses because they supported the RIC all through the troubles and because a daughter of Michael Keane was married to a member of the police force. They claimed a total of £4,958 13*s* 5*d* for damages and they were awarded the significant sum of £2,340.[357]

Cumann na mBan

Towards the end of May, Miss Katie O'Brien, a young woman from Clarecastle and a daughter of a prosperous timber merchant, was arrested by the military in Ennis after being searched. Along with her bicycle, she was taken to her home in Clarecastle in a military lorry; her home was then subjected to a 'rigorous but fruitless search'. The young O'Brien sisters, Katie and Netta, were members of the Ennis No. 1 branch of Cumann na mBan. They and many other republican women did invaluable work for the independence movement.

Cumann na mBan was founded on 2 April 1914 as an Irish republican women's organisation, and as an auxiliary to the Irish Volunteers. The organisation was quite active as a support group during the Easter Rising, the hunger strikes of 1917 and the conscription crisis of early 1918. When the War of Independence began in 1919, Cumann na mBan gave huge support to the IRA. In Clare, Cumann na mBan was structured in a similar way to the IRA, with three brigades divided along the east, west and middle of the county; these brigades, in turn, were divided into battalions and companies. By July 1921 there were over 1,500 Cumann na mBan members in Clare organised into seventeen battalions: six in east Clare, six in mid-Clare, and five in west Clare.

The pension applications made by some of these republican women gives us some insight into their work for the cause of Irish independence during 1919–21. Mary Falvey of Darragh, who joined Cumann na mBan in 1917, was officer commanding of the Ballyea Company, 2nd Battalion, Mid-Clare Brigade. In her application for a pension (which was granted) she states that her republican work included the following:

> organising; catering; raising funds; dispatch work, intelligence gathering; receiving letters and parcels and under-cover communications, often at night time; storing arms and ammunition, and removing them in times of danger; delivering rate money, which was deposited at her home, which was the company HQ, and she was also involved in transport.

Her home was also used as a safe house, where IRA men found temporary refuge. Other pension applicants mentioned that they undertook guard duty for IRA men that were resting; they also mentioned nursing the wounded and being involved in propaganda. Clearly, the women of Cumann na mBan did valuable work as an auxiliary support group for the IRA during the War of Independence.[358]

Conclusion

In 1921, up to the truce on 11 July, the IRA were responsible for the deaths of fourteen policemen, seven soldiers and two marines – a total of twenty-three men. One soldier was also severely wounded in the Cratloe plane ambush in October 1920 and died of his wounds on 3 March 1921, resulting in a total of twenty-four members of the Crown forces killed by the IRA. Sixteen of these victims were shot by members of the East Clare Brigade, seven were shot by the Mid-Clare Brigade, and one was shot during the combined operation of the East and West Clare brigades at Kilrush.

Several civilian deaths were also attributed to the IRA this year, including two alleged spies: John Reilly and Patrick Darcy. Joseph Falsey was shot while filling in a road trench and Joe Greene was allegedly killed for his defiance of Sinn Féin courts. During this year, at least seven civilians were killed by the Crown forces – many for 'refusing to halt' – and a child, Patrick Morrissey, was shot dead during an IRA ambush in Ennis. Therefore, between the IRA and Crown forces, at least twelve civilian deaths were caused by the war in Clare, and many others were injured, physically or psychologically.

As has previously been indicated, there were few things worse than being labelled as an informer – if they were caught in a time of war, the penalty was usually death. In recent times, Sean O'Callaghan, a prominent member of the IRA, who, in his own words, had become disillusioned by the sectarianism and futility of the IRA campaign in the late 1970s, decided to become an informer on his IRA comrades in 1979. In his memoir *The Informer* (carrying the same name as the Liam O'Flaherty novel), published in 1998, O'Callaghan states:

> I knew what I was getting into and I did it voluntarily with the full knowledge of what would happen if I was caught: interrogation and torture, followed by a bullet in the back of the head in a ditch in some quiet road [...] I had been brought up to believe that the worst thing anybody could do was to be a police informer. Better by far to be a rapist, a murderer, anything but an informer.[359]

Clearly informers were despised people, in fiction, folklore and reality, throughout much of Irish history. This was also the case during the War of Independence. Many people, including at least two priests, were accused of spying during this time, and some people, whatever their motives, took grave risks to pass on vital information to the police. The price if they were caught was usually death, and at least three civilians in Clare paid the ultimate sacrifice for their actions after the IRA perceived them to be informers. Besides the three Clare civilians who were executed by the IRA for alleged spying, three soldiers and one policeman were also killed for this reason between 1919 and 1921. The execution of the three civilians, Martin Counihan, John Reilly and Patrick Darcy, was, and still is, a controversial subject. The killing of Martin Counihan was a badly executed operation in which Counihan was shot and left mortally wounded, surviving for a few hours after making his way to the village of Bodyke. The execution of John Reilly, an ex-soldier, seems to have been carried out efficiently, and he had the consolation of a priest to pray with and comfort him before his death by firing squad. The execution of Patrick Darcy seems to have been carried out after what can only be described as a kangaroo court. The unfortunate Darcy allegedly denied the accusation that he was an informer to the end; he forgave his executioners and apparently did not have the benefit of spiritual consolation before he was shot. His case is still a matter of emotional controversy in west Clare.

In a time of war, desperate times required desperate measures. The trials of the alleged informers took place in secret military courts conducted by the IRA; the normal legal checks and balances of jurisprudence, aimed at proving guilt 'beyond reasonable doubt', were not possible then. The main primary sources relating to their guilt are IRA witness statements, but these must be treated with some caution, as they were written between thirty and forty years after the War of Independence. Gearoid O'Tuathaigh, emeritus professor of history at National University of Ireland, Galway, warns of the hazards of such recollections in which memories and impressions written long after the events may conflict with historical facts. Traditionally, he said, 'historians are suspicious of memory [...] beware the treachery of memory [...] "facts" may be omitted, suppressed or embellished by the narrator.'[360] Furthermore, there is the question of bias in these IRA witness statements. The civilians who were shot as spies were despised and deemed to be outcasts because they were accused of associating with police, 'an act of high treason'. As Fr Gaynor remarked, 'West Clare reeked with spies.' Perhaps we will never know whether these three unfortunate men were guilty of being informers.[361]

In contrast with the deaths of twenty-four members of the Crown forces, the IRA only lost four members this year. Each of them were from the East Clare Brigade, and each of them died in June. Patrick White died in Spike Island, Christopher McCarthy and Patrick Gleeson died in the Cratloe ambush and ex-RIC clerk Tom Healy died of a heart attack during the Carrigoran ambush. Overall, between civilians, IRA men and Crown forces, at least forty people were killed in Clare this year up to the truce on 11 July 1921. Three Clare-born members of the RIC were also killed outside of the county.

Therefore, over the two years of conflict between July 1919 and July 1921, nearly one hundred people were killed and many more were wounded. This included forty-four policemen (including fourteen Clare-born policemen), twenty-five civilians, seventeen IRA men, nine soldiers and two sailors. Besides these victims, hundreds of people, both combatants and civilians, were injured during the conflict, and many of these people died prematurely because of their injuries.

The testimony of several IRA men from all three brigades suggests that, in 1921, the IRA was finding it difficult to engage the enemy with any chance of success. Patrick Devitt (Mid-Clare Brigade) recalled:

> From the date of Moanreel [December 1920] up to the Truce it was very hard to get a chance in North or Mid-Clare to attack the enemy, convoys were strengthened with armoured cars, the best we could do was to hamper communications by road cutting, destroying telephone lines and long distance sniping etc.

Michael Brennan (East Clare Brigade) stated:

> The fight at Mountshannon had seriously depleted our ammunition supply and some smaller encounters by different groups during our absence in Galway had brought it to a critical stage. We were down to about a dozen rounds per rifle and in the face of this, we daren't risk any operations, which didn't offer good prospects of capturing arms. We occupied ourselves in holding up trains and mail cars, road blocking and trenching and sniping, the column remained in small groups.

John Flanagan (West Clare Brigade) wrote, 'The British always travelled in strength from 1920 onwards in convoys of lorries. Our brigade, with poor equipment, eight to ten rifles and between twenty five and thirty shotguns, could not hope to deliver a serious attack on the enemy.' The Mid-Clare and East Clare brigades co-ordinated many ambushes, but the enemy often didn't show up, or else they arrived in forces too strong for the IRA to ambush them.[362]

Martin Chambers corroborated John Flanagan's opinion and was also critical of the leadership:

> I always held the view that it was not a country which lent itself to guerrilla warfare in a big way. It is relatively flat, possesses few suitable ambush positions, affords little cover and is traversed by numerous roads and by-roads which an enemy holding all points of vantage and equipped with fast transport could avail of to surround and intercept I.R.A. columns. As well, their intelligence was more efficient in the area than in most places. I am not putting forward these points as an excuse for the fact that West Clare had not more military activities to its credit during the struggle for independence during the Black and Tan war, as I believe that more successful fighting could have taken

> place if the men in charge of the area had more heart in their work.[363]

Truce

By July 1921 the IRA and the Crown forces were almost in a stalemate position, with neither side able to defeat the other. The Crown forces controlled the towns, while the IRA were dominant in rural areas. After the Glenwood attack in late January, the police and military convoys were too well armed for the IRA to ambush them successfully. The county was under military rule, and after the attacks on Ennis (16 April) and Kilrush (23 April), severe restrictions were imposed on the people of these towns, with curfews from 10 p.m. until 5 a.m., and bans on fairs and markets within a 5-mile radius of these towns. The ban on fairs and markets was a severe economic penalty imposed on a largely agricultural county in which about 70 per cent of the population depended upon agriculture. Curfew was also imposed on Killaloe at this time. The British were still exacting revenge for attacks on them by burning IRA supporters' houses. People were rounded up around the county in order to repair roads, which had been trenched, and several people were killed in suspicious circumstances 'while running away'. More than forty houses were burnt this year in reprisals; at least nine of them belonged to the Protestant minority, who were unionists or loyalists.

The IRA had caused major damage to the road network – by trenching roads and blowing up bridges – which 'seriously hampered Crown forces' by June 1920 and also caused major inconvenience to the general public. The IRA also seriously affected other communications in the county by damaging railway lines, robbing mail and cutting telephone and telegraph wires around the county. The county administration, which was seriously compromised during the War of Independence, was suffering from a severe financial crisis; there was a huge burden of debt on the ratepayers due to compensation for criminal injuries, and the collection of rates was taken over by the IRA. By July the county was in a bad state, economically and politically. The legal system was boycotted by the vast majority, who resorted to the Sinn Féin courts instead. Under martial law, even the use of bicycles by civilians was banned from 1

July. There was a 'reign of terror' in the county, and many people yearned for peace.

David Fitzpatrick opines that the time was ripe for a truce:

> By mid-1921 the IRA had reached an impasse [...] it was too poorly armed to have much hope of dislodging the enemy from his heavily fortified strongholds [...] But the opposing forces, and the government behind them had also reached an impasse. On 11 July 1921 both sides acknowledged defeat by agreeing to a Truce.[364]

I do not totally agree with Fitzpatrick in this conclusion. Though the heavily armed Crown forces controlled the main towns in Clare, the lightly armed IRA controlled the countryside, and neither side could defeat the other. The IRA were not defeated in July 1921 and could have carried on a prolonged guerrilla conflict against the Crown forces, but their chances of defeating the Crown forces were slim.

The IRA were hampered by a shortage of ammunition at this time. An IRA inspector in east Clare reported to Richard Mulcahy on 15 June:

> Of course we are all aware of the poor armaments of this whole area, but it was not advisable to send anything owing to the bad conditions which existed there. I think the best we could do would be to supply East Clare with stuff [ammunition] and let him [Michael Brennan] dispose of it in South Galway as he thinks fit.

In his report of April 1921, Michael Brennan highlighted the shortage of ammunition:

> I must emphasise the frightful position we find ourselves in through lack of ammunition [...] it is very easy to imagine how long twenty five rounds of ammunition per man would have lasted.[365]

Dan Breen, an IRA leader in Tipperary, also mentioned a shortage of ammunition at the time of the truce:

> The Truce [...] In many ways we welcomed the respite. For some time our area had been running out of ammunition [...] everywhere we were acclaimed as heroes, even by the people, who two years before had been denouncing us as assassins. It was a delight to relax from the hard life of campaigning and enjoy the blessings of peace.[366]

At the national level, major political developments were occurring that paved the way for a truce. Having successfully opened the parliament at Stormont in June, copper-fastening partition and appeasing the unionists of the six counties, the British government was anxious to reach an accommodation with the nationalists in the twenty-six counties, as the British military campaign in Ireland was damaging to the British reputation abroad. Many nationalists were also anxious for peace in Ireland; behind the scenes, leading churchmen and politicians were negotiating with the British. King George V made an emotional appeal for peace at the opening of Stormont on 24 June, and following some tentative preliminary negotiations between de Valera and Lloyd George, arrangements were made for a truce at midday on Monday, 11 July. On this occasion – unlike the time of Archbishop Clune's negotiations, which took place in December 1920 – the British did not insist that the IRA should surrender their weapons as a preliminary to talks.[367]

Michael Brennan, in his memoir, describes the emotional surge and excitement he experienced when the truce came into effect on 11 July:

> I was in the Kilmaley district [in mid-Clare, probably on county council business] when the orders for the Truce reached me on the 9th or 10th of July. Just after midday on July 11th I went into Ennis with some comrades and when our car stopped at the Clare Hotel we were surrounded by an almost hysterical crowd. One of the most excited was a British sergeant (named Doyle, I think) wearing the ribbon of the Victoria Cross on his tunic. We were of course, fully armed and equipped and our appearance was tangible proof that 'the Terror' was ended. This was probably the real cause of the emotion.[368]

The truce was warmly welcomed in Clare, but, tragically, it was not the end of the conflict.

APPENDICES

Appendix I: Number of deaths from 1 January 1919 to 11 July 1921

Year	RIC/Black and Tans	IRA	Army	Navy	Civilians	Resident magistrate	Total
1919	2	1	0	0	0	0	3
1920	14 (+10*)	12	2	0	11	1	50
1921	14 (+3*)	4	7	2	12	0	42
Totals	30 (+13*)	17	9	2	23	1	95

This table is based on the best estimates of those that died between 1 January 1919 and 11 July 1921. It does not include republicans whose health was undermined, who died prematurely after 1921 as a result of being 'on the run', who died from the long-term effects of hunger strikes, or who died from an accident. It includes two IRA men, killed outside Clare, Peadar Clancy (Dublin) and Joseph McMahon (Cavan), and one civilian, Conor Clune, killed in Dublin..

*The figures in brackets refer to Clare-born members of the RIC who were killed outside of the county.

Source: R. Abbott, *Police Casualties in Ireland, 1919–1922* (Cork: Mercier Press, 2000).

Appendix II: Crown mortalities in Clare (according to brigade territories) from January 1919 to 11 July 1921

Brigades	East Clare	Mid-Clare	West Clare	Total
Police	14	13	3	30
Army	6	3	0	9
Navy	0	2	0	2
Totals	20	18	3	41

Appendix III: IRA members killed in actions against Crown forces during the years 1919–1921*

Year	East Clare	Mid-Clare	West Clare	Total
1919	0	0	0	0
1920	4	3	6	13*
1921	4	0	0	4
Totals	8	3	6	17

The table includes two IRA members, Peadar Clancy and Joseph McMahon, who were killed outside of the county.

Appendix IV: Inventory of arms in the Mid-Clare Brigade from records kept by Sean O'Keefe, quartermaster of the Mid-Clare Brigade

1917: Martini rifles bought from GHQ Dublin; 2 Lee–Metford rifles bought from GHQ

1917–1918: 5 Lee–Enfield rifles seized from soldiers on leave

1918–1920: 5 Lee–Enfield rifles bought by Bill McNamara from soldiers in Ennis

1918–1920: 2 Lee–Enfield rifles bought by Peadar O'Loughlin from soldiers in Ennis

1918–1920: 3 Lee–Enfield rifles bought by Lehane's from soldiers in Lahinch

1918–1920: 5 Winchester rifles seized in raids on private houses

24/02/1918: 2 carbines seized from police in Derrymore

05/07/1919: 1 police carbine seized during attack on RIC at Kilshanny

05/08/1919: 2 police carbines seized during attack on police at 81 Cross in Islandbaun

23/06/1920: 7 Lee–Enfield rifles captured from military in Ennis

17/07/1920: 1 Lee–Enfield rifle seized from soldier by Michael Nestor at Ennistymon

20/07/1920: 4 Lee–Enfield rifles seized from military party at Ennistymon

22/09/1920: 6 Lee–Enfield rifles captured during Rineen ambush

18/10/1920: 14 Lee–Enfield rifles captured at Ruan barracks

This inventory from O'Keefe included the following note:

NB – only two or three of these weapons were lost to the enemy, one at Moanreel, and the others at Crowe's Bridge in January 1920. Dozens of revolvers were acquired from individuals who were involved in land agitation, then common in Clare. Some revolvers were purchased from soldiers; about a dozen revolvers were got by raids on private houses, the Webley and the Bulldog predominated. We had a few hundred shotguns, but most of these had become defective by use and abuse. By the time of the Truce we had three or four dozen serviceable shotguns at the disposal of the Brigade. I recollect at the Truce on 11 July 1921 the brigade held a total of about 80 serviceable rifles and about 50–60 revolvers and automatic pistols.

Source: Sean O'Keefe, Quartermaster, Mid-West Brigade, WS 1261.

Appendix V: IRA membership by brigade on 11 July 1921

Battalion	East Clare Brigade	Mid-Clare Brigade	West Clare Brigade
1st Battalion	391	336	450
2nd Battalion	368	431	594
3rd Battalion	146	319	566
4th Battalion	380	509	425
5th Battalion	468	380	455
6th Battalion	367	265	N/A
Totals	**2,120**	**2,240**	**2,490**

According to these records, there were 6,850 members of the IRA in Clare at the time of the truce on 11 July 1921. The majority of these were from rural areas around the county, rather than from urban areas. It must be remembered, however, that the majority of these IRA men were passive supporters of the movement. The most active IRA men in Clare were in the flying columns, and there were about 150 men among the flying columns of the three brigades combined.

Source: Military Archives, MSPC/RO/207-213; 214-220A; 221-226.

Appendix VI: Cumann na mBan membership in Clare on 11 July 1921

Battalion	East Clare Brigade	Mid-Clare Brigade	West Clare Brigade
1st Battalion	108	139	64
2nd Battalion	105	100	146
3rd Battalion	40	130	124
4th Battalion	90	67	46
5th Battalion	121	35	90
6th Battalion	108	120	N/A
Totals	**572**	**591**	**470**

The total membership of Cumann na mBan in Clare on 11 July 1921 was 1,633.

Source: Military Archives, CMB Rolls 70-84.

Appendix VII: List of battalions of the Clare brigades

East Clare Brigade

1st Battalion: Carrigoran, Newmarket, Quin, Clonmoney, Sixmilebridge and Ballycar.

2nd Battalion: Cratloe, Meelick, Clonlara, Truagh and Oatfield.

3rd Battalion: Kilbane, Garranboy, Bridgetown and Ogonneloe.

4th Battalion: Caherhurley, Scariff, Mountshannon, Cooleenbridge and Tuamgraney.

5th Battalion: Bodyke, O'Callaghan's Mills, Tulla, Knockjames and Glandree.

6th Battalion: Feakle, Annaghneale, Killanena, Flagmount Caher and Dromondoora.

Mid-Clare Brigade

1st Battalion: Crusheen, Barefield, Ballinruan, Clooney, Ennis and Doora.

2nd Battalion: Ballyea, Inch, Connolly, Lissycasey, Ballycorick, Kilmaley and Clarecastle.

3rd Battalion: Kilnamona, Ruan, Kilseedy, Dysart, Rath, Corofin and Kilnaboy.

4th Battalion: Ennistymon, Inagh, Lavareen, Lahinch, Moy, Glandine, Miltown Malbay, Letterkelly and Ballyea.

5th Battalion: Kilfenora, Clouna, Liscannor, Ballyculliney, Moymore, Doolin, Kilshanny and Kilnaboy.

6th Battalion: Ballyvaughan and Noughaval, Carron, Murrough, Toovahera, Ballinalacken, Lisdoonvarna and New Quay.

West Clare Brigade

1st Battalion: Coolmeen, Kildysart, Cranny and Labasheeda.

2nd Battalion: Knockerra, Kilmurry McMahon, Kilmihil, Glenmore, Killimer and Kilrush.

3rd Battalion: Cooraclare, Monmore, Cree, Doonbeg, Bealaha and Clohanemore.

4th Battalion: Mullagh, Coore, Knocknahilla, Kilmurry Ibrickane and Quilty.

5th Battalion: Carrigaholt, Kilkee, Kilferagh, Doonaha, Querrin, Moveen, Cross, Lisdeen and Kilbaha.

Source: Military Archives, MSPC/RO/207-226.

Appendix VIII: Diary of Mid-Clare Brigade activities, April 1921

The following is a diary of operations for the Mid-Clare Brigade; it was contained in a letter from Frank Barrett to Richard Mulcahy:

1 – no activity

2 – no activity

3 – sniping parties on look-out for enemy in 5/6 Battallion areas, no contact.

4 – sniping parties of 2nd Batt on look-out, enemy not on road expected.

5 – DI and five constables attacked at Corofin in 3rd Batt. area, two of party believed killed and three injured.

6 – no activity

7 – no activity

8 – all roads in Batt. areas 4/5/6 entrenched and barricaded.

9 – enemy expected at Kilfenora fair – eighteen riflemen in position, officers and men of 5/6 Battn., no show by enemy

10 – no activities
11 – three roads held by sections, six snipers – no show by enemy, mails raided at Kilfenora, 3rd Batt., Torraline(?) sixth Battn., more barricades on roads and pits dug in Batts. 1/2/3 areas.
12 – mails raided at Liscannor, 5th Battn., – all roads in 2nd Battn. again held, no enemy activity.
13 – all roads in 2nd Batt held in vain. Mails raided at New Quay, 6th Batt.
14 – all roads held in 2nd Batt. in vain, mails raided at Turnpke, 2nd Batt; mail raid 4th Batt.
15 – all roads in 2nd Batt again held in vain; party of 5th Batt waited in vain for four lorries expected to travel from Ennis to Ennistymon.
16 – mixed party of military and Auxiliaries attacked in public house in Ennis with revolvers and bombs resulting in the death of one military sergeant and wounding of two B & Ts and two women by 1st Batt. A party of 2nd Batt searched public houses in Tiermaclane where some of the local RIC were reported drinking, proved to be erroneous. The RIC in this fortress are certainly confined. They have information of the activity of the Battalion and never move about.
17 – no activity
18 – a column of 2nd Batt. moved to Kildysart to attack a patrol of eight RIC who were reputed to come out daily at Kildysart. The column commanders were informed of the landing there of an armed party from the West Clare Brigade. The RIC were aware of this party in their vicinity, consequently they were confined to barracks. In view of this coincidence, the 2nd column retreated to its own area. Mails were raided at Ballycorick by the 2nd Batt.
19 – mails raided again at Ballycorick
20 – Three roads in the 2nd Batt area were held by the column, but no enemy appeared.
21 – house of H [Harry] Mills, Ennis, destroyed as counter-reprisal by 1st Batt. Mails raided at Crusheen by 1st Batt. Two roads held by column of 2nd Batt., but no enemy activity.
22 – all roads through 2nd Batt area again seized.

23 – all roads through 2nd Batt area again seized.
24 – fifteen men of 5th Batt attacked RIC returning from Mass to barrack at 180 yards range, inflicting three casualties and causing considerable damage to the roof of the barracks.
25 – no activity reported.
26 – fresh barricades and pits dug on roads in Batt. 4/5/6 areas
27 – no activity reported
28 – fresh barricades erected and pits dug on roads in 1/2/3 Batt. areas.
29 – no activity reported.
30 – mails raided at Ballyea by the 2nd Batt.

[Note: it is remarkable that in this report of activities for April, Frank Barrett did not mention the killing of Constable Stanley Moore, who was shot dead by the IRA in Miltown Malbay on the night of Thursday, 7 April. Neither does he mention the killing of two marines at Ballyvaughan on 20 April. Both incidents were within the Mid-Clare territory. Perhaps the battalion commandants of battalion areas 4, 5 and 6 did not inform the brigade commandant about these events.]

Source: Letter from Frank Barrett OC Mid-West Brigade to chief of staff, Richard Mulcahy Papers, UCD Archives, P7/A/19.

Appendix IX: Military activities of the Crown forces in the Mid-Clare district during April 1921*

The following is a list of activities based on intelligence compiled by the Mid-Clare Brigade and signed by Frank Barrett:

1 – no activity
2 – no activity
3 – store and shop destroyed in Miltown Malbay by local RIC, (unofficial)
4 – a large party of RIC cyclists raided the area of 3rd Batt in search of 'wanted men'
5 – no activity
6 – a mixed party of RIC and military raided for dog licences over a small area in the 5th Batt. The military in the 4th Batt area filling in trenches and rebuilding bridges. Three RIC tenders went from Corofin to Ennis returning the same day.
7 – no activity
8 – wholesale activity all over different Battalions as a result of

Volunteer operations cutting road trenches, barricading bridges, felling trees and cutting telegraph poles and wires, together with raids on mails and post men notably in Batt. areas 4/5/6.

9 – ditto, in all cases co-operating with the military

10 – ditto in all cases co-operating with the military, mostly over Batt. areas, 4/5/6

11 – surrounding Roman Catholic churches in Batt. 4/5/6 and coercing the congregations to fill in trenches and repair bridges etc., which were torn down nightly over the week previously.

12 – no activity

13 – again employed in removing barricades and filling trenches between 4 am and 8 am in Batt. areas 4/5/6

14 – no activity reported

15 – three RIC trucks travelled between Ennis and Corofin through the 3rd Batt area; also four lorries (mixed), travelled between Ennistymon and Ennis.

16 – four lorries, two RIC, two military, travelled between Ennistymon and Lisdoonvarna; the leading lorry crashed into a road block and got smashed completely, they immediately fired about 200 rounds at people working nearby.

17 – no activity reported.

18 – volunteers fired upon by Black & Tans and military in Lahinch.

19 – Ballyvaughan, A company area of 5th Batt was raided by a mixed force as a result of marines being fired upon.

20 – no activities except 'official' reprisals in Ennis.

21 – RIC raided in E company, 3rd Battn. For wanted men.

22 – RIC raided in D company of 6th Batt area under threats to civilians in connection with a raid on mails.

23 – sixteen lorries (mixed forces), met at Bellharbour, A coy, 6 Batt area, and ill-treated all pedestrians they came into conflict with as a result of a raid on mails coming to marine station, Ballyvaughan, and RIC Lisdoonvarna. These forces were a mixture of RIC, B&T's, Auxiliaries and military, the two latter from Gort and Galway.

24 – RIC activity in Ennistymon as a result of morning attack on barracks.
25 – RIC raids in Lahinch (D Coy area), 4th Battn. and E Coy, 3rd Batt. area
26 – three lorries (one RIC, two military) raided Kilfenora (A Coy 5th Batt), and searched six houses.
27 – Lahinch and Liscannor raided for 'wanted men', raids carried out by mixed forces.
28 – RIC again visit Kilfenora at 4 am taking two prisoners, prisoners released in the evening. Sixteen RIC also raided part of B Coy, 5th Batt at 4 am same morning.
29 – Liscannor again raided by mixed force
30 – no activity reported.
Military activities – same as RIC, they always work in conjunction with each other except in the 3rd Battn. area; there are no Auxiliaries within the brigade area.

Source: Correspondence between Frank Barrett and Richard Mulcahy, 30 April 1921, Richard Mulcahy Papers, UCD Archives, P7/A/19.

Appendix X: Weekly intelligence summary, 6th Division, copy no.43 G/18/89/2

The following is a weekly intelligence summary based on captured British documents:

17/05/1921

Mid-Clare Brigade

Mid Clare Brigade has been inactive and has not been located.

West Clare Brigade has been active in the Doonbeg-Cooraclare-Kilmihil area and intended attacking the RIC barracks at Kilkee on 6th inst. It is now believed to have moved up towards Quilty. Its only activity has been the cutting of roads in the southern part of the county.

The following information re the attack on the Kilrush barracks on 22 April has been obtained and corroborated: the attackers comprised about 40 men of a flying column from Kerry or

County Cork and the Cooraclare Battalion and West Clare Flying Column.

The Kilrush members of the IRA were used as guides, very unwillingly and apparently on point of the bayonet.

Simon Breen's house at Kilmacduane, Cooraclare was used as a meeting place for arranging the attack.

John Liddy, Michael Honan and Michael Killoughrey have been living in a dug-out in the townland of Clonreddan, which was discovered on the 8th inst. This was large enough to hold six men and apparently a tent had been erected, as a number of tent pegs were found.

Liddy's party were rationed from Cooraclare and obtained money and despatches through a woman who cycles from Ennis to Clonreddan once a week. Willie Haugh is reported to have taken over command of this brigade. One of the rebels who was killed is reliably reported to have been buried at Doonbeg on the 24 ult.

Willie Haugh and twenty others had been living in a dug-out in a bog in Moyasta–Shragh district.

West Clare Brigade IRA – This column is still believed to be north of Scarriff except for a small section under Harry O'Mara at Flagmount, which met at Caher Cross Roads during the latter half of last week. It is now reported to be in the vicinity of the West Limerick Brigade.

Michael Brennan is now reported to be touring County Galway. He is stated to have taken over command of the Galway IRA in addition to the East Clare Brigade. The man he took over from comes from Kincarra and was reduced in rank for inefficiency. The above incidents suggest that the IRA are forming divisional headquarters in certain areas. This is mere conjecture.

Information has been received that the Marine Detachment at Seafield, Quilty, is to be attacked, and that a hedge which is situated about 100 yards is to be used by the rebels to fire from.

The murder gang in West Clare have decided to assassinate Sergeant Monaghan, Constables O'Keefe and Kelly, RIC, Kilkee, for having arrested Michael Roche on 12/4/21

18th Brigade area

Michael Brennan of Clare is, apparently, Commander-in-Chief, IRA in the West. He calls himself Lieut. General of Flying Columns, and states that it is his job to rouse the West and is confident of his ability to do so.

The Madigans of Banmore, Moyasta, and Miss Irene Kennedy of Lisdeen, Kilkee, Co Clare are in the habit of harbouring rebels.

John Coots of Spancel Hill, near Ennis, who was acquitted of carrying arms etc., is an itinerant tailor and also a deserter from the MGG. His tailoring is only a cloak, in reality he is a machine gun instructor to the Clare IRA.

John Naylon [*sic*] of Kilfenora, who is serving a sentence for taking rates from a rate collector by threats, was in charge of all the administrative side of the IRA in North Clare. If the prison authorities, where he now is, use their influence he might supply some very useful information, although he did not do so when arrested.

Source: Florence O'Donoghue's *No Other Law: The Story of Liam Lynch and the IRA, 1916–1923* [see Appendix One, pp. 311–30]. Smoke-damaged copies of these reports are found in University of Limerick, Special Collections, the East Limerick Brigade papers, P46/71 and P46/72.

BIBLIOGRAPHY

Abbott, R., *Police Casualties in Ireland, 1919–1922* (Cork: Mercier Press, 2000).

Andrews, C.S., *Dublin Made Me* (Cork: Mercier Press, 1979).

Augusteign, J., *From Public Defiance to Guerrilla Warfare: The Experience of Ordinary, Volunteers in the Irish War of Independence, 1916–1921* (Dublin: Irish Academic Press, 1996).

Barry, T., *Guerrilla Days in Ireland* (Cork: Mercier Press, 1955).

Béaslaí, P., *Michael Collins and the Making of a New Ireland* (London: The Phoenix Publishing Co., 1926).

Breen, D., *My Fight for Irish Freedom* (Tralee: Anvil Books, 1989).

Brennan, M., *The War in Clare, 1911–1921* (Dublin: Four Courts Press, 1980).

Browne, K.J., *Éamon de Valera and the Banner County* (Clare: Glendale, 1982).

Buckland, P., *Irish Unionism 11: Ulster Unionism and the Origins of Northern Ireland, 1886–1922* (Dublin: Gill and Macmillan, 1973).

Bury, R., *Buried Lives: The Protestants of Southern Ireland* (Dublin: The History Press, 2017).

Cahill, S., 'The life and death of Tomas Shannon', *The Other Clare*, 41 (2017), 26–9.

Carroll, A., *Sean Moylan: Rebel Leader* (Cork: Mercier Press, 2010).

Clancy, C., 'The experiences of a Sinn Féin priest: Fr Pat Gaynor and self-government in Clare 1919–1921', *The Other Clare*, 31 (2007), 51–8.

Crowley, J., D. O'Droisceoil and M. Murphy (eds), *Atlas of the Irish Revolution* (Cork: Cork University Press, 2017).

Deasy, L., *Brother against Brother* (Cork: Mercier Press, 1998).

Deasy, L., *Towards Ireland Free* (Cork: Mercier Press, 1972).

Devas, N., *Two Flamboyant Fathers* (London: Collins, 1966).

Dooley, T., *The Irish Revolution, 1913–1923: Monaghan* (Dublin: Four Courts Press, 2017).

Dorney, J., *The Civil War in Dublin: The Fight for the Irish Capital, 1922–1924* (Dublin: Merrion Press, 2017).

Dowd, C., *Faith, Ireland and Empire: The life of Patrick Joseph Clune, Cssr, 1864–1935*(New South Wales: St Paul's Press, 2014).

Dwyer, T.R., *Tans, Terror and Troubles: Kerry's Real Fighting Story, 1913–23* (Cork: Mercier Press, 2001).

Durney, J., *The War of Independence in Kildare* (Cork: Mercier Press, 2013).

Enright, S., *The Irish Civil War: Law, Execution and Atrocity* (Dublin: Merrion Press, 2019).

Ferriter, D., *A Nation and Not a Rabble: The Irish Revolution, 1913–1923* (New York: The Overlook Press, 2015).

Fitzpatrick, D., *Politics and Irish Life, 1913–1921* (Dublin: Gill and Macmillan, 1977).

Fitzpatrick, D., *The Two Irelands, 1912–1939* (Oxford: Oxford University Press, 1998).

Fitzpatrick, D., 'Protestant depopulation and the Irish Revolution', *Irish Historical Studies*, 38, 152 (2013), 643–670.

Foster, R.F., *Modern Ireland, 1600–1972* (London: Penguin, 1988).

Foster, R.F. (ed.), *The Oxford History of Modern Ireland* (Oxford: Oxford University Press, 2001).

Garvin, T., *1922: The Birth of Irish Democracy* (Dublin: Gill and Macmillan, 1996).

Griffin, G., *The Collegians* (London: Atlantic Books, 2008).

Hart, P., *The IRA and Its Enemies: Violence and Community in Cork, 1916–1923* (Oxford: Clarendon Press, 1998).

Hayes, B., *The IRA: A Documentary History* (Dublin: Gill and Macmillan, 2010).

Heffernan, B., *Freedom and the Fifth Commandment* (Manchester: Manchester University Press, 2014).

Herlihy, J., *Royal Irish Constabulary Officers, 1816–1922* (Dublin: Four Courts Press, 2005).

Herlihy, J., *The Royal Irish Constabulary* (Dublin: Four Courts Press, 2016).

Hopkinson, M., *Green against Green: The Irish Civil War* (Dublin: Gill and Macmillan, 1988).

Hopkinson, M., *The Irish War of Independence* (Dublin: Gill and Macmillan, 2002).

Jackson, A. (ed.), *The Oxford History of Modern Ireland* (Oxford: Oxford University Press, 2014).

Keane, H., *Memories of My Childhood in Co. Clare* (printed for private circulation, 1990).

Kee, R., *Ireland: A History* (London: Abacus, 2000).

Kee, R., *The Green Flag* (Penguin: London, 1989).

Kennedy, G., *The Crusheen Volunteers and Their Role During 1916* (Clare: published by the author, 2013).

Kissane, B., *The Politics of the Irish Civil War* (Oxford: Oxford University Press, 2005).

Laffan, M., *The Resurrection of Ireland: The Sinn Féin Party, 1916–1923* (Cambridge: Cambridge University Press, 1999).

Leeson, D., *The Black and Tans: British Police and Auxiliaries in the Irish War of Independence, 1920–1921* (Oxford: Oxford University Press, 2001).

Lyons, F.S.L., *Ireland Since the Famine* (Glasgow: Fontana, 1971).

MacLysaght, E., *Changing Times: Ireland since 1898* (Buckinghamshire: Colin Smythe, 1978).

McArdle, D., *The Irish Republic* (London: Victor Gollanz, 1937).

McCarthy, C., *Cumann na mBan and the Irish Revolution* (Cork: The Collins Press, 2007).

McCarthy, D., *Ireland's Banner County: Clare from the Fall of Parnell to the Great War, 1890–1918* (Clare: Saipan Press, 2002).

Mac Conmara, T., *Days of Hunger: The Clare Volunteers and the Mountjoy Hunger-strike of 1917* (Clare: Dallan Publishing, 2017).

Mac Conmara, T., *The Time of the Tans: An Oral History of the War of Independence in County Clare* (Cork: Mercier Press, 2019).

Mac Conmara, T., '"These four Claremen have taken on the British Empire", the Clare Volunteers and the transformation of Ireland in 1917', *The Other Clare*, 36 (2012), 27–32.

Matthews, A., *Dissidents: Irish Republican Women, 1923–46* (Cork: Mercier Press, 2012).

Morrison, G., *The Irish Civil War: An Illustrated History* (Dublin: Gill and Macmillan, 1981).

Mulcahy, R., *My Father, the General: Richard Mulcahy and the Military History of the Revolution* (Dublin: Liberties Press, 2014).

Murphy, E.D., 'The Patrick Hennessy letters', *The Other Clare*, 30 (2006), 13–15.

Murphy, J.A., *Ireland in the 20th Century* (Dublin: Gill and MacMillan, 1975).

Murray, P., *Oracles of God: The Roman Catholic Church and Irish Politics, 1922–37* (Dublin: UCD Press, 2000).

Neeson, E., *The Civil War in Ireland* (Cork: Mercier Press, 1966).

O'Brien, P., *The Glynns of Kilrush County Clare, 1811–1940: Family, Business and Politics* (Dublin: Open Air, 2019).

O'Brien, G.R., *These My Friends and Forebears: The O'Briens of Dromoland* (Clare: Ballinakella Press, 1991).

O'Callaghan, J., *The Irish Revolution, 1913–23: Limerick* (Dublin: Four Courts Press, 2018).

O'Callaghan, S., *The Informer* (London: Transworld Publishers, Ltd., 1998).

O'Conchubhair, B., *Limerick's Fighting Story, 1916–21: Told by the Men Who Made It* (Cork: Mercier Press, 2000).

O'Corrai, C., and S. O'Corrai, *Peadar Clancy: Easter Rising Hero, Bloody Sunday Martyr* (Galway: Cranny Publications, 2016).

O'Dea, S., 'Clare in 1920', *The Capuchin Annual*, 14 (1970), 276–86.

O'Doherty, G. (ed.), *With the IRA in the Fight for Freedom: The Red Path of Glory* (Cork: Mercier Press, 2010).

O'Donoghue, F., *No Other Law: The Story of Liam Lynch and the Irish Republican Army, 1916–1923* (Dublin: Irish Press Ltd., 1954).

O'Brien, P., *Havoc: The Auxiliaries in Ireland's War of Independence* (Cork: The Collins Press, 2017).

O'Flaherty, L., *The Informer* (Dublin: Wolfhound Press, 2006).

O'Gadhra, N., *Civil War in Connaught, 1921–23* (Cork: Mercier Press, 1999).

O'Leary, C. and P. Maume, *Controversial Issues in Anglo-Irish*

Relations, 1910–1921 (Dublin: Four Courts Press, 2004).

O'Malley, E., *On Another Man's Wound*, (Dublin: Anvil Books, 1990).

O'Malley, E., *The Singing Flame* (Dublin: Anvil Books, 1978).

O'Malley, K.H. and A. Dolan (eds), *No Surrender Here: The Civil War Papers of Ernie O'Malley, 1922–24* (Dublin: Lilliput Press, 2007).

O'Murcadha, C., 'Dr Donough MacNamara's memoir of the War of Independence', *The Other Clare*, 40 (2016), pp. 16–26.

O'Murcadha, C., 'Prison letters of Canon O'Kennedy', *The Other Clare*, 37 (2013), pp. 21–5.

O'Reilly, S., *Clare GAA: The Club Scene, 1887–2010* (Clare: published by the author, 2010).

O'Reilly, T. (ed.), *Our Struggle for Independence*: *Eyewitness Accounts from the Pages of An Cosantoir* (Cork: Mercier Press, 2009).

Ó Ruairc, P.Ó., *Blood on the Banner: The Republican Struggle in Clare* (Cork: Mercier Press, Cork, 2009

Ó Ruairc, P.Ó., 'Missing in action-British servicemen secretly buried in Clare during the War of independence', *The Other Clare*, 36 (2012), pp. 77–80.

Ó Ruairc, P.Ó., *Revolution: A Photographic History of the Revolutionary Ireland, 1913–1923* (Cork: Mercier Press, 2011).

Ó Ruairc, P.Ó., *Truce: Murder, Myth and the Last Days of the Irish War of Independence* (Cork: Mercier Press, 2016).

Ó Ruairc, P.Ó., '"The distinction is a fine one, but a real one," Sectarianism in County Clare during the War of Independence', *The Other Clare*, 34 (2010), pp. 35–42.

Ó Ruairc, P.Ó. (ed.), *The Men Will Talk to Me: Clare Interviews by Ernie O'Malley* (Cork: Mercier Press, 2016).

O'Sullivan, D.J., *The Irish Constabularies, 1822–1922* (Kerry: Brandon Books, 2000).

Pakenham, F., *Peace by Ordeal* (London: Weidenfeld and Nicholson, 1935).

Pike, D.H. (ed.), *Australian Dictionary of Biography* (Melbourne: Melbourne University Press, 1981).

Power, J., *A History of Clare Castle and Its Environs* (Clare:

published by the author, 2004).

Power, J., *The GAA in Clare Castle, 1887–1987* (Clare: GAA, 1987).

Power, J., *Clare and the Great War* (Dublin: The History Press, 2015).

Price, D., *The Flame and the Candle: War in Mayo, 1919–1924* (Cork: The Collins Press, 2012).

Ryan, M., *Tom Barry: IRA Freedom Fighter* (Cork: Mercier Press, 2003).

Ryan, M., *Liam Lynch: The Real Chief* (Cork: Mercier Press, 2005).

Shanahan, E., *The Hand that Held the Gun: Untold Stories of the War of Independence in West Clare* (Clare: Clare Books, 2019).

Share, B., *In a Time of Civil War: The Conflict on the Irish Railway* (Cork: The Collins Press, 2006).

Sheedy, K., *The Clare Elections* (Dublin: Bauroe Press, 1993).

Spellissy, S., *The Ennis Compendium: From Royal Dun to Information Age Town* (Clare: The Book Gallery, no date).

Smith Walsh, E., *Kilkenny: In Times of Revolution, 1900–1923* (Dublin: Merrion Press, 2019).

Stacpoole, J., *Stacpoole: The Owners of a Name* (Auckland: published for private circulation, 1991).

Stewart, A.T.Q., *The Shape of Irish History* (Belfast: The Blackstaff Press, 2001).

Townshend, C., *The Republic: The Fight for Irish Independence, 1918–1923* (London: Allen Lane, 2013).

Valiulis, M.G., *Portrait of a Revolutionary: General Richard Mulcahy and the Founding of the Irish Free State* (Kentucky: University of Kentucky Press, 1992).

Walsh, M., *Bitter Freedom: Ireland in a Revolutionary World, 1918–1923* (London: Faber and Faber, 2015).

Williams, T.D., *The Irish Struggle, 1916–1926* (London: Routledge & K. Paul, 1966).

Weeks, L. and M. O'Fahartaigh (eds), *The Treaty: Debating and Establishing the Irish State* (Dublin: Irish Academic Press, 2018).

Younger, C., *Ireland's Civil War* (London: Fontana/Collins edition, 1970).

Newspapers

Clare Champion
Clare Journal and Saturday Record
Cork Examiner
Freeman's Journal
Galway Advertiser
Irish Independent
Irish Times
Limerick Leader

Magazines
Capuchin Annual
History Ireland
The Other Clare

ENDNOTES

1 J. Power, *The GAA in Clare Castle, 1887–1987* (Clare: Clarecastle GAA, 1987), pp. 95–6.
2 E. Smith Walsh, *Kilkenny in Time of Revolution, 1910–1923* (Dublin: Merrion Press, 2019), pp. 97–100.
3 Police reports for County Clare, October–December 1917, National Archives of Ireland (NAI), MFA/54/62.
4 See letter from John Devoy published in the *Clare Champion*, 16 August 1924; J. Power, *A History of Clare Castle and its Environs* (Clare: published privately at Ennis, 2004), pp. 370–86, passim; F.S.L. Lyons, *Ireland since the Famine* (Glasgow: Fontana, 1971), pp. 247–59, passim.
5 RIC reports, precis of information received by the Special Branch, April 1905–November 1913, NAI, CO MFA/54/74.
6 P.Ó. Ó Ruairc, *Blood on the Banner: The Republican Struggle in Clare* (Cork: Mercier Press, 2009), p. 27; Sean O'Keefe, Bureau of Military History, Witness Statements (WS) 1261.
7 RIC reports, NAI, CO MFA/54/74.
8 Art O'Donnell, WS 1322; RIC reports, 1908, NAI, CO MFA/54/74. See also John Joe Neylon, WS 1042; Andrew O'Donoghue, WS 1326; Joe Barrett, WS 1324; Michael Brennan, WS 1268; Michael O'Dea, WS 1152, and Hugh Hehir, WS 683; also, C. O'Comhrai and S. O'Comhrai, *Peadar Clancy: Easter Rising Hero, and Bloody Sunday Martyr* (Galway: Cranny Publications, 2016), p. 24.
9 J.E.A. Connell, Jr, 'Home Rule rally on Sackville Street, Dublin, March 1912', *History Ireland*, 2, 20 (March/April 2012).
10 D. Fitzpatrick, *Politics and Irish Life, 1913–1921* (Dublin: Gill and Macmillan, 1977) pp. 89, 105.
11 J. Power, *Clare and the Great War* (Dublin: The History Press, 2015), chapters 2, 3 and 4 passim.
12 R.F. Foster, *Modern Ireland, 1600–1972* (London: Penguin Books, 1989), pp. 471–6.
13 Ernest Blythe, WS 939, pp. 34, 35, 42–4, 55.
14 *Saturday Record* (*SR*), 17 July 1915. Note that the *Saturday Record*, along with another Ennis paper, the *Clare Journal*, was owned by the Protestant Knox family and was pro-British government in its editorial policy.
15 M. Brennan, *The War in Clare, 1911–1921: Personal memoirs of the Irish War of Independence* (Dublin: Four Courts Press, 1980), p. 11.
16 Art O'Donnell, WS 1322.
17 *Clare Journal* (*CJ*), 3 June 1915.
18 *CJ*, 15 November 1915.
19 Episcopal correspondence, Fogarty to O'Dwyer, 9 December 1915, Limerick Diocesan Archives (LDA), BI/ET/7.
20 *Clare Champion* (*CC*), 15 November 1915.
21 Police reports from County Clare, NAI, MFA/54/57.

22 *CJ*, 15 April 1916.

23 P.Ó. Ó Ruairc, *Blood on the Banner*, p. 39. There were more than a dozen Irish Volunteer branches in the county by Easter 1916, including the following: Carrigaholt, Cloonagh, Corofin, Cratloe, Crusheen, Darragh, Feakle, Inagh, Inch, Kildysart, Killaloe, Meelick, Newmarket-on-Fergus and Tullycrine.

24 Fr Charles Culligan's speech was given at a Sinn Féin meeting at the Ennis workhouse on 29 January 1916, see D. Fitzpatrick, *Politics and Irish Life, 1913–1921*, p. 139; J.A. de Weil, *The Catholic Church in Ireland, 1914–1918: War and Politics* (Dublin: Irish Academic Press, 2003), p. 18. Also, Police reports for County Clare, MFA/54/58.

25 See witness statements of Clare Volunteers such as Art O'Donnell, WS 1322; Joe Barrett, WS 1324; Michael Brennan, WS 1068; Sean McNamara, WS 1047; and Éamon Fennell, WS 1252. Also, P.Ó. Ó Ruairc, *Blood on the Banner*, pp. 42–52; G. Kennedy, *The Crusheen Volunteers and Their Role during 1916* (Clare: published by the author, 2016), pp. 21–30; M. MacMahon, *The Parish of Corofin: A Historical Profile* (published by the author, 2013), p. 289.

26 *CJ*, 6 May 1916.

27 *CJ*, 15 May 1916.

28 The inquiry was held at the Shelbourne Hotel, Dublin; *CC*, 3, 10 June 1916; *SR*, 10 June 1916; M. Brennan, *The War in Clare*, pp. 18–19.

29 *SR*, 24 June 1916.

30 *CC*, 5 May 1916.

31 *CJ*, 27 April 1916; *SR*, 6, 13, 20 May; *CC*, 5 May; K. Sheedy, *The Clare Elections* (Dublin: Bauroe Press, 2000), p. 786.

32 *CC*, 5, 20 May 1916.

33 Episcopal correspondence, Fogarty to O'Dwyer, 31 July, 7, 10, 12 and 17 September 1916, LDA, BI/ET/07. See also, T.J. Morrissey, SJ, *Bishop Edward T O'Dwyer of Limerick, 1842–1917* (Dublin: Four Courts Press, 2003), p. 380.

34 *CC*, 10 June, 1 July, 19 August, 9, 30 September, 7, 28 October 1916; *SR*, 10 June 1916; Police reports for County Clare, dated 11 May 1916, according to Mr Gelston, County Inspector, NAI, MFA/54/59

35 Michael Brennan, WS 1068.

36 Police reports for County Clare, December 1916, NAI, MFA/54/60.

37 Police report for County Clare, February 1917, NAI, MFA/61/54.

38 Police reports for County Clare, March 1917, NAI; *CC*, 10 March 1917; NAI, MFA/54/63; P.Ó. Ó Ruairc, *Blood on the Banner*, p. 73.

39 *CJ*, 26 February 1917; *CC*, 28 April 1917.

40 *CC*, 12 May 1917.

41 Police Reports for County Clare, May 1917, NAI, MFA/54/62.

42 *CC*, 15, 22 June 1917; *SR*, 15 June 1917. At the meeting in the Clare Hotel, the following attended: Rev. A. Clancy, PP; Rev. J. O'Donoghue; Rev. M. Crowe; Rev. T. Molloy; Rev. W. O'Kennedy (president of St Flannan's College, Ennis). Besides the clergy, the following also attended: Messrs Sean McNamara, Con Kearney, M. Nugent, P.C. Casey, M. O'Brien, M. Hegarty, A. Brennan, J. Barrett, J. Spellissy, M. Quin, D. Bugler, J. Crowe, T. McGrath, P. Brody, T. Considine and M. McInerney.

43 *CC*, 7 July 1917; *SR*, 7 July 1917.

44 Police reports for County Clare, June 1917, NAI, MFA/54/62.

45 E. MacLysaght, *Changing Times: Ireland since 1898* (London: Colin Smyth, 1978), p. 111. MacLysaght, from Tuamgraney, was a Sinn Féin representative at the Irish Convention set up by Lloyd George in 1917 to strive to reach a political consensus in Ireland. MacLysaght, a moderate, stated, 'the people as a whole do not want revolution and the country is looking for a settlement.' But he prophetically declared at the convention, which he regarded as 'a hostile assembly', 'if the Convention fails,

it will require revolution and bloodshed to arrive at the inevitable result, Irish freedom.' E. MacLysaght, 'Some memories of the Irish Convention, 1917–1918', *Capuchin Annual* (1968), pp. 345–52.

46 *CC*, 11 July 1917; de Valera's quote cited in *Capuchin Annual* (1969), 'Chief of Staff', an article by General Richard Mulcahy, p. 343; O'Callaghan to editor of the *Irish Times*, dated 25, 30 June 1917, pp. 848, 850, George O'Callaghan Westropp Papers, Archive Collections, UCD, Letterbooks P38/3.

47 The development of these national organisations can be seen in extensive coverage in the *Clare Champion* during the months of June–December 1917. J. Cronin, *The Munster GAA Story* (Clare: Clare Champion, 1986), p. 107; also, R. McElligott, 'The GAA, the 1916 Rising and its aftermath to 1918' in G. O'Tuathaigh (ed.) *The GAA and Revolution in Ireland, 1913–1923* (Cork: The Collins Press, 2015), pp. 152–8. The advertisement for the Clarecastle GAA fundraising sports meeting for de Valera's election fund was in the *Clare Journal*, 28 September 1917.

48 Michael Brennan, WS 1068.

49 Police reports for County Clare, July 1917, NAI, MFA/54/62.

50 T. MacNamara, *Days of Hunger: The Clare Volunteers and the Mountjoy Hunger Strike of 1917* (Clare: Dallan Publishing, 2017), passim.

51 *CC*, 29 September 1917; J. Power, 'Censorship of the Clare Champion in 1917–1918', *The Other Clare*, 42 (2018), pp. 68–76.

52 See copy of the letter in pamphlet form in police reports for County Clare, 1917, NAI, MFA/54/61/62.

53 *CC*, 24 November 1917; see comment by Dr J. Power, 'Commemorating Clare 1917 Hunger Strikers', *CC*, 1 December 2017, p. 10.

54 Police reports for County Clare, September–December 1917, NAI, MFA/54/62; *CC*, 6 October 1917.

55 *The Great Bishop of Limerick* (Dublin: MH Gill and Co., 1917), p. 18; de Weil, *The Catholic Church in Ireland, 1914–1918*, pp. 185, 195; Fogarty to O'Dwyer, 5 May 1917, LDA, BI/ET/0/7.

56 Police reports for County Clare, October–December 1917, NAI, MFA/54/62; Police reports for County Clare, January–February 1918, MFA/54/63.

57 Police reports for County Clare, October–November 1917, NAI, MFA/54/62; and J. Power, *Clare and the Great War*, pp. 120–32.

58 For a contemporary opinion on that role, see *Clare Champion*, 3 November 1917. The unattributed article was probably written by the editor, Sarsfield Maguire.

59 See witness statements of Joe Barrett, WS 1324; Michael Brennan, WS 1068; Thomas MacNamara, WS 1077; Andrew O'Donoghue, WS 1326; and Peter O'Loughlin, WS 985. Police reports for County Clare, January–February 1918; J. Power, *Clare and the Great War*, pp. 199–201 and note 8, p. 319.

60 *CC*, 29 February 1918; Police Reports for County Clare, January–February 1918, NAI, MFA/54/63.

61 J. Power, 'Censorship of the Clare Champion in 1919–1918', pp. 68–76.

62 *SR*, 27 April 1918; de Weil, *The Catholic Church in Ireland, 1914–1918,* p. 213; *SR*, 22 June; J. Power, *Clare and the Great War*, pp. 204–11.

63 *SR*, 10 August 1918.

64 Police reports for County Clare, September 1918, NAI, MFA/54/65.

65 Police reports for County Clare, November–December 1918, NAI, MFA/54/65.

66 J. Power, *Clare and the Great War*, p. 320, note 37; E. Gaynor, *The Memoirs of a Tipperary Family: The Gaynors of Tyone* (Dublin: Geography Publications, 2008), p. 85.

67 P. O'Brien, *The Glynns of Kilrush: Family, Business and Politics* (Dublin: Open Air, 2019), p. 134.

68 Police reports for County Clare, January, February, April and August 1919; P. O'Brien (in *The Glynns of Kilrush*, pp. 133–4) states that the home of Mr Glynn of Pella House, Kilrush, along with those of the widow Lyons, Mrs Fitzpatrick and Mr Costello of Kilrush were also raided for arms in January; Police report for County Clare, November 1918, NAI MFA/54/65.

69 *CC*, 11, 18 January, 24 May 1919.

70 *CC*, 11, 18, 30 January, 6 February, 22 February, 19 April, 12 July 1919. The East Clare Sinn Féin *combhairle ceanntair* represented clubs in the following parishes: Ballinruan, Ballyvaughan, Ballycorick, Barefield, Bodyke, Bridgetown, Carron, Clarecastle, Clonlara, Corofin, Cratloe, Clooney, Crusheen, Doora, Inagh, Ennis, Feakle, Garranboy, Inch, Kilaneena, Kilnaboy, Kilnamona, Kilmore, Kilkeedy, Meelick, Newmarket-on-Fergus, Nuaghoville, O'Callaghan's Mills, Oatfield and Ballycar, Quin, Rath, Ruan, Scariff, Sixmilebridge and Tulla.

71 *SR*, 18 January, 1 March 1919; *CC*, 22 February, 11 October 1919.

72 *SR*, 18 January, 1 October 1919; *CC*, 9 August, 23 October, 6, 20 December 1919.

73 E. O'Malley, *On Another Man's Wound* (Dublin: Anvil Books, 1979), p. 96; M. Brennan, *The War in Clare*, see chapter one; P.Ó. Ó Ruairc, *Blood on the Banner*, pp. 90–1.

74 Police reports for January 1919, NAI, MFA/54/66.

75 Mr Gelston, Police report for January 1919, NAI, MFA/54/66.

76 *CC*, 11 January 1919; *SR* 11 Jan, 1919.

77 Police report for March 1919, NAI, MFA/54/66.

78 D.J. O'Sullivan, *The Irish Constabulary, 1822–1922* (Kerry: Brandon Publications, 1999), p. 283.

79 *CC*, 19 April, 24 May; *SR*, 19 April 1919; Police report for April 1919, NAI, MFA/66; Art O'Donnell, WS 1322; John Flanagan, WS 1252; E. O'Malley, *On Another Man's Wound*, pp. 34–6.

80 *SR*, 5 July 1919; P.Ó. Ó Ruairc, *Blood on the Banner*, pp. 78–9.

81 Martin Chambers, WS 1251; Joseph Daly, WS 1253; and John Flanagan, WS 1316, all from the West Clare Brigade. Also, Andrew O'Donoghue, WS 1326; and Thomas Shalloo, WS 1075, from the Mid-Clare Brigade. M. Brennan, *The War in Clare*, p. 38; Joe Barrett, WS 1324; Sean McNamara, WS 1072; and Pat Kerin, WS 977, from the Mid-Clare Brigade; see correspondence between Frank Barrett and Michael Collins, 25 July, and 8, 9, 26 August 1919, Military Archives, (B3), p. 915; Barrett to Collins, 4, 8 November 1919, Michael Collins Papers, Military Archives, IE/MA/CP/2/31/(xvii, xxiii); E. O'Malley, *On Another Man's Wound*, pp. 104–6.

82 See D. Fitzpatrick, *Politics and Irish Life, 1913–1921*, chapter one, for estimates of the Crown forces in the county; J. Herlihy, *The Royal Irish Constabulary* (Dublin: Four Courts Press, 1997), p. 104.

83 Police report for County Clare, January 1919, C.I. Gelston to Inspector General, NAI, MFA/54/66.

84 P. Béaslaí, *Michael Collins and the New Ireland* (London: The Phoenix Publishing Co., 1926), p. 225.

85 *CC*, 9 August 1919; Police reports for August 1919, NAI, MFA/54/67; Andrew O'Donoghue, WS 1326; Martin Chambers, WS 1251. Meda Ryan records that in July 1919, GHQ informed Liam Lynch that he, as commandant of a brigade in Cork, could disarm any military provided there were no casualties. M. Ryan, *Liam Lynch: The Real Chief* (Cork: Mercier Press, 2012), p. 42.

86 *SR*, 12, 19 July; *Irish Times*, 12 July 1919.

87 *CC*, 12 July; *Irish Times*, 11 July 1919.

88 *CC*, 26 July 1919; Operations of Active Service Unit members of Mid-Clare Brigade during Anglo-Irish War, notes compiled by Joe Barrett, copy in Local Studies Centre,

Ennis. Barrett states that there were seven RIC men in the hut, who were equipped with rifles and revolvers. Joe Barrett, in his witness statement (WS 1324), also states that two serviceable rifles, with a small quantity of ammunition plus a few shotguns and a few dozen home-made bombs, were used in the attack on Inch, which lasted about two hours, and that one IRA man was severely wounded by a premature explosion. Barrett gives a list of fifteen men who were involved. About fifteen men also took part in the Connolly attack led by Ignatius O'Neill. They had two rifles and about thirteen shotguns. But their home-made bombs did not arrive in time for the attack. The attack was called off after about an hour, as the RIC refused to surrender and ammunition was being wasted. See Edward Lynch, WS 1333; John Joe Neylon, WS 1042; Pat Devitt, WS 1044; Pat Kerin, WS 977; and Anthony Malone, WS 1076. See also Police reports on County Clare for July 1919, NAI, MFA/54/67.

89 *CC*, 15 July 1919; Police reports for July 1919, NAI, MFA, 54/67; General Richard Mulcahy, 'Chief of Staff', *Capuchin Annual* (Dublin: Capuchin, 1969), pp. 349–51. By contrast, when more than £16,700 was stolen from a bank in Cork, Liam Lynch, commandant of the Cork No. 2 Brigade, ensured that every penny was returned to the bank and the culprits were punished, see M. Ryan, *Liam Lynch*, pp. 52–3.

90 *Irish Times*, 1 August 1919.

91 *SR*, 23 August 1919; *CC*, 23 August 1919; Records of the Irish Distress and Irish Grants Committee, British National Archives, Kew, London, file ref. no. CO 762, copy in Local Studies Centre, Ennis, ref. no. 55/10 p.840. Cahir was awarded £100 for his distress.

92 *Irish Catholic*, 9 August 1919; see also *SR*, 13 August and *CC*, 13 August 1919.

93 *CC*, 23, 30 August 1919.

94 John Joe Neylon, WS 1042, 'At 81 Cross on August Monday 1919, along with Martin Devitt and Seamus Connolly we attacked two policemen [...] we had a Martini rifle, a carbine and a revolver [...] we shot the police dead, a sergeant and a constable [...] we got two revolvers [...] Martin Devitt was wounded'; T.S. McDonagh, WS 1540, 'At 81 Cross, where Sgt Riordan and Constable Murphy were killed by IRA Volunteers Martin Devitt, 'Tosser' Neylon and Seamus Connolly [...] Devitt was wounded [...] the RIC were the first police to be killed in Clare during the War of Independence'; also Seamus Connolly (Cullinagh, Ennistymon, officer commanding of the 5th Battalion, Mid-Clare Brigade), WS 976; and Joe Barrett, WS 1324, 'Attack at Illaunbawn [...] two policemen shot dead [...] Martin Devitt was wounded [...] John Joe Neylon, shot the police dead and collected their weapons.' Frank Barrett to Michael Collins, 11 August 1921, Military Archives, Michael Collins Papers, IE/MA/CP/2/31 (x; xiii); GHQ to Barrett, 25 August 1919.

95 *CC*, 9, 23 August 1919; Police reports, August 1919, NAI, MFA/54/67.

96 Sir Lucius O'Brien to Donough O'Brien, 6 August 1919, from the Inchiquin Papers, courtesy of Grania Weir, née O'Brien, Whitegate.

97 *CC*, 13 August; *SR*, 13 August 1919; Police reports, August 1919, NAI, MFA/54/67.

98 *CC*, 20 August; Police reports, August 1919, NAI, MFA/54/67.

99 *CC*, 23 August; Police reports, August 1919, NAI, MFA/54/67.

100 Police reports, July–December 1919; *SR*, 13 October, 27 December 1919, NAI, MFA/54/68; Considine to Adjt. General, no date, Michael Collins Papers, Military Archives, IE/MA/CP/3/40 (iii). In a public statement in the *Clare Champion* dated 5 June 1920, Michael Whelan of Shragh denied that shots were fired at him and that his wife was attacked; Gerald Griffin, *The Collegians* (London: Atlantic Books, 2008), p. 437; Liam O'Flaherty, *The Informer* (Dublin: Wolfhound Press, Dublin), pp. 12, 15, 21, 157, 163 ; *SR*, 13 September 1919. Michael Kearney was a member of the 2nd Battalion, Mid-Clare Brigade and took part in several operations during

the war. See notes compiled by Joe Barrett, 'Mid-Clare Operations' in Local Studies Centre, Ennis.

101 *CC*, 23 August, 27 September, 4, 18 October 1919; *SR*, 13 December 1919; Police reports, August–December 1919, NAI, MFA/54/68.

102 Police reports, July–November 1919, NAI, MFA/54/67/68.

103 *SR*, 15, 22 November; CC, 15 November, 20 December 1919.

104 *CC*, 6 December; *SR*, 6 December 1919; *SR*, 3 January 1920.

105 *SR*, 20 August, 20 September; *CC*, 20 August, 20 September 1919; Police report for County Clare, August 1919. Tomas Mac Conmara – in *The Time of the Tans* (Cork: Mercier Books, 2019), pp. 242–8 – reveals the huge emotional impact that this tragedy had upon the Murphy family.

106 *CC*, 6 September 1919.

107 *CC*, 9, 23, 30 August, 4 October.

108 *CC*, 20 September; *SR*, 15 November 1919.

109 *CC*, 23 August 1919.

110 *SR* 11, 25 October, 15 November; CC, 13 December 1919; O'Callaghan Westropp to Viscount French, dated 18 October 1919, George O'Callaghan Westropp Papers, Archives Collections, UCD, Letterbooks, P 38/4, pp. 87–90, 115; Colonel O'Callaghan Westropp's letter to the editor of the *Morning Post*, on the state of Clare, 9 December 1919.

111 Police report for January 1919, NAI, MFA/54/66.

112 Police reports for September 1919, NAI, MFA/54/68; *SR*, 11 October, 8 November 1919.

113 *SR*, 29 November 1919; *Irish Times*, 24 November 1919; *CC*, 31 January 1920; Anthony Malone, WS 1076.

114 *SR*, 13 December 1919.

115 *SR*, 6 December; *Irish Independent*, 5 December 1919; *Irish Times*, 5 December; *CC*, 3, 31 January 1920; Irish Independent newspaper cutting of the attack, 5 December 1919, Military Archives, Michael Collins Papers, IE/MA/CP/2/31 (xxviii).

116 Letter from Sir Lucius O'Brien, Dromoland to his son Donough O'Brien, dated 7 December 1919, courtesy of Grania Weir, née O'Brien, Whitegate.

117 Andrew O Donoghue, WS 1326.

118 Thomas Shalloo. WS 1075; Note, at a trial in Dublin in April 1921, Thomas Gannessy, a herdsman for H.V. McNamara, was found not guilty of the attack. *CC*, 23 April 1921; *SR*, 23 April 1921.

119 Letter from Lord Inchiquin to his son Donough O'Brien, Dromoland Castle, 7 December 1919, courtesy of Grania Weir, née O'Brien, Whitegate.

120 *SR*, 6, 20 December 1919; Frank Barrett to Michael Collins, 13, 16 October 1919, Military Archives, Michael Collins Papers, IE/MA/CP/2/31 (xix, xxi).

121 William McNamara, WS 1135.

122 Peter O'Loughlin, WS 985.

123 Andrew O'Donoghue, WS 1326.

124 Patrick Devitt, WS 1044.

125 Seamus McMahon, WS 984.

126 Peter O'Loughlin, WS 985.

127 Police reports, February 1920, NAI, MFA/54/69.

128 P.Ó. Ó Ruairc, *Blood on the Banner*, pp. 91, 106–7.

129 *SR*, 21 February 1920; *CC*, 21 February 1920.

130 Patrick Devitt, WS, 1044.

131 Seamus McMahon, WS 984.

132 Military Archives, Michael Collins Papers, IE/MA/CP/2/32, (ii-xi), dated 30 July 1919–24 November 1919; Art O'Donnell, WS 1322.

[133] *CC*, 10 January; *SR*, 31 January, 28 February, 14 August 1920; Police reports, January, February, July, August and September 1920; H. Keane, *Memories of My Childhood in County Clare* (printed for private circulation, 1990), pp. 3, 33. I am indebted to George Stacpoole, Adare, for bringing this memoir to my attention. O'Callaghan Westropp to Blackwood, 6 January 1920, George O'Callaghan Westropp Papers, Archive Collections, UCD, P 38/4, p. 129.

[134] *CC*, 6 March 1921.

[135] Letter from Lady Inchiquin, Dromoland Castle, to her son Donough in India, 15 January 1920, courtesy of Grania Weir, née O'Brien, Whitegate.

[136] Unionist description of the state of Clare, 23 April 1920, Report from Captain RF Hibbert of Woodpark, Scariff, Co. Clare, Irish Historical Documents 1914–1925, pp. 166–7 No. 101.

[137] *CC*, 21 February 1920; *SR*, 21 February 1920.

[138] *SR*, 24 January 1920; *CC*, 24 January 1920; E. Shanahan, *The Hand that Held the Gun: Untold Stories of the War of Independence in West Clare* (Clare: Clare Books, 2019), see chapter 'The drowning of Michael Darcy ', pp. 92–98, passim.

[139] *CC*, 28 February; *SR*, 28 February 1920; Police reports, February 1920, NAI, MFA/54/69; Patrick Devitt, WS 1044; John Joe 'Tosser' Neylon, WS 1042; T.S. McDonogh, WS 1540; and Andy O'Donoghue, WS 1326.

[140] *SR*, 6 March 1920; *CC*, 6, 27 March 1920.

[141] D.J. O'Sullivan, *The Irish Constabulary, 1822–1922*, p. 309.

[142] *SR*, 13 March, 10, 17 April 1920.

[143] *CC*, 7, 14 February, 15 May 1920; George O'Callaghan Papers, Archives Collections, UCD, P38/4, p. 149, dated 9 March 1920. The resolution by the Grand Jury of County Clare was sent to the Lord Lieutenant of Ireland, Viscount French.

[144] C. O'Comhrai and S. O'Comhrai, *Peadar Clancy*, chapter 6, 'The Hunger Striker', pp. 121–32, passim; *SR*. 17 April 1920; C. Townshend, *The Republic: The Fight for Irish Independence, 1918–1923* (London: Allen Lane, 2013), pp. 142–4.

[145] *SR*, 17, 24 April 1920; *CC*, 17, 24 April, 8 May 1920; *Irish Times*, 29 April 1920; Edward Lynch, WS 1333; Police reports, 14 April 1920, NAI, MFA/54/69.

[146] *Irish Times*, 19, 20 April 1920; *SR*, 24 April, 15 May 1920; CC, 15 May 1920.

[147] Bill Haugh, WS 474; T. Mac Conmara, *The Time of the Tans*, pp. 228–42.

[148] E. Gaynor, *The Memoirs of a Tipperary Family*, pp. 174–5.

[149] *SR*, 28 August; *CC*, 28 August 1920; *Irish Times*, 23 August 1920; Bill Haugh, WS 474; John Flanagan, WS 1316.

[150] *SR*, 28 February, 28 August 1920; R. Abbott, *Police Casualties in Ireland, 1919–1922* (Cork: Mercier Books, 2000).

[151] *CC*, 24 April, 10 June, 10 July 1920; *SR*, 24 April 1920.

[152] P.Ó. Ó Ruairc, 'Sectarianism in County Clare during the War of Independence', *The Other Clare*, 34 (2010), pp. 35–41, passim; *Irish Times*, 21, 23 September; *SR*, 25 September 1920.

[153] *CC*, 1 May, 19 June 1920; *Irish Times*, 20 April 1920; *CC*, 1, 8 July; *SR*, 1, 8 July 1920; Police reports, June 1920, NAI, MFA/54/69; E. Gaynor, *The Memoirs of a Tipperary Family*, pp. 175–6; Irish Distress Committee, Kew London, file CO762, Nora Logan, ref 96/3, p. 1609; Katie McNamara, ref 68/1, p. 1093; and Susan O'Keefe, ref 172/1, p. 2958; also correspondence, Mrs K Shinnors, Market Street, Ennis, to Pensions Board, 26 May 1941, Military Archives, MSPC-CMB-70.

[154] *CC*, 10 June 1922; *CC*, 1 July; *SR*, 1 July; Police reports for County Clare, June 1920, NAI, MFA/54/69.

[155] *SR*, 17 April; Police reports, June, October and December 1920, NAI, MFA/54/69/70; *SR*, 9 July 1921; E. Gaynor, *The Memoirs of a Tipperary Family*, pp. 130–2; see also, C. McCarthy, *Cumann na mBan and the Irish Revolution* (Cork: Collins Press, 2007);

Irish Distress Committee, British National Archives, Kew, CO 762, refs Peter Blake, 157/20, p. 2668; Michael Garrahy, ref 95/1, p. 1584.

[156] Police reports, October 1920, NAI, MFA/54/70; *SR*, 5 June 1920.

[157] Police reports, April and June 1920, NAI, MFA/54/69; *CC*, 4 September 1920.

[158] *SR*, 12 June, 25 September, 2 October 1920; Police reports, April 1920, NAI, MFA/54/69.

[159] Police report, August 1920, NAI, MFA/54/69.

[160] Letter from Sir Lucius O'Brien to his son Donough, 22 July 1920, courtesy of Grania Weir, née O'Brien, Whitegate.

[161] *SR*, 24 April, 14 August; *CC*, 17 July, 4, 11, 25 September; Police reports for June and July 1920, NAI, MFA/54/69.

[162] Irish Distress Committee and Irish Grants Committee, British National Archive, Kew, London, CO 762. The applications by Joseph Brown, Batt Culligan, William C. Doherty, William T. Hogan, Joseph McInerney and William T. Corbett can be viewed in the alphabetical index. A copy of the County Clare applicants can be viewed in the Clare Resource Centre, County Library, Ennis. Christopher Kelly did not apply to the Irish Distress Committee for compensation. The sources for his case are in the County Clare police reports for June and July 1920, NAI, MFA/54/69, and in *SR*, 14 August 1920

[163] E. Gaynor, *The Memoirs of a Tipperary Family*, p. 144.

[164] Joseph Daly, WS 1251.

[165] *CC*, 22 January 1921.

[166] C. Townshend, *The Republic*, p. 130, 134; D. Fitzpatrick, *Politics and Irish Life*, pp. 174–5. Also, Fitzpatrick states, 'A detailed scheme for civil courts complete with guards in each parish to preserve the peace was devised for West Clare by the sentimental poet Brian O'Higgins', see D. Fitzpatrick, 'The two Irelands' in J. Crowley, D. O'Droisceoil and M. Murphy (eds) *Atlas of the Irish Revolution* (Cork: Cork University Press, 2017), p. 83.

[167] Art O'Donnell, WS 1322.

[168] *CC*, 24 July; *CC*, 15, 22 May, 5, 12, 19 June, 17, 24 July, 7 August.

[169] For Brehons in the Sinn Féin courts, see witness statements of Thomas Shalloo, WS 1075; Peadar O'Loughlin, WS 985; Andy O'Donoghue, WS 1326; Patrick Kerin, WS 977; Seamus Connolly, WS 976; Éamon Fennell, WS 1251; Thomas McNamara, WS 1077; Hugh Hehir, WS 683; and Joseph Daly, WS 1252.

[170] E. Gaynor, *The Memoirs of a Tipperary Family*, pp. 121–6.

[171] *SR*, 26 June; *CC*, 26 June 1920; a report in the *Saturday Record* of 3 July stated that ash plants were not used by the IRA on the soldiers. See document, 'Operations of the 2nd Batt, Mid-Clare Brigade' by Joe Barrett, dated 12 February 1941, Local Studies Centre, Ennis.

[172] Joe Barrett, WS 1324; Sean O'Keefe, WS 1261; William McNamara, WS 1135; Andrew O'Donogue, WS 1326; and Hugh Hehir, WS 683. Joe Barrett's account of the operation has been re-published in *With the IRA in the Fight for Freedom: 1919 to the Truce* (Cork: Mercier Press, 2010), pp. 125–31; see also notes on *Operations of the Mid-Clare Brigade*, copy in Local Studies Centre, Ennis.

[173] *SR*, 17 July, 7 August 1920; Police reports, July and August 1920, NAI, MFA/54/69; Sean O'Keefe, WS 1261; P.Ó. Ó Ruairc, *Blood on the Banner*, p. 142; *CC*, 24 July 1920.

[174] *CC*, 4 December 1920. Sources for Joe Hawes: F. Brew, *The Parish of Kilkeedy: A Local History* (Clare: 1998), pp. 214–16; see also J. Hawes, 'Mutiny under the sun' in T.P. Kilfeather, *The Connaught Rangers* (Dublin: Anvil Books, 1969), chapters 12–14, passim; also O'Muircearthaigh, *The Connaught Rangers*, p. 47; *CC*, 4 July 1970, 19 January 1973, 11 January 2013. Grave at Shanakyle, Kilrush. He is also named

on the Connaught Rangers memorial, erected by the National Graves Association at Glasnevin, Dublin in 1983. *History Ireland*, spring 2001, vol 9; *History Ireland*, Spring 1998, issue 1, vol 6, article by Tom Bartlett; see Lot 603 James Adams, auctioneers Dublin, sale of effects of Jim Daly, executed on 2 November 1920, letter written by Joe Hawes to his friend, James Daly; J. Power, *Clare and the Great War*, pp. 258–9.

175 Police reports, August 1920, NAI, MFA/54/69.

176 Anthony Malone, WS 1076; John Joe 'Tosser' Neylon, WS 1042; Patrick Kerin, WS 977.

177 *SR*, 25 September, 2 October 1920; *CC*, 25 September, 2, 9 October 1920; *Irish Times*, 23 September 1920.

178 *SR*, 2 October 1920.

179 *Irish Times*, 27 September; *CC*, 2 October 1920; *SR*, 2 October 1920.

180 *Irish Times*, 25 September 1920; *CC*, 2 October 1920.

181 *Irish Times*, 30 October 1920; *CC*, 2 October 1920.

182 *SR*, 2 October 1920; *Irish Times*, 23, 25 September 1920.

183 *SR*, 2 October 1920; *CC*, 30 October 1920.

184 E. O'Malley, *Raids and Rallies* (Cork: Mercier Press, 2011), pp. 95–126.

185 Police report for September 1920; Major C.R. Davin, temporary county inspector, police report for October, 31.10.1920, NAI, MFA/54/70.

186 F.S.L. Lyons, *Ireland since the Famine*, pp. 415–18; C. Townshend, *The Republic*, pp. 161–8.

187 C. Townshend, *The British Campaign in Ireland, 1919–1921* (Oxford: Oxford University Press, 1975), pp. 95, 100; Lloyd George's speech was quoted in *Irish Independent*, 10 November 1920; also cited in C. Townshend, *The Republic*, p. 134.

188 Anthony Malone, WS 1076; Anthony Kerins, WS 977; John Joe 'Tosser' Neylon, WS 1042.

189 E. O'Malley, *Raids and Rallies*, pp. 107–8.

190 *CC*, 21 August 1920.

191 *London Gazette*, 30 July 1919; *Irish Times*, 2 October 1920; *CC*, 9 October 1920.

192 *SR*, 25 September 1920.

193 *Irish Times*, 28 September 1920; *CC*, 2, 9, 16 October 1920; *SR*, 2, 9, 16 October 1920; *CC*, 23 October; *SR*, 23 October 1920.

194 *CC*, 2, 9 October 1920; *Irish Times*, 2, 5 October 1920; David Joseph Conroy, WS 809.

195 Bill Haugh, WS 474.

196 E. Gaynor, *The Memoirs of a Tipperary Family*, pp. 126–7.

197 E. Shanahan, 'Telling tales: the story of the burial alive and drowning of a Clare RM in 1920', *History Ireland*, 1 (Jan/Feb 2010); E. Shanahan, *The Hand that Held the Gun*, pp. 190–204; Fr Pat Gaynor, *The Memoirs of a Tipperary Family*, pp. 126–7.

198 C. Townshend, *The British Campaign in Ireland, 1919–1921*, pp. 95, 158.

199 D. Leeson, *The Black and Tans: British Police and Auxiliaries in the Irish War of Independence, 1920–1921* (Oxford: Oxford University Press, 2001), pp. 371–3; *SR*, 12 June 1920; J. Borgovono, 'Army without barriers, the IRA, 1920–1921', *Atlas of Ireland*, p. 395.

200 R.C. Grey, *The Auxiliary Police* (London: Peace with Ireland Council, no date), copy in Bureau of Military History, Dublin, CD 227/16/9; another copy in Local Studies Centre, Ennis.

201 *SR*, 16 October.

202 *SR*, 23 October 1920; *CC*, 23 October 1920; *Irish Times*, 20 October 1920; Sean O'Keefe, WS 1261; Andy O'Donoghue, WS 1326; Joe Barrett, WS 1324; and John Joe 'Tosser' Neylon, WS 1042.

[203] Police reports, October 1920, NAI, MFA/54/70; and September 1921, MFA 54/72, dated 3 November 1921.
[204] Michael Brennan, WS 1068; *The Times*, 28 June, 30 July 1920; P.Ó. Ó Ruairc, *Blood on the Banner*, p. 142.
[205] Col. J.M. McCarthy, WS 883; B. O'Conchubhair, *Limerick's Fighting Story, 1916–21: Told by the Men Who Made It* (Cork: Mercier Press, 2000), pp. 260–1; Thomas McNamara, WS 1077; Henry O'Mara, WS 1653; Michael Brennan, WS 1068.
[206] Michael Brennan, WS 1068; *CC*, 2 October 1920; Police reports, September, October 1920.
[207] *CC*, 6 November 1920; *CC*, 5 February 1921.
[208] *Irish Times*, 6 October 1920; *CC*, 9, 30 October 1920.
[209] *CC*, 13 October 1920; *SR*, 13 October 1920.
[210] Tom Tuohy, WS 983.
[211] *SR*, 27 November 1920; *CC*, 20, 27 November 1920.
[212] Michael Brennan, WS 1068; Joe Clancy, WS 1370.
[213] Thomas McNamara, WS 1077; Harry O'Mara, WS 1652.
[214] Michael Brennan, WS 1068.
[215] Michael O'Dea, WS 1152; Harry O'Mara, WS 1652; Thomas McNamara, WS 1077.
[216] Michael Brennan, WS 1068.
[217] Joe Barrett, WS 1324; Peter O'Loughlin, WS 985; Andy O'Donoghue, WS 1326; John Joe 'Tosser' Neylon, WS 1042.
[218] William McNamara, WS 1135.
[219] Joe Barrett, WS 1251.
[220] Bill Haugh, WS 474; E. Gaynor, *The Memoirs of a Tipperary Family*, p. 177.
[221] Art O'Donnell, WS 1322.
[222] Martin Chambers, WS 1251; E. Shanahan, *The Hand that Held the Gun*, pp. 160, 289–92; Police reports, May 1921, NAI, MFA,54/72.
[223] Bill Haugh, WS 474.
[224] Martin Chambers, WS 1251.
[225] See National Library of Ireland, Ms 5368, for the official report from Dublin Castle on the deaths at Croke Park; T. Carey, 'GAA Centenary Bloody Sunday Outline', *History Ireland*, 2, 11 (summer 2003); C. O'Comhrai and S. O'Comhrai, *Peadar Clancy*, pp. 40–53, 158–79; E. MacLysaght, *Changing Times*, pp. 97–102, 104–10.
[226] *Irish Times*, 20 December 1920; *SR*, 25 December 1920; *CC*, 25 December 1920.
[227] John Joe Neylon, WS 1042; see also John Burke's opinion of the ambush at Moanreel in P.Ó. Ó Ruairc (ed.), *The Men Will Talk to Me: Clare Interviews with Ernie O'Malley* (Cork: Mercier Press, 2016), pp. 86–8.
[228] Joe Barrett, WS 1044.
[229] Police reports for December 1920, NAI, MFA/54/70; M. MacMahon – in *The Parish of Corofin*, pp. 291–6 – has a recent appraisal of the Battle of Moanreel.
[230] *CC*, 25 September, 23 October 1920; *SR*, 2, 9, 23 October 1920; H. Keane, *Memories of My Childhood in County Clare*, pp. 4, 6, 21, 54; Irish Grants Committee, PRO, Kew, London, CO 762, ref.193/22, p. 3443, dated 6 January 1927. See copy of this file in Local Studies Centre, Ennis.
[231] *SR*, 23 October 1921.
[232] *CC*, 30 October, 20 November 1920; Paddy 'Con' McMahon in P.Ó. Ó Ruairc (ed.), *The Men Will Talk to Me*, p. 99. Fr Pat Gaynor states that the execution of this soldier was bungled and ugly, 'he was still alive next day and was able to drink a cup of tea that some kind person in the locality gave him. He had been left lying inside a hedge and ultimately – so Éamonn Waldron told me – was battered to death by a stone'; E. Gaynor, *The Memoirs of a Tipperary Family*, p.178.
[233] *SR*, 27 November; *CC*, 27 November 1920; P.Ó. Ó Ruairc, *Blood on the Banner*, p.

194.

[234] *Irish Times*, 23 December 1920; *SR*, 1 January 1921; *CC*, 1 January 1921, 21 January 1921; for allegations that Captain Michael McNamara and Commandant Willie Shanahan were tortured before being killed, see Glucksman Library, University of Limerick, Special Collections, West Clare Brigade papers, compiled by Moss Twomey, *c*.1930, P4520(2) and P 45/15 (2); E. Shanahan, *The Hand that Held the Gun*, pp. 212–23.

[235] Police reports for October 1920, NAI, MFA/54/70; *Irish Times*, 29 October 1920; *CC*, 30 October 1920; *SR*, 30 October 1920; Thomas Tuohy, WS 983; Pat McDonnell in P.Ó. Ó Ruairc (ed.), *The Men Will Talk to Me*, pp. 161–2, 202, 209.

[236] J. Power, *Clare and the Great War*, pp. 138–9; for the private correspondence between Bishop Fogarty and Dr Edward O'Dwyer, Bishop of Limerick, on the morality of the 1916 Rising, see letters from Bishop Fogarty to Bishop O'Dwyer in Limerick Diocesan Archives. Bishop Fogarty became a public supporter of Sinn Féin after the East Clare by-election and was an outspoken critic of British policy, e.g. during the hunger strikes of 1917 and the slaughter at Canada Cross, Miltown Malbay in 1920; Bishop Fogarty, WS 271. Also, original letter from the National Bank to Bishop Fogarty 13/4/22 acknowledging receipt of £7,674 to be lodged to account of M. Fogarty, E. de Valera and S. O'Mara, Trustees of Sinn Féin funds, Killaloe Diocesan Archives, Ref 1.9. B. 1–Box 34.

[237] D. Fitzpatrick, *Politics and Irish Life*, pp. 138–41.

[238] Thomas Tuohy, WS 983; John Ryan, WS 1136.

[239] *Irish Catholic*, 19 July, 16 August, 23 August 1919, 2, 30 October 1920.

[240] B. Heffernan, 'The Catholic Church and the War of Independence' in *Atlas of the Irish Revolution*, p. 504; T. O'Fiaich, 'The Catholic Clergy and the Independence Movement', *Capuchin Annual* (1970), p. 484; for a comprehensive study of this topic, see B. Heffernan, *Freedom and the Fifth Commandment* (Manchester: Manchester University Press, 2014), passim.

[241] *CC*, 24 April 1920; *SR*, 15 May 1920.

[242] *SR*, 1 January 1921; *CC*, 1 January 1921.

[243] *CC*, 21 August, 11 September 1920; E. Gaynor, *The Memoirs of a Tipperary Family*, pp. 134–9.

[244] *SR*, 16 October 1920.

[245] *CC*, 20 November; *SR*, 27 November 1920.

[246] Monsignor J.T. McMahon, WS 362.

[247] *SR*, 11 December; CC, 11 December 1920.

[248] Police reports, December 1920, NAI, MFA/54/70.

[249] *Irish Independent*, 14 December 1920; *CC*, 18 December; *SR*, 18 December 1920.

[250] F.P. Crozier, *Ireland Forever* (London: Jonathan Cape, 1932), p. 107.

[251] *SR*, 18 December 1920.

[252] *SR*, 1 January 1921.

[253] B. Heffernan, *Freedom and the Fifth Commandment*, p .74.

[254] Letters from Sir Shane Leslie of Castle Leslie, Co. Monaghan to Dr Fogarty, 5 Nov 1920, 30 April 1921, Killaloe Diocesan Archives, Westbourne House, Ennis, Box 15, FA 321.

[255] Tom Tuohy, WS 983.

[256] Police report for County Clare, October 1920, NAI CO MFA/54/70.

[257] E. Gaynor, *The Memoirs of a Tipperary Family*, pp. 127, 129, 138, 140, 150; Irish Distress Committee, British National Archives, Kew, London, CO762, ref no. 72/3, p. 1172, Fr James Russell.

[258] C. Dowd, *Faith, Ireland and the Empire: Patrick Joseph Clune, Cssr, 1864–1935* (New South Wales: St Paul's, 2014), pp. 190–225; Monsignor J.T. McMahon, WS

362; C. Younger, *Ireland's Civil War* (London: Fontana/Collins edition, 1970), p. 131; Michael Brennan, WS 1068; *CC*, 8 January; *SR*, 8 January, 12 March 1921; article by D.F. Bourke, *Australian Dictionary of Biography*,(Melbourne: Melbourne University Press, 1981).

[259] R. Fanning, *Fatal Path: British Government and Irish Revolution, 1910–1922* (London: Faber and Faber, 2013), pp. 246, 256–7.

[260] Monsignor J.T. McMahon, WS 363; Michael Brennan, WS 1068.

[261] National Archives UK, WO 141 93 213, Record of the Rebellion in Ireland, Vol IV, part 2, ch 7, cited in E. Shanahan, *The Hand that Held the Gun*, p. 255 and note 7 p. 413; Police reports for County Clare, October 1920, NAI CO MFA/54/70.

[262] *SR*, 8 January 1921; *CC*, 8 January 1921; 'Military proclamation: Use of bicycles prohibited from 1 July in Martial Law area', *SR*, 2 July 1921.

[263] *SR*, 8 January 1921; Police reports for January 1921, NAI, MFA/54/71; *SR*, 8 January 1921; *CC*, 22 January 1921.

[264] *Irish Times*, 21 January 1921; *SR*, 22 January; *CC*, 22, 29 January 1921; Michael Brennan, WS 1068; Michael O'Dea, WS 1152.

[265] *Irish Independent*, 22 January 1921; *CC*, 29 January 1921; Bodkin Report, February 1921.

[266] Police reports, January 1921, NAI, MFA/54/71; Michael Brennan, WS 1068; Joe Clancy, WS 1370; *CC*, 5 February 1921.

[267] Joe Clancy, WS 1370; Correspondence, OC, (M. Brennan) to adjutant-general, 29 March 1921, Richard Mulcahy Papers, UCD Archives Collections, P7/A/38.

[268] Michael Brennan, WS 1068; GHQ to Brennan, dated 8 February 1921, Military Archives, Michael Collins Papers, IE/MA/CP/5/2/22 (v).

[269] Police report, March 1921, NAI, MFA/54/71.

[270] *SR*, 5 March; *CC*, 5 March 1921; *CC*, 5 February 1921.

[271] Police report, February 1921, NAI, MFA/54/71; *SR*, May, 16 July 1921.

[272] *SR*, 22 January 1921.

[273] Police reports for October, December 1920, and May 1921, NAI, MFA/54/70/72.

[274] Bill Haugh, WS 474; Martin Chambers, WS 1251; John Flanagan, WS 1316; Anthony Malone, WS 1076; Hugh Hehir, WS 683; Michael Brennan, WS 1068.

[275] See the extensive reports in the local papers, *CC* and *SR*, between January and July 1921 on road cutting etc., e.g., 2 February, 5, 12, 19, March, 23, 30 April, 14, 21, 28 May, 11, 18 June, 9 July 1921; H. Keane, *Memories of My Childhood in County Clare*, p. 1.

[276] Correspondence, Mulcahy to Barrett 31/3/1921, and Barrett to Mulcahy, 11/4/1921, Richard Mulcahy Papers, UCD Archives, P7/A/17.

[277] *SR*, 19 March 1921; *CC*, 26 March 1921; 21, 28 May 1921.

[278] Police report for May 1921, NAI, MFA/54/72.

[279] Police reports, February 1921, NAI, MFA/54/71; *SR*, 23 April, 25 June 1921.

[280] *SR*, 5 February 1921; CC, 26 March 1921; Bill Chambers, WS 474.

[281] Police report, February 1921, NAI, MFA/54/71; *CC*, 5 March; *SR*, 5 March 1921.

[282] *CC*, 30 April 1921.

[283] *SR*, 28 May 1921; *CC*, 28 May 1921.

[284] *CC*, 9 July 1921; Correspondence, Frank Barrett to R. Mulcahy, 28 May 1921, Richard Mulcahy Papers, UCD Archives, P7/A/19.

[285] *CC*, 12 February, 30 April 1921; *SR*, 21 February, 19 March 1921; John Burke, in P.Ó. Ó Ruairc (ed.), *The Men Will Talk to M*e, p. 91; Bill Haugh, WS 474.

[286] Correspondence, Mulcahy to Barrett, 31/3/1921 and Barrett to Mulcahy, 11/4/1921, Richard Mulcahy Papers, UCD Archives, P7/A/17.

[287] Police reports, William Attridge, CI, Ennis, 31 January 1921, NAI, MFA/54/71; Communications between Director of Intelligence and Frank Barrett, 11 May, 1, 7

July 1921, Military Archives, Michael Collins Papers, IE/MA/CP/5/2/21 (xxxii, xliv, xlvi).

288 Police reports from March to June 1921, NAI, MFA/54/71/72.

289 *SR* 21 May, 11 June 1921; *CC*, 11 June 1921; *SR*, 26 February, 5 March, 11 June 1921; *CC*, 5 March, 11 June, 16 July 1921; Police reports, 7 March 1921, NAI, MFA/54/71; Peter O'Loughlin, WS 985; E. Gaynor, *The Memoirs of a Tipperary Family*, pp. 132–3.

290 *SR*, 26 February 1921; *SR*, 5 March 21; Police reports, January–June 1921, NAI, MFA/54/71/72.

291 *CC*, 28 May 1921; Police reports, January–June 1921, NAI, MFA/54/71/72.

292 C.E. Glynn, 4 May 1921, 22 August 1921 and T. MacDonnell, for chief secretary, Dublin Castle, 30 June 1921 – copies of the letters are included in Police reports for County Clare, June 1921, NAI, MFA/54/72.

293 *SR*, 10 July 1920; *CC*, 12 February 1921.

294 *SR*, 2 October, 1920, 12 February, 21, 28 May 1921; *CC*, 12 February, 28 May, 9 July 1921; Police reports, February, April 1921, NAI, MFA/54/71/72; D.J. Conroy, WS 809; Bill Haugh, WS 474; Art O'Donnell, WS 1322; D. Fitzpatrick, *Politics and Irish Life*, p. 189; K. Sheedy, *The Clare Elections*, pp. 339–40; Gaynor, *The Memoirs of a Tipperary Family*, pp. 158–69.

295 John Joe 'Tosser' Neylon, WS 1042; Thomas McDonagh, WS 1540; *SR*, 12 March; Intelligence Summary from captured police intelligence, Police reports, May 1921, NAI, MFA/54/72; Correspondence Frank Barrett to chief of staff, May 1921, Richard Mulcahy Papers, UCD Archives, P7/A/19.

296 D. Fitzpatrick, *Politics and Irish Life*, pp. 188–97, and notes pp. 332–4; for their role in collecting rates, see the witness statements of Bill Haugh, WS 474; M. Hayes, WS 1173; Seamus Connolly, WS 976; Pat Kerin, WS 977; Thomas McDonagh, WS 1540; Sean Murnane, WS 1048; Hugh Hehir, WS 683; Thomas Shalloo, WS 1075; Peter O'Loughlin, WS 985; Andy O'Donoghue, WS 1326; Sean McNamara, WS 1072; Anthony Malone, WS 1076; Art O'Donnell, WS 1322.

297 D. Fitzpatrick, *Politics and Irish Life*, pp. 195–7, and notes, pp. 332–4; John Quinn, WS 1661; *SR*, 8 July 1922; Police report, William Attridge, CI, 30 September 1921, NAI, MFA 54/72.

298 Sean O'Keefe, WS 1261; Bill Haugh, WS 474; and Tom Tuohy, WS 983; *Irish Times*, 21, 22 January 1921; Police report, 19 January 1921, NAI, MFA/54/71; William McNamara, WS 1134; Peter O'Loughlin, WS 985

299 Peter O'Loughlin, WS 985; Joe Barrett, WS 1324; Correspondence, Frank Barrett to adjutant general, 14 June 1921, Richard Mulcahy Papers, UCD Archives, P7/A/19.

300 *CC*, 25 June 1921.

301 Andrew O'Donoghue, WS 1326; Thomas Shalloo, WS 1075; *CC*, 8 July 1921.

302 Chief of Staff to OC Mid Clare Brigade, 4, 30 April, 23 May 1921, Richard Mulcahy Papers, UCD, Archives Collection, P7/A/19; Chief of Staff to Acting OC, Mid-Clare Brigade, 4 March 1921, UCD, Archive Collections, Richard Mulcahy Papers, 7A/11/17; *CC*, 9 July 1921; *SR*, 9 July 1921; Reports from West Clare, director of organisation to the chief of staff, 30 June 1921, Richard Mulcahy Papers, UCD, Archives Collection, P7/A/21; Michael Brennan's report of operation at Kilrush, 8 April 1921, Mulcahy Papers, P7/A/38; Barrett to Director of Intelligence, 29 April 1921, Military Archives, Michael Collins Papers, IE/MA/CP/5/2/21(xvii).

303 *CC*, 2 July; *SR*, 2, 9 July 1921; Police reports, June 1921, NAI, MFA/54/72; Joe Clancy, WS 1370; Correspondence, M. Brennan to adjutant general, 30 June 1921, Mulcahy Papers, UCD Archives, P7/A/20.

304 Michael Brennan, WS 1251; Police reports, June 1921, NAI, MFA/54/72; *SR*, 25 June 1921; Extract of report from Michael Brennan to the chief of staff, 22 June

1921, Mulcahy Papers, UCD Archives, P7/A/20; correspondence M. Brennan to chief of staff, 6 July 1921, Mulcahy Papers, UCD Archives, P7/A/20.

305 *CC*, 11 June 1921; P.Ó. Ó Ruairc, *Blood on the Banner*, p. 247.

306 *SR*, 18, 25 June; *CC*. 18 June 1921; Police report, June 1921, NAI, MFA/54/72; Michael Brennan, WS 1251; Correspondence, Michael Brennan to chief of staff, 6 July 1921, Mulcahy Papers, UCD Archives, P7/A/20; P.Ó. Ó Ruairc, *Blood on the Banner*, pp. 248–9; K. Sheedy, *The Clare Elections*, pp. 626–7; Correspondence between Barrett and Director of Intelligence, 14 April, 7, 19 May 1921, Military Archives, Michael Collins Papers, IE/MA/CP/5/2/21(xviv-xvii; xxxiii); GHQ correspondence with Brennan, 26 April and 9 June 1921, Military Archives, Michael Collins Papers, IE/MA/CP/5/2/22(xxiii and xxx).

307 Michael Brennan, WS 1068; see also Joe Clancy, WS 1370; Michael O'Dea, WS 1152; Police report, William Attridge, CI, 30 April 1921, NAI, MFA/54/72; Correspondence, Michael Brennan to adjutant general, report of operations on 8 April 1921, Mulcahy Papers, UCD Archives Collections, P7/A/38. In this report, Brennan states that the date of this long march of about 20 miles was 3 April. He states that there were fifty armed IRA men being chased by the British, who came in seven Crossley Tenders and were armed with two Lewis guns. On this occasion, Brennan highlighted the 'frightful shortage of ammunition, with only twenty five rounds per man'.

308 *CC*, 12 March, 9 April, 28 May 1921; Police reports, March, May, June 1921, NAI, MFA/54/71/72; Joe Barrett Papers, courtesy of Dr Paul O'Brien, Mary Immaculate College, Limerick.

309 Barrett to Director of Intelligence, 14 April 1921, Military Archives, Michael Collins Papers, IE/MA/CP/5/2/21(xvii); Michael Brennan, WS 1068; Bill Haugh, WS 474; Correspondence Michael Brennan to adjutant general, 29 April 1921, Mulcahy Papers, UCD Archives Collections, P7/A/38.

310 *SR*, 30 April, 14 May, 18 June; *CC*, 30 April, 4 June 1921; *Kilrush Herald*, 6 May 1921; Police report, April 1921, NAI, MFA,54/72; Michael Brennan, WS 1068; for a detailed account of the operation at Kilrush, see Bill Haugh, WS 474.

311 *SR*, 12 March, 23 April, 30 April 1921.

312 Police report for July 1921, NAI, MFA/54/72; P.Ó. Ó Ruairc, *Blood on the Banner*, pp. 229–30; *CC*, 18 May 2018; RTÉ 1 documentary *Ar son na Poblachta*, broadcast on 29 October 2019 at 7.00 p.m.

313 Joe Clancy, WS 1370; Brennan to HQ, 23 March 1921, Military Archives, Michael Collins Papers, IE/MA/CP/5/2/22.

314 *SR*, 6, 29 August 1921; *SR*, 21 January 1921.

315 Police reports, February 1921, NAI, MFA/54/71; P.Ó. Ó Ruairc, *Blood on the Banner*, pp. 230–1. See also, by P.Ó. Ó Ruairc, Irish Story (2011) 'Deserters or spies? British Soldiers Executed At Lough Attorick', https://www.theirishstory.com/2011/02/18/deserters-or-spies-british-soldiers-executed-at-lough-attorick/#.XsJ-WGhKhyw, accessed 18 May 2020. Note, according to Geneva Rules of Warfare, it would be normal practice during wartime that enemy forces found in civilian attire behind enemy lines would be shot as spies. However, the official report, if it is credible, states that the soldiers were in uniform. Thomas McNamara, in his witness statement, stated, 'we shot three British officers as spies'. Thomas McNamara, WS 1077; *SR*, 26 February 1921.

316 *SR*, 9, 16 April; *CC*, 9, 16 April 1921; Police reports, April 1921, NAI, MFA/54/72.

317 *CC*, 23 April 1921; *SR*, 23 April 1921; Peadar O'Loughlin, WS 985; *SR*, 29 October 1921; Police report for County Clare, William Attridge CI, 30 April 1921, NAI MFA/54/72.

318 *SR*, 23, 30 April; *CC*, 23, 30 April, 21 May, 4 June 1921; P.Ó. Ó Ruairc (ed.), *The*

Men Will Talk to Me, pp. 100–1; Peter O'Loughlin, WS 985; Police reports, April 1921, NAI, MFA/54/72; Correspondence Frank Barrett to the chief of staff, April report (Barrett states that O'Shaughnessy's shop was 'an enemy den'), Mulcahy Papers, UCD Archive Collection, P7/A/38; Correspondence from Richard J. Stacpoole, Eden Vale to Dr Fogarty, dated 23 April 1921, Killaloe Diocesan Archives, Ennis; O'Callaghan Westropp to T. Edwards, 26 October 1921, George O'Callaghan Westropp Papers, Archive Collections, UCD, P38/3, pp. 153–4 and 277–8; O'Callaghan Westropp to W.T. Cosgrave, 8 December 1922, George O'Callaghan Westropp Papers, Archive Collections, UCD, P38/4, p. 342.

319 *SR*, 28 May, 4 June 1921; *CC*, 28 May, 4, 11 June 1921; Police reports, April 1921, NAI, MFA/54/72; Andrew O'Donoghue, WS 1326; Sean McNamara, WS 1072.

320 *SR*, 4, 11 June; *CC*, 4, 11 June, 9 July 1921; Police reports, June 1921, NAI, MFA/54/72; Correspondence Frank Barrett to Richard Mulcahy, 28 May 1921, Richard Mulcahy Papers, UCD Archives, P7/ A/ 18.

321 Police report, June 1921, NAI, MFA/54/72; *SR*, 2, 9 July 1921; *CC*, 2 July 1921; Joe Clancy, WS 1370; M. Brennan to adjutant general, 29 March 1921, Mulcahy Papers, UCD Archives, P7/A/38.

322 *SR*, 16 July; *CC*, 9, 16 July 1921; Police reports, July 1921, NAI, MFA/54/72.

323 *SR*, 7 May; *CC*, 14 May, 11 June 1921; R. Abbott, *Police Casualties in Ireland, 1919–1922* , see the alphabetical index. For further insights into the history of the RIC, see J. Herlihy, *The Royal Irish Constabulary*; D.J. O'Sullivan, *The Irish Constabulary, 1822–1922*; J.A. Gaughan, *The Memoirs of Constable Mee* (Cork: Mercier Press, 2012); and also, E. Malcolm, *The Irish Policeman, 1822–1922: A Life* (Dublin: Four Courts Press, 2006), passim.

324 Police reports, for July 1921, NAI, MFA/54/72; Correspondence, Frank Barrett to Mulcahy, 11 April 1921, also diaries at end of April, May and June 1921, Richard Mulcahy Papers, UCD Archives, P7/A/19; Michael Brennan, WS 1068; E. O'Malley, *On Another Man's Wound*, p. 336; P.Ó. Ó Ruairc, *Truce: Murder, Myth and the Last Days of the Irish War of Independence* (Cork: Mercier Press, 2016), passim. See appendices one and two for IRA operations and Crown forces activities for April 1921.

325 Andrew O'Donoghue, WS 1326.

326 *CC*, 8 January 1921; *SR*, 9 April, 28 May 1921; *CC*, 9 April, 28 May, 29 October 1921; E. Gaynor, *The Memoirs of a Tipperary Family*, pp. 134–57.

327 *SR*, 9 July 1921; *CC*, 9 July 1921; C. O'Murcadha, 'The prison letters of Canon O'Kennedy'. *The Other Clare*, 37 (2013), pp. 21–4; Frank Barrett to Director of Information, 3 February, 18 March, 7 May 1921, Military Archives, Michael Collins Papers, IE/MA/CP/5/2/21(vi, xiv, xxxi).

328 *SR*, 16 April; *CC*, 21 May 1921; Police report, March 1921, NAI, MFA/54/71; Bodkin Report, February 1921.

329 *SR*, 4 June 1921.

330 Seamus Connolly, WS 976.

331 Sean Murnane, WS 1048.

332 John Quinn, WS 1073; Correspondence, Brennan to Mulcahy, undated, and Mulcahy to Brennan, 22 April 1921, Mulcahy Papers, UCD Archives Collections, P7/A/17; Military Archives, Michael Collins Papers, IE/MA/CP/5/2/22 (viii; xiv), dated 19 February 1921 and 14 March 1921.

333 P.Ó. Ó Ruairc (ed.), *The Men Will Talk to Me*, Appendix II, 'The execution of Patrick D'Arcy', pp. 178–203. P.Ó. Ó Ruairc concludes, after a thorough study of this case, 'that the British acceptance of liability in these cases, though not conclusive proof, gives a strong indication that those killed [Counihan, Darcy and Reilly] were involved in espionage.'

334 *SR*, 25 June, 15 October 1920; *CC*, 25 June 1921.
335 Martin Chambers, WS 1251.
336 Bill Haugh, WS 474; Correspondence, B. Haugh to the adjutant general, monthly report, 30 June 1921, Mulcahy Papers, UCD Archives, P7/A/20.
337 County Inspector's Report for February, March 1921; P.Ó. Ó Ruairc (ed.), *The Men Will Talk to Me*, p. 171, note 15; E. Shanahan, *The Hand that Held the Gun*, pp. 232, 278–80; S. Cahill, 'The life and death of Thomas Shannon', *The Other Clare*, 41, pp. 26–9; Glucksman Library, University of Limerick, Special Collections, West Clare Brigade Papers, compiled by Moss Twomey on 18/9/1930, P45/21(2). Moss Twomey states that Thomas Shannon was shot on the night of 13 March 1921 by a party of Black and Tans. Twomey said that a Castle statement alleging that he was shot by a party of rebels to whom he refused to pay rates was a vile and false statement; Thomas Shannon was a true and trusted member of the organisation and is honoured as a republican martyr by the Old IRA.
338 Michael Russell, WS 1226; Typed letter signed and dated by Commandant Joe Barrett, Barrett Papers, Mary Immaculate College, Limerick, courtesy of Dr Paul O'Brien; E. Shanahan – in *The Hand that Held the Gun*, pp. 271–305 – thoroughly investigates the tragic and controversial execution of Patrick Darcy, but concludes, 'This book makes no pronouncement about the guilt or innocence of Patrick Darcy, nor does it seek to speculate about the rights or wrongs of his murder'; *Sunday Press*, 13 November 1955; Conversation with Brendan Daly of Cooraclare, former Fianna Fáil Councillor, TD and Minister for Fisheries, and a nephew of Patrick Darcy, at Ennis on 26 November 2019, Military Archives, MPSC, MD/6954; S. Enright, *The Irish Civil War: Law, Executions and Atrocity* (Dublin: Merrion Press, 2019), pp. 121, note 11, 174.
339 *CC*, 21 May 1921; Police report, May 1921, NAI, MFA/54/72.
340 Cited in F. O'Donoghue, *No Other Law: The Story of Liam Lynch and the Irish Republican Army, 1916–1923* (Dublin: Irish Press Ltd., 1954), Appendix III.
341 *CC*, 12 February 1921; *SR*, 12 February, 16 April 1921.
342 *SR*, 22 October 1920; Police report, May 1921, NAI, MFA/54/72; Bill Haugh, WS 474.
343 *SR*, 18 June, 29 October 1921.
344 Unionist description of the state of Clare, 23 April 1920, Report from Captain R.F. Hibbert of Woodpark, Scariff, Co. Clare, Irish Historical Documents 1914–1925, pp. 166–7, No. 101; *SR*, 18 June, 22, 29 October 1921.
345 *SR*, 25 June, 22 October 1921; *CC*, 25 June 1921.
346 *SR*, 2 July, 22 October 1921; *CC*, 2 July 1921; Correspondence, F. Barrett to C/S 25 June 1921, 28 June 1921, reply C/S to F. Barrett, 5 July 1921, Mulcahy Papers, UCD Archives, P7/A/21.
347 *SR*, 9 July, 22 October 1921.
348 *SR*, 16 July 1921; Correspondence F. Barrett to Adjt. General, 8 September 1921, Mulcahy Papers, UCD Archives, P7/A/ 24; Correspondence between F. Barrett and W.J. Corbett, 27 August 1921 and 30 August 1921, Mulcahy Papers, UCD Archives, P7/A/ 24.
349 *SR*, 26 March; Police report, March 1921, NAI, MFA/54/71; Correspondence, Frank Barrett to chief of staff, 4 April 1921, Richard Mulcahy Papers, UCD Archives Collections, P7/A/16.
350 *CC*, 4 June 1921; Police reports, June 1921, NAI, MFA/54/72.
351 Paddy, 'Con' McMahon, in P.Ó. Ó Ruairc (ed.), *The Men Will Talk to Me*, pp. 102–3; *SR*, 4 June 1921; Police report, June 1921, NAI, MFA/54/72; Correspondence Barrett to Mulcahy, dated 6 June 1921, Richard Mulcahy Papers, UCD Archives, P7/A/19; S. O'Reilly, *Clare GAA: The Club Scene, 1887–2010* (Clare: published by

the author, 2010), pp. 122–32.

[352] *SR*, 2 October 1920; D. Fitzpatrick, *Politics and Irish Life*, p. 76; *SR*, 9 July 1921; H. Keane, *Memories of My Childhood in County Clare*, pp. 1–2; see D. Fitzpatrick, *Politics and Irish Life*, pp. 70, 74, 278, and p. 308, note 40, and p. 351, note 57.

[353] M.M. Bodkin, *A Considered Judgement: Report of Judge Bodkin* (Dublin: The Talbot Press, 1921).

[354] *SR*, 2 July 1921; *CC*, 2, 9, 16 July 1921; See Paddy 'Con' McMahon's account in *The Men Will Talk to Me*, pp. 119–20.

[355] *SR*, 25 June, 30 July 1921; *SR*, 6 August 1921; *CC*, 9 July, 6 August 1921; Police report, May 1921; S. Enright, *The Irish Civil War*, p. 38 and p. 149, note 9; Enright cites the case of *Egan* vs *Macready* (1921), 1 IR 265.

[356] D. Fitzpatrick, *Politics and Irish Life*, p. 228; Michael M. Brennan, *The War in Clare*, pp. 38, 100–1, 106–7; Report of the deputy chief of staff on the Clare Inquiry, 27 October 1921, Mulcahy Papers, UCD Archives, P7/A/28, report of the deputy chief of staff, (General O' Duffy), on the Clare Inquiry, 27 October 1921. Mulcahy Papers, UCD Archives, P7/A/28, report dated 28 October 1928; Commandant-General Brennan's appointment was accepted on 15 November 1921, Mulcahy Papers, UCD Archives Collections, P7/A/37.

[357] *SR*, 18 June 1921; Correspondence, letters from J.J. Keane to the minister of defence, 18, 31 October 1921, Richard Mulcahy Papers, UCD, Archive Collections, P7/A/34; Report by Michael Brennan to chief of staff, 5 November 1921, Richard Mulcahy Papers, UCD, Archive Collections, P7/A/34; Chief of staff to M. Brennan, 16, 30 November 1921, Richard Mulcahy Papers, UCD, Archive Collections, P7/A/34; Irish Distress Committee and Irish Grants Committee, UK National Archives, Kew, CO762, reference 153/6, p. 2587, (copy in Local Studies Centre, Ennis).

[358] *SR*, 28 May 1921; J. Power, *Clare and the Great War*, pp. 208–10; Military Archives, MSPC/CMB/70; C. McCarthy, *Cumann na mBan and the Irish Revolution* (Cork: Collins Press, 2007), passim; E. Shaw, 'The Clare election of 1917 and the O'Brien – Sheedy Autograph Book' in *Clarecastle and Ballyea, Land and People 2* (Clare: Clarecastle and Ballyea Heritage Group, 2016), pp. 149–52; Dr Catherine O'Connor, 'Cumann na mBan in Clarecastle and Ballyea' in *Clarecastle and Ballyea, Land and People 2* (Clare: Clarecastle and Ballyea Heritage Group, 2016), pp. 73–80; Margaret Houlihan, 'Cumann na mBan activity in County Clare 1917–1921', *The Other Clare*, 42 (2018), pp. 84–92.

[359] Sean O'Callaghan, *The Informer*, (Kent: BCA, 1998), pp. 92–93.

[360] G. O'Tuathaigh, 'The Irish Revolutionary Decade, 1913–1923: voices, narratives and contexts' in C. Boylan, S. Buckley and P. Dolan (eds), *Family Histories of the Irish Revolution* (Dublin: Open Air, 2018), pp. 23–32, passim; also interview between Mary O'Malley and Gearoid O'Tuathaigh at Cuirt International Festival of Literature, 'Memory and in Literature and History' at Nun's Island Theatre, Galway, 14 April 2019.

[361] P.Ó. Ó Ruairc (ed.), *The Men Will Talk to Me*, p. 252.

[362] Patrick Devitt, WS 1044; Michael Brennan, WS 1068; and John Flanagan, WS 1316. See also, corroborating statements by Andrew O'Donoghue, WS 1326; Sean O'Keefe, WS 1261; Tom Tuohy, WS 983; and Bill Haugh, WS 474.

[363] Martin Chambers, WS 1251.

[364] D. Fitzpatrick, *Politics and Irish Life*, p. 230.

[365] Correspondence, QMG to chief of staff, 15 June 1921, Michael Brennan, WS 1068; Mulcahy Papers, UCD Archives, P7/A/20; Michael Brennan to chief of staff, April report 1921, Mulcahy Papers, UCD Archives Collections, P7/A/38.

[366] D. Breen, *My Fight for Irish Freedom*, pp. 166–7.

[367] R. Fanning, *Fatal Path: British Government and Irish Revolution, 1910–1922*,

chapter ten, pp. 246–76, passim; C. Townshend, *The Republic*, pp. 306–13.

368 M. Brennan, *The War in Clare*, pp. 104–5. Incidentally, the British army sergeant Martin Doyle, VC, mentioned here was sympathetic to the IRA and gave them information around this time, see M.J. Whelan, 'The impact of ex-British soldiers on the Irish Volunteers and the Free State army, 1913–1924', MA thesis, National University of Ireland, Maynooth, Maynooth, 2018.

INDEX OF NAMES

INDEX OF PLACES